Major scholars on Japan explore the Japanese style of learning in this important volume, drawing upon ethnographic and experimental studies of learning throughout the life span. The reader gets an inside view of Japanese teaching methods, where the emphasis is on the process of learning rather than the end product. Applications across contexts, from religion to music to mathematics to guidance, are handled very differently than in the West.

Contributors analyze various models of learning within and without the Japanese school system. Together these analyses comprise an example of a nation, a landscape of learning. The examples considered here allow us to understand better the rich coherence of systems in the broader social context. A carefully articulated Introduction and Conclusion by the editors provide salient comparisons of East and West and caution that we do not simplify our model of either one.

D0190726

Teaching and learning in Japan

Teaching and learning in Japan

EDITED BY

Thomas P. Rohlen
Stanford University

Gerald K. LeTendre
University of Georgia

CAMBRIDGE
UNIVERSITY PRESS

PUBLISHED BY THE PRESS SYNDICATE OF THE UNIVERSITY OF CAMBRIDGE
The Pitt Building, Trumpington Street, Cambridge

CAMBRIDGE UNIVERSITY PRESS
The Edinburgh Building, Cambridge CB2 2RU, United Kingdom
40 West 20th Street, New York, NY 10011-4211, USA
10 Stamford Road, Oakleigh, Melbourne 3166, Australia

First published 1995
First paperback edition 1998

Printed in the United States of America

Library of Congress Cataloging-in-Publication Data is available.

A catalog record for this book is available from the British Library.

ISBN 0 521 49587 3 hardback
ISBN 0 521 65115 8 paperback

Contents

Contributors

Clea Fernandez, Stanford University, School of Education

Rebecca Irwin Fukuzawa, Tokyo, Japan

Theresa Graham, University of Nebraska, School of Education

Thomas Hare, Stanford University, Department of Oriental Languages and Literature

G. Victor Sōgen Hori, McGill University, Faculty of Religious Studies, Montreal

Lauren J. Kotloff, Consultant, Philadelphia, PA

Shin-ying Lee, University of California, Los Angeles, Department of Psychology

Gerald K. LeTendre, University of Georgia, School of Teacher Education

Catherine C. Lewis, Child Development Center, Oakland, CA

Lois Peak, U.S. Department of Education

Thomas P. Rohlen, Stanford University, School of Education

Nancy Ukai Russell, Princeton, NJ

Nancy Sato, Stanford University, School of Education

Harold W. Stevenson, University of Michigan, Department of Psychology

James W. Stigler, University of California, Los Angeles, Department of Psychology

Ineko Tsuchida, Child Development Center, Oakland, CA

Makoto Yoshida, University of California, Los Angeles, Department of Psychology

Introduction: Japanese theories
of learning
THOMAS P. ROHLEN
AND GERALD LETENDRE

We see teaching and learning more clearly today, not just in
Japan, but in all advanced societies. Learning is a major component of the intellectual consciousness of our day; we understand
learning as something that occurs not just in schools and among
children, but throughout society and throughout life. It is central
to organizational change, social order, economic competition,
and a host of other social processes. Viewed inclusively, the
world of learning is rich in practices and understandings that
vary in historical time, cultural space, and institutional context.
The range of "things" to be learned is enormous – facts, endurance, maturity, peace of mind, empathy, physical coordination,
judgment, persistence, morality, faith, concentration, trust, and
so on. How these things are taught differs greatly from society
to society and reflects basic understandings about such matters
as human nature and the nature of knowledge. Our growing
awareness of the importance of teaching and learning allows us
to see not only how ubiquitous these processes are, but also
how varied and interconnected.

Most research on learning focuses on distinguishing the psychological factors and processes performed by individuals in
relation to specific tasks. Our formal theories of learning and
teaching derive largely from the Anglo-American tradition of
educational psychology. We are finding that the often reified
Western theories that have dominated our perceptions and research seriously hinder our ability to perceive the numerous
uncodified worlds of teaching and learning that abound in each
society. Knowledge of these worlds, especially comparative
knowledge, promises to be of great practical and heuristic value
in our continuing pursuit of the goal of opening up our under-

standing of learning and teaching to the great variety that exists.

We also want to understand the way patterns of learning are organized in whole societies, in institutions, in groups, and in individual experience. To do this, we must look at more than just individual task performance or the standard curriculum of schools. Ours is an age of information, of thinking rather than manufacturing, of whole societies competing with each other using various kinds of collective intelligence. It is an age increasingly defined by the necessity to reflect upon ourselves collectively and to transform how we learn as a result. For premodern societies, "How do you teach?" or "What do you learn?" are, as a rule, nonquestions. But for industrial societies, such questions strike at the heart of the process of adaptive change.

The studies gathered in this volume are united by the common goal of understanding teaching and learning in Japan as it actually occurs. All of them seek to answer questions about the actual conduct of learning in different settings and at different points in the life cycle. The authors in this volume have set out to explore the expectations and associations found in specific Japanese situations. The methodologies employed are diverse, but the focus remains on grasping the details of practice and their implications for our understanding of basic Japanese themes and formulas for learning. Each is based on intense firsthand observations. Some are ethnographic in nature, some are experiential, and some are based on formal methods. All seek to reveal the richness of everyday activity.

The overarching questions the book as a whole seeks to explore include the following: (1) Can we begin to define the range of contexts (traditional and contemporary, private and public) that the Japanese have perfected as learning environments? (2) What do these contents have in common? (3) How and why do they differ? (4) Can we fathom underlying cultural formulations that distinguish Japanese teaching and learning? Can we perceive an overall structure to this variety in cultural time and space (a single landscape, so to speak)? Although each chapter seeks to describe a specific context, the overall goal is to construct a whole picture embracing the diversity and underlying commonalities. We seek to discover dynamics among the parts of the larger landscape. We recognize the existence of many other contexts that could also be included if we had enough space. (Traditional apprenticeships and company small-group learning are two of the most obvious.)

Collectively, the studies presented here help us to see how the Japanese understand learning. The understandings are naive, cultural, controversial, and even contradictory in many cases, but they are real in that they are embedded in practice. In this there is both good news and bad news. The good news is that by the end of this book, readers can expect to have learned a great deal about teaching and learning in Japan and to have grasped certain common patterns, even "philosophies," that underlie the diversity. The bad news is that readers will just as certainly have come away with an uncomfortable sense of the complexities involved, the internal ironies, and the fact that this or that Japanese approach may seem an exemplar on the surface, but the deeper we dig the more we have to face the fact that it contains implications and cultural trade-offs that are far from attractive. If there are lessons from Japan in what follows, there are also some sobering realities.

The paradoxes and contradictions found in the Japanese culture of learning should stand as a warning: We simplify Japan at the risk of adequate understanding. Japan's contradictions reflect our own expectations – for example, a culture that makes sense because it is homogeneous in its basic values and assumptions. The contradictions of our own beliefs become apparent when we attempt to view Japanese ideas through them. This has much to do with our wish to learn from Japan. Rather than borrowing certain instructional techniques, the most important lesson may be to be able to see more clearly, via a rich comparison, what we do and why: to become conscious of the basic assumptions we make about learning.

Most of the learning we do will *not* be done in schools. Learning occurs within institutions such as the family, the factory, the office, or various leisure groups. But schools and school learning do provide powerful models or paradigms of teaching and learning in industrial societies. By expanding our inquiry into various areas, we can explore basic, universally recognized models of learning. We can ask: Are the practices the same? Are the understandings the same? Using a variety of case studies and relating them to each other, we can assemble a description of the landscape of learning within a given society.

The present world system is also colored by the perception that some societies are better at this "learning business" than others. We have mountains of reports and papers that enjoin us to boost education in order to increase our economic success, social justice, individual creativity, and even the democratic process. Here again, systems of public education dominate our attention and set the limits of our inquiry into teaching and learning. We pay enormous attention to the school and the classroom, but rarely, if ever, do we seek to locate the topic of learning within the totality of human activities. The crucial and ubiquitous interface of daily interaction between someone designated as a "teacher" (including "experience") and others designated as "learners" occurs in a variety of settings, day after day, year after year. The accumulation of thousands of such experiences forms patterns and produces monumentally important differences in the formation of both human resources and social forms. Whether we are comparing school systems, companies, or whole national populations, what happens in face-to-face learning environments remains the most difficult area to fathom cross-culturally – and therefore, despite its critical importance, one that is easily neglected.

Taken as a whole, any society's landscape of learning is rich in contradictions and complementarities. Institutions may reinforce each other, echoing common themes in their pedagogical patterns, or they may contradict each other in their approaches, producing jarring learning experiences for large sections of a given populace.

Each nation seems to have its own emphases, blind spots, and styles. In this book, these issues emerge as the authors analyze various models of learning. Together, these analyses comprise an example of a national landscape of learning. The examples considered do not exhaust the great variety in Japan by any means, but they allow us to understand better (1) the rich coherence of specific contexts, (2) the variability even within Japan, and (3) the place of school-based systems in the broader social context.

During the conference at which the papers in this volume were first assembled, the authors discussed their separate case studies and became increasingly aware of underlying patterns and themes. The ubiquity of these patterns (produced primarily at the level of face-to-face interaction) is stunning when the range of social circumstances is considered. Much of the socialization of children, the transmission of traditional knowledge and values, the adaptive efforts of organizations, the development of adult resources, and the transmission of new knowledge in nonschool settings rests, it appears, on remarkably common and taken-for-granted basic practices associated with learning.

What are the sources of this hidden unity? All Japanese experience many forms of teaching and learning as they mature, first of all, and these forms serve as a reservoir or set of micromodels for learning and teaching that form the basis for such activities in adult institutions. Having participated in many variations of the common learning patterns as children, every Japanese has a developed set of core expectations about how teaching and learning should occur. A cultural code of appropriate behavior, learned early, is thus available throughout society and throughout the learner's life.

These expectations include beliefs about the correct or true nature of relations between a teacher and a learner, between one teacher and another, between student and student, and between school and parents. "Teacher" (*sensei/shidosha*) is a social role in schools, companies, and artistic pursuits, part of a set of fundamental relationships that include emotional and social obligations not conveyed by the equivalent English term; in Japanese, "teacher" is a symbol that triggers a range of associations and emotions for virtually all members of society. Whether in a monastery or a factory, those Japanese designated as *sensei/shidosha* are understood and judged within a framework of culture-specific expectations.

It is obvious that human development embraces much more than childhood, and learning is not limited to schooling. For our purposes, then, let us define the timeline of learning we are addressing here as beginning with the entrance to school and lasting until the individual ceases to have a desire or capacity to continue learning. Within this framework we ask: What sequences or stages in the process of learning do people see? Do these stages differ between different kinds of learning? How do these sequences of learning fit with conceptions of adulthood, personal growth, and spiritual fulfillment? Are gender differences significant? Is there an overall structure? To combine these queries into one: How do Japanese models of human

nature and personal growth that exist for early childhood relate
to those found in adult life?

Time: developmental expectations and ideals
of learning

The entrance of the child in school is perhaps the single most
basic step along the road to adulthood. At home the child is the
central (often the sole) focus of parental attention. It is known
that the ideal Japanese mother's life is carefully orchestrated
around high standards of care for the young child. Entrance into
preschool is a transition clearly understood in Japan to mark the
beginning of a socialization process by which the child comes to
see himself or herself as part of larger social groupings (Hendry,
1986; Lewis, 1989; Peak, 1989). The schooling process takes the
child from a familial environment where individual attention and
dependency are predominant through middle school, where the
child is but one of many students in an increasingly formalized
structure.

   This intense socialization to group processes apparently does
not produce the traumatic results we as Americans would expect (Peak, 1991). Critics of the Japanese system of education
(both here and in Japan) continue to denounce the system as
one that stifles individuality and produces a docile body politic.
As Nancy Sato and Catherine Lewis make clear in this volume,
before we can definitively say how Japanese education affects
individuality, we need to look closely at various stages and to
know the basic transformations that individuals are expected to
make in their development.

   The social context of elementary schooling has many positive
aspects that have been largely ignored to date. The most basic
orientations defining the stage of early schooling (K-4) are the
focus on a group context (referred to in Japan as *shudan seikatsu*) and the notion that children of this age develop best if
left to follow their own curiosity and find their own concentration levels. This latter understanding is rarely discussed explicitly, but one encounters it in the literature on childrearing
(Lewis, 1989). A range of Japanese practices indicate that it is
commonly assumed that children up to the age of 10 develop
best when allowed to follow their own inclinations. The natural
child is quite individualistic and idiosyncratic, and spontaneous

expression generally receives much toleration in elementary schools. Instructional approaches adapted to the nature of the young child are characterized by a facilitative role for teachers and considerable student–student interaction. Group emphases do not overwhelm individual inclinations at this stage.

The socialization into different learning environments from preschool to high school is surprisingly persistent, incremental, and consistent in its direction. Peak (1991) and, in this volume, Lewis and Kotloff offer a persuasive portrait of this transition that allows us to see how family attachments are gradually shifted to peer groups and how demands on the child are slowly increased over the years of elementary school. Given the relative encouragement of dependency by parents and the pressures of exam competition beginning in late elementary school, we would expect and often find some stress and trauma associated with the discontinuities involved. The essays by LeTendre and Fukuzawa describe the key transitional role that middle schools play in this transition. The gradual trend in early education, then, is sharply mediated in middle school and again at the point of entry into postsecondary education.

As we know from work on high schools (Rohlen, 1983; Okano, 1993), secondary-level teaching employs a pedagogy almost entirely dependent on teacher-centered lectures to large classes of students engaged in note taking for the purpose of passing exams. The use of small groups for instructional purposes is extremely rare, and student presentations are limited. Classroom proceedings center on the teacher, who elaborates at length on a fixed lesson. Indeed, comparing elementary and high school instruction, one wonders if they are part of the same system.

The basic routines established in K-9, it appears, make possible the subsequent, rather dramatic change in academic teaching style at the secondary level. In this volume, numerous authors provide rich evidence of routines that later serve as foundations for the basis of instructional order in many adult contexts. Small-group discussions, cooperative chores, peer pressure to manage disruptions, and *hansei* (self-reflective criticism) are all examples that are subsequently found in high schools, university clubs, and company training programs. The rotation of leadership responsibilities in small groups, as well as many other such practices, are also in evidence throughout the Japanese landscape of learning. What seems to change, then, is not the fundamental habits and routines or guidance practices, but rather the basic focus of the development effort.

Having by high school mastered the basic routines, students and teachers need not focus their energies on organizational ordering. Instead of spending time on this, they concentrate in most schools on the looming entrance examinations to university. Middle school and high school together are a time when students are expected to move beyond being well socialized to being challenged to strive for personal attainment in a narrowing and competitive field of knowledge.

It is safe to say that the successes of Japanese high school students on comparative math and science achievement tests rest heavily on a foundation of prior teaching and socialization that had nothing to do with the cramming or rote learning associated with high school instructional processes. The crucial routines and values of elementary and middle school education, which researchers in both Japan and the United States are only recently emphasizing, are critical but not highly visible aspects of most high schools. The topography of instruction gradually shifts as exams approach, so to speak, but the underlying geology does not change. We need to keep this complexity in mind when judging the Japanese system, for to fail to see its stages as part of a larger whole is to distort what is clearly a 12-year process. Although shifts may be far-reaching, as the essays on middle school illustrate, they are all well within a single process.

Constructing a general framework of differences

Is there an underlying conceptual framework that gives meaning to this process, or is it largely the accretion of historical forces and cultural eclecticism: a long history of cultural borrowing, occupational reform superimposed on previous nationalist and militaristic practices, economic growth, and so forth? Although many educators would hesitate to suggest a broad and underlying frame of meaning, there are persistent similarities that point to such a framework.

If we think of the educational process as enmeshed in developmental ideals of the life course derived from indigenous, Confucian, and Buddhist ideas, such a framework can be recognized. From the perspective of character building (Rohlen in this volume), stricter discipline and increasing challenges must be part of the adolescent experience for a successful transition from childhood to adulthood to occur. In this perspective, the ordeal of exam preparation and the increasing severity of teachers are necessary and positive aspects of growing up. One might even say that the stages of development move from a focus on curiosity, spontaneity, energy, and collective activity to one that emphasizes individual work, suffering, and attainment through personal spiritual development. This transition has many parallels in the transition from Shinto to Buddhism. In this regard, there is even reason to argue that ontogeny appears to replicate cultural history. Although teachers, for example, decry the distortions of teaching to the entrance exams, it is evident that they also feel students need to be challenged in order to advance spiritually and emotionally. Exams are a character-building challenge. By grades 8 and 9, children are seen as ready for an adult-like seriousness, a controlled, purposeful course of action. Without the focus of the entrance examinations, teachers would have to invent new challenges in order to realize their conceptions of how children should be guided into adulthood.

If socialization to the group is the goal of stage one, and stage two is a matter of increased challenge, self-discipline, and concentrated effort, stage three is far more varied. Some students go to university, where they may spend most of their time in intense group activities. Others go to work and encounter another cycle of socialization, formal instruction, and apprentice-like on-the-job training. We can make sense of these disparate stages if we see a thread of spiritual maturation running through nearly all learning after about age 10. The guidance of middle schools, with its attendant and often rigorous discipline, is centered on building the child's character. Precisely because the child is approaching adulthood, there is an increase in the focus on perfecting the self by facing severe challenges. Such a focus, whether found in the obsession within university student clubs or devotion to one's job, recurs throughout the lives of modern Japanese.

This underlies the powerful tendency to perfectionism in Japanese culture. Perfecting the self means perfecting one's attitudes and, more important, one's performance. This emphasis has a long history in Confucian thought (see Tu Wei-ming,

The Self as Creative Transformation). Rohlen (1973, 1976) has labeled this ideology "spiritualism" (*seishin*) and has shown that it plays an increasingly central role in the Japanese understanding of learning. Although this ideology is associated with adult learning, it flows out of a socialization model for childhood that is different, inherently (and culturally) prior, and less well articulated. What is constant is the group context.

When the child or learner is in an initial stage, all that can be expected is that they learn to behave in a particular group context. Children naturally play and learn to get along with each other; the potter's apprentice sweeps the floor and tries to keep out from underfoot. Only after the basic socialization to the group's activities is complete is the learner ready to accept the more demanding tasks needed for mastery and for reflection (*hansei*). Both the rationale and model for good behavior and the justification for self-perfection derive from the prior assumed importance of the group context.

Not even most adult training is done in the name of the company. A great deal of personally meaningful learning also occurs among adults that is strictly voluntary and unrelated to practical ends. Pursuits such as the tea ceremony or ink painting occupy people's free time. These pursuits are typically highly structured by Western standards, and they intensify as retirement approaches. A high proportion of the population participates, and given Japan's relatively early retirement and its longevity rates, a significant proportion of the normal life course is open for self-reflection and self-perfection.

As Hare (this volume) relates, many of those who pay for instruction in Noh acting are people who will never perform. Having mastered the basics of life – family, job, and friends – most Japanese apparently hunger for more learning. Not only do private organizations (such as the systems of licensed teachers and schools that dominate the traditional arts) offer a variety of things to be learned, but the government itself spends a tremendous amount on "social education" (*shakai kyōiku*) aimed at providing a range of classes for the "silver set."

Yet this path is also a trap. Hori (this volume) shows that merely to memorize a hundred sutras brings no enlightenment. Just doing routines does not guarantee insight. The form can become a false promise. In the end, to truly move beyond the authority of highly perfected forms represented by memorization and repetition, the Japanese student must in some sense leave the well-trod path, set aside the dictates of convention and form, and find the key to a realm of understanding that is personal. This journey to true independence cannot be misunderstood as a shortcut, however, since only a thorough mastery of what is given establishes the foundation to move beyond it. Ironic as it may seem, this final stage of adult advancement begins to replicate, in style and philosophy, the spontaneity and playfulness of early childhood education.

Old age, ideally the age of mastery and self-perfection, is a time (as Hare, this volume, relates) to descend again (developmentally speaking) and have fun. In line with Confucian and Shinto views, mastery of life gives license to experiment and create, to circle back to the playfulness of childhood. It should not come as a surprise to Westerners, then, to see the transformation of their friends in the first few years of retirement: The ostensibly rule-bound, workaholic company man may now be spending much of his time perfecting his watercolors or Chinese cooking skills. A woman who has rushed from her job to her home in order to make dinner and run errands now practices her folk dance form late into the night in preparation for her group's coming performance. These persons are simply exercising the earned right to follow their own fancies and to study whatever they wish, typically still in the name of self-perfection.

The overall picture of Japanese learning as it relates to the life cycle, then, is one quite different from our stereotypes. It begins by confronting the reality of a shared social experience. The notion of childhood differs and moves toward increased discipline with adolescence. Adulthood is not a plateau of learning; rather, it is an extended period rich in challenges and opportunities to improve.

For over one hundred years, public schools have occupied the attention of educational researchers both in and out of Japan. However, before 1872, childhood learning experiences were far more diverse than they are today. Boys may have been apprenticed at about age twelve, they may have attended a local "school" in a temple or neighbor's house, or they may have attended a fief school if they were part of the warrior elite. Knowledge was not readily codifiable, nor was there a clear image of teaching as a profession. Prospects for boys and girls differed enormously.

The rapid implementation of a national school system not only eliminated many of these traditional forms of learning and teaching but also subordinated those that survived. The serious business of national development and the rising power of the state took center stage, embodied in a nationwide uniformity of public schooling. All preexisting forms were made peripheral and, to a degree, dependent. They survived by doing what the public school system chose not to do. Although apprenticeships, for example, exist today, they are found only in the traditional arts and crafts. Moreover, although today's tutoring academies (called *juku*) have premodern origins, they are dependent on their role of supplementing the character of the public school system. In other words, the Westernized version of school dominates the learning scene, and most other learning situations are defined in reference to it.

Learning, however, is not confined to the space defined by public schooling. Beginning in childhood, most children are exposed to the peripheral worlds of academic tutoring, artistic expression (i.e., music lessons, calligraphy classes), and character-building activities (judo or kendo). Indeed, the public schools have become tacitly reliant on these supplementary activities to a degree. That is, teachers can expect slower students to get outside help and can expect motivated parents to provide a range of educational experiences for their children. Where cram schools are numerous, for example, teachers are under less pressure to teach to a low common denominator; they are also less obligated to do exam preparatory work.

This implies that a symbiotic relation exists between the public schools (under the jurisdiction of the monolithic bureaucracy of the Ministry of Science, Culture, and Education) and the diverse private teaching activities for children (*juku*) – organized as commercial enterprises.

The cram school is the most common and notorious form of *juku*. Before we decry the degradation of *juku*-based learning as simply rote memorization, however, we must examine our own prejudices and assumptions about learning. Americans have developed a fine dichotomy between rote and critical thinking; one is good, the other bad. How valid is this distinction, especially outside our cultural sphere? Certainly, accomplishments in the arts, in athletics, and in much else begins with repetitive imitation. We learn to walk and talk and think largely by imitation, too. If this is true, why should it not be true of academic learning, at least to some degree? Japanese tutoring schools often help children master subjects by giving them supplemental exercises (a kind of rote learning) by which they "deepen the grooves of their learned patterns" (i.e., their memory of relationships as well as of details). Math speed tests are an example, but so is repeated practice in solving word problems or filling in names on blank maps. Russell's study of kumon *juku* (this volume) helps us grasp the interrelationship of such institutions and the public schools. As she illustrates, cram schools may actually permit responsiveness to other pedagogical approaches within the public system. The exercises, drills, and rote learning of *juku* serve as the basis for problem solving and practical application as taught in a more discovery-based and critical (or "constructivist") manner by public school teachers. There is reinforcement, and even tacit mutual dependence, between the two.

Programs like the Suzuki Method (Peak, this volume), flower arranging classes, and the martial arts also have complex relationships to the public system. Their general claim is that they cultivate self-improvement and build character. Their argument is that public schools pay insufficient attention to these matters. They too are part of a larger developmental formula. The cultivation of both spiritual and academic pursuits outside of school points to the high expectations Japanese parents have of the learning process: Their ambitions are not situated within the school alone or within modern Western notions of human development.

Turning from the centrality of the public schools to actual classroom teaching, we encounter many details of instruction that resonate with our general discovery of a distinctly Japanese approach to methodologies and technique. A number of essays (by Shin-ying Lee and colleagues, by Tsuchida and Lewis, and by Stigler and coauthors) document the attention to detailed lesson planning typical of Japanese teachers.

Compare the lesson plans that Stigler and his colleagues present. The typical American lesson plan is a bare outline – literally less than a paragraph. The Japanese outline is a detailed set of concepts complete with illustrations, comprising several paragraphs of dense text. What does this tell us about the differences in our views of learning and knowledge? In this one document, the comparative insights are often profound.

The American outline is designed for one day, and one day only. It is a throwaway plan, little more than a grocery list of ideas to hit on – a reminder note. The teacher, like so many American teachers, expects to add what she feels is important at the moment. She wishes to change her direction at a moment's notice if she judges it necessary and to ad lib what she needs. The knowledge is reduced to a few grand concepts, and the teacher decides how best to communicate these ideas to her students at a given time.

The Japanese lesson plan, and the hundreds like it we have seen, is meant to be used repeatedly. Each year it will be dusted off, with perhaps a few adjustments made or a small part deleted, but it will be used again. The lesson plan itself is based on a set body of pedagogical knowledge that is organized in as accurate or true a way as possible. The teacher has consulted the text, tapped several sources of accumulated knowledge on the subject, typically talked with other teachers about it, and summarized it in detail in a series of precise steps. The grand concepts are less central than in the American lesson plan; what is important here is detail. The exact details of the process of understanding the material must be explicitly conveyed. Missing also are the American teacher's concerns about whether today's class may need a radically different set of instructions from yesterday's or last year's or whether one student may learn very differently from another. The Japanese teacher usually assumes that if the details of the knowledge acquisition process are presented in a time-tested and precise way, the grand concepts will reveal themselves to all students.

This thoroughness (a form of perfectionism) is coupled with an intense interest in understanding the minutiae of the child's cognitive development, lesson by lesson. Russell's account of the Kumon Method and Peak's discussion of the Suzuki Method underscore the same points. Japanese teachers, furthermore, seem to be more comfortable with group discussions, mistakes, confusion, and other aspects of a discovery-oriented (or constructivist) approach. This requires a less hurried, time-constrained approach and confidence in the process on the teacher's part. In essence, then, when we look closely at elementary classroom teaching, we discover many attitudes that echo points made about Zen monastic training, as analyzed by Hori. We do not think these parallels are accidental.

The organization of this book

This book is ordered as follows: First are two essays that provide accounts of historically older learning systems that predate the public school system. They introduce a number of general themes that will recur in subsequent chapters. We then turn to the early stages of schooling to examine the place of feelings, of supportive peer group development, and of other aspects of socialization to school. Next, we consider the practices and concepts underlying school guidance; notions of maturation, teacher responsibility, and transition are examined. Then we move to issues centering on cognitive development and the teaching of subject knowledge. Finally, we consider two of the literally hundreds of major artistic pathways open to nearly all Japanese, one centering on young children and the other largely the domain of older Japanese.

In the Conclusion, we review the major themes underlying learning and teaching across the many case studies and contexts presented. These themes are the Japanese cultural components of teaching and learning. We also discuss the implications for further research on learning as conceptualized as part of a broad social landscape. We invite the reader to join us in exploring the varied terrain of this fascinating landscape.

Fundamental approaches

The historical span of institutionalized teaching and learning in Japan is ancient, dwarfing the hundred or so years of public schooling. This obvious point carries a less obvious implication – that much that is taken for granted about the subject actually has deep historical roots. We begin this book with two portraits of training in contemporary institutions, a monastery and a corporation, where approaches to teaching and learning are clearly derived from premodern ideas and practices.

As will be evident, both the Zen monastic training and character-building exercises in a particular bank are similar in having personal growth as their primary focus. Unlike formal schooling, they are not preoccupied with the ultimate goal of teaching knowledge deemed useful to life in an industrial society. Very little in either approach rests on the written or spoken word, and a great deal depends on experiences designed to teach via psychic and physical challenges. Confusion, pain, loneliness, and many other sources of disequilibrium are thus utilized as teachers.

How old or uniquely Japanese are such approaches? The question of historical roots is easier to answer in the case of the Zen monastery. Zen Buddhism entered Japan in the seventh and eighth centuries from China, where it had already been established for over a century. The roots of Zen trace back to India and the centrality of meditation (*dhyana*). An elaborate monastic tradition evolved in China and Japan, embracing a considerable diversity of practice, as it was influenced by the tenets of Taoism, the teachings of Confucius, and the rites of Shinto. The intense emphasis on learning by doing described by Hori seems to be unique to Zen. Descriptions of life in Tibetan monasteries or in the Theravada tradition do not reveal such emphasis.

The character-building exercises, part of one bank's training for new employees, are also old, at least in their basic conceptualization and intention. Developed in the 1950s and 1960s, corporate training of a spiritual kind borrowed its practices from many sources – the military, the Olympics, Zen Buddhism, apprenticeship programs, and other religions more uniquely Japanese. Its deeper roots, historically speaking, lie primarily in the conviction that character development arises from suffering and hardship, and the belief that these experiences can be intentionally manipulated for the learner's benefit.

Another aspect common to both forms of teaching is their intention to foster social adhesion and peer bonding through a process that makes the sharing of difficult experiences the basis of greater attachment. The fact that learning is essentially accomplished in a collective environment and is experienced largely collectively characterizes an outlook that we find typical of schooling in Japan as well. Cooperation is not only a major goal, it is a critical foundation for other kinds of learning.

All this makes teaching different from the typical and expected role established by the model of classroom instruction. The task is not to convey explicit information effectively. Nor is it to order and lead. Rather, the teacher plants seeds of insight, facilitates processes that are carefully designed to cause change, and monitors unobtrusively to see that all is going according to plan. In the Zen tradition, metaphors like the "transmission of the lamp" or "transmission outside the scriptures" are common. These convey the belief that wisdom (enlightenment) does not come from a reading of the scriptures but rather from a direct and penetrating apprehension of the ultimate nature of the phenomena – be it one's self or the object of one's actions.

Are these techniques exclusively Japanese? Certainly not. We find such ideas and practices throughout the world in initiation rites, in military and other "boot" camps, and in the practices of mystical or evangelical organizations. What distinguishes the Japanese case is that these kinds of learning and teaching are not relegated to the periphery. Central social institutions such as corporations, schools, and factories may readily incorporate them if they desire. The intensity and thoroughness the Japa-

nese bring to most of these undertakings also gives such practices a Japanese flavor. Finally, the language of the self and self-
development in Japan is closely tied to the philosophy embodied
in such training, giving it a culturally generated importance not
found in the modern West.

Teaching and learning in the Rinzai Zen monastery

G. VICTOR SŌGEN HORI

Popular images of Japan tend to cluster around two conflicting cultural stereotypes. One depicts Japan as a ritualistic, rule-governed, hierarchical society where obsession with preserving traditional form and with conformity to group goals stifles individual creativity. The other pictures Japan as the repository of a mystical culture that produces gentle, creative, slightly foolish sages. These two stereotypes clash. How can one society be both? A closer look at teaching and learning in the Japanese Zen monastery allows us to see how ritual formalism coexists with mystical insight.

I propose to divide the spectrum of human learning into three domains: (1) ritual formalism, (2) rational teaching and learning, and (3) mystical insight. In modern Western society, we have focused upon, and greatly developed, what I have labeled rational teaching and learning, but we seem to have less interest in, or confidence about, the two ends of the spectrum. A Japanese Zen monastery, on the other hand, substantially discounts rational teaching and learning and teaches both ritual formalism and mystical insight. In fact, it teaches mystical insight by *means of* ritual formalism.

I wish to express my appreciation to the following people: to Thomas Rohlen of the School of Education, Stanford University, both for inviting me to the Conference on Teaching and Learning in Japan and for very helpful comments on an earlier draft of this paper; to the other conference participants for several days of rewarding intellectual discussion and good fellowship; to the Department of East Asian Studies at Brown University for inviting me to give a presentation of some of the ideas in this paper; and to the referees and editors of *The Journal of Japanese Studies* for very helpful criticism.

By "ritual formalism," I am stretching one term to cover several kinds of behavior: repetition, rote memorization, behaving according to traditional prescription. In ritual formalism, students imitate form without necessarily understanding content or rationale. They are instructed in "what" to do but given very little instruction in "why" and "how" to do it.

By "rational teaching and learning," I refer to that pattern of education in which a teacher of a body of knowledge and/or skills usually formulates its general principles, even if crudely, and then through instruction seeks to transmit an understanding of those general principles to the students. Instruction is usually by verbal explanation, demonstration, conducting drills, or some combination of these and other techniques. It is not part of rational teaching and learning to teach students to perform tasks without an understanding of general principles (the "reason why"), nor is it part of rational teaching and learning to expect the student to perform the required particular tasks without prior instruction.

I am using the term "mystical experience" to refer to that moment when one experiences oneself as no longer fundamentally distinct from the objective world, when there occurs a breakdown in the usual distinction we make in ordinary life between the self as subject of experience and the world about us as the object of experience. I make no judgment about whether that experience is in some sense genuine or false. My description of mystical experience in these terms no doubt presupposes some hidden assumptions to which someone will object (see Katz, 1978, 1983; Proudfoot, 1985; Foreman, 1990). If this essay stimulates such criticism, it may then be necessary to rethink this definition.[1]

I was first struck by the connection between the formalism of rote learning and the spontaneity of insight long before I entered the Zen monastery. As a graduate student in philosophy, I taught propositional logic to first- and second-year university students and noticed that the class divided into two groups, those who could solve the logic problems and those who could not. Those who could solve them started by memorizing the basic transformation formulae of propositional logic. These formulae are to propositional logic what multiplication tables are to arithmetic or the basic equivalence equations are to algebra. Having committed these formulae to memory, these students were thereby able to solve the logic problems because they could "just see" common factors in the equations and then cancel them out or could "just see" logical equivalences. However, the other students, those who had not committed the transformation formulae to memory, were more or less mystified by the problems, though many made serious attempts to "reason" their way through. Some of these latter students said that the ability to solve such problems was like musical ability, that successful problem solvers had a special ability to "just see" the answer to the logic problems, just as people with musical ability can "just hear" when a note is flat or sharp. And they excused themselves by saying that they had not been born with that particular gene. But in fact, those who had done the rote memory work had developed logical insight, while those who had not developed logical insight were the ones who had skipped the rote memory work, thinking they could reason their way through the logic problems. . . .

It is a long way from logic problems in a philosophy classroom to the Zen Buddhist monastery. Teaching and learning occur in both places, but they are directed toward quite different goals. Education in the school classroom is directed toward giving students knowledge and skills, but it is not primarily concerned with developing a certain kind of personal character or religious outlook. A monastery, on the other hand, is deliberately trying to develop a certain kind of religious person and transmits a body of knowledge and skills as a means to that end. Yet despite the distance between these two kinds of teaching and learning, I believe there is a connection. Rote repetition and memorizing on a larger and institutional scale grows into ritual formalism in the Zen Buddhist monastery, while the logical insight of the philosophy classroom expands into what I call mystical insight.

Thus, the connection between ritual formalism and mystical insight, which I will attempt to describe in this paper, is matched by a connection between rote memorizing and logical insight in the academic classroom:

Ritual Formalism	Rational Teaching and Learning	Mystical Insight
Rote Memorizing	Reasoning	Logical Insight

In the "just seeing" of logical insight, a logical formula shifts position across the subject-object line in experience. At first, the logic formula is the object of my attention, a piece of information I try to memorize just as I do a line from the multiplication tables. But in the experience of "just seeing," the logic formula is no longer the object I am *attending to;* it becomes part of what I, as subject of experience, am *attending with.* The logic formula becomes, so to speak, part of the conceptual lens through which I now look at the objects to which I am attending. Logical insight is not mystical insight, of course, but the two share family resemblances: what was once an object of experience becomes (part of) the subject of experience. And in this essay, I hope to show a further resemblance: that both the logical insight of the philosophy classroom and the mystical insight of the Rinzai monastery are taught through ritual formalism.

Right from the beginning, some people will not want to agree with this thesis. . . . Those who advocate rational teaching and learning affirm that schools should not teach students to memorize facts merely to regurgitate them on tests. The educational mission must be to teach students to "analyze," "explain," "articulate," "generalize," "contextualize," and "apply to concrete situations." . . . Rote methods are blamed for making classroom education boring for children and for deadening their innate creativity. Given freedom, children will find the learning process intrinsically interesting and will enthusiastically teach themselves, so it is said. I remember a traditional Japanese tea ceremony teacher saying, "Don't ask questions. Just do it this way for three years and you will know." Many educators are offended by such ritual methods, which seem to demean the students' sense of self-esteem and belittle students' confidence in their own ability to understand. The moral vision of the student as an autonomous individual full of rational and creative potential continues to propel educational theory. But when this moral vision causes people to reject rote teaching methods out of hand, then moral vision blinds rather than illuminates.

These are dangerous waters, I realize, for I am talking about what distinguishes the culture of Japan from that of the West. In recent years, . . . critics have said, explanations in terms of culture really explain nothing at all ("Such and such way of doing things is typically Japanese"), or such explanations reify culture, creating the illusion of an "ethno-centric, culture-bound notion of common moral impulses, common values, located like a little pacemaker in each person's heart" (Wold, 1988:755) in a society. In addition, these days, any item of cultural difference is liable to be taken by *Nihonjinron* theorists as further evidence of the uniqueness of the Japanese race. Not surprisingly, in reaction, there are now many people who are impatient with discussions of how different Japanese culture is. . . . I write this description of monastery life to try to describe that difference, but I realize that many will find "naive" or "implicit" theories here and take me to task for taking sides in these intellectual and ideological disputes. Here, let me just make a small defensive move against possible critics. . . .

. . . My overall conclusion in this essay is that the Japanese Zen monastery employs a style of teaching and learning not found, to the best of my knowledge, in the West. While recognizing that such a conclusion can be used ideologically, I would hope that ideological argument does not prevent us from first trying to assess its truth.

In 1976 I was ordained as a Zen Buddhist monk and for 13 years, from 1977 to 1990, lived, worked, and practiced in Rinzai Zen Buddhist monasteries and training halls in Japan. In this essay, I write not as a scholar-observer bent upon maintaining "objectivity" . . . but as a practitioner speaking from within the tradition. Please pardon my use of very general words like "the Japanese" and "Westerners," as if there were no individual differences among the members of these groups. Each instance of these terms should be prefaced by some quantifier like "a few," "many," or "most." But to do this could invite a challenge to show statistical evidence – evidence that does not exist.

Also, I use male pronouns throughout and write as if only men engage in Buddhist practice. It is manifestly not true that only men engage in Buddhist practice; it has not been true of Buddhist practice in Japanese history, and especially it is not true now of Buddhist practice in the West. But Rinzai Zen monasteries for women no longer exist in Japan. Sōtō Zen nuns have reestablished monastic practice for women but, according to a recent study, theirs is a very different style of teaching and learning (see Arai, 1993). Unfortunately, it does seem that at present only men engage in the style of teaching and learning depicted in this essay.

Temples and monasteries[2]

Japanese Zen Buddhism divides into three schools: the Sōtō School, the Rinzai School, and the Ōbaku School. Sōtō Zen is by far the largest school, with almost 15,000 temples spread across the country (Foulk, 1988). Rinzai has fewer than 6,000 temples and Ōbaku has fewer than 500. There is consequently no single temple which represents all of Japanese Zen, nor is there any single priest who heads up the entire priesthood. The Rinzai Zen temples are further divided into 16 lineages, each led by a head temple called a *honzan* (literally "main mountain"), which is usually a large temple with a prestigious history. The local Zen temple is normally a branch temple (*matsuji*) of a *honzan*. The larger *honzan* maintain monasteries (*semmon dōjō,* "halls dedicated to training," or *sōdō,* "monks' halls") where the next generation of priests receives its training. A few *honzan* are large enough to support more than one monastery.

In order to become the resident priest of a temple, a monk is required to spend some time in training at a monastery, the exact duration to be determined by local tradition and *honzan* regulations (Suzuki, 1965). Most monks probably spend between one and three years at a monastery, but some manage to get away with shorter stays (Sato and Nishimura, 1973). On the other hand, a priest of one of the Daitokuji *honzan* temples is required to have at least five years of monastery training behind him. A Rinzai Zen monastery then functions somewhat like a Christian theological seminary by training monks for parish priesthood. However, the ethos and style of training make it a very different place. The Zen monastery has a reputation for fierce discipline. For those associated with it, it embodies the essence of Japanese manhood, fierce samurai loyalty, unswerving dedication, and strength of character.

The monastery itself is under the sole direction of the Zen Master, called *rōshi* (literally "aged teacher"). Under him are the monks, who are divided into two unequal halves. The larger half, called the *dōnai* ("within the [meditation] hall"), includes all monks who for that term have no office, along with a few officer monks associated with the *dōnai.* Chief of these is the *jikijitsu,* head of training. The smaller half is the officers' quarters, called the *jōjū* (literally "permanently resident"), which includes the cooks, attendants to the *rōshi,* and other officers.

In Rinzai Zen, monastic practice is centered around *zazen* (meditation) and the *kōan,* a paradoxical problem assigned by the *rōshi* to the monk to be used as the focus of concentration during meditation. The monks meet daily with the *rōshi,* in a one-to-one meeting called the *sanzen,* to present their response to the *kōan.* Other formal teaching includes the *rōshi*'s regular lectures. Although there is a great deal of rhetoric about Zen understanding being beyond books and texts, right from their first year Zen monks study a text called the *Zenrin kushū* (Zen phrase collection) as part of their *kōan* practice. In the advanced stages of *kōan* practice (which most monks do not experience because they leave at less advanced stages), monks spend a great deal of time researching Zen and other texts in order to compose essays in Japanese and poetry in classical Chinese, which they write in brush and submit for approval to the *rōshi.*

This description so far may give the impression that the monks are engaged in a quite ordinary style of teaching and learning, but it is not so.

Teaching without teaching

A new monk arriving at the gate of a Japanese Zen monastery is called a *shintō* (new arrival). Once admitted to the monastery, the *shintō* has much to learn. Immediately, he must learn monastery routine: where things are kept, what happens when, who is responsible for what. He must learn proper language, deportment, attitude, and pace. He must memorize sutras and ceremonial procedure. He must learn how to do *zazen* and how to penetrate the Zen *kōan.* After an initial period of six months to a year, he will be assigned to one of the offices such as *tenzo* (cook), *enzu* (vegetable gardener), *densu* (keeper of the shrine), or perhaps even *sannō* (attendant to the *rōshi*). If he remains at the monastery for many years, he may in time become a *yakui* (senior officer), one of the group of head monks who hold the positions of senior responsibility, which include *jikijitsu* or leader of training in the *zendō* (meditation hall), *fusu* (administrator), and *daiten* (head cook). A monk constantly moves back and forth between the officers' quarters and the communal *dō-nai,* usually spending one term (a half year) in office and then one term in the *dōnai* concentrating on meditation. During his entire career, the monk is constantly learning.

Ancient tradition rests heavily upon new monks. The *rōshi* and older monks remind the new arrivals that the robes, rituals, sutras, language, personal relations, and the entire life of Zen training itself date back to the ancient past and that the new monks must do their share in preserving this ancient tradition against the encroachments of modern life. Much of a monk's life consists of committing sutras and Zen texts to rote memory, practicing traditional forms of ceremony and ritual, and in general eating, dressing, speaking, and living in a style reminiscent of medieval Japan. One could then be pardoned for thinking that teaching and learning in a Buddhist temple consists of nothing more than exercises in rote memory and formalized ritual. But in the Rinzai Zen monastery, Zen monks are expected to learn the ancient tradition without really being taught.

Twice a year offices change. At seven o'clock on the evening before the day of the change, the names of the new officers are announced. At eleven o'clock the following morning, the new officers take over and from that moment forward are on their own. The brand new cook must prepare nourishing and tasty meals for 20 monks every day; the brand new keeper of the shrine must perform all the detailed ritual and ceremony for the many sutra services; the brand new attendant to the *rōshi* must heat the *rōshi*'s bath to just the right temperature and iron his laundry just so. But there is no break-in period when the old officer shows the new officer what to do; the incoming officer cannot apprentice himself to the outgoing officer to learn the ropes. The new officer must perform his duties without receiving prior instruction.

If the new *tenzo,* or cook, makes a mistake in the ringing of the gong which calls everyone to meals, a senior monk will surely give him a tongue-lashing in front of everyone. The cook will be criticized if the rice is too hard, the soup is too salty, the vegetables have been cut too small, the tea is lukewarm, the faucet is left dripping. If the monks eat up all the food he has served, he must scurry around and cook more food while the monks wait impatiently at table. If he makes too much food, he is forced to eat all the leftovers. After the meal is over, one of the head monks may further criticize him for not using the heaps of cabbage sitting ripe in the fields, or for overcooking the squash, or for always making the same few dishes. He may choose to criticize the cook in private or to humiliate him in public. The new cook suffers this constant harassment until he can cook properly, manage the kitchen without making mistakes, and use all the temple's food supplies resourcefully. He is greatly motivated to learn all this as soon as possible.

Let us call this method of teaching "Teaching Without Teaching." At first glance, this may not seem to be a teaching method at all. Some observers here will only see a form of hazing, an initiation ritual for inducting new members into a group. If the goal is to teach the new cook how to do his job, there seem to be much more direct and efficient methods of teaching. For example, if we were teaching a new officer "rationally," perhaps a week or so before the change of office, we would have the incoming officer apprentice himself to the outgoing officer. The outgoing officer would explain in careful detail the various tasks as he performed them on the job and gradually during the week would allow the new officer to try his hand at each task. By week's end, under the watchful eye of the outgoing officer, the new officer would be trying to do all the jobs by himself. Here emotional tone is a factor. A skillful instructor would try not to embarrass or humiliate the new officer since he believes that students learn better in a supportive atmosphere where they feel accepted and can maintain self-dignity. Most certainly, the outgoing officer would not engage in any deliberate verbal and physical abuse of the new officer. Let us call this rational, reasonable way of teaching "Teaching By Teaching."

Opposite or complementary?

. . . In the Rinzai Zen monastery, the daily meditation and meetings with the *rōshi* over the Zen *kōan* provide the main focus for this training, but all activities in the daily life of the monastery – chanting the sutras, growing vegetables, sweeping the garden, cooking, etc. – are nevertheless systematically used as arenas of Zen practice. The entire regime of monastery life is not task-oriented but person-oriented, done not just to get the work done, but to help monks test and train their powers of egoless concentration, so that they may eventually achieve awakening or enlightenment.

Monastery-style Teaching Without Teaching thus does not, on the surface, seek to find the most efficient or convenient way of doing the job. In fact, in order to test the monk, Teaching

Without Teaching deliberately requires that the jobs be done in what appear to be inefficient or inconvenient ways. Thus the cook has no budget for shopping and is expected to make his meals entirely from the vegetables that grow in the garden and from whatever donations of food the monastery has received. He may not use the conveniences of electricity or gas but instead must cook everything over a wood fire. If he wants hot water, he first brings water from the well in a bucket, pours it into a cauldron, and lights a fire under it; 20 minutes later he has hot water. Some few concessions to modernity have been made. A pump and faucet have been attached to the well so that hauling up water by rope is no longer necessary. Most monasteries probably have refrigerators now and vacuum cleaners as well. But nevertheless monastery life is still deliberately kept at a fairly primitive level: no heat in the winter, no chairs to sit on, no money to spend, no flush toilets, no creature comforts – all this creates an appropriate ascetic environment and gives the monks more room to use their ingenuity in resourceful ways.

In rational Teaching By Teaching, on the other hand, once a person is designated to do a job, that person is encouraged to do it in the most convenient and efficient way possible. Thus the modern cook uses not only gas and electricity but also microwave ovens, refrigerators, automatic potato peelers, electric vegetable choppers, dishwashers, and, of course, the cook also submits an ever-increasing budget to maintain all this mechanical support. Little thought is given to what effect such mechanized convenience has on the cook as a person, his resourcefulness and self-discipline when using scarce ingredients, his respect for the tools he uses daily, his awareness of the farmers who grew his produce, his attitude toward the people whose food he prepares, or his mindfulness as he chops carrots.

Although Teaching Without Teaching offers no advance instruction and leaves the monk on his own, the monk cannot do anything he wishes. He must maintain the traditional formalized ritual life of the monastery. The monastery system prescribes precisely what the monk is required to do but gives little direction on why or how to do it. Since he receives no instruction, the monk must constantly use his own insight and intuition, be original and resourceful, in maintaining that prescribed form. How does one get both the spinach and the noodles cooked ready to be served at exactly 10:20 A.M.? A novice would cook one, wash out the cauldron, and then cook the other. But under the pressure of a tight schedule, the monk suddenly realizes that he can cook the spinach in the still hot, leftover water from the noodles and save himself 20 minutes. Every monk who has spent time as a cook will have tried and abandoned the standard cookbook way of slicing radishes. The cookbook says to first cut off the leaf and stem and then slice thinly. But it is impossible to slice the entire radish this way since one cannot slice the part held by the fingers of the left hand. Before the monk gets scolded for serving radishes sloppily sliced, he will have seen some better way of slicing radishes (retain the leaf and stem and use it as a handle) which will slice the radishes thinly as required by tradition, use the radishes more efficiently, and get the food on the table on time.

Despite the ritualized form of monastery life, efficiency thus is very highly valued. And every cook is under great pressure to devise ever more efficient ways of work. Constantly he is scrutinizing every step of his actions, asking is it faster to reverse the order of these two jobs, can I use the residual heat from this fire for some other task, do I get a better cut if I hold the blade of my knife this way, and so on. Although "what" he is required to do is prescribed for him, the cook subjects every detail of "how" he does the task to minute examination in a constant search for improvement.

The term I am using, "ritual formalism," includes a variety of activities: repetition, rote memorization, behaving according to traditional prescription, and more. Common to these various activities is the idea that the performers are imitating form without first learning why or how those activities are to be done. But although the very notion of ritual seems to imply the unthinking repetition of tradition, the Zen monastery requires its monks to carry on that tradition while at the same time refusing to teach it to them. The monastery deliberately does so, intending to create monks who are innovative and resourceful. The monastery teaching tradition ridicules the *tanpankan,* "the fellow carrying a board" on his shoulder, who thus can see only one side of things, and instead urges monks to develop *rinki ōhen,* "on the spot adaptability." Under this system of training, each monk develops his own untraditional solution to maintaining the traditional, his own original way of continuing the established convention. Necessity is the mother of invention, but in a Japanese

Zen monastery, maintaining ritual form is the unexpected father of insight.

Confucianism I: motivation

Few Zen monks question why Zen monasteries teach in this way. For them, it is just the tradition. But I have met two older priests who have reflected on the matter. They quote Confucius:

The Master said, Only one who bursts with eagerness do I instruct; only one who bubbles with excitement do I enlighten. If I hold up one corner and a man cannot come back to me with the other three, I do not continue the lesson. (Waley, 1938:8)

In this passage Confucius is teaching a student how to lay out a field plot and insists that, having shown the student where to lay out the first corner, the student should have enough initiative and resourcefulness to determine the other three on his own. Older Zen priests who are familiar with the Confucian classics go on to quote further passages such as:

He hears one part and understands all ten. (Waley 1938:8)

In the Zen temple, colorful traditional verses are often quoted to express the same point:

With a good horse, does one need to use even the shadow of a whip?

Seeing just the shadow or hearing just the sound of the whip, a good horse will at once know the rider's wishes and begin to gallop.

In other words, the key factor in successful teaching and learning is not so much the ability of the teacher. It is whether or not the student is strongly motivated and has initiative.

The Master said, If a man does not continually ask himself 'What am I to do about this?, what am I do to about this?' there is no possibility of my doing anything about him. (Waley 1938:15)

I once heard the priest of a Zen temple say, "That new disciple is no good. You have to tell him everything."
   . . . Teaching Without Teaching insists that the ability or inability of the student to understand all ten parts from seeing only one part is not merely a matter of native intelligence, about which nothing can be done; it is also a matter of motivation, and

there is much that we can do to motivate the student. Thus, the fundamental problem facing a teacher is not in teaching the content of any lesson but in motivating the student to seek for himself. The entire discipline of monastery teaching and learning is constructed upon this assumption, that true teaching and learning cannot occur while the student remains a passive recipient of the teacher's instruction but occurs only when the student is actively motivated to learn. . . .

The learning process is student-initiated not only when senior monks teach junior monks the concrete tasks of monastery life, but also when the *rōshi* trains the monks in the *kōan*, the practice which is often thought to be the mystical heart of Zen. By the nature of the case, the *rōshi* cannot teach the point of the *kōan* to a monk. He could, of course, merely tell the monk the traditional answer to the *kōan*, in the same way that a tax accountant informs his client that his total tax for the year is $5,231. But just as the tax client does not know why his tax is $5,231, so also the monk would not understand why that answer was a correct response to the *kōan*. He must see for himself the connection between *kōan* and answer. If the monk makes no effort and listlessly proffers only "I don't know" at his encounters with the *rōshi,* the *rōshi* cannot direct him in any way. Only when the monk first makes great effort, and concomitantly makes many mistakes, does the *rōshi* have any opportunity to teach the monk. The *rōshi* is likened to a bell. First, one must strike it.

The *rōshi*'s teaching consists primarily in motivating the student and very little in teaching the content of the *kōan*. He assigns the monk a *kōan* such as "Two hands clap and there is a sound; now, what is the sound of the single hand?" and gives no hints about how this question is to be answered. The monk usually meets the *rōshi* over the *kōan* twice a day; during intensive retreats they meet three, four, and even five times a day. Very quickly the monk exhausts his list of possible replies. The *rōshi* continues to pressure the monk to bring an answer. He sometimes ridicules the monk, sometimes presents a stony face, sometimes ignores the monk. He scowls, he jeers, he feigns astonishment at the stupidity of the monk. But he is relentless in demanding an answer. The monk feels cornered and helpless; he is confused; he vows to make a great effort and when his efforts yield nothing, he may fall into great disappointment or even depression. But he is desperate to know what that *kōan* means and would give anything to be able to penetrate it. There is no better student than one so desperate to learn.

Confucianism II: mutual polishing

Though Teaching Without Teaching can work in one-to-one situations, it develops a special dynamic in groups. Monks do not reserve their criticism and admonishments just for the new monk. Teaching Without Teaching is not merely hazing, an initiation ritual for newcomers. Long after initiation is over, monks continue to constantly admonish, warn, reprimand, and lecture each other:

The seam of your robe is crooked. Fix it!
Your collar is dirty. Wash it!
Chant louder. Put more guts into your voice!
The floors are dirty. Are you sure you mopped them today?
Walk quietly. Make no noise when walking!
Shut up! No talking!
Your sitting cushions aren't in line. Fix them!
If you have so much time on your hands, go sit!
Your attitude is wrong. Be grateful when someone corrects you!
No running away!

Whether or not he has experienced awakening, every Zen monk is expected to lead the life of enlightened action in all his daily behavior. A monk may not know the enlightened way to act in any given situation, but if he does anything clumsy or mistaken or selfish or in any way unenlightened, some monk senior to him will be sure to chastise him.

In a large community, of course, a single *rōshi* cannot monitor the daily behavior of all his monks. The community of monks thus monitors itself. This self-disciplining action is called *sessa takuma,* another Confucian phrase (Waley, 1938:15), which means, literally, "cutting, chipping, filing, polishing" but which I translate here as "mutual polishing." The image is of a pile of rough stones all placed into a stone mortar and constantly stirred. The rough edges of the stones cut and chip each other away, rubbing against each other in constant friction until they become round, smoothly polished gems. No one stone is superior to any other, but through mutual friction all become gems together revealing the unique individual nature of each. Through the constant abrasive action of their criticism upon each other, all monks learn though no single teacher teaches. Through mutual polishing, each attains an individual uniqueness. . . .

Generalizability and genuineness

In defense of traditional monastery-style teaching, I have heard Zen *rōshi* offer two arguments: (1) a monk taught the traditional way generalizes his ability to learn beyond the original context, while a student taught by the new, rational methods must be retaught for each new task; and (2) a student taught the traditional way genuinely knows for himself why he is doing what he is doing, while a student taught the rational way is merely following someone else's example.

After a monk has survived his first assignment to office, usually he returns to the communal *dōnai* to spend a term without office. But he knows that in the following term, he may very likely be appointed cook or attendant to the *rōshi*. In his off-term, he watches every move those officers make, remembers the stories that older monks tell of their terms in those offices, and every now and then will ask them what the cook is normally doing at 7:30 in the morning or what is the *rōshi*'s favorite food and how it is to be prepared. If the monk happens to be near the kitchen, he will observe where all the kitchen utensils are kept, the order in which the cook does his many jobs, the way the cook works together with the *rōshi*'s attendant, and so on, trying to deduce the overall pattern of the cook's job from a few observations. Long before he actually gets appointed cook or *rōshi*'s attendant, he tries to build up a picture of the daily routine of these jobs. He is learning without being taught in a situation outside his first learning experience. He is generalizing.

During my time in the Zen monastery, we were told stories of how model students learned without being taught. In the traditional carpenter's shop, we were told, a new apprentice would spend his first three years doing nothing but drudge work. He would arrive first at the shop in the early morning to light the fire, bring in the water, wash the toilets, make tea, and do all the other little tasks of getting the shop started. During the day he would not be allowed to touch a tool. Instead he would have to haul lumber, clean up cuttings, deliver a cabinet to Mr. So-and-So, and so on. In the evening, when everyone had left, he would do a final sweep of the floor. During this initial period, no one would actually teach him any carpentry. But after three years when his formal training began, the older carpenters would expect him to know already what wood to use for what kinds of job, how that wood is cured, where that wood is kept, etc. Though no one would have taught him, he would be expected to know the names and uses of all the tools, all the language and terminology used to describe joints, types of construction, methods of finishing, etc., as well as the names of all the customers and suppliers of the shop. Like a carpenter's apprentice, a Zen monk is urged to be always observant, to be able to understand the entire task long before he is required to do it.

In Teaching Without Teaching, the student genuinely learns. In using the English word "genuine," I am constructing a concept to correspond to the casual, everyday Japanese phrase *hontō ni* as in *hontō ni wakaru,* which normally is translatable as "truly understand." Let me try to explain what this ordinary-sounding phrase implies in the monastery. When a student is told in advance and in detail what to do and how to do it, he has no opportunity to test out different ways of doing the task and to discover through his own exploration which methods work and which fail. Probably the rationale for this procedure would be efficiency: why ask the student to reinvent the wheel? But if asked how the method he has learned from the teacher or text-book compares with other methods, the student cannot answer from his own experience of those other methods. He has never tried the other methods and failed; he has only succeeded at the one method which he has been taught is successful. In that sense, he does not really know why he is doing what he is doing; his understanding is not entirely first-hand, not based on personal experience, not entirely genuine.

Power and hierarchy

To some, the Rinzai monastery's method of teaching may appear to be nothing more than indoctrination or brain-washing, especially since the teaching method is imbedded in a hierarchical social structure. Here it is necessary to make a few comments about power and hierarchy in the monastery.

The monastery has an explicit hierarchy. The *rōshi* warns the head monk, who will afterward scold one of the middle-ranking monks; the middle-ranking monk, in turn, will deliver a blistering lecture to the *shintō*. Except for the single monks at the very top and very bottom of the hierarchy, every monk is simultaneously subject to discipline by higher-ranking monks and in turn responsible for disciplining lower-ranking monks. An outside observer may object, first, that since the monastery is a hierarchical system, teaching and learning are not truly reciprocal since younger monks may not criticize senior monks, and second, that such a system of hierarchy must inevitably encourage senior monks to abuse the power of their position. . . .

Against the charge that the monastery hierarchy encourages abuse of power and that younger monks surely must suffer, I can say that in my experience, this did not happen often. There were occasions in which a senior monk would try to use his position to personal advantage, but this did not happen enough times to be a problem. There was one monk, however, who consistently disregarded monastery rule and very often took advantage of others. He was detested by many but, strangely, he was also admired by others. Eventually after many years, he was expelled from the monastery. But this charge raises the question of what we mean by "abuse of power," and here, I believe, different cultural perspectives produce quite different expectations and divergent moral evaluations. When a young monk enters a monastery, he expects to be ordered around in very rough language, to be humiliated in public, to be slapped, cuffed, and hit with a stick quite often. Yet he does not consider himself "abused" or think himself the victim of injustice. In fact, he may very well look back upon this experience with great gratitude, as I do.

A *sesshin* is a week devoted to intensive practice. In the yearly calendar, *rōhatsu* is the most intense *sesshin* because it commemorates the Buddha's own enlightenment, celebrated on December 8. In my second year, I went through the entire week of *rōhatsu* without once passing my *kōan*. Since first- and second-year monks are required to announce after every meeting with the *rōshi* whether or not they have passed their *kōan,* my failure to progress was public knowledge. As encouragement, the *jikijitsu,* head of the *zendō,* hit me with the stick with increasing frequency each succeeding day. At first, I attempted to keep count of how many times I was hit with the stick. By the fourth day, my count had risen to more than 500 times. During the second half of the *sesshin,* the *jikijitsu* was even more ferocious with the stick, and although I lost count, I estimate that I received well over a thousand hits with the stick by the end of the week. At the end of *sesshin,* the *jikijitsu* showed me a blister on his right hand and said, "You gave that to me, I had to hit you so often I got a blister on my hand." We laughed and I thanked him for his efforts on my behalf. . . .

Back and front

. . . To the outside world, the Rinzai Zen monastery appears to be a disciplined group of dedicated and sincere monks all committed to maintaining the purity and severity of the monastic institution. Behind this facade, however, the monks carry on an active life not revealed to the public. Monks look forward to *takuhatsu* (begging) days since they have a chance to leave the monastery for the morning and remove themselves from the watchful eye of the head monk. Sometimes they enjoy themselves so much that they come back from begging rounds slightly drunk. Late at night after the last *zazen* (meditation) is over, some of the monks may gather for a cigarette behind the woodshed where the firewood is stacked. Carefully pulling a thick piece of firewood from the stack, one of the monks will reach into the open space and pull out a bottle of whiskey. Suddenly everyone has a teacup in hand and little pieces of dried fish are being passed around. In monastery language, this is *sarei,* "tea ceremony," and on a winter's night, after sitting out in the open until almost midnight, a little drink is most welcome before crawling into a very cold mattress. Other monks may climb over the wall to go to the local public bath and afterward enjoy a bowl of noodles. Some of the more adventurous ones may even head downtown to sing in the *karaoke* bars, always mindful that wake-up is 3:30 or 4 A.M. Of course, in the monastery there will be one or two monks who are very fussy about keeping all the rules, and they will receive their share of good-natured kidding, perhaps even be dragged against their will on some outrageous escapade.

The formal life of disciplined obedience masks an informal

life of pranks, deceptions, and even betrayals. The *densu* is responsible for waking everyone up at 3:30 (summer) or 4 A.M. (winter) every morning. If he fails to get up, everyone sleeps in late, an event appreciated by all. To make that much-appreciated event occur more often, monks are not above sabotage. A careless *densu* who leaves his alarm clock near a window will likely find that during the night a hand from outside the window has reached in and turned off the alarm. The next morning as the head monk chastises the *densu* for his idleness, everyone will sympathetically agree that the *densu* certainly has a difficult office. Slipping back and forth between the formal life of strict discipline and the informal life of play, monks constantly slide in and out of inconsistent, and sometimes contradictory, relations with each other.

To outside observers, such behavior may seem to be the epitome of hypocrisy, but in the monastery not only is it tolerated, it is considered quite necessary. Few people can live entirely and completely in the abrasive world of strict discipline. In fact, one might even argue that monks can practice with such strict discipline only because they play so hard on the shadow side. But although the shadow life of pranks and play is a break from the strict discipline, it is still considered an integral part of monastery practice. Monks are required to make great effort in both the formal and informal sides of monastery life. Because the *rōhatsu ōzesshin* commemorates the Buddha's own enlightenment, all other activities are cancelled so that the monks can devote all their energy to *zazen* and *sanzen*. As the daily 22-hour schedule begins with wake-up at 2:00 A.M. and ends after midnight, a late-night snack of hot noodles is served at about 10:00 every evening. The *jikijitsu,* of course, wants to get his monks finished with eating as quickly as possible in order to return to the *zendō* to continue sitting. But the monks deliberately eat as slowly and as much as possible in order to extend the eating time to a maximum. With effort, they will be able to cut off an entire half-hour, a full period of *zazen,* from the time they spend afterward sitting in the cold *zendō* under the stick. The *jikijitsu* cannot complain since the rule is that everyone may have as many second helpings as desired. In this way, the monks silently and playfully resist the *jikijitsu.* . . .

However, one year an interesting incident occurred. During

this particular *rōhatsu ōzesshin,* the monks were not eating much; the evening noodles were quickly eaten and within 15 minutes, everyone was back in the *zendō* for further *zazen.* This attitude was symptomatic of the entire *sesshin* that year for the monks in general moved and sat with an air of tired lassitude. After noodles one night, the *jikijitsu* gave us a furious scolding for failing to eat more noodles, criticizing us for not making effort, for being passive, for not arousing fighting spirit. Later that night, as we brushed our teeth, we all agreed our performance at noodle-eating had been shameful. From the next day on, everyone ordered second and third helpings and the general air of lassitude lifted from the entire *sesshin.* With that, the *jikijitsu* told us that we had finally worked up some of the fighting spirit required for the most important *sesshin* of the year.

Much more can be said about this aspect of monastery life, but here it is worthwhile only to make two points. First, in addition to allowing monks time and space for rest and relaxation, the behind-the-scenes life of play teaches monks not to make a religion out of Zen practice, not to treat monastery practice as something holy. A beginning *shintō* quite naturally is rigid about trying to maintain as strictly as possible all the rules and regulations of monastery life. But in time he soon learns the concrete meaning of the teaching that the *samadhi* (state of consciousness attained in deep meditation) of the advanced Zen practitioner is *yūge zammai,* "the *samadhi* of play." Second, while the formal life of monastery discipline often isolates a monk and tests his individual personal resources, the shadow life affirms that beyond distinctions of rank and office, all monks share common social bonds and a fundamental humanity. This sense of shared life is often expressed in the traditional Japanese way by taking a bath together and sharing a drink.

All social organizations have a formal and an informal aspect. But in other contexts, while the informal behavior is often thought to be antithetical to the formal, perhaps even a degeneration or corruption of an ideal, in the Zen monastery, both the formal and the informal life of the monastery are thought to be equally important arenas of Zen practice. The informal life is neither antithetical to, nor a corruption of, the formal; it is the partner or complement of the formal.

Development or self-discovery?

In thinking about how we conceptualize personal development and how we attempt to understand other cultures, I have found it useful to use a typology of models: a Development model and a Self-Discovery model.[3]

The Development model presupposes that the learner has a set of innate dispositions to develop in a certain way. The process of learning is a gradual response to external stimuli in the learner's environment. If there are no traumatic occurrences to impair or truncate development, the learner will develop naturally, actualizing all innate dispositions in a sequential development. Biological metaphors, expressed in language such as "nurturing," "organic," and "blooming," come easily to mind. The process of learning is depicted as systematic and reasonable; innate dispositions work their way out according to their own internal logic. The learner in the beginning is the passive receiver of nurturing from the physical and social environment, and the self comes to full form only through interaction with the environment.

On the other hand, the Self-Discovery model presupposes that buried within the learner is a fundamentally pure, true self. But from earliest childhood, we are socialized to accept a self-image imposed by our parents, a morality imposed by society, a set of conventional beliefs about our place in the world sanctified by tradition. It is only when the true self breaks free of this false consciousness that a person attains true self-knowledge, maturity as a person, and individual creativity. The Self-Discovery model therefore depicts learning and personal development as the destruction of the encrusted, unnatural shell around the self, a struggle often described as traumatic, liberating, and very sudden. Mythic metaphors of "quest," "ultimate ordeal," and "rebirth" come easily to mind. Although one may encounter guides along the way in one's journey, in contrast to the rational and interactive learning of the Development model, learning in the Self-Discovery model is fundamentally solitary; the lonely self wells up from inside, breaking through its environment in an irrational thrust to come to the light.

Zen has appealed strongly to Westerners because it seems to be one of the few areas of Japanese culture that embodies Self-Discovery. However, in this essay, I am questioning whether the Self-Discovery so often associated with Zen is truly part of actual traditional monastery practice. Is the attainment of mystical insight in the Rinzai Zen monastery Self-Discovery or Development?

Ritual practice

We are now starting to close in on the problem of how ritual formalism can reside together with mystical insight. Let us start by pointing out that this is not a problem for Japanese people, who are quite used to the idea that one goes to a Zen monastery to engage in a highly ritualized form of life in order to gain spiritual enlightenment. It is in the secular West that a conjunction of ritual formalism and mystical insight is difficult to grasp.

Traditional Buddhism and Confucianism employ ritual in many ways. Actions are ritualized to endow them with special or sacred meaning; ritual acts function as symbols; ritual is done for cathartic effect; and so on. There is also an educational use of ritual formalism: it trains consciousness. Each particular ritual act in Confucianism has not only a prescribed behavioral form but also a prescribed attitude, emotion, or state of mind. The making of prostrations or the offering of food to deceased ancestors, for example, is to be done with an attitude of repentance or devotion. The ritual fails if not done with sincerity. Meditation, one of the central ritual practices of Buddhism, similarly is often explicitly directed toward the cultivation of feelings, emotions, and attitudes such as loving kindness, compassion, or sympathetic joy. Other ritual practices aim at the eradication of the attachments found in ordinary consciousness. One repeats and repeats the prescribed act with the prescribed state of mind until one no longer has to will them consciously, until one can act naturally with sincerity, or devotion, or loving kindness.

Buddhist meditation practices here exemplify the simplest form of rote repetition. In many sects, the beginning student repeats again and again the mere watching or counting of the breath going in and out of the body. In some forms of Tibetan Buddhist practice, the beginner starts off with 100,000 full-body prostrations, 100,000 repetitions of a short mantra, 100,000 creations (and destructions) of a mandala, and 100,000 repetitions of a longer mantra. These practices are merely repeated again and again, with little attempt made to understand why or how one is to do them. In fact, often students are cautioned that too much thinking about the practice inhibits the practice. All of these are ritual practices performed with the explicit intention of disciplining consciousness.

Practitioners perform these meditation exercises, at least in the beginning, in the belief that to do so leads eventually to Buddhist enlightenment. But Zen priests also teach that wanting enlightenment is itself a form of attachment and thus a hindrance to the attainment of the non-attachment of enlightenment. This makes enlightenment seem especially mysterious, for what, then, can one do to gain enlightenment if the very attempt to gain enlightenment is what prevents it? Despite this rhetoric about the apparent futility of practice, the very existence of monasteries and of monastic discipline presupposes that one can engage in concrete practices that advance one toward the goal of enlightenment. And the concrete practices that form the path to that spiritual insight consist of ritually performed acts.

The Zen kōan

In the Rinzai Zen monastery, monks are given *kōan* upon which they focus their attention during long periods of *zazen,* sitting meditation. The traditional beginning *kōan* include, for example, Hakuin's famous "Two hands clap and there is a sound. What is the sound of the one hand?" and Jōshū's Mu: "A monk asked Jōshū, 'Does a dog have Buddha-nature?'; Jōshū replied 'No!' " (pronounced *mu* in Japanese). Sitting in meditation, the monk blindly repeats the *kōan,* posing the problem of the *kōan* to himself again and again. The *kōan* has a correct response – a single response, which that monastery's lineage considers correct – and the monk is under enormous pressure to produce it. The remarkable point of the *kōan* method is that with concentrated effort, monks regularly do start to penetrate the *kōan,* usually within six months of their arrival in the monastery.

Some critics have charged that the *kōan* question and answer is mere ritual, that the monk merely presents a set response which the *rōshi* ritually approves. If the monk is too dull-witted to come up with the appropriate answer on his own, then the *rōshi* will just tell the monk the answer, so it is thought. In fact, a "crib" of set answers to *kōan* has been published in both Japanese and English, and the existence of this book leads many people to believe that the encounter between *rōshi* and monk is little more than a *pro forma* stage play. But the fact that a crib exists proves nothing. A high school algebra crib will provide all the answers to the algebra problems, but the student who wants to pass the final test in algebra must not only know the final answer but also understand the reasoning that leads from the problem to the answer and be able to perform the necessary intermediate calculations correctly. Similarly, giving the correct response in *kōan* training can degenerate into merely an exercise in rote memory, but understanding the connection between the *kōan* and the correct response requires insight. In order to test whether the monk has true insight into the *kōan,* the *rōshi* asks numerous "checking questions" called *sassho.* For the *kōan* "The Sound of One Hand," the checking questions include "Cut the sound of one hand into two with one slash of the sword," "Did you hear the sound of one hand from behind or from the front?" "The sound of one hand – let me hear it too," and many more. If the monk has true insight into the *kōan,* he will be able to answer these checking questions as well. If he is merely a parrot repeating a set phrase, he will not.

Nothing is more mysterious than the way in which rote repetition of the *kōan* triggers the mystical insight called awakening or enlightenment. The monk repeats to himself over and over again, "What is the sound of one hand?" constantly posing anew the question to himself. The repetition becomes so ingrained that without conscious effort the *kōan* always rises to consciousness whenever attention is not fixed on anything else. As he drifts off to sleep at the end of the day, the last thing involuntarily drifting through his mind is the *kōan* endlessly repeating itself. And on arising in the morning, the first conscious thought is again the *kōan* continuing its ceaseless repetition from the night before.

In the beginning, the monk seeks the answer to the *kōan,* expecting that the answer will arise someday in his consciousness like an object illuminated by a spotlight. But as he continues to work on the *kōan* and yet still fails to penetrate it, he starts to react to his own inability. He begins to have doubts about the *kōan* practice. He will doubt his own abilities. He may fall into a deep disappointment or depression. He challenges himself to have faith and pushes himself beyond what he thought were the normal limits of endurance and willpower. In this region beyond his normal limits, he panics, turns desperate, becomes frantic. Here all self-consciousness is gone. No longer is there a self constantly watching the self. By such forceful techniques, the Rinzai Zen monastery pushes monks into a state of mind beyond the dualism of ordinary consciousness.

At the extremity of his great doubt, there will come an interesting moment. This moment is hard to describe, but on reflection afterward we might say that there comes a point when the monk realizes that he himself and the way he is reacting to his inability to penetrate the *kōan* are themselves the activity of the *kōan* working within him. The *kōan* no longer appears as an inert object in the spotlight of consciousness but has become part of the searching movement of the illuminating spotlight itself. His seeking to penetrate the *kōan,* he realizes, is itself the action of the *kōan* which has invaded his consciousness. It has become part of the very consciousness that seeks to penetrate itself. He himself is the *kōan.* Realization of this is the response to the *kōan.*

The Zen Buddhist term for enlightenment or awakening is *kenshō,* often translated in English as "seeing one's nature." This translation and the usage of this term in English is extremely misleading for several reasons. It suggests that there is seeing, on the one hand, and an object of seeing, called "one's nature," on the other. This is misleading because awakening occurs at the breakdown of the subject–object distinction expressed in "seeing" (subject of experience) and "one's nature" (object of experience). Further, *kenshō* in Japanese is as much verb as noun: "How do you *kenshō* this?" is a typical Zen challenge.[4] Finally, in Japanese *kenshō* is used to cover anything from a slight insight to a total spiritual transformation of character and personality, unlike the English usage, which tends to use it only to label something total and absolute.

In *kōan* training, the insight comes precisely in the fact that the traditional distinction between a subject of consciousness and an object of consciousness ("two hands clapping") has broken down. The subject seeing and the object seen are not independent and different. "One's nature" and "seeing" are not two. To realize, in both senses of "realize," this fundamental nonduality is the point of *kōan* practice and what makes it mystical insight. One gets to this fundamental realization not through the rational understanding of a conceptual truth, but through the constant repetition of the *kōan*. One merely repeats the *kōan* without being given any instruction on why or how. Ritual formalism leads to mystical insight.

Self

Does monastery Zen practice fit the model of Self-Discovery or of Development? The more prominent elements of Zen practice – it is chaotic, full of anguish, capped by *kenshō* ("seeing one's nature," a translation that suggests a pure original self) – fit the Self-Discovery model nicely. These are the elements emphasized both in the rhetoric of native Zen practitioners and in descriptions by outside observers. But there is an important point that does not fit the model nicely. Whereas the Self-Discovery model attributes the false consciousness that obstructs our self-awareness to the conditioning that our parents, schools, and society in general forced upon us, Zen follows traditional Buddhism in attributing that false consciousness not to society and external forces but to us ourselves. Not "them" but the self's own attachments, its own anger, greed, and ignorance, are responsible for the distorted way it perceives the world and for its own alienation from itself. For those who thought Zen justified rebellion against society, this is not good news.

Rinzai Zen monastery practice, however, brings monks to the point of insight through practices that fit only into the Development model. Despite the emphasis on sudden enlightenment in Zen literature, the Rinzai Zen monastery creates a ritualized environment that encompasses all daily activity, formal and informal. Far from playing the role of the suffocating environment that prevents the self from true self-awareness, as depicted by the Self-Discovery model, monastery life provides a complete environment structured to stimulate the personal growth of the monk through an organic sequential development, as depicted by the Development model. The very existence of the Zen monastery as an institution presupposes the belief that the social environment is not a barrier, but rather an aid, to the monk in his quest to attain enlightenment.

Behind these two models are two different conceptions of

self. The Self-Discovery model describes personal growth and development as getting in touch with the independent self buried beneath the obstructing layers of false consciousness created by the social environment. The Development model rests on the assumption that the self does not exist fully formed prior to its contact with its environment and that personal growth occurs through the self interacting with it. The rhetoric of Zen, with its dramatic accounts of the struggle for self-awareness, would lead one to believe that Zen monastery practice is a pure form of Self-Discovery, but actual monastery practice with its ritualized environment more closely fits the Development model. The Zen phrase that denotes enlightenment, "seeing one's nature," seems to invoke an independent autonomous self, but in fact, "seeing one's nature" refers to the collapse of subject and object of experience. Self-Discovery in Zen is discovery that the autonomous self is not real (although neither is it unreal).

Reflections

At the end of this essay, there are many loose ends.

Against the dominant attitude in education, I have argued that ritual and rote methods are necessary in teaching and learning. The ability and disposition to imitate is both primitive and widespread. Young animals, soon after they are born, begin to imitate the adults of their species; the behavior they learn is said to be "imprinted." Children imitate their parents and also other people around them, including other children. Teenagers imitate popular idols and students take professors as role models. A great deal of learning goes on outside the classroom, and some huge portion of it is accomplished through imitation, without any accompanying rational explanation.[5] Yet in the classroom, rote repetition is not highly valued as a method of teaching. In this essay, I have tried to show that there is a connection between ritual formalism and insight, that there is a connection between instructing a student merely to imitate and repeat without explaining "why" or "how" and the student's development of insight later. From the point of view of specialists in psychology or philosophy of education, I have probably made several blunders in trying to argue for this. The ideas in this essay would benefit from their criticism.

This essay tries to describe some phases of the actual *kōan* practice as it is conducted in the Rinzai monastery. I am afraid, however, that this essay gives the mistaken impression that the *kōan* is merely a means, a clever irrational instrument, to induce the experience of *kenshō*. The *kōan* however has more than one function, as Hee-Jin Kim points out (Kim, 1985: 1–47). The *kōan* as instrument may be non-rational, but the *kōan* as realization is discursive and says something. Furthermore, different *kōan* have different things to say. The entire *kōan* curriculum takes more than ten years to complete, each *kōan* expressing some new facet in the total Zen teaching. It would be unfortunate if readers took away the impression that a *kōan* is merely an irrational paradox whose function is to create a psychological crisis as a precedent to Buddhist enlightenment. To explain this would, however, require another essay. . . .

An unintended but relevant consequence is that my description of the operation of the Zen monastery reveals features of the monastery that resemble what has been called the Japanese managerial style. The work-group autonomy of the Japanese corporation corresponds to the autonomy given to a monk newly appointed to office. The explicit vertical structure of the corporation is paralleled by the explicit hierarchy of the monastery. Both the corporation and the monastery give a great deal of attention to detail. *Kaizen,* the constant step-by-step analysis, standardization, and improvement of tasks in, for example, a Japanese automobile factory nicely parallels the monk's constant attempt to make his way of working more and more efficient (Adler, 1993:97–108). Corporation *hansei,* "reflection," is paralleled by the criticism of mutual polishing in the monastery, and both are institutionalized ways of learning from failure. In her study of the Japanese Red Army, Patricia G. Steinhoff discovered that despite their revolutionary stance against the mainstream values of Japanese society, over the years the members of the Japanese Red Army developed, through trial and error, a working style that spontaneously reinvented several features of the Japanese managerial style (Steinhoff, 1989:724–40).

What is the significance of the fact that such diverse organizations – the business corporation, the Zen monastery, and the Red Army – should share such a resemblance? Do all Japanese, by virtue of the fact that they are Japanese, carry a genetically determined template that causes them to create very similar social organizations wherever they find themselves? Or is there some other explanation? Patricia Steinhoff speculates that the source of "this quintessentially Japanese style of organization can be located explicitly in the culture of the postwar Japanese elementary school" (Steinhoff, 1989: 733). Her point is that Japanese children, including those who later went on to become members of the Red Army, learned non-traditional decision-making procedures introduced by the American educational reformers during the postwar occupation period. In similar fashion, Paul Adler, in his study of the Toyota automobile production system, shows that it was originally inspired by the time and motion studies of the American, Frederick Winslow Taylor, the original efficiency expert. Is the present social organization of the Rinzai monastery similar? Is the social organization of the Rinzai Zen monastery a recent, postwar creation, too? Is there some non-traditional influence in its formation? These questions need further investigation. . . .

Finally, in order to show how teaching and learning function in the Rinzai Zen monastery, I have also had to describe some monastic teaching practices and sketch the different cultural assumptions that underlie them. Without this exploration into cultural assumptions, I fear that a mere surface description of monastic practices will be misunderstood. To point out cultural differences almost inevitably leads to comparisons which in turn will inevitably cause someone offense. Critics of earlier versions of this essay justly criticized me severely for making invidious cultural comparisons. I stand chastised. Nevertheless, it is a legitimate problem for intellectual study to ask why people in one culture construct and reconstruct certain fixed images of other cultures.

Notes

1. Part of my purpose in this essay is to demystify the notion of "mystical insight." The rhetoric of both the Rinzai Zen monastery and Western language descriptions of Zen describe *kenshō*, the Zen experience, as if it were totally transformative of the human experience, as if its genesis were completely indescribable in words. There is a point to this rhetoric, but one should not get carried away by it. The entire monastery *kōan* curriculum operates on the assumption that beginning monks start with a slight

insight which further training systematically deepens and makes intelligible. The training system presupposes, although this is never expressed in so many words, that Zen mystical insight is in some sense connected to ordinary experience (negation is a kind of connection) and that there is a logic to its development.

2. For a fuller description, see T. Griffith Foulk, "The Zen Institution in Modern Japan," in Kenneth Kraft, ed., *Zen: Tradition and Transition* (New York: Grove Press, 1988), pp. 157–77.

3. I do not know who first coined these terms. They are used by Yearley (1990). However, I have extended and amplified these terms in my own way. I would like to thank Harold Roth of Brown University for pointing me to this text.

4. This point will be of interest to those who are interested in whether mystical consciousness has intentional content. The form of this question, "How do you *kenshō* that?" is similar to "How do you interpret that?" and other questions that clearly imply that the state of mind in question has intentional content.

5. At the Teaching and Learning in Japan Conference, April 9–12, 1992, Thomas Hare of Stanford University pointed out that the original meaning of the Japanese word *manabu* is "to imitate."

Building character

THOMAS P. ROHLEN

Basic categories of human development are not necessarily sorted out the same way in every society. A case in point is what Japanese call "spiritual training" (*seishin kyōiku*), a range of experience based on forms of instruction that entail a mixture of physical ordeals, lessons in social morality, and character building.

The basic logic is that to grow spiritually, to mature, and to gain character strength, one must suffer one or another kind of hardship. Creating instructive hardships or challenges to mind and body (here, a false dichotomy) is the foundation of the teaching enterprise. Certainly, the degree of difficulty to be endured and the size of the challenge to be overcome are not without limits. Thus, the techniques involved have as much to do with calibrating the right amount of hardships as with explaining them in a manner that links the experience to understanding. We find this kind of learning to be common in such places as Outward Bound, military training, sports, summer camps and the like. The Japanese approach is eclectic, inclusive, and expansive. Because there is much Japanese interest in the possibilities, there is much creativity and variation. Americans locate these activities on the private side of the public–private ledger because they involve personal growth and because they are painful to some degree – things we see as matters of personal choice and voluntary submission to a particular

The fieldwork on which this essay is based was supported by NIMH Pre-doctoral Fellowship No. 5-F01-MH-36190-04.

Much of this essay appeared first in "Spiritual Education in a Japanese Bank," *The American Anthropologist*, No. 75, N. 5 (October 1973), pp. 1542–62.

training regimen. To endure physical hardships or to be "improved" morally are aspects of human experience generally left up to the individual in the West.

In Japan, by contrast, activities of this kind are frequently encountered in company employee training programs, in public schools, in student clubs, and in a host of other circumstances such as religious organizations, police departments, traditional psychotherapies, prisoner reform, traditional artistic pursuits and the martial arts.[1] "Spiritual training" is presumed to be good for everyone and therefore the responsibility of those in authority. While there are many opportunities for voluntary adult learning of this kind, schools and companies rarely leave such important matters to individual choice alone.

Spiritualism (*seishin-shugi*) is a key to much that Japanese regard as traditional and foreigners regard as Japanese in the nation's ongoing cultural pattern. Spiritualism provides a very definite philosophy of socialization and human development. At one time it inspired the training of the country's samurai and, more recently, its pre-war youth. Spiritualism establishes a perspective by which individual character continues to be widely judged today. It is, in summary, but the most recent manifestation of a very long and still quite vital Japanese orientation to issues of human maturity.[2]

Here I wish to focus on a particular example, one belonging to a large regional bank which I participated in during 1969. Given routinely at the time to all new male recruits, it began within several weeks after their graduation and lasted for three months. During that time the 120 young men lived together in the bank's training institute. Sessions lasted between ten and sixteen hours per day, six days a week. The time devoted to character building was about one-third of the entire program. The remaining two-thirds was devoted to numerous job-related technical skills. This estimate of the division of time between "spiritual" training and technical training, however, ignores the fact that the task of learning job skills was commonly interpreted from a character-building perspective. Even many aspects of recreation, such as the songs taught the trainees, were vehicles for related messages. A character-building intention finds opportunities in nearly every kind of learning activity.

While unquestionably this bank's program varies in many details from other programs, the underlying goals, philosophy and methods involved are very much alike across Japan. It is the purpose of this essay to clarify and document what these are.

The bank example

The most dramatic means for teaching character development were a series of special training events. The five reported here – *rotō, zazen,* military training, a weekend in the country, and an endurance walk – were the most fascinating of a larger group of such activities.

Rotō

For two days the group stayed at a government youth center in an agricultural region. Early on the morning after arrival, we were instructed to go down into the market town and find work from the residents. Instructions were to go singly from house to house, offering to work without pay. We were to do whatever our hosts asked of us. It was strongly emphasized that each was to go alone and work alone for the entire day. In addition, the trainees were disallowed from making any explanation for themselves or their reasons for volunteering to work. They could offer no more than their name and their willingness to be of service. Patently, the prospect of performing this very unusual exercise made the Japanese uneasy.

Dressed in white, nondescript athletic uniforms, and without benefit of a social identity or a reasonable explanation for themselves, the trainees were sent out to make a most unusual request of strangers. Their reliability would not be vouched for by their relationship to a known institution. This situation, difficult as it would be anywhere, is of particular difficulty in Japan, where, as a rule, strangers ignore one another and social intercourse between them is unusual and suspicious. Approached by an unknown person with a request like this, the common response would be a hurried and not very polite refusal. It was with considerable consternation that the trainees left for the town below.

At first they wandered about from street to street, reluctant to leave their friends and go alone to the front gate of some house where they would have to place themselves at the mercy of some stranger who was more than likely to refuse them.

Some walked four or five blocks together before anyone mustered the courage to make a first approach. Gradually dispersing, the common experience was to be refused two or three times before finally locating a house or a shop that allowed them in and gave them some form of work. All agreed to having been very anxious about the first approach, but found the second and the third easier to make as long as people were polite. An impolite refusal created considerable upset.

Taken in at last, the trainees all had similar experiences. Their hosts they saw as warm and understanding people. They found themselves happy to work hard and long. They volunteered to do things that even the host did not ask. This, they said, was partly to avoid having to go out again to seek a new situation and partly from a felt desire to be of help to those who had generously taken them in.

When all had returned, a discussion of the day's experience was held in the auditorium. The instructor in charge had each small group talk over their experiences and then discuss their relevance to the meaning of work. A variety of opinions emerged. In general, the trainees had had such an interesting and pleasant time with their hosts that it had not occurred to them to think of their tasks as "work." The instructor latched on to this point to ask whether the enjoyment of work had more to do with the kind of work performed or with the attitude of the worker to it. The bank's reasons for utilizing *rotoo* centered on establishing precisely the right answer to this question. The trainees, of course, concluded that "attitude" was critical. The gratitude they had felt to their hosts had made menial and even demeaning tasks easy to accept.

The deeper intent of *rotō,* as it is used by some Buddhist temples, is a bit different. It is used as a method of shocking people out of spiritual lethargy and complacency. The word *rotō* actually means something like "bewilderment" and refers to a state of insecurity established when the individual is divorced from his comfortable social place and identity. In the course of begging for work – that is, begging for acceptance by others – the subject is forced into a realization of how much is taken for granted in his daily life – especially one's dependence on affiliations, titles, ranks, and a system of support. Perhaps for the first time, the trainee begins to ask who he really is outside his fixed social identity. This is not a typical Japanese question. *Rotō* also provides a unique opportunity for a trusting and compassionate interaction between strangers. After such an experience, it is unlikely that the person will continue to disregard the humanity of others, and it is hoped that the experience will foster greater warmth and spontaneity in the individual.

The bank, however, had a different agenda. As the trainees themselves observed, the anxiety of rejection and isolation mounts with each refusal until finally, when some kindly person takes one in, a cathartic sense of gratitude arises. No matter what the work, even cleaning an outhouse, the sense of relief, of gratitude and of being trusted makes the work seem pleasant and satisfying. Work that is normally looked down upon is, in this circumstance, enthusiastically welcomed.

After such an experience, it is difficult to deny the assertion that any form of work is intrinsically neither good nor bad, satisfying nor unsatisfying, appropriate nor inappropriate. Pleasure in work, it must be concluded, varies according to one's attitude and circumstances. Failure to enjoy one's work, it was pointed out, was essentially a matter of improper attitude, and any work can be enjoyable with the correct, that is, positive, attitude. Since it must assign rather dull and methodical tasks to many of its employees, this lesson was of obvious value to the bank, but also, on reflection, to each of the trainees who would have to perform the work.

Zen meditation

We practiced Zen meditation (*zazen*) on three occasions.[3] The longest and most thorough of the three took place during the second month, when we visited a large and well-known Zen temple several hours by bus from the training institute. This temple, with its many fine buildings and lovely gardens, has the tradition of being the foremost institution in the region for the training of new Zen priests and, although the number of new priests has diminished, the temple has become extremely busy, providing two- to three-day Zen training sessions for sports teams, student groups, and business trainees.

On arrival the trainees were lined up and marched into a small room, where they deposited their shoes and baggage, and were then conducted to a large hall and made to sit formally on their knees. A priest informed them of the temple's rules and procedures and explained in detail the special manner of eating meals in a Zen temple. He left and the group sat for some time in silence. When he returned, he brought with him the head priest. We were instructed to bow our heads to the floor and to stay in that position until the head priest's greeting was ended. For about three minutes we bowed in this manner while he spoke of the tradition, rigors, and purpose of Zen.

The instructor next asked the group to try to sit in the lotus position, and while we struggled with this, he went on to explain that it was very important to sit up straight. "This will bring one's 'spirit' (*kokoro*) and body together in harmony," he said. "Sit up straight and you won't waver, either in spirit or in body. If you don't waver, you won't go astray or become confused." He then explained the method of counting breaths, telling us to breathe in and out very slowly, taking as long as possible without becoming uncomfortable. "This, too, serves to preserve the unity of spirit and body. It may be quite helpful for you in your work, since it will teach you the power of spiritual concentration. When you are bothered or worried, you can overcome such interference and perform more efficiently," he added.

Next, the 4-foot wooden paddle, the *kyosaku*, was introduced. "You are struck by the *kyosaku* or, more literally, 'given' the *kyosaku* for the purpose of supporting your determination." Being hit was an aid to concentration, he explained. He then demonstrated how he would walk up and down the room carrying the paddle. Stopping before someone, he showed how the person was to bring his hands together in a praying position in front of him, bow, and receive two blows across the back, between the base of the neck and the top of the shoulder blade. Before assuming the regular *zazen* position, the person was to bow once again to the *kyosaku*, this time with gratitude. The effect of this introduction, needless to say, generated considerable anxiety.

We next underwent two half-hour sessions of meditation. There was no tranquillity or concentration, however, since everyone was obviously uncomfortable and there was constant fidgeting. The priest walked up and down, stopping frequently to apply the *kyosaku* to individual backs. The loud "whack, whack" as it struck only created more anxiety in the rest of us. I tried maintaining the proper count and rhythm, but the noise and motion and the recurring thought that perhaps the priest would stop and strike me made even the seemingly simple task of counting up to 10 over and over very difficult. The more I tried to forget my concern with the progress of the priest, the worse my anxiety grew. When I was finally struck by the priest, I was surprised to find that the pain was inconsequential compared to the relief and physical release I experienced. Afterwards, for a few minutes at least, I relaxed enough to begin to concentrate.

In between the interminably long half-hour sessions, we were instructed to walk in single file around the hall, maintaining the concentration on breathing and counting as we walked. These brief walking sessions were designed to provide respite from the pain and discomfort of sitting, yet just as the circulation in our legs began to return, we began another painful sitting. The moments when the walking sessions ended were poignantly ones of regret and resignation.

At one point, the group was marched single file into an adjoining room, where all again sat in the lotus position along low, narrow tables. Hymnals were passed out, and for five minutes the trainees chanted Buddhist hymns, following the lead of the priest. Eating utensils were passed out, and first soup and then an unappetizing rice gruel were dished out by younger priests running in a squatting position along the line of tables. The recipients were told to bow when accepting food. Without a word we ate. There was an opportunity for seconds, but most, hungry as they were, refused. Next, hot water was poured, and, using it, we cleaned each bowl in turn until only the final one contained warm water and residue. This awful stuff we were told to drink as if it were tea. The entire proceedings had not taken twenty minutes. During the short subsequent break the trainees complained bitterly about the food.

We returned to the large hall for more painful sitting. Although tranquillity was the goal, most continued to struggle uncomfortably. Some stealthily glanced at their watches, yet most seriously attempted to breathe and concentrate as the priests instructed. This, in fact, was the best way to survive the endless discomfort. At one point the priest explained that it was quite natural to feel pain and impatience. Just to learn to sit correctly takes considerable practice, he said. Enduring the pain was just the beginning of Zen. He repeated that a straight back, counting, the half-opened eyes, and a position of weightlessness for the shoulders were the keys to learning to sit without discomfort. This was the first step in learning to concentrate one's spirit.

There was considerable relief when a ninety-minute temple-cleaning exercise was announced. Some went to clean the outhouse and others helped clean up around the kitchen. My detail raked leaves and pulled grass along a path. The priest ordered us to be meticulous in pursuit of the tiniest weed.

We did more *zazen* and then had dinner exactly on the pattern of the previous meal. From six o'clock to seven we were given time to wander about the temple. Some trainees found a small snack stand in a park adjoining the temple grounds and, against instructions, purchased snacks which they greedily consumed. All seemed miserable. Without exception, they observed that all one could possibly think about was enduring each half-hour session until the bell rang and the walking began. Their discomfort and distraction were so great that little or nothing of Zen as a religious experience could be appreciated.

For two more hours that night, the practice continued. The temple hall by that time was dark and quite cold, the temperature below freezing, but there was no relief for the seated trainees. At nine o'clock we went to sleep right where we had been sitting. There was some talk and some illicit eating of food bought at the snack stand, but very soon everyone was asleep.

It was pitch dark and bitterly cold at 3:00 A.M. when the trainees were awakened and brusquely told to get up, to fold their sleeping gear, and to assume the lotus position. Soon we were marched to the main hall, where, once more sitting, we joined fourteen priests in an hour-long chanting of prayers and occasional prostrations. There were no cushions and this floor was excruciatingly hard. My stomach was empty. The cold seemed unendurable. My knees and legs were in agony. I doubted I could endure much more.

Breakfast, at 5:30 A.M., was no different from the two previous meals, and yet many famished trainees asked for seconds. The hot soup tasted good on such a cold morning. From six o'clock to seven, we were given another free period. Most trainees tried to sleep, covering themselves with the cushions as best they could, too tired, shocked, and unhappy to talk with one another. I recalled the treatment of prisoners of war a number of times, and found it easy to understand the breakdown of morale and cohesiveness under stress. All I wished to do was escape into sleep.

The next hour was spent again sitting and chanting. Then the head priest gave a half-hour lecture. . . .

For the rest of the morning we meditated. No one seemed any more comfortable or adapted to the sitting position, and the squirming continued. My legs continued to become numb, and often I could not stand in order to walk around at the end of the half-hour sessions. The only consolation during the last two and one-half hours was the knowledge that with each minute we were getting nearer the end.

During the ride back to the bank's training center there was much comment about the pain, and the terrible food, and how one of the hardest events of the three-month training was over. While very few of the trainees were impressed by what they had learned of themselves or the nature of the Zen experience, many were deeply impressed by the strict discipline and dedication of the younger priests training at the temple. Some indicated that in the future, when they felt depressed or sorry for themselves, they would remember the stern, simple lives of those priests. *Satori* ("enlightenment"), *mushin* ("selflessness"), and other Zen concepts were no more comprehensible after the two days than they had been previously, but the Spartan ways of Zen living had become tangible realities.

Visits to military bases

The first trip to a Japanese military installation for training came in the second week of the program. The trainees, sixty at a time, went to an army base not far from the city. The purpose, we were told, was to learn group order. The young men were noticeably nervous on the bus going to the base. Most rode silently looking out the window. After arrival, we were assigned to several barracks and given army cast-off fatigues to wear.

In the afternoon of the first day, after a lunch in the enlisted men's mess, we were run through an obstacle course and then given the Japanese army physical fitness test. Nothing particularly frightening occurred, and people grew more relaxed. Then for a whole afternoon we practiced close order drill, eventually taking turns as drill sergeants ourselves, calling our commands and marching one another around the parade grounds in teams of twelve, awkward and chaotic at first. We became reasonably competent as the day passed under the tutelage of the regular army supervisors. During the occasional breaks, there was much joking about being in military uniforms. In particular, the trainees took great pleasure in saluting one another. A respectful appreciation for the precision of passing regular army units also developed.

The mood on the bus home was in marked contrast to the gloomy atmosphere going out. There was much ebullient yelling back and forth and noisy rubbernecking at girls along the way. Everyone gaily saluted the driver and his female assistant as we descended from the bus.

Near the end of the three months, we again went to a military base, this time the former Naval Officer Candidate School at Edajima – Japan's Annapolis. Today it is still in use as a school for the Self-Defense Force Navy. Some years after World War II, a museum for the various personal effects, diaries, reminiscences and other illustrations of the brief days of Japan's suicide pilots was established on the base. The director of this museum is a man who began collecting these mementos after the war as evidence of the true attitudes and character of the pilots. He has given himself the mission of explaining or reinterpreting the *kamikaze* to a generation of younger Japanese who knew very little of their actual lives or character. The day-and-a-half visit to Edajima was primarily to see the museum and hear the director's explanation.

Our group was prepared for the visit by watching several recent commercial movies depicting the life of midshipmen training there during the war. According to these movies, only the cream of Japan's young men could enter Edajima after having passed the most rigorous academic and physical tests. In one movie it was described as the most difficult school to enter in Japan. The movies emphasized the spiritual or character strength and camaraderie of the young men, qualities making more tragic the fact that most were destined to die shortly after graduation. Having seen these dramatic portrayals of Edajima, the young bankers were duly impressed with its tradition and its almost sacred quality for prewar Japanese.

In an hour-long lecture, the director of the museum told of his impressions of the suicide pilots and the lessons their example might hold for young people in a peaceful, modern Japan. His lecture, entitled "What Is Man's Mission in Life?", made a stirring impact on the trainees.

He began by describing the education given at Edajima. In addition to physical and intellectual skill, perfection and alertness were demanded at all times. Midshipmen arriving at the top of a long flight of stairs might be asked, for example, to say how many steps they had just climbed. Discipline was so strict that many grew to hate their officers, and yet they would never complain openly, for to do so was to fail training. Teachers also accepted great personal suffering without complaint, for the spirit of the place was endurance and sacrifice for the nation. Newcomers gradually acquired this spirit and passed it on. The epitome of this was that after 1941, young men coming to Edajima realized that they were in fact volunteering to die. In the classrooms of Edajima, he claimed, there was much discussion of the small possibility Japan had for winning the war. He stressed that preparation to serve one's country up to and including death was not something that began with the suicide pilots. It was the spirit of Edajima long before the war. He told of a pilot of one of the miniature suicide submarines that set off for Hawaii at the time of Pearl Harbor departing with the final words, "We are bound to lose."

Such stories of courage and uprightness continued a while longer and then he observed:

Nobody wishes to experience unpleasant things, but unpleasant things are part of life and nothing of significance can be achieved without suffering. Today's individualism ignores this fact and easily becomes empty egoism. The men at Edajima had a kind of individualism and independence, one that focused on their mission to serve one's country, not on the pursuit of pleasure. The trouble with today's students is that they know nothing of the discipline and sacrifice required to change society for the better.

There was a young cadet at the academy who, because he opposed a certain rule at the school, sat in the same place for many weeks, fasting and drinking only water to show his opposition. His action was respected by the others because he didn't complain or criticize, but rather demonstrated the sincerity of his complaint by personally suffering. How many so-called revolutionaries today are prepared to do that kind of thing?

The director then told a story about the novelist Kawabata Yasunari. During a visit to a grade school near the end of the war, Kawabata asked the youngsters if there were any in the class willing to die for Japan. One young boy stepped forward and said, "I will." Kawabata asked his reasons with the observation, "If Japan loses, do you think your death will be regarded as a loss? If Japan wins, do you think you will be honored?" The little boy replied, "Mister, aren't you being misleading? I know that Japan is going to lose." Kawabata bowed to the little boy.

Through such anecdotes the simple courage of Japan's wartime young, particularly those volunteering to become suicide pilots, was presented. Their inner strength, not their zealousness or their naiveté, was emphasized. The *kamikaze* were Japan's best, the museum director concluded. They were the best informed about Japan's impending defeat, and yet they volunteered to die without even, in most cases, an opportunity to see family or friends a last time. There is a popular song about the fellowship of the suicide pilots and the fact that they would never again meet at cherry blossom time. The image of these young men taking off on warm spring afternoons is truly a tragic one, and the museum director at the end recalled this scene. Sitting very straight in their chairs, the trainees, to a man, were weeping silently as he finished.

The visit to the museum proper the next day was made in silent interest, with none of the troublemaking spirit that the trainees usually brought to their excursions. Once inside, they were allowed to wander about on their own, looking at the many rooms of paintings and other mementos of naval history, until they reached the rooms containing the personal stories of the suicide pilots. The trainees were deeply affected by the similarity in age between themselves and the young men who died in 1945. They noticed how beautifully written the pilots' diaries were. According to their own statements, it was a moving experience.

After inspecting the base, we were assigned to row heavy, cumbersome longboats, traditionally part of Edajima training. The difficulty of developing coordination in a crew was stressed, and as we clumsily knocked oars and hit one another with them, the point seemed easy to grasp. What I had thought might be interesting turned into a frustrating and mildly traumatic experience. Teamwork, here as elsewhere, was an almost perpetual theme.

A weekend in the country

We spent several days on a small island about an hour's boat ride from the city. According to our leaders, we were expected to learn something of self-reliance and the kind of ingenuity engendered by simple, rural living conditions. The weekend's activities were also to provide opportunities to let off steam and be as boisterous and rowdy as we wished. Several activities would also be conducted to teach us a greater appreciation for social interdependency and social service, we were told. Finally, living together in a cramped and primitively built lodge where meals were cooked on wood-burning stoves would be another experience helping us appreciate the oft-mentioned *shu-udan seikatsu* (group living). I was reminded of Boy Scouting more than anything else.

With our unpacking completed, we gathered in the main room of the lodge to listen to a short explanation from the head of the training section:

"In the city, in our modern training institute, we have no chance to let loose and become rough and tumble (*takamashi*), so we have come out here to let you express your energy and youthfulness. While all of you are bankers, and are normally expected to be proper and decorous, we want you to have a more aggressive spirit burning inside. This weekend will be a chance for you to find out just how boisterous and full of fight you can be. So don't hold back. Throw yourself into the activities we have planned as completely as you can. Finally, we are going to help some farmers in their fields, and we hope that all of you will learn and benefit from this experience."

The leader then divided the room into groups, had them face each other and instructed everyone to yell out in a loud voice, *"washoo, washoo,"* one group alternating with the other. We then began doing squat jumps thrusting our arms high over our heads, yelling *"washoo."* The two groups alternated and a piston-like effect was created, one group jumping up and yelling, followed by the other. After ten or fifteen minutes of this, the room seemed filled with a weird frenzy. The heat, constant rhythmic yelling, and unceasing motion made me feel a bit afraid, as if I had been locked in a boiler room with a monstrous engine. When the exercise ended (and it seemed interminably long), we collapsed with exhaustion. This was our introduction to what the trainers had in mind when they said they wanted us to be full of energy and boisterousness. I was fascinated to realize that our training went from the extremes of silent Zen meditation to this mass explosion of energy and noise.

The next morning before dawn the group ran in formation (i.e., our regular smaller groups) to a wide, empty stretch of beach facing the open air. A light rain was falling and, with the wind off the ocean, soaked our thin athletic outfits. After the usual calisthenics, we made a long line facing into the wind. Rotating leadership in each squad, we screamed commands at the top of our lungs. Most were quite inhibited at first, but eventually all were yelling as loud as possible. Next, we practiced swinging wooden swords up and down, as one would in practicing Japanese fencing. Intersquad *sumo* matches, marked by more effort than skill, were the last events held on the beach before breakfast. The run through the rain back to the lodge for breakfast seemed particularly dreary.

During the morning we went off with the various farmers who had agreed to put us to work in their fields. We were provided with scythes and other farm equipment, and under the farmers' direction we weeded gardens and cut grass in tangerine groves. Some of the trainees worked strenuously, while others loafed. The farmers were not inclined to make the trainees work harder, and the project was much like other work details we had experienced, even though it was explained to us as service (*hoshoo*) to the farmers.

That afternoon we were asked to comment on the experience. The general opinion was that being directed to go out and help farmers who had obviously been rounded up by our instructors and persuaded to allow us to work for them provided very little sense of actual service. Some said they enjoyed the work; others said they found it inappropriate to training as bankers. It was agreed that to learn about service to others, the work should be voluntary. The lesson was largely a failure, as I saw it, and only later did I learn that the bank's president, feeling that Japan's traditional values rested on its agricultural tradition, had personally ordered this element of the program.

The second afternoon was spent playing contact sports on the beach. Stripped to our waists and divided into two teams, we played several games popular in the old Japanese navy, *kiba gassen* and *boo-taoshi*. Another *sumo* wrestling tournament was the day's final event. In the first game, each side creates mounted warriors, with one man riding on the shoulders of three compatriots. Starting from opposite sides of the field, the two teams charge, and the side that forces the other's men to the ground first is the winner. The second game involves the defense of standing poles, one for each team. The object is to attack and tear down the opponents' pole while preserving one's own. At each end of the field the attackers assault the other's defenses by leaping upon the group, surrounding the pole, tearing people away from it, and wrestling with the people who come to reinforce the defenders. Neither of these two games took much more than fifteen minutes, but they were fiercely contested, and some of the less aggressive trainees were quite evidently frightened to have to fight their fellow trainees. The same consternation was apparent during the round robin *sumo* tournament. The roughhousing was not discussed afterward, and only later did I realize that it was part of a toughening-up regime in preparation for the marathon walk we all knew was the culminating ordeal of our training.

During the time on the island, squads were assigned cooking, clean-up, and other chores, and the conditions and organization of life in the lodge followed the usual camp patterns, even as far as singing songs around a great bonfire the last night. After the entertainment and singing, the program ended with all standing arm-in-arm in two great circles around the fire, swaying back and forth, singing the bank's song and the very sentimental song of the *kamikaze* pilots. As a bonding ritual, the time on the island worked very effectively.

The endurance walk

Ever since the first day, we had heard about the twenty-five-mile endurance walk to be held at the end of training. Our daily one-mile run and the other climbing and hiking activities were explained as preparation for this event. On the morning of the walk, there seemed to be a high level of anticipation and readiness, even among the weaker and less athletic trainees.

The program was simple enough. The trainees were to walk the first nine miles together in a single body. The second nine miles were to be covered with each squad walking as a unit. The last seven miles were to be walked alone and in silence. All twenty-five miles would be accomplished by going around and around a large public park in the middle of the city, each lap approximately a mile. A number of rules were set out by the instructors. It was forbidden to take any refreshment. During the second stage, each squad was to stay together for the entire nine miles and competition between squads was discouraged. Finally, it was strictly forbidden to talk with others when walking alone during the last stage.

The training staff also walked the twenty-five miles going around in the opposite direction, thus passing us face-to-face frequently. Some dozen or so young men from the bank, recent graduates of previous training programs, were stationed along the route and instructed to offer the trainees cold drinks, which, of course, they had to refuse. This was the program, and there was no emphasis at all placed on one person finishing ahead of another. Instructions were to take as much time as needed, as long as the entire twenty-five miles was completed. The walk began around 7:30 A.M. and finished around 3:00 P.M. There was no time limit and many had not gone the full twenty-five miles, but the collapse from heat prostration of a few led the instructors to call the event off at a point where most had a lap or two remaining.

On the surface, this program was simple enough, but in retrospect it seems to have been skillfully designed to maximize certain "spiritual" lessons. When we began, the day was fresh and cool, and it seemed as though we were beginning a pleasant stroll. Walking together in one large group, everyone conversed, joked and paid very little attention to the walk itself. The first nine miles seemed to pass quickly and pleasantly, and the physical hardship that we had been expecting seemed remote.

Forming up into squad groups at the beginning of the next nine miles, we were reminded again not to compete with other squads. But discovering squads close before and behind, the pace began escalating and resulted in an uproarious competition. As a team came up from the rear, the team about to be overtaken would quicken its pace. Before long, trainees found themselves walking very fast, so fast that those with shorter legs had to run occasionally to keep up. There was much yelling back and forth within each squad, the slower and more tired people crying out for a reduction in speed, the others urging them to greater efforts. A common solution was to put the slowest person at the head of the squad. This not only slowed the faster ones down but forced the slow ones to make a greater effort (a pattern I realized typified the way Japanese organizations order work and also what happens in elementary classrooms). Competing like this kept us from noticing how hard a pace we had been keeping. By the end of the second nine miles the toll was obvious. Many, besides suffering from stiff legs and blisters, were beginning to have headaches and show evidence of heat prostration. Some lay under a tree by the finish line sucking salt tablets. It was noon by that time, and the park baked under the full heat of a mid-June sun.

Any gratification the leading squad found in their victory was soon forgotten. At the finish line, there was no congratulation and no rest. Squads were sternly instructed to break up and continue walking, this time in single file and in silence. Soon a long line of trainees stretched over the entire circumference of the course. Having already covered eighteen miles, the last nine at a grueling pace, all were very tired. . . .

My own experience was to become acutely aware of every sort of pain. Great blisters had obviously formed on the soles of my feet; my legs, back and neck ached; and at times I had a sense of delirium. The thirst I had expected to be so severe seemed insignificant compared to these other afflictions. After accomplishing each lap, instead of feeling encouraged, I plunged into despair over those remaining. My awareness of the world around me, including the spectators in the park and the bank employees tempting us with refreshments, dropped almost to zero. Head down, I trudged forward. Each step was literally more painful than the one before. The image of a dazed prospector lost on the desert kept recurring in my mind. The temptation to stop and lie down for a while in the lush grass was tremendous. Near the end, I could do no more than walk for a minute or two and then rest for much longer. The others around me seemed to be doing the same thing. . . . For some reason, it was heartening to discover that six or eight of the trainees had fainted and were prostrate under a shady tree at the finish line, where they were receiving some medical attention. I, too, wanted to lie there with them, and yet I felt encouraged by the fact that I had not yet fallen. "I am stronger, I can make it," I thought to myself as I passed by. Other moments brought feverish dreams of somehow sneaking away. I reasoned that no one would notice if I slipped out of the park and returned just when the event was closing. Bushes became places I could hide behind, resting until the group was ready to go home. I kept going, I suppose, because I feared discovery. Although in a feverish state, I was surprisingly capable of looking objectively at my response to this test of endurance. The content of lectures about "spiritual" strength came back to me. I could see that I was easily tempted and inclined to quit. Under such stress, some aspects of my thoughts were obviously not serving my interest in completing the course. Whatever will power I had arose from pride and an emerging, almost involuntary, belief in the importance of character. If I was to finish, I needed just what I had been told – spiritual strength.

It angered and amused me to realize how cleverly this exercise had been conceived. I vowed over and over never to get involved in such a situation again. And yet, within days, when the memory of the physical pain had dimmed, I was taking great pride in my accomplishment and viewing my completion of the twenty-five-mile course as proof that I could do anything I set my mind to.

Discussion

These were the most notable activities of this particular program. In addition, there were a number of other, less dramatic and more day-in, day-out aspects that deserve our attention.

In order to sponsor an intense "group life," all leadership and direction of daily activities was placed in the hands of the trainees themselves, who took turns commanding the various twelve-man squads and assuming overall leadership. Such things as clean-up, kitchen and service details, the morning and evening assemblies, scheduling, and travel were all directed by the young men on a rotating basis. It was expected that a strong appreciation for the burdens of leadership and the need for cooperation would develop under such conditions. The most poignant illustrations of the necessity for order in group living came whenever the entire retinue traveled as a unit. The value of group discipline and coordination learned in the many exercises, starting with our training at the army base, quickly proved useful. At stations and elsewhere the young men enjoyed watching other, less orderly groups of young people struggle with the problem of keeping together.

Closely related to the matter of group living was the popular theme of teamwork (*chiimu waaku*). The form of organization for most competitions was the team. Studies related to banking, pursuit of hobbies, and other, less obviously group pursuits were arranged to require teamwork. While competition between individuals was seldom encouraged, group competition was a major means of motivation. It should be stressed that emphasis on "group living" and teamwork are so common in Japanese society that none of the young trainees, even those who were critical of other aspects of the program, complained of these things.

The physical had a definite role in character building. Each morning and evening, group exercises were held. On three occasions lectures on health and physical fitness were delivered. Whenever feasible, the instructors had the trainees hike, even run, to their destinations. It was not unusual for lectures at the institute to be interrupted by an instructor for the purpose of correcting trainees' posture. Underlying these efforts was the common assumption that good physical condition and proper posture are fundamental to the development of spiritual power.

Newcomers who had trouble developing enough skill and speed to pass the bank's standard abacus test found that the exercise had strong "spiritual" overtones. The practice required was long and tedious, and there were no shortcuts to developing speed. Practice was left entirely to each trainee, but the instructors watched with great interest. Trainees who did not practice or who gave up easily were privately cautioned (in *seishin* terms) and encouraged to try harder. The moral that dogged persistence would solve the problem lay at the heart of this exercise. One night I stumbled by accident upon an instructor and three trainees sitting on their knees on the concrete roof of the institute, all in obvious pain. The instructor had invited these poor performers to strengthen their will by joining him in this ordeal. . . .

How may we then define the term "spiritual"? If the frame of reference is a very general one contrasting physical and mental, the concept would be placed in the mental column. Attitudes, will power, concentration, and many other mental qualities are important aspects of spiritual power. Yet this kind of distinction obscures more than it clarifies, for the physical–mental distinction is not central to the concept. It is true that the "mind over matter" and "power of positive thought" philosophies approach the meaning of *seishin,* but there are differences. In the case of traditional Japanese thought, the mind–body is overridden by the concept *kokoro* (heart), important in Zen and in many traditional forms of education. *Kokoro* represents the broad area of individual psychosomatic unity. The state of an individual's *kokoro* may be composed or disturbed, and there are numerous terms for both of these conditions. Composure implies that both the mind and the body operate properly, efficiently and in harmony; in the state of disturbance, the mind and the body are accordingly upset, undependable, and involved in an adverse way with one another. Both of these states may be distinguished as to degree. Learning to achieve composure is one goal of *seishin* training, and a composed *kokoro* is regarded as a major source of *seishin* strength.

Many lessons in the bank's training were specifically aimed at teaching the trainees how to attain composure, or at least to awaken in them a greater awareness of the interrelationship of the physical and mental aspects of disturbance. Zen meditation and the emphasis on posture are two outstanding examples. Yet, composure is not an end in itself as much as it is a basis for more effective individual action. The standard by which spiritual strength is measured is performance. The outward manifestations of strength are such things as the ability to endure trouble and pain, coolness in the face of threat, patience, dependability, persistence, self-reliance, and intense personal motivation – qualities we would associate with "strong personal character." Yet spiritual strength is not measured by performance, no matter how spectacular, that results solely from cleverness or physical power, although these qualities are often interpreted as products of spiritual strength.

True strength hinges on difficulties that test a person's will, particularly one's will to carry on in some socially useful purpose. They include fear, disillusionment, depression, boredom, loneliness, and lack of confidence, as well as the more obvious problems of physical pain and temptations of all kinds. Any form of stress that tempts a person to resign his effort or to escape a problem is relevant as a test of spiritual strength and an opportunity for improvement. Similarly, any quality that helps the individual pass such tests is part of spiritual strength. For this reason, verbal instruction in the proper moral outlook can be regarded as contributing directly to spiritual power. It provides conviction and strengthens the individual's resolve.

Training for spiritual strength, as we have seen, uses artificially created tests to build up staying power for life's actual tests. The designs for tests are usually quite well considered, for there are a number of factors governing their success. First, they must not be too easy or too hard. The danger of excessive stress is real. Second, the experience of passing the ordeals must reveal to the trainee both the process of temptation and the methods of dispelling it. That is, the trainee must be prepared to experience the test in spiritual terms, and this often requires considerable teaching, in the normal sense, before the event. The goal is a new understanding as well as a formative experience.

Third, the test must be of some relevance to the trials of real life. An endurance walk may not seem very relevant to work in a bank, but the instructors pointed out that the temptation to take a forbidden drink of water "which costs nothing" is like the temptation to steal from one's own bank. An analogy was also made between the arduousness of sitting in *zazen* and the problem of maintaining concentration during mundane clerking. Spiritual growth is also typically connected to well-known public figures' successes. Japanese life is rife with Abraham Lincoln stories.

No matter what form of test is devised, the key element in the whole process is the experience of emotional wavering and the "spiritual" struggle within to carry on until the test is completed. Passing any test is not a matter of scoring high or coming in ahead of others. Competition is within the self and success is marked by completion of the ordeal. Enduring one test to its conclusion will make completion of subsequent similar tests less difficult, it is assumed, and in this way maturation occurs. During the moments of greatest wavering, the individual experiences his own weaknesses with heightened awareness, and on the basis of this self-knowledge he can proceed to gain equanimity, self-confidence and will power.

According to spiritualist thought, "incorrect" attitudes are typically the source of personal difficulty.[4] What is meant by "attitudes" in this instance is not opinions, such as political opinions, but rather a person's general attitude toward difficulties to which he must personally respond. For example, the bank's purpose in using *rotoo* was to teach a better attitude toward work, one that is accepting, positive and enthusiastic. The basis of a proper attitude, in this context, begins with acceptance of life's necessities and responsibilities. Instead of fighting such requirements, the most satisfactory attitude is to acknowledge and accept them. To regret or attempt to avoid one's duties only leads to frustration, disappointment, and upset.

The dimension accepting–resisting, which is consistently important throughout Japanese life, is a key to evaluating the correctness of a person's attitudes. Complaining, criticizing, arguing, and other forms of resistance constitute evidence of improper attitudes and are predictive of behavioral problems. Ready acceptance of unpleasant or difficult tasks, on the other hand, illustrates a correct attitude.

While this approach to learning seeks to sponsor an accepting attitude[5] toward all of life's necessities, in Japan the greatest attention is paid to developing the proper attitude toward social responsibilities. The interdependent nature of society generates duties and obligations that make the diligent performance of every role important. This is a basic assumption taught as a fact of life. The necessity of responsibility to one's social role follows from this fact. In the bank's training, furthermore, society itself was portrayed as greatly dependent on everyone cooperating.

While such social realities are underlined, individual differences are ignored or treated as unimportant. It is a firm principle that individual needs and desires are properly challenged and controlled as part of the program to develop spiritual strength, and there are numerous historical cases in which the coincidence of a desire to toughen up trainees on the part of the instructors and a desire to demonstrate spiritual strength on the part of the trainees have resulted in tests going to extreme and dangerous levels.

For any person, the correct and most satisfying goals, according to this kind of thinking, are fulfillment of one's social role and achievement in one's chosen personal pursuit. These goals are assumed to be self-evident. The spiritually mature person is, by definition, a contributor to society. The evidence lies in cooperation and service to others. This agenda allows for a limitless differentiation of levels of accomplishment and recurrent perceptions of incompleteness. Spiritual maturation is a lifelong pursuit, one assisted by all manner of specialized programs.

A few more characteristics of the approach should be noted briefly as they relate to classroom education.

1. Emphasis is placed on non-verbal forms. A well-behaved class, for example, is not necessarily an indication of lethargy, stupidity, or the failure of the teacher. It is likely to be interpreted as evidence that students are well disciplined, receptive, and respectful. Spiritualism, furthermore, takes a skeptical view of verbal logic when it generates excuses for resistance, non-participation and failure to be responsible.

2. Rather than viewing difficulties and hardships that students face as barriers to education, and therefore as things to be overcome by better facilities or improved methods of instruction, a spiritual perspective is likely to regard hardship in an educational situation as an asset to the training process itself. Discomforts, for example, pose challenges and are therefore useful. Arduous cramming for entrance exams is likely to be interpreted as good for one's character.

3. Knowing how difficult a test should be and evaluating each student's capacity are key teacher tasks. This insight is analogous to what parents in "tough love" programs are called upon to develop. Being appropriately challenging is an art.

4. A knowledge of self and self-reflection (*jikaku* and *hansei*) are stressed in this approach. Blame for difficulties or failure, individual or social, will be placed most heavily on spiritual weakness rather than on a lack of knowledge or inadequacy in the social environment. The spiritual perspective thus gives precedence to spiritual reform over social reform. Schooling is certainly viewed as an instrument of change and improvement, but its influence should be on individual character.

5. Rather than encouraging students to consider themselves as different from one another, and thus sponsoring individualistic thought and creativity, spiritual education sponsors outward conformity to teachers' examples and group standards. Non-conformity is viewed as disruptive of group unity and a sign of character weakness. It is thought that conformity is made from conviction, not dullness, and that to conform to the group is difficult rather than easy.

6. Spiritual education also aims to help the individual achieve contentment through the development of an ordered and stable psyche free from confusion and frustration. This is to be attained through the gradual conquest of *waga* or *ga* (one's primitive self, or id in Freudian terms). The phrase expressing this process, *waga o korosu* (literally "kill the self"), is a common expression related to this approach. While students in elementary and middle schools are too young for this emphasis, it begins to creep into education as high school and university entrance exam preparation looms.

7. Whenever possible, competition is organized along group rather than individual lines and many events have no obvious competitive quality. This is not because competition hurts feelings, but because it disrupts group unity and because the real competition takes place *within* each individual.

8. The unchanging nature of spiritual problems and their solutions is a basic assumption of the approach. Teachers, parents, and senior students are, by virtue of greater experience and training, spiritually more advanced and therefore worthy of respect and authority. Age does not become a sign of outdatedness, and intergenerational continuity and concord in the unchanging pursuit of spiritual strength are encouraged. Authority in school is much cleaner as a result.

The similarity between the bank's program and processes and methods found in middle schools (Fukuzawa and LeTendre, this volume), in certain Japanese forms of psychiatric therapy (see, for example, Reynolds, 1969), in Zen training (Hori, this volume), in religious rituals of individual reform (Wimberley, 1969), and in practices of reform for criminals in Japanese prisons illustrates a simple lesson, namely, that educational efforts which seek some kind of character change or improvement are best studied within a single theoretical framework, one that will also adequately account for other kinds of psychological transformations. At various points in the training reported here, for example, anxiety or deprivation was artificially intensified and then reduced, creating a strong sense of relief and catharsis which served to strengthen certain intended directions of change in a trainee's view of himself and of his relationship with society. The parallels between education and such processes as initiation, therapy, and conversion are undeniable.

Whether spiritual training is to be labeled education, initiation, socialization, conversion, or therapy is not, however, a profitable question. We have a strong academic inclination to understand education as verbal instruction leading to improved storage and manipulation of symbolic information; this is the reason for cognitive psychology's centrality. This is what we see happening in schools between teachers and students. Yet learning and maturation are far more complex and may be sponsored by many means, not just verbal instruction. Personal and social experiences and the development of spiritual strength are undeniably critical too. Actual spiritual training exercises are a peripheral part of contemporary Japanese schooling; nevertheless, the attitude itself permeates schools, and to Japanese parents and teachers it is a crucial part of the preparation for adulthood and central to the understanding of personal growth.

This is also why the bank chose to emphasize it in its introductory training, marking, as it were, a critical point in the life cycle.

Notes

1. See, for example, Nitobe (1905), Benedict (1946), and Suzuki (1959). Unfortunately, explanations of Japanese arts and sports in English seldom mention *seishin* foundations or much of their methodology.
2. Many of the most commonly encountered values – fortitude (*nintai*), patience (*gaman*), endurance (*shimboo*), tenacity (*gambaru*), and the like point to this form of behavior. Of course, loyalty is hardly meaningful without the ingredient of persistence.
3. Kapleau (1965) offers a thorough account of the procedures and philosophy of *rinzai* Zen, the same sect as the temple visited by the trainees.
4. I have in mind the expressions *kokoro-gamai, taido, kokoro no mochikata,* and *mono no kangaekata,* all of which translate as attitude.

The emotional foundations
of early learning

From monastic training and a "boot camp" for bankers, we turn our attention to children and the entrance to public school. Considering the radical shift in context and purpose of this new direction, we should not expect to find much similarity of philosophy or practice. But similarities do exist. In fact, some of the most glaring incongruencies in descriptions of Japanese teaching can be uncovered by comparing studies of different levels within the public school system. Compare Rohlen's 1983 description of high schools with Peak's 1992 description of early learning. We can begin our detailed exploration of the Japanese landscape in earnest by trying to see what essential foundations the Japanese lay and expect will be sustained throughout life.

Our choice of the word "emotional" in the title of this section deserves comment. For us it contrasts rather neatly with the cognitive, drawing attention to the important matters preschool teachers focus on: the inner world of the child; connections between the child and the whole class; and integrating aspects of the child's personality. Japanese preschool and early elementary education have been generally portrayed as nurturing and "child centered" (White, 1987; Peak, 1989). Teachers try to gain the attention of the learners and engage them in in-depth questioning. In elementary school, the emphasis is on the class (*kumi*) and small group (*han*) as organizational units. The classroom organization of elementary school focuses heavily on the close, "wet" emotional relations of peers that Lewis describes.

Thinking and understanding in Japanese involve the "heart" (sometimes translated as "mind" but definitely having a somatic location in the chest). When in everyday English we refer to mental processes or to thinking, we have the head in mind. The cognitive domain works best if it is not influenced by too much emotion – then "cool reason" can prevail. The Japanese, too, value inner calm as an enhancement to thinking, but they focus on the child's emotions as an integral part of the learning process.

Everyone progresses together. *Minna to issho,* or "all together," is a prime curricular goal in the early years of education. At this time, teachers focus on laying the basis for meaningful participation in the social order. This consistent approach to the classroom as a community leads teachers to seek to harness the child's feelings for others (empathy, the need to play and belong). Although this purpose may be couched in statements like "just letting the children play," this play is extremely significant because it is highly organized by the teachers. It is organized to use community building and emotional support as antecedent to critical thinking and cognitive skill development.

This means, of course, that students who learn exceptionally quickly or slowly will chafe at the group's pace. Much of this irritation is alleviated by an emphasis on emotional harmony and sharing. Individual contributions, like Tomoko's song that Kotloff describes, are assimilated as part of the group effort. In this regard, some researchers see a suppression of both the student's individuality and creativity. Teachers of this age group have an intimate grasp of the social and psychological processes that occur in a group of young children. These insights are sometimes used in ways analogous to Zen training or *seishin kyōiku.*

One criticism frequently raised about the Japanese capacity and wish to generate group feelings is that it leads to conformity and a denial of the individual. Sato's study of a fifth-grade classroom in Tokyo addresses this issue and arrives at some enlightening conclusions. Although individuals must subordinate themselves to the group, group and individual are not dialectically opposed, as in American thought. Rather, group and individual are joined by complex dynamics in which supportive groups can make it safe to explore one's feelings.

In direct opposition to our stereotypes of Japanese education as "killing the individual," elementary school and classroom organization offers children more time to talk and more time to interact with the teacher. Unpalatable as it may be to some researchers, Japanese elementary teachers maintain a boisterous, engaged atmosphere while simultaneously getting children to do significant amounts of academic work. Why then is the emotional life of the child apparently so neglected in subsequent years of schooling? Has the task been accomplished? Does maturity demand a new focus? The refocusing of the teacher's efforts in subsequent years is addressed by LeTendre in the next section.

By American standards, there is great compliance and conformity in Japanese early education. There is also remarkably little worry among Japanese school children about being scolded by the teacher for the wrong answer (at the elementary level). Teachers and children are united in a search. Similarly, teachers' lives are organized to promote a sense of common struggle. By organizing learning as a set of goals to be achieved by the group, much of the invidious comparison of American schools (and of later Japanese education) is avoided.

The social and emotional life of the child is the teacher's primary focus. And there is an assumption that the social atmosphere largely determines the emotional balance. Not unlike U.S. elementary schools, where first-grade walls are covered with pink lambs and smiling whales, Japanese schools emphasize the effect of the environment. But the focus is on the social, not the physical, environment. The most important objects in the child's landscape are other children.

Entrance to middle school, as we see in the next section, is a major disjuncture in children's lives. In middle school, children are held to be ready for rigorous training and shaping. The concern with group living will be replaced with a concern for hierarchy and organization. In the clubs of middle school, children will be abruptly introduced to senior–junior relations. Individual commitment to the group and near-total involvement with the institution are expected.

Both Japanese and American thinkers have wondered whether there is a contradiction between the intense group processes found in Japanese public schools and the creative expression of the individual. Many Japanese criticize their own system for this failing and look to the "creative" American classrooms. The problem of the collectivist inclination surfaces early in the landscape of learning and will figure again as a major theme in subsequent sections of this book. Are complex problems requiring many contributions likely to be a Japanese strength, whereas problems best solved in relative isolation by independent thought likely to be a weakness? When is the emotional life of the group supportive of individual needs and when does it demand support?

Fostering social and intellectual development: the roots of Japan's educational success

CATHERINE C. LEWIS

When schools care about children, children care about schooling.
Thomas Sergiovanni

Recently, I interviewed a group of Japanese elementary teachers who had toured American elementary schools. They were eager to share with Japanese colleagues several features of American elementary education they had just observed: multicultural curricula; integration of computers into classroom life; drama and role-playing used to help students understand history. Yet they were puzzled and troubled by other aspects of American elementary school life: ability grouping of children; discipline systems that put the names of misbehaving children on the blackboard for all to see; the ever-changing membership of elementary classes as students were pulled out or added for special activities, remedial help, or "gifted" education. Echoing the questions of dozens of other Japanese teachers I have interviewed over the past decade, they gently asked how the practices that struck them as so different from those in Japan – ability grouping, public rewards and punishments doled out by the teacher, variable class membership – affected the social fabric of elementary school life. "Don't American parents complain that ability grouping violates children's right to equal educational opportunity?" they asked. "Don't children in the low-

This essay draws on the material presented in *Educating Hearts and Minds: Reflections on Japanese Preschool and Elementary Education*, by Catherine C. Lewis (New York: Cambridge University Press, 1995). I wish to acknowledge the support of the Abe Fellowship Program of the Center for Global Partnership, the Nippon Life Insurance Foundation, the Social Science Research Council, the Spencer Foundation Small Grants Program, and the Association for Asian Studies.

ability group feel like less valued members of the class?" "When children are publicly warned about misbehavior, aren't other children reluctant to be their friends?" "How do American teachers develop a feeling of 'classhood' when all class members and their teacher do not spend the whole day together?"

One is hard pressed to find an American who *hasn't* heard that Japanese students excel on international tests of academic achievement. Yet, how many Americans know that the Japanese accomplish this without ability grouping or tracking of students during the elementary and junior high years? Or that about thirty days of Japan's famed longer school year are devoted to activities – school festivals, field days, picnics, overnight trips – designed to build a sense of community and camaraderie within the school? Japan's educational achievements are often credited to the rigorous, challenging curriculum that all children are expected to master and the skillful way it is taught. These are important, I believe, but they are only half the story. Rigor is emphasized, but so is caring. Pervading Japanese elementary education is a deliberate, thoughtful effort to make the school like a family: a friendly, supportive place that meets children's social and emotional needs, as well as their intellectual needs.

In the history of American education, the pendulum has swung back and forth between concern with intellectual rigor and with students' social adjustment. The two are often thought of in a hydraulic relationship: Increasing the rigor of the curriculum undermines children's social development; increasing attention to children's social development means retreating from a demanding curriculum. This chapter argues that Japanese elementary education attends to both social and intellectual development: Children pursue a challenging curriculum in an environment that is caring and supportive. How is this done? Looking at Japanese elementary education from three vantage points – curriculum, human relationships, and explicit values – we will ask how the demands of intellectual and social development are integrated in each.

Observational method

The account that follows draws heavily on observations I have conducted in Japanese elementary schools over the past decade.

In 1985, I spent a minimum of one full day in each of 15 different first-grade classrooms in 13 Tokyo public schools (a convenience sample). The diverse sample included schools in wealthy and poor neighborhoods of Tokyo; the oldest as well as one of the newest elementary schools in Tokyo; classes that ranged in size from 23 students (in central-city areas of declining enrollment) to 45 (in rapidly expanding industrial areas); and teachers ranging from one to forty years of teaching experience. Subsequently, I observed classrooms in grades one through six and interviewed teachers in Tokyo, Kyoto, and Nagoya during four additional stays in Japan (in 1987, 1989, 1990, and 1993). The longest of these was in 1993, when I observed in two Nagoya elementary schools intensively for four months, and when my own sons attended the local preschool and elementary school in our mixed factory and residential neighborhood in Nagoya.

In my visits to Japanese schools, I interviewed teachers after observing them teach. I asked them standard questions about classroom organization and discipline and specific questions about incidents I had observed. These questions were ethnopsychological in focus: I asked teachers why they used particular instructional techniques, and tried to elicit the thinking about children's learning and development that underlay the techniques. The sample of teachers I observed and interviewed cannot be assumed to be a representative sample. Yet some practices were so pervasive that it seems almost certain that they would be prominent in any sample. For example, in all of the more than 30 elementary schools that I studied, in three cities, in observations that spanned six years, (1) children assumed responsibility for many aspects of classroom management, such as quieting the class and calling it to order; and (2) all used fixed, small groups of children (*han*) as the basic units for many daily classroom activities. Compared to a long-term ethnography, in which the observer spends many months or years at a single site, my observations no doubt give a more "model" view of educational practices: I saw less behind-the-scenes action and presumably more of what teachers and principals wanted me to see. Yet what I found is remarkably consistent with the independent observations of long-term ethnographers like Nancy Sato (1991a).

Many of the practices that I describe below – such as the use of *han* and children's assumption of responsibility for much classroom management – are long-term practices that could not possibly have been marshalled for the visit of a foreign researcher. On the other hand, lesson content or disciplinary force could more easily have been modified with my presence in mind.

Although this essay focuses only on Japanese classrooms, it is worthwhile to note that my implicit comparative framework is based on classroom observations and teacher interviews with U.S. elementary teachers, many of whom were observed or interviewed as part of special research projects or school change efforts. Like their Japanese counterparts, they were not randomly or representatively sampled and, as volunteers, they were probably among the more capable and confident teachers.

Curriculum

How does the Japanese elementary curriculum address the dual demands of social and intellectual development? As other researchers have documented, all Japanese elementary students are expected to master a rigorous academic curriculum; by late elementary school, the lowest-performing Japanese classes outperform the highest-performing U.S. classes in mathematics (Stevenson and Stigler, 1992). But as William Cummings and others have noted, the Japanese elementary curriculum is focused on the whole child, not just on the intellect: "Japanese teachers believe in 'whole-person' education. . . . they feel that their most important task is to develop well-rounded 'whole people,' not just intellects."

Nonacademic subjects – art, music, physical education, homemaking, and special class activities – account for more than one-third of instructional hours at first grade and more than 40 percent of instructional hours by sixth grade (Monbusho, 1989b). First-graders spend as much time in art and music (combined) as they do in mathematics. The Ministry of Education's official Course of Study for Elementary Schools is striking in its focus not just on academic development but on social, emotional, and ethical development as well. Its goals for the elementary years include, for example, children's "interest in language," "affection for our country and its history," "love of nature," "love of music," "richness of sentiment," "fondness for exercise" and "reverence for life." To be sure, Japanese teachers lead their students in learning mathematics, Japanese, and other academic subjects. But they also lead them in brushing their teeth, thinking about ways to ease their mothers' workloads at home, discussing what it means to "do your utmost" at the upcoming athletics festival, and talking about whether all class members are building friendships.

Approximately thirty days of Japan's school year are devoted to special activities and ceremonies – carnivals, sports days, school excursions, service projects, art and music festivals – designed to bring all members of the school together in a shared, memorable event. Some of these events are preceded by weeks of preparation in which, for example, students craft invitations to send to local senior citizens, organize brigades to walk them to the school, decorate the school grounds, and practice for the event. There are times for seriousness, when students talk about what it means to "do their utmost" at the upcoming sports day or learn to use the kerosene stoves and sharp cleavers they will use on their upcoming camping trip. But there are also times for hilarity: when principal and teachers dress up like rock stars and perform a skit for the school or when children carry off an elaborate "aliens' squirt-bottle battle" they've planned as the final event of the school festival. In planning and reflecting on these various school events, teachers ask themselves questions, many based on the goals of the national curriculum. Did the event build a feeling of cohesiveness (*matomari*) within the school? Did children of different ages and from different classes work together well? Did the event help children develop persistence and responsibility? Did we create happy memories? Children's personal development, their connection to the group, and the development of the whole child – through athletics, art, outdoor activity, service, or just plain fun – are the goals of these thirty days a year devoted to special activities.

As American educators are being pressed to show "accountability," measured by achievement tests, the Japanese national curriculum enshrines outcomes that are matters of heart and soul as well as mind: "richness of sentiment," "an active attitude, as one family member, of wanting to improve family life." Japanese teachers need not feel that their attention to children's social and emotional development is a distraction from their real role as educators; along with intellectual development, social and emotional development are central to education as defined by national goals.

From the child's point of view, Japan's whole-child curriculum may create an image of the "good student" that goes well beyond academic performance. In the 19 first-grade classrooms where I recorded school, class, or group goals, only 8 percent of these goals focused on intellectual development. The vast majority focused on children's social development ("Let's be a friendly class"; "Let's help each other"), persistence ("Let's persist until the end"), and energy or enthusiasm ("Let's play outside energetically"). Although these goals are closely based on the national curriculum, they are discussed and sometimes chosen by students – particularly the weekly class and group goals, which often reflect children's own language and experiences: "Let's play dodgeball without the boys hogging the ball," "Let's become a class where it's okay to make mistakes," and "Let's become children who easily say 'I'm sorry' and 'Thank you.' "

Researchers interested in "multiple intelligences" have noted that U.S. schooling heavily emphasizes verbal and mathematical intelligence and neglects other kinds of intelligence: musical, kinesthetic, visual-spatial, and interpersonal (Gardner, 1985). Because of its emphasis on art, music, social development, physical education, and other areas beyond verbal and numerical skills, Japanese elementary education may extend a somewhat broader welcome mat to children, providing more arenas where children can express themselves and develop competence.

In Japanese elementary schools, the dual concern with social and intellectual development is evident not just in *what* is taught but also in *how* it is taught. After visiting local playgrounds as part of social studies, first graders worked together in cooperative groups of four to design their "ideal park" and build a three-dimensional model of it. The teacher announced at the outset that the lesson had two goals: "to make the most wonderful park you can and to listen kindly to the ideas of every member of your group." Similarly, the goals of a first-grade science lesson were to "find out which bottle holds more and explain to your classmates how you found out" and "to share water without grabbing, so it won't get spilled, and if we do have water spills, to help each other clean up without saying things like 'It's not my fault' or 'You did it.' "

Human relationships

A Japanese teacher once described her goal for first grade as "developing a 'thread' to each child"; this thread would enable her to feel what the child felt, and the child to feel what she felt. On-the-job training for new Japanese elementary teachers focuses not on techniques for conveying subject matter but on techniques for building trusting relationships with children and for understanding how children feel and think (Shimahara and Sakai, 1995). *Kizuna* – the bond or tie between students and teacher – is seen as the central principle of good education; to develop this bond, new teachers are urged to "mingle with students without disguise and pretense" (Shimahara and Sakai, 1995). Here's the kind of advice experienced Japanese elementary teachers give their new colleagues:

Teaching is a kind of art. Emphasis should be placed on the relationship of hearts, the nurturing of bonding between the teacher's and children's hearts.

It is important to understand children as human beings whose characteristics are expressed in their activities. It is my belief that all children can do their best and concentrate on work. But it depends on the teacher's approach and desire. I am not concerned with how to teach children; rather I try to understand them first by developing personal relations, *kakawari*. When I get a new class I do not teach subject matter immediately. Instead I play with children intensely for a week to gain a good understanding of them. Then I will begin to know what kinds of children they are and gradually direct them toward the goals of learning on the basis of happy and trustful *kakawari* with them. (Shimahara and Sakai, 1995:156–7)

The concern with developing strong, positive bonds – among children and between children and teachers – extends to every corner of Japanese elementary education. We will examine three aspects of elementary school life that illustrate this concern with human bonds: the investment in a sense of community within the school; discipline practices; and fixed small groups.

Investment in classroom and schoolwide community

Why do Japanese elementary schools devote approximately thirty days a year to shared activities such as festivals and school trips? These events are not required by the national curriculum, yet they are accorded great importance by teachers and students alike. *Matomari* (cohesiveness or unity) is commonly mentioned as a goal for these schoolwide activities. The events are meant to create happy, lifelong memories. Many a principal has regaled me with the story of a difficult student who finally stopped being disruptive after "touching hearts" with classmates and teachers on the school camping trip or during the shared hard work preparing for the school festival.

Similarly, teachers' investment in *gakkyuzukuri* (creating classhood) is meant to connect children to a larger entity – the class – that is meaningful and important to them. Children talk about what kind of class they want to be and what chores, "promises," and goals they will need to become that kind of class. Children meet briefly twice a day, and for a longer period once a week, to discuss their progress in becoming a class and to plan enjoyable, shared activities. Many of my friends in their forties and fifties still attend reunions of their elementary school classes and reminisce over events that are still very much a part of elementary school life: sports day, class trips, and carnivals planned by the upper grades to entertain the younger students.

Japanese elementary students and teachers typically stay together for two years, providing a long time to create and experience a sense of community. Except for the ten-minute or twenty-minute breaks between each academic lesson (when students are often completely unsupervised), teachers spend the whole day with their students: Students and teacher eat lunch together in the classroom, and the classroom teacher is responsible for all or nearly all subjects, including science, art, music, and physical education. Likewise, activities that fragment the class – such as pull-out programs and ability grouping – are eschewed (Kajita, Shiota, Ishida, and Sugie, 1980).

Teachers help build connections among children through lessons that draw out children's personal experiences and ideas. In many classrooms, the day begins with the two daily student monitors giving "one-minute speeches." Often, these focus on what they did the previous day after school – extracurricular classes, TV programs, family activities, and so forth. Class members then question them for five minutes or so: Where do you play baseball? What do you play with your dog? What's your favorite character on the Ultraman show? Like many other activities, these speeches are designed to help children get to know one another as people. Children compose and deliver oral reports on "my most precious possession," tell about their grandparents, draw in each class member's house on a class map, and discuss what each class member likes most and least about school. In a society known for "groupism" and "conformity," teachers' interest in drawing out each child's experience is somewhat surprising. Yet, as one teacher pointed out, "To nurture the group, you must nurture each individual."

In addition to helping children get to know one another as human beings and providing shared, enjoyable experiences that built a sense of unity, teachers scrupulously avoided practices that would foster competition among children. If student work was posted, it was usually the work of every single student in the class. Prizes and awards (for behavior or academic work) were rare, and even sports day events were designed to showcase group effort and cooperation rather than individual achievement. Finally, rather than being segregated by ability, children worked in mixed-ability, family-like groups, which are the topic of the next section.

Familylike small groups

In their familylike small groups, Japanese elementary students work, play, and socialize together many times each day. These fixed groups (*han*) of about four children, which are found in virtually all Japanese elementary schools, differ sharply from the groups commonly found in American elementary schools. Each *han* includes children with diverse abilities and personal qualities, who together pursue a wide range of activities from art projects to science experiments to eating lunch together. Japanese teachers often liken these groups to families; the same groups are maintained for an average of two months in elementary school. A primary goal of the groups is to provide a familylike home base for children. As teachers said, "It's hard for children to feel connected to a big class, much easier to feel connected to a group" and "It's easier to express your ideas to a small group than to talk in front of the whole class." Teachers conducted many "group-building" activities designed to give children shared, pleasurable experiences within their groups: Children built art and social studies projects together, played games, and interviewed one another about their interests.

As each group learned to work together, the entire class began to function smoothly. In the words of one teacher, "Everything's easier if you have groups, because each group provides order." Teachers told me that a good group is "one that works well together" and has *matomari* (cohesiveness, or a sense of unity). They explained that, once groups had *matomari,* the class could easily take field trips, eat lunch outside the classroom, or undertake a complicated science experiment.

Third, teachers designed groups in ways intended to foster individual children's development: "I try to place a distractible child with a child who likes to take care of others, a generous child with a shy child." Teachers also mentioned that they spread various abilities across groups, so that children had ready access to another child who could read, explain mathematics, or was good at sports. Like the teacher interviewed by Ineko Tsuchida (this volume), who first grouped students to build leadership and then to help students who were falling behind in mathematics, teachers used groups to accomplish the dual goals of social and intellectual development.

Groups in Japanese elementary schools are familylike: They bring together children of various abilities, who stay together for a considerable time and together pursue a wide range of activities, from sports to art to academic lessons. In contrast, groups in American schools are more often factorylike: They temporarily join children of a particular skill level to accomplish a particular task (e.g., reading or math). Several portraits of American education suggest that ability grouping is "as common as daily recess" (Goodlad, 1984; Hallinan, 1987). A 1992 study of 24 elementary schools in six districts across the United States found that 60 percent of the 472 teachers grouped their children for reading, and 72 percent of these used same-ability grouping at least some of the time (Developmental Studies Center, 1992). Although one shouldn't make too much of metaphors, the contrast between the familylike groups of Japanese elementary schools and the worklike, task-specific groups of American elementary schools may well reflect larger themes: that Japanese schools are organized, like families, to promote children's development in all areas (social, intellectual, emotional, etc.); that American schools are organized, like factories, primarily to produce certain targeted "products" (in this case, academic skills).

Discipline

Discipline is a third aspect of Japanese school life that demonstrates the strong focus on relationships within Japanese elementary education. In a first-grade classroom in central Tokyo, six-year-old Shoji Itoh repeatedly jumped up from his seat during the reading lesson. Each time, he shouted *"baka yaro"* ("you're a jerk") at the teacher so loudly that it could be heard several classrooms away. Each time little Itoh yelled, Ms. Nakanishi went over to his seat, put her arm around him, and pointed out the sentence currently being read out loud. The class read aloud, with intermittent outbursts from Itoh, for about fifteen minutes. Then they began an activity Ms. Nakanishi called "collecting words." Up and down the rows, each of the 35 students named a favorite object in a picture projected on the front wall; Ms. Nakanishi wrote each named object on the board, so that students could later notice the different alphabets used for Japanese-origin and foreign-origin words. When Itoh's turn came, he named "electric rice cooker." Ms. Nakanishi asked him to come to the front of the class, put her arm around him, and praised him extravagantly: "You are very smart. Most second and third graders don't even know a word as difficult as 'electric rice-cooker.' See how smart Itoh-kun is? Let's all clap for him. Today he's done so well." Itoh gave a theatrical bow to the class's applause and took his seat, beaming.

Why did Ms. Nakanishi single out for praise a child who had been so disruptive just moments earlier? I saw this strategy used by several other first-grade teachers as well. Teachers explained that disruptive children needed to strengthen their bonds to other children. Ms. Nishimura explained her strategy for handling Itoh: "I try to find something to praise him for during each period in order to let him feel spiritually relaxed and to keep his classmates from giving up on him." What I saw as issues of control and misbehavior, teachers talked about as issues of community; they transformed my questions about discipline into discussions of the teacher–child bond and the bonds among children. What interested the teachers seemed to be not so much the misbehavior itself but what it signified about the child's bonds with the teacher and with other children. For example, a teacher who had to wait seventeen minutes for the student monitors to quiet the class for a lesson told me, "I could have gotten the class to begin the lesson by saying one word, but I didn't. I wanted to know what the students were feeling."

Teachers often described their disciplinary choices as attempts to balance the need for order with the need to maintain the child's bonds to other children. Even as they scolded children, they often tried to help them preserve their identity as "good children" and save face with classmates. For example, when a first-grade boy repeatedly left his seat and ran around the classroom during social studies, his teacher told the class: "Ichibashi-kun came to my house over summer vacation several times, and we had a very good time together, and he studied hard, but now he needs to act like a first grader when he's with the whole class too." Another first-grade teacher scolded a boy who had repeatedly tried to distract classmates with antics of dumping unwanted objects on others' desks, and who had finally taken his arms out of his sleeves and whipped his empty sleeves around, hitting nearby children during class: "You have been inconveniencing us all since earlier today. You are good. You can do it." A first grader who put a paper bag over his head and left his seat during social studies elicited the scolding "You are really a good child. So you can understand what I'm saying. You can understand. You're in first grade now."

Discipline appealed to feelings. Teachers made comments such as "If you break that hat, your mother will cry," "Your pencil-san will feel miserable if you peel it," "Your pianica is crying" (to a girl about to drop her pianica), and "Please behave properly on parents' day. If you don't, the parents won't laugh at you, they'll laugh at me." When teachers appealed on behalf of the "feelings" of objects or people, they were asking for children's help – in a way that masked the conflict between the desires of child and teacher. In contrast, a direct request would have underlined this conflict.

In summary, when misbehavior occurred, discipline tended to be emotional, not legalistic or mechanical. It appealed to feelings, and to the child's bonds to the teacher and other children. Often, it tried to strengthen those bonds. The Japanese discipline I saw contrasted sharply with behavioral approaches such as "assertive discipline" that are found in many American schools (Hill, 1990). Behavioral approaches focus on controlling immediate behavior – through rewards and punishments – rather than on building the child's bonds to others or promoting the child's long-term internalization of values. The stickers, "motivators," point systems, and rewards that are common features of American classrooms were rare in the Japanese classes I studied; one problem, Japanese teachers pointed out, was the competition among children that such rewards engendered.

Japanese teachers also tended to keep a low profile as authority figures, tolerating a fair amount of misbehavior during the early elementary years and allowing children to take much authority (see Lewis, 1995). "I don't do anything when students forget things they are supposed to bring to school, because if I did anything, it would be too strong. I let the children handle it," explained one first-grade teacher. Elaborate systems were developed so that the children could, indeed, handle much classroom management and discipline: Two rotating daily monitors were responsible for bringing the class to order at the beginning of each lesson, dismissing it at the end of each lesson, leading twice-daily class meetings, and many other roles. All children became monitors in turn, not because of their skills or good behavior but simply because they were members of the class.

Children discussed what chores and jobs needed to be done to keep the class running smoothly, and they did these. At the daily meetings, chore group members often thanked classmates for their help or asked for more cooperation: "A bunch of library books were left on the floor. Please help the library chore group by reshelving them yourself!" "Thanks from the flower group to everyone who brought in flowers for our lunch tables this week." "Last week we playground equipment group members complained because some people wanted to keep jumping rope when it was time to put away the rope. This week everyone's stopping right away. Thanks!"

Hansei (critical self-reflection) was an integral part of classroom life, as students asked themselves at the end of each lesson, day, or week, questions like "Have I done anything kind for others?" "Have I done anything naughty?" "Have I tried my hardest to help groupmates?" Teachers relied on the gradual, cumulative effect of children's self-examination, rather than on direct intervention, to bring about discipline. Often the teacher's role was to dispense mercy: to remind children not to identify one another by name when reporting a problem to a class meeting; to recall that kindness and helpfulness were class goals, and that even criticism could be given in a kind and helpful way; to interpret children's misbehavior in the most positive light.

As several researchers have noted, Japanese teachers tend not to attribute malicious motives to children (Tobin, Wu, and Davidson, 1989; Peak, 1992). Children do not purposefully break rules; they "forget their promises" or "don't understand." Misbehavior is called strange (*okashii*) behavior. Belief in children's inherent goodness is a dominant theme in Japanese child-rearing, both historical and contemporary (Hara and Wagatsuma, 1974; Kojima, 1986; Boocock, 1987).

Values

To enter a Japanese elementary classroom is to confront clear, explicit values. Students study beneath banners proclaiming their school, class, or group goals – a total of 94 goals in the 19 classrooms I studied, all written in *hiragana* (a simple phonetic script) so that the first graders could read them. As noted above, many goals closely followed the Ministry of Education's guidelines for moral education for first graders (which emphasize friendship, cooperation, and caring for one's belongings and oneself), but others grew out of the children's own experiences ("Let's play dodgeball without the boys hogging the ball"). Of the 94 goals, about half focused on friendship, cooperation, and other aspects of social and emotional development: "Let's become friends," "Let's get along well and put our strength together."

The remaining half of the goals fell approximately equally into five categories: persistence, responsibility, enthusiasm, healthy habits, and academic striving. Persistence (*gambaru, doryoku, konki*) included goals such as "Let's become children who persist until the end." When children discussed persistence, they often chose specific personal goals they wanted to try hard at. A lesson that I saw many times – variously as part of social studies, moral education, and class meetings – was for children to choose goals for self-improvement. Often, these goals ranged across many aspects of development: "I want to run around the whole track without stopping," "I'm going to eat my whole lunch, even the vegetables," and "I'm going to stop punching my little brother."

The emphasis on energy or enthusiasm (*genki*) was reflected in goals such as "Be energetic" and "Let's play energetically." When children answered roll call, sang, responded in unison, or danced, a teacher's comment that "there's not much *genki* today" would result in loud voices and exuberant gestures. That Japanese teachers value exuberant, enthusiastic behavior – perhaps because it shows wholehearted connection to the group – has been noted by other researchers (Peak, 1992).

The emphasis on responsibility included general goals such as self-reliance (*jibun no koto o jibun de suru*) and specific behaviors such as being on time, keeping one's desk contents neat, and keeping the area around oneself neat. All of the 19 first-grade classrooms had charts designed to help children self-manage. For example, lesson schedules posted in all classrooms allowed students to prepare for the upcoming lesson during the break that preceded it by laying out the right notebooks and textbooks or by changing into gym clothes. These schedules also showed the length of the breaks between lessons (usually ten or twenty minutes) and reminded children of options for that time: use the bathroom, play outside, and so forth. Charts showed what should be brought to school each day and how desk contents should be arranged. Charts showed the agenda for the daily class meetings so that students could lead these meetings. Additional charts listed the members and tasks for each chore group. In most classes, students reflected on some responsibility daily: Had they completed their chores? Remembered to bring from home all required items? Kept their desks neat? Been ready for lessons on time? Finally, 8 percent of goals focused on academics. These goals emphasized effort, not outcomes – for example: "Let's become children who take initiative in learning," "Let's think carefully," and "Let's try hard at Japanese."

Values did not just inhabit banners. They found their way into the content or process of many – perhaps most – academic lessons. Social studies lessons had first graders discuss the reasons for the rules in nearby parks, identify ways children could ease their mothers' workload, and study the ways adults help one another in the daily life of the school. As noted above, how children worked together was as important as what they learned when children worked together in science, social studies, and other areas.

Although social skills (such as "listening with your eyes") and classroom rules are often illustrated and posted in U.S. classrooms, core values (such as kindness, responsibility, fairness) are not prominently featured. The difference seems an important one: Japanese education is unabashedly concerned with children's social and ethical development in its emphasis on values such as kindness, helpfulness, and friendliness; the American emphasis on social skills strikes one as more pragmatic. Children should listen well in order to make the central work of the classroom, academic learning, more efficient. Despite the overwhelming public consensus in the United States that public schools should be concerned with children's character development (Elam, 1989), U.S. educators may be understandably wary of doing this in a society far more diverse than is Japan.

The very fact that values are made so explicit in Japanese elementary schools – in classroom goals and in weekly moral education classes – is striking because it places ethical and social development squarely within the mission of schooling. The particular content of the values is also striking. Would U.S. educators choose to emphasize friendship as strongly as it is emphasized in Japan, where both classroom goals and moral education lessons often center on friendship? When I asked 19 Japanese first-grade teachers what is the most important thing for children to learn in the first few months of first grade, none of them mentioned academic skills; most of them mentioned friendship. Japanese elementary students routinely discuss topics such as how friends greet each other (by name, with a smile) and how nice it feels for all classmates to be greeted that way; how all the children of the class can build friendships with one another; what friendly things happened in their class that week; how it feels to be excluded from a playground game or not greeted by classmates. Some Americans may consider friendliness a rather soft and fuzzy value, without the moral weight of, say, responsibility, fairness, or helpfulness. When I once suggested teasing, exclusion, and other issues related to friendliness to U.S. educators as one focus for a moral education curriculum, they told me potential funders would laugh at my ideas and asked that I stick to more "weighty" values such as honesty, fairness, and responsibility. Yet children's friendships undoubtedly provide critical grist for their ethical development by helping children to see things from the perspectives of others, and by helping to provide the motivation to care about how others are treated and to act upon what one knows to be right.

Another striking value of Japanese education is the emphasis on children's enthusiasm and energy. One day in a Japanese first-grade classroom, as I watched children run around the classroom during the ten-minute break between lessons, playfully hitting each other with gym bags and jumping out of the ground floor windows, under a banner that said "Let's become energetic children," I wondered how educators in their right minds had chosen to emphasize energy. As discussed elsewhere (Lewis, 1995), the emphasis on energy is both a recognition of children's need to be active and evidence, like wholeheartedness, persistence, and volunteering one's ideas, that children are engaged with schooling. As noted by Tsuchida and Lewis (this volume), the emphasis on participation in Japanese classrooms sometimes overshadows other values, such as personal comfort; participation is not a right but a responsibility. Both lessons and classroom management in Japanese elementary schools are designed so that children's energy, initiative, and participation are essential (Lewis, 1995). For example, children's ideas about what sinks or how to multiply fractions must be expressed for those lessons (which draw on children's various ideas) to proceed; children's discussions decide classroom chores and rules, and their recognition of problems is the catalyst for making the classroom run more smoothly. So it may not be surprising that energy and enthusiasm are key goals from the early years.

We have briefly explored some of the key values of Japanese elementary schools – friendliness, cooperation, persistence, energy. What are the key values of U.S. elementary schools and how are they transmitted, both explicitly and implicitly? There is no room to explore this here, but I invite readers to reflect on their own experiences and to explore the considerable research literature in this area (Sarason, 1983; Kliebard, 1987; Nicholls, 1989; Jackson, 1990; Jackson, Boostrom, and Hansen, 1993; Kohn, 1993).

Conclusions

A hydraulic model of children's social and intellectual development seems to underlie much U.S. thinking about education. We see rigorous curriculum and attention to children's social development as competing forces. Japanese elementary education gives great importance to *both* social and intellectual development. How is this possible?

As we have seen, in looking at the curriculum and pedagogy, the discipline, the organization of children into groups, and the explicit values, Japanese elementary schools refuse to privilege intellectual development over social development. The quick-fix methods that might boost academic outcomes – competition, ability grouping, honors and awards – are rejected because they are potentially damaging to children's bonds with one another, and hence to their social and ethical development. Similarly, the rewards and punishments that might keep Japanese children on task in the short run are rejected because they do nothing to promote children's self-discipline and personal commitment to good behavior in the long run (and indeed, are likely to undermine it; Lepper, 1981). Though Japanese early elementary classrooms often look chaotic to Westerners, their investment in children's relationships with one another, in children's personal commitment to classroom values, and in children's leadership yields impressive long-term dividends. Eventually, Japanese students are off task a tiny fraction of the time that their American counterparts are, with less direction from adults and more student responsibility (Stevenson and Stigler, 1992).

When educators are serious about both social and intellectual development, it greatly constrains what they can do in the classroom. If children are not to be motivated by competition or awards, then lessons must appeal to them for other reasons – because the subject matter strikes children as inherently interesting and important, because the lessons are connected to children's own efforts to make sense of the world, and because the lessons enable children to accomplish something they care about. Likewise, if children are not to be grouped by ability, then lessons must be designed so that children with disparate skills all find something of value and challenge, and children must develop the disposition and skills to help one another. And so, attention to social and intellectual development – which are themselves interwoven in Japanese practice – depend on aspects of Japanese practice addressed by other chapters in this volume: an engaging curriculum taught in ways that enable children to take an active, thoughtful role.

". . . And Tomoko wrote this song for us"

LAUREN J. KOTLOFF

Introduction

At Dai-ichi, a Japanese preschool, two classes of five-year-olds have been working together to write and develop a play for a holiday school assembly. Tomoko, who is particularly fond of writing stories and poems, decides to write a song for the play. She brings lyrics to school one morning and works on them during the free play period. With the help of her teacher and two classmates, Tomoko sits at the piano and sets her words to music, amid much laughter and chatter. Afterward, the class has its Morning Class Meeting, where the teacher explains to the group that Tomoko has written a song for their class play. She thanks Tomoko, as well as the two classmates who helped her, for writing "such a nice song for us" and begins to sing it to the class. They begin to sing along with her, and after several repetitions, most of the children have learned the song. Saying, "Here the girls wrote such a nice song," she prompts the children to agree to use it as the finale of their play.

A few days later, when I heard the teacher refer to the song as "the song that we all wrote together," I realized that what I had regarded as Tomoko's song had become the class's song. Indeed, when the children performed the play at the assembly, the teacher made no mention of Tomoko's special contribution. She simply introduced the play as "the play that the five-year-old classes wrote together."

The teacher's neglecting to give Tomoko special recognition conflicted with my instincts as an American and as a former

This research was supported by grants from the Japan Foundation and the Social Science Research Council.

teacher, for whom singling out individuals for special recognition is considered a method to develop self-esteem, reward effort, and increase motivation. However, through my year of observation in this Japanese preschool, I came to realize that the source of both Tomoko's motivation and her reward was a set of expectations and values that are central to life in Japan – the desire to work for the sake of the group and the capacity to gain satisfaction from doing so. This essay is an attempt to explain how the teachers and classroom activities in this Japanese preschool developed this set of expectations and values in the children under their care. Specifically, I will illustrate how these group orientations were instilled through classroom processes that fostered the children's emotional attachment to the group, their commitment to group projects, and their sense of collective identity.

Japanese group processes

A central feature of Japanese group processes is the readiness of group members to identify with and contribute to collective goals. In Japan most work, social activities, and recreational activities are carried out as collective endeavors, and the high productivity and loyalty of Japanese workers, as well as the high degree of social order maintained within the society, rest to a large extent on the ability of Japanese group members to sustain a sense of common purpose. Thus the willingness to align personal goals with those of the group is important both to the individual's psychological well-being and to the society as a whole.

This sense of loyalty and personal commitment to the group is related to two aspects of Japanese group processes. First, as Rohlen (1989) observes, groups in Japan have an affective as well as an instrumental dimension. The group is more than a collection of individuals who come together to accomplish a task or a goal; it serves an emotional function as well. Groups in Japan provide their members with a sense of belonging and acceptance. Plath (1975) notes that the group is the place where individuals can feel assured of getting sensitive responses to their human needs. As a result of this affective dimension of group life, Japanese individuals tend to form strong emotional attachments to their groups. Rohlen (1989) suggests that the willingness to conform to group standards in Japan is seen as a measure of personal commitment and loyalty to the group. Thus, Japanese individuals' readiness to commit their energy and talent to collective endeavors can be understood as an expression of the affective bond that develops among group members.

The second aspect of Japanese group processes influencing loyalty and commitment involves the development of collective identity. Group members come to define themselves in terms of their group affiliation and incorporate aspects of the group into their own individual identities. This sense of collective identity enables group members to adopt the goals of the group as their own, and to feel a sense of personal pride and achievement in the attainment of these collective goals.

The strong emotional bonds and sense of collective identity that the Japanese feel toward their group motivate the desire to work for the sake of the group. This group orientation does not spring forth fully developed when the individual reaches adulthood, but rather is the product of a socialization process that begins in early childhood and is reinforced throughout the individual's lifetime.

Much of this socialization is achieved through the schooling experience, which for most Japanese children begins with entry into preschool. As recent studies indicate, Japanese parents and teachers of preschool children consider learning to function as a member of the group to be the primary goal of preschool education (Shigaki, 1983; Hendry, 1986; Tobin, 1987). Because learning to identify with and work toward group goals is an important characteristic of a good group member, we would expect this to be a central part of the preschool experience.

Dai-ichi Preschool: a case study

This essay is based on an ethnographic case study, which I conducted from 1985 to 1986, of one Japanese preschool. The focus of this study – Dai-ichi Preschool – is located in Kanazawa, a mid-sized city on the western coast of the island of Honshu. During the study, the school had an enrollment of approximately 103 students, aged three to five, who were divided into five classes according to age.

Dai-ichi is somewhat different from the preschools that have been reported in the literature to date. It is a Christian preschool whose educational approach has been influenced by Western models. However, this is not as unusual as might first appear. The first Japanese preschools were established by American missionaries. In fact, Dai-ichi, which celebrated its 100th anniversary the year of my study, enjoys the status of being the oldest Christian preschool in Japan. This Western influence continues to this day. Tobin (1989) reports that while Christians make up only 1 percent of the Japanese population, approximately 15 percent of Japanese preschools are Christian, and Christian and Western ideas and values about child development exert a strong influence on Japanese preschool education.

In spite of its Christian affiliation, the vast majority of the children at Dai-ichi come from non-Christian families. In the year of my study, only two of the students were Christian. The school is popular with non-Christian families because of its reputation as an excellent preschool and, interestingly, because the parents agree with the values that the school tries to instill.

During the thirteen months of my study of Dai-ichi, I rotated among the five classrooms. I spent one day per week with each class and took detailed observational notes of classroom activities. In addition, I gave a daily ten-minute English lesson using two hand puppets. Because the children loved these puppets and were greatly amused by their antics, I was able to gain their acceptance and confidence faster than I would have otherwise. In addition to classroom observation and teaching, I conducted periodic informal interviews of the teachers and the headmistress, attended formal talks given by the headmistress to students' mothers, and translated articles written by the headmistress on the educational philosophy that formed the basis of Dai-ichi's program. For comparative purposes I also observed classroom activities in four other, more typical Japanese preschools during site visits that ranged from two days to five months.

Although activities in the older classrooms were more complex and demanded greater skill than those in the younger classrooms, the curriculum was basically the same throughout the school. Moreover, due to the tight control that the headmistress exerted over her teachers to ensure the undiluted implementation of her educational philosophy, there was very little variation in the teaching styles among the eight teachers. This resulted in a high degree of consistency in the educational philosophy, teaching style and curriculum content among the five classrooms.

Fostering emotional bonding to the group

Ideally, the desire to work hard for the sake of the group is motivated by the emotional bond that the Japanese individual feels toward his or her group. High worker productivity is believed to be a function of the degree to which workers feel a sense of belonging to and connection with the corporate group, and much effort is spent by management creating and maintaining positive relations within the group to facilitate this bonding process. In his study of Japanese banks, Rohlen (1975, 1989) found that bonding within the work group is a stated goal of training programs for new employees, which typically include many group social and athletic events planned by management to promote a sense of belonging and fellowship.

Similarly, Japanese teachers believe that the children's attachment to the classroom group is a necessary precondition for successful adjustment to school. In fact, they delegate much of the responsibility for maintaining classroom order and discipline to the children themselves, believing that children follow their classmates' directives because of the bonds that develop among the classroom peer group (Lewis, 1984).

As the next sections illustrate, the teachers at Dai-ichi, like corporate managers in the adult world, spend considerable time and effort establishing positive and supportive peer group interactions that foster the children's attachment to the group and commitment to group projects.

Fostering attachment to the group in Morning Class Meeting

Although teachers encouraged positive group interaction throughout the day, the group bonding process was most obvious during the daily Morning Class Meeting. Each day at Dai-ichi opened with an hour-long free-choice play period during which the children chose from among a variety of arts and crafts projects and play equipment. They worked individually or in small groups while the teacher acted as a facilitator and consultant, allowing each child to pursue his or her interests. Morning Class Meeting immediately followed this free play period. As the children finished cleaning up from their play period, they arranged their chairs in a semi-circle, sang a song, and stood to deliver formal morning greetings to the teacher and to themselves as a classroom group ("Good Morning, Everyone!"). These unison activities, as well as the physical arrangement of their chairs, brought the children together and reinforced the cohesion of the group after the helter-skelter of the free play period. Following these opening activities, the teacher took the roll and then had individual children present their free play projects to the group. As the following section illustrates, the teachers conducted this daily fifteen-minute activity so that each child could feel accepted and valued as a member of the group.

Roll call

At Dai-ichi, roll call was not simply a matter of establishing who was present and who was absent. Rather, the teachers used it as an occasion for fostering a warm group dynamic. They opened the Morning Class Meeting by telling the group who was absent that day and providing small details of the illnesses or personal problems that were the cause of the absences. Then they welcomed back any child who had been absent the day before. If a child was still absent after several days, the teacher sometimes said that she would call the child's home after school to inquire about his or her health and report her findings to them the next day. After a period of several days in which many children had been absent, one teacher remarked to the group how nice and cheerful it was that everyone was together once again. In this way, the teachers expressed not only their own sympathy and concern, but also the sense that their classmates' welfare is a matter that concerned the whole group – each child was missed when absent and welcomed back upon returning. The loneliness of being outside the warmth and friendliness of the circle of the group was expressed in the arrangement of the absent children's chairs. Each child in the class had his or her own small wooden chair with a personalized seat cushion tied to it, sewn and decorated by the child's mother. As the children seldom used each other's chairs, the chairs seemed to take on the quality of their owners. Each morning as the children arranged their chairs in a semicircle for Morning Class Meeting, they lined those of their absent classmates against the wall, where they stood for the remainder of the day – silent reminders of absent friends.

Presentations

Having established a supportive group dynamic through the routines surrounding roll call, the teacher moved on to the heart of the Morning Class Meeting, which was to give the children a chance to present to their peers the projects they had worked on during the preceding free play period. These presentations played a key role in building group relations based on trust, mutuality, and respect.

The teacher usually had several children's free play projects on a table next to her. She held up a piece of work while either she or the child explained to the group what it was and how it was made. She tried to sustain the listening children's interest and involvement through her own enthusiasm and by eliciting their comments. The following two excerpts, taken from observations of Morning Class Meetings in the two classrooms of four-year-olds, illustrate this point:

> The teacher holds up one child's origami-paper project and asks the group, "What do you think this is?" She lets some children call out their guesses; then she has the child who made it explain that it is a warrior's helmet. The next child explains to the group that her origami is an animal. The teacher asks her to explain that she can make it talk by moving the mouth. The rest of the children listen quietly.

> Several children have made paper puppets this morning. The teacher shows some of these to the group. One child used the puppet-making materials to make not a puppet but her own original creation. The teacher holds it up so that everyone can see it, and with a tone that expresses her own excitement and admiration says, "This one is not a puppet. . . . Can you guess what it is? It's a merry-go-round!"

As this excerpt suggests, these presentations were never conducted in a critical or competitive atmosphere. Rather, the teachers worked hard to make Morning Class Meeting a pleasant time of sharing one's work with one's friends. The teachers told me that the children are very proud to have their work shown to their peers, and that this builds their self-confidence. In the teachers' view, it is the positive response of the peer group, rather than of the teacher, that enhances the child's feeling of self-esteem. In fact, through their own enthusiastic response to each child's work, they served as a model to the listening children, encouraging them to respond to their classmates' work with genuine interest, respect, and admiration.

The way the teachers praised a child's work also served to develop positive group relationships. Rather than speaking their praise to the child directly, the teachers tended to praise the child's work to the group, as in the following two examples:

The teacher in a class of four-year-olds shows one girl's origami project to the group. After explaining what it is, she praises the child by saying to the group, "She worked really hard and thought of this by herself," and then asks the child to explain to the others the technique she used.

The teacher shows her class of three-year-olds the paintings that some children finished this morning. Using a voice that conveys almost exaggerated admiration, she comments on each picture: "This is great, isn't it? This was done so prettily, wasn't it, with black crayon, then yellow crayon."

In the second example, the teacher not only praised the child to the group but tried to elicit their agreement with her own positive assessment of the work. In addition to using this praise style, the teachers often ended the discussion of a child's work by saying, "We're all looking forward to seeing the finished product." At such times the teachers acted as if they were merely a spokesman for the group, when in actuality they composed their message. By mediating their praise through the group and speaking for them in this way, the teachers controlled the flow and tone of the discussion to ensure that the children received support and encouragement from the group for their creative efforts.

Through Morning Class Meeting, the children also learned to rely on one another for advice and ideas as well as praise. For example, one girl in a class of five-year-olds was having problems with her project during free play one morning. In Morning Class Meeting the teacher explained the problem to the group and asked if anyone had any ideas for solutions. This sparked a lively round of suggestions from the children. It is hard to capture the earnestness with which they offered their suggestions:

The children had been making thank-you cards to give to their mothers at their graduation ceremony. (As part of the graduation ceremony, the children present their mothers with cookies and cards in appreciation for their love and care.) The teacher has three or four cards on the table before her to show to the group. She holds up one that is in the shape of a rabbit's head and explains that the child who made it did not know what to do with it next. Because the teacher did not have any good ideas either, she told the child she would ask the group for some suggestions. As usual, many children stand up, one at a time, and offer their ideas: "You could attach a body!" "You could put white around the head!" Four or five children give suggestions, and the teacher clarifies, extends, and repeats each idea so that all can hear. When no further suggestions are offered, she says to the child who created the card, "Well, here are lots of ideas you can think about!"

In all of the classrooms, the teachers conducted Morning Class Meeting as a discussion within and between the peer group, rather than as a series of dyadic teacher–pupil exchanges. They engineered the discussions so that the children presented their projects and offered their suggestions and comments to their peers rather than to her. By mediating their praise through the peer group and by modeling and shaping positive peer group responses, they enabled each child to receive the esteem of the group, not simply of the teacher. And because the teachers discussed the children's failures as well as successes within the non-competitive atmosphere of Morning Class Meeting, the children learned that they did not have to hide their failures, but could turn to their peers for advice if they ran into a problem. Because all children eventually got a turn as "presenter" and as "audience," they learned to support their peers and to expect such support in return.

Through the daily Morning Class Meetings, the teachers tried to develop the kind of supportive group that Plath described as the Japanese ideal, a group to which the children could turn to receive "sensitive responses to their human needs" (Plath, 1975). Through the practices described above, teachers fostered the children's emotional bonds to the group – bonds that could motivate and direct their efforts toward achieving collective goals.

Besides fostering the children's emotional attachment to the group, several classroom practices developed the children's commitment to group projects. Two of these practices involved the ways in which decisions concerning group projects were made and the ways in which special privileges were distributed within these projects.

Fostering commitment to group projects

One of the reasons often given to explain why Japanese managers succeed in winning such a high degree of commitment from their workers is that they routinely extend decision-making processes to their workers, enabling them to feel a sense of participation and personal investment in the company. That is, rather than impose decisions that they have made unilaterally, decisions are reached through an often lengthy process of discussion involving the whole work team, and consensus is sought before any decisions are implemented. These same processes characterized the way decisions were made in the classrooms at Dai-ichi.

Whole-class projects were a major part of Dai-ichi's curriculum. The teachers strictly adhered to the child-centered educational philosophy of the school, which dictates that children should have a major role in designing their own activities. Thus, the children in each of the classes wrote and developed dramatic skits, puppet plays, and percussion accompaniments to music, and multifaceted projects centered on a variety of themes. All decisions concerning their projects were made through group discussions and consensus, which encouraged the children's commitment to and personal investment in the projects.

"Minna de soodan-site kara kimeru" (We'll decide after we discuss it together). When it came time to work on a group project, the teacher would call the children together and tell them that they were going to discuss what needed to be done next. One teacher introduced a discussion by assuring the children that if they all put their heads together, they would come up with lots of ideas. In the four- and five-year-old classrooms, the teachers sometimes had the children work on their projects in small groups. At such times they would instruct each group, "Decide what to do after you discuss it together" (*Minna de soodan-site kara kimete*). Indeed, the word *soodan*, which means discussion, was used by the teachers and children alike

to describe how practically all aspects of classroom life were decided.

The teachers expected the children to carry on these discussions and arrive at a consensus with minimal supervision. On one occasion, the teacher asked a group of four-year-olds to write steps for a dance. When a child asked for too much help from her, she directed him back to his group, saying, "Discuss it by yourselves, please" (*Jibun-tachi de soodan-site, kudasai*). Even when the teachers participated in the discussions, they acted as facilitators, prompting the flow of ideas from the group with prompts like "Well, everyone, what should we do?"

Everyone in the group was encouraged to contribute to these discussions, and the teachers allowed them to continue until everyone's ideas were heard. But no idea was implemented without the group's consensus.

I observed many instances of teachers seeking the consensus of the group before adopting or implementing an idea for a project. In the following observation, the children in one class of five-year-olds were writing the dialogue for a dramatic skit. Taking the role of discussion leader and scribe, the teacher guided the discussion but sought agreement from the others before incorporating any one child's idea into the skit:

> Another child gives an idea for the next part. The teacher repeats it to the group and asks them, "Is it okay with you?" She repeats this consensus-seeking behavior after another child offers an idea for the next line.

During the same writing session, one child's idea for a character's name was not used because it did not win everyone's approval. A name on which all could agree was chosen instead:

> The teacher asks, "What will you name him?" One child calls out his idea. The teacher repeats it, eyeing the group to see if they agree. Some children protest, and she says, "Well, what should we do?" Then a girl gives an alternative idea, and the teacher again checks this out with the others, saying, "Is that okay?" This time all the children seem to agree, and the teacher writes it down.

If consensus could not be reached, the teachers would try to help the children find a way to compromise; occasionally, they would simply drop the matter for another time.

If I asked the teachers or the children how an idea for a

project had come about, they would usually tell me that they had decided it as a group. This was the case even if the ideas in question had originated with individual children acting on their own. For example, when the five-year-olds met to plan the next steps for their airplane project, the teacher opened the session by referring to their previous group discussion, saying, "After our discussion yesterday, we all combined our efforts and made lots of things for the airplane this morning." In fact, some children had bypassed the group discussion process and had implemented their own ideas on the airplane during free play that morning. However, what seemed important to the teacher was to maintain the collective spirit of the project by defining all aspects of a project as the result of group decision-making processes. It was as if, by referring to these self-initiated efforts as the outgrowth of group discussion, the teacher conferred legitimacy upon them by bringing them into the collective fold.

Group discussions fostered a sense of commitment to group efforts by allowing all of the children to participate in the evolution of the project. Seeking consensus before implementing ideas gave dissenters a chance to be heard, and once consensus was reached, everyone could feel a sense of ownership of the project.

Sharing leadership roles and special privileges. Another practice that promoted the children's commitment to group projects at Dai-ichi was the way the teachers distributed leadership roles, responsibilities, and privileges among the children. In classroom projects such as dramatic skits and orchestra ensembles, children must often compete with one another for the few lead roles. When teachers give special roles to only a few children, they run the risk that the others will be disappointed and their sense of investment and engagement in the project will be diminished. To avoid this problem, the teachers at Dai-ichi rotated special roles and responsibilities among all of the children, thus giving each child equal access to leadership positions. This prevented discord and schism from developing within the group and strengthened each child's sense of being a full participant in the group project. For example, when the children begin rehearsing their dramatic skits, the teachers let them choose the parts they wanted to play. However, in order to give everyone a chance to play each part, over the weeks leading up to the performance they had the children change their parts at each rehearsal. Furthermore, all special parts – such as major roles or special musical instruments – were rotated among volunteers. Thus, there was a different bass drummer at each run-through of a music piece and different actors in each role at each play rehearsal. Because the teachers continued to rotate the parts throughout the rehearsal period, by the time of the performance most of the children had gotten a turn to play each part. As the head teacher explained to me, this practice gives each child a chance to play the role he or she wants, and because each child has to learn each part, their sense of involvement in the project is enhanced.

The teachers came up with some rather creative strategies to ensure that all of the children had a turn. For example, in order to give all of the children a chance to play the various instruments in a music ensemble, the teachers tape-recorded the piano music they were using for the project and made both the tape and the instruments available to the children during the free play period to use as they wished. Thus children who did not get a chance to play the bass drum in rehearsal could do so to their heart's content during free play. This practice yielded some unexpected results. One morning I walked into the three-year-olds' free play period to find three children standing on "conductor's boxes" waving their batons in time to the tape-recorded music. Their obvious pleasure in conducting did not seem to be the least bit diminished by the fact that their "orchestra" consisted of one lone castanette player; they were getting their turn at the baton.

Perhaps the most striking example of this strategy was the teachers' practice of allowing the children to play the main characters of their plays in pairs or in small groups. For example, if the children were using a fable about an old couple bewitched by a sprite as the basis for their play, the original cast of three characters was changed to a small group of men and their wives who were contending with a troupe of spirits. In this way, everyone got to play a major role.

During rehearsals for the Christmas play that the two classes of five-year-olds put on each year, the children played the major characters (Joseph, the Innkeeper, and so on) in groups of two or three so that everyone got a chance to play the role of his or her choice. At some point before the actual performance, the children were expected to decide who would play what role the night of the performance. However, if a decision could not be reached, a child's sense of investment in the play was not sacrificed for the sake of fidelity to the original script. Thus, one year the Christmas play was performed with two children playing the role of Mary together because, as the headmistress laughingly told me, "No matter what, they both absolutely insisted on doing it!"

Fostering collective identity

Ideally for the Japanese, group effort does not entail sacrificing personal goals for the sake of the group, but rather identifying with the group to the extent that the individual feels a sense of personal pride and satisfaction when collective goals are reached. How is this sense of collective identity developed in preschool children? Studies of Japanese preschools have discovered some means by which group identity is fostered in children. For example, preschoolers often wear identical school uniforms, with badges or other markers identifying their classroom subgroup (Shigaki, 1983; Hendry, 1986). They are expected to identify themselves and are referred to according to their classroom group – for example, "Taro from Rainbow Class" (Tobin, 1989). Lewis (1984) found that in classrooms where the children were divided into subgroups, the teachers frequently referred to them collectively by subgroup name and conferred rewards and privileges on subgroups rather than on individuals. These studies also reveal that most activities in the preschool curriculum are group rather than individual activities.

I found these practices at Dai-ichi as well, and they no doubt contribute to the socialization of group identity. My extended stay at Dai-ichi enabled me to follow the development of class projects over several weeks and thus gain further insight into how, through participation in these projects, children learn to feel a sense of satisfaction from knowing that "We did this together" rather than simply "I did this myself." The following is a discussion of how group activities at Dai-ichi instilled a sense of group identity in the children, encouraging them to see themselves as part of a collective and to view their accomplishments as the result of collaboration and cooperation rather than of individual effort.

Collective ownership of ideas and projects

Through my observations in each classroom at Dai-ichi, I became aware of a central principle that seemed to guide the development of group projects: the principle of collective ownership. That is, in the way the teachers developed and referred to the children's projects, they communicated the idea that the projects were not the property of any individual child or small group of children, but were collaborative efforts shared and owned equally by everyone.

The teachers reinforced the principle of the collective ownership of projects through a practice that I observed frequently in all of the classrooms at Dai-ichi. They routinely took the ideas of individual children and used them to launch whole class projects to which everyone was invited to contribute. In this way, ideas did not remain the property of the child who originated them but became part of the collective domain. For example, a four-foot-high cardboard giraffe that one four-year-old girl made during free play was painted bright pink by four of her classmates. Similarly, an airplane built out of large wooden blocks by a small group of children in the five-year-old class developed into a six-week-long, multifaceted class project to which the whole class contributed.

The teachers transformed individual children's ideas into whole class projects through the Morning Class Meeting. The case of the airplane project is a typical example. The teacher first let the three children show their airplane construction to the class, but then she opened the project to the whole group by asking everyone for their ideas on what else to make for the airplane:

The teacher asks the group, "What else can we do to make this airplane look even more like a real airplane?" Several children offer ideas and suggestions. One little girl suggests making a TV for the passenger section. The teacher picks up on this and asks the group what they think about making it out of a cardboard box. This sparks another round of discussion about what to make for the TV and how to make it. One child says that they need to make an antenna. Another suggests making control dials. The teacher allows the discussion to continue until most of the children have had a chance to offer their ideas and opinions. She ends the discussion by reviewing their suggestions and promising to set up the materials for them to make the TV in free play the next day.

Through this group discussion, the teacher turned the three children's airplane into a whole-class project. From that point on, the airplane "belonged" not to the three children who had originated it, but to everyone.

Flexible and fluid division of labor. The way the tasks were divided within a work group also reinforced the notion of collective ownership. All finished projects at Dai-ichi were the product of group cooperation and collaboration. Teachers did not assign responsibility for tasks within a project to individual children. Rather, the division of labor within a project was completely fluid, and anyone could work on any task at any time. The teachers generally left the children alone to work out who was to do what, and as a result, the children tended to pool their talents. If one child could not do something well, he or she was expected to let a more skillful child take over. For example, in one of my observations, a group of five-year-olds were huddled around a table writing a script for their puppet play. A few children were dictating their ideas to three boys, who were taking turns writing them down, not each on his own paper but all on a single piece of paper. Another child was helping them with the spelling. When one of the boys criticized the other's handwriting, that child asked a girl standing nearby to write it correctly for him. Thus, the finished script was not the product of one child's efforts but was a combination of several children's ideas, copied down by three scribes, who had been assisted by two spellers.

Cooperative effort was indicative of most group projects at Dai-ichi. They were collaborative endeavors in which it was usually impossible, as well as unnecessary, to keep track of individual contributions. Most finished products were the result of several children's ideas elaborated upon and discussed by the whole group and worked on by a variety of different children. Such flexible division of labor is characteristic of adult groups in Japan as well, where who does what depends on the requirements of the situation at hand, and any group member can be asked to perform any task needed to get the job done (Pelzel, 1970). The central concern is the quality of the final product, and the children at Dai-ichi were encouraged to combine their efforts for the sake of achieving their common goal.

Individual efforts praised as contributions. Viewing the children's ideas and efforts as part of the collective endeavor does not mean that individual children were never praised at Dai-ichi. However, when a child's work was singled out for special mention, the teachers praised that child's work in terms of the contribution it made to the group effort. This can be illustrated through the incident described at the opening of this essay, when Tomoko, with the help of two friends, wrote a song for the class play. After presenting the song to the group, the teacher did not praise her for her creativity or self-initiative, but instead thanked her for writing such a nice song "for us," thus defining and praising Tomoko's work as a contribution rather than as an individual achievement. Moreover, in thanking Tomoko, the teacher used the honorific verb form *tukutte kudasatta,* which is rarely used with children and is reserved for speaking to or about an adult held in high esteem. In this context, the teacher's use of the honorific amplifies the praise, and frames it in terms of the group's great gratitude and appreciation. In internalizing adult values in the process of socialization, children learn to value in themselves what others value in them. At Dai-ichi, the children learn that their talent and creativity are praiseworthy because they make a meaningful contribution to the group effort.

Individuality tied to the group. Not all of the activities at Dai-ichi were group projects in which the whole class worked together to produce a single product. There were also activities designed to be carried out by individual children working independently. During the morning free play period, the children used a variety of art materials or play equipment to work on individual projects. This daily free play period was the heart of the school's Western-influenced "open education" program. It was designed to promote aspects of Western individualism and did in fact present the children with opportunities for individual autonomy and creative self-expression. But even this highly individualized free play period had a cooperative group context. That is, these individualized activities that the children worked on during free play grew out of, or were later integrated into, whole-class cooperative endeavors. For example, puppet making was a free play activity in each of the classrooms. Although each child could design his or her own puppet, these puppets were later used as the basis of a puppet-play project that the children wrote and developed as a group. Similarly, the children always made their individual costumes for their class plays during free play. Although each child could use his or her own creative ideas to develop the costume, their ultimate purpose was for use in the class play. Those free play activities that are not part of a group project at all were also given a cooperative group context. They were used as the basis of the Morning Class Meeting, where they were shared with the group and used to instruct and inspire others.

Because of the cooperative group component that was part of all activities at Dai-ichi, even the children's individuality was used to serve the group effort. Working hard on one's own costume ultimately improved the class play. Making a puppet that is different from all of the other children's was an act of individual self-expression, but one that contributed to the overall quality of the group's puppet play. Even if children went completely off on their own and rejected or ignored the group's project (e.g., the little girl, described earlier, who used the puppet-making materials to construct a merry-go-round), the teachers held up their creations as models of creativity from which they could all learn. Thus, the children at Dai-ichi always acted within a group context. They learned to regard their own and other's work not as the expressions of individuals acting in isolation, but as arising from and contributing to the group.

Learning to value collective membership

The teachers' ultimate goal was not simply to develop the children's cooperative work and interpersonal skills. Rather, their goal was for the children to feel a sense of pride in being part of a group effort. One major means the teachers used to achieve this goal was by giving the children opportunities to show off their group projects to the other children in the school. When major group projects such as dramatic skits, puppet plays, and theme projects were completed, the teachers had the children present the finished product to the children in the other classes.

For example, if a class finished a puppet show, they usually performed it in front of the other classes. When the five-year-olds spent an afternoon making cookies, rather than eating the cookies themselves they threw a party and served them to their three-year-old guests.

The teachers made sure that these events were gala affairs. The children spent a great deal of time planning and preparing for them. They made personalized invitations for their guests and hung posters announcing the time and place of the event throughout the school. The teachers of both the presenting class and the guests communicated a sense of anticipation marking the specialness of the event to their students. The excitement and anticipation generated by these events, and the mixing of older and younger children that was part of the events, increased their power to serve as teaching opportunities. Thus, the teachers used these occasions to instill not just pride in group projects but social decorum, self-control, and responsibility for the welfare of others as well.

Perhaps the most dramatic examples of this during my year in the school were the two occasions on which one of the five-year-old classes presented their completed projects to the rest of the school. The first was the presentation of the airplane project. Planned and developed by the children over a six-week period through the group processes described above, the airplane was an amazing accomplishment by any standard of preschool education. It was built out of large wooden blocks, ran the whole length of the classroom, and was equipped with everything from landing lights to seatbelts, from maps to murals of "things you can see from the plane," all made by the children themselves. When the project was finished, the five-year-olds posted invitations throughout the school inviting the other classes to come and play on it. However, the purpose was not simply to let the other children play on the airplane, but also to allow the five-year-olds to bring their airplane to life for their guests.

As the passenger-guests from each class arrived, two five-year-olds seated at the entrance to the room sold them tickets and boarding passes and guided them through a painted cardboard boarding gate to their seats. Screaming "IRRASSYAIMASU! IRRASSYAIMASU!" (Welcome! Welcome!), five-year-old stewardesses, wearing aprons, took the passengers' meal orders (from menus they had made) and dashed off to the plane's kitchen to heat up the plastic and paper food they had prepared. Five-year-old flight attendants showed a picture story through the cardboard TV mounted in the passenger section to some wide-eyed four-year-old guests who sat buckled in their seats. A five-year-old pilot sat in the cockpit, and as the plane was about to take off, the teacher turned on the tape recording of airplane sound effects and waved goodbye.

This same procedure was followed later in the year when the five-year-old class completed a large wooden bus, similarly equipped, and turned their classroom into a city to which all were invited. The city scene included an art museum housed behind curtains. When a busload of children from the other classes stopped there, the curtains were dramatically opened to reveal a display of the five-year-olds' completed arts and crafts pieces.

Having the opportunity to present their finished products to an appreciative (and sometimes awestruck) audience of their peers, and to have so much fun doing so, was a powerful learning experience, and allowed all of the children to share equally in the rewards of the group effort. It was through this concrete, positive experience of the benefits of group work that the school instilled a sense of pride in group ownership and collaboration.

Conclusion

Schools play a major role in socializing children to the values and norms of their society. The management and organization of daily classroom life, and the patterns of interaction among students and teachers, both reflect and perpetuate these norms. Preparing children to participate in cooperative group life was a major socialization goal of the preschool program at Dai-ichi. This essay has described the various practices through which the teachers fostered collaborative work habits, a sense of collective identity, and a sense of pride and comfort in group participation.

By having the children present and discuss their work in the daily Morning Class Meeting, the teachers encouraged the children to relate to their peers as collaborators and colleagues rather than as competitors. By having them share leadership roles and special privileges, they minimized the chance that some children would stand out while others felt left out, passed over, and eventually alienated. The teachers' practice of basing decisions regarding classroom life on group discussion and consensus reinforced the collective nature of classroom life and taught the children that, as group members, they might have to modify their own ideas in order to move the project forward. By framing their praise for individual children's accomplishments as contributions to group efforts, and by using these accomplishments to inspire and instruct the other children, the teachers built individual self-esteem on a social foundation. The children could feel proud of themselves because they helped the collective effort. Finally, the teachers' practice of giving the children opportunities to win the respect of the school by showing off the fruits of their collective labors was a powerful lesson in the benefits of collaboration.

These were important lessons for the children to learn. The capacity to function well in group contexts will be essential to their success in their future as students and, ultimately, in their lives as adults. Because groups are central elements of the social organization of Japanese schools and society, the individual's ability to gain satisfaction from the achievements of his or her group's goals is a major ingredient in the Japanese individual's feelings of personal and professional self-worth.

Honoring the individual
NANCY SATO

Introduction

No one seems to dispute the common notion that Japan is a group-oriented society, whereas the United States is an individualistic society (Nakane, 1970; Smith, 1983). But, rather than group oriented, the Japanese may be *relations oriented,* where one's relations to the social world are highlighted. A relations orientation emphasizes the importance of one's relational situation in the world, but the relation is not always to the group. The relation can be with one or more persons, with the surrounding environment, with aspects of oneself, and with experiences. Breaking away from the "group-oriented" theory allows one to see that group orientation is not necessarily the starting point; rather, it is the end product of a complex web of mutual obligations and responsibilities, with individual relations as the building blocks. Defining group membership and dynamics occurs in this layered architecture of individuals and their interdependent relations carefully crafted over time. This raises a provocative question: can group orientation and individualism be distinguished, as they are in Western thought?

Within this framework, I argue that individual and group dimensions are complementary aspects of teaching–learning processes in Japan, and that both individual and group orientations are nurtured in Japanese elementary classrooms. This essay begins with a brief examination of the Japanese notion of self, and then explores the educational implications of a relational focus through a description of school and classroom practices. The data are derived from research conducted in many classrooms from 1987 to 1989, primarily an intensive, daily observation period from November 1987 through August 1988 at two Tokyo public elementary schools with highly contrasting educational attainment expectations (one upper-class *yamanote* school and one lower-class *shitamachi* school).[1]

The teaching–learning process is an intricate, complicated one that unfolds in the daily interactions between teachers and students over the course of a year, not during the brief visits to classrooms that most researchers undertake. Therefore, my research strategy involved attending school with the same students all day, every day, Monday through Saturday, from 8:00 A.M. until the students went home, in order to perform a systematic examination of classroom practices.

Complementarity: individual-capacity building in tandem with group-community building

The label "group oriented" is not as dangerous as the common stereotypes that accompany U.S. thinking about it. Because of an unquestioned acceptance of "group oriented" to describe Japanese culture and society, words like "homogeneous," "standardized," "uniformity," and "rigid" are too easily accepted without proper examination. Similarly, our inclination is to imagine schooling that restricts individual expression, creativity, and initiative, and therefore lacks diversity. Images of mechanical robots, rote cramming for entrance exams, and faceless, rule-bound students uniformed in military-looking garb evoke pity from an American audience.

Two major misconceptions may result. One is not appreciating when individual expression, creativity, initiative, and diversity do occur. Actual classroom life is teeming with evidence that contradicts our images. Students can be rowdy or aligned in uniform postures. The second misconception is not realizing the salient role of opposing images and forces when conceived as complementary processes across a continuum of relations. I discovered uniformity as the starting point for diversity, standardization as a catalyst for creativity, and individualization as a means to become group oriented.

The cultural veneer of homogeneity is fabricated by standardized practices, and conceals the actual diversity and individuality expressed in local, particular contexts and in more private spheres – the culturally appropriate venues for such expressions. Importantly, the degree to which homogeneity, standardization, and uniformity are regarded as a basis for commonality, and for creating shared experiences, actually *cultivates the relationships* from which diversification and individualization are generated. For example, the standardized curriculum offers a meeting ground for national educational discourse and teacher professional community building in Japan. The common framework also constitutes a shared base from which creative, individual adaptations evolve. Although teachers complain about the restrictions imposed by a national curriculum, their dedication and initiative are not crippled. The Ministry of Education monitors the written curriculum, but not the curriculum process. The prescribed curriculum becomes a living curriculum as students and teachers collectively encounter materials, teach and learn from each other, and construe new meanings in unpredictable ways: a creative, individual and group process.

Granted, social and systemic pressures limit the range of adaptations, and Japanese privately resent these constraints, but local flexibility allows the overall structure to maintain itself and to appear rigid. Ironically, in some ways, Japanese teachers seem to have more professional latitude that "engenders more diversity at the classroom level than does the apparently less controlled American system" (Sato and McLaughlin, 1992:3). The interplay between opposing forces surfaced as a key aspect of the observed teachers' instructional techniques. They skillfully maneuvered between moments of activity and passivity, noise and silence, verbalizing and sensing, doing and listening; they attended at once to qualities of emptiness and fullness, individual and group, uniformity and diversity. Among the Japanese educators I met during the course of this study, I encountered a way of thinking that allowed much goofing off one moment in order to engender disciplined, hard work the next; a mindset that viewed boisterous rowdiness (unacceptable in U.S. classrooms) as a necessary antecedent to quiet concentration; and a perspective that accepted rote practice as a catalyst for creativity. As complementary rather than competing forces, they coexist naturally. Meticulous attention to individual involvement from moment to moment nurtures social cohesion and smooth group processes. Well-functioning groups rely heavily on individual responsibility and initiative.

Individual development is both bound and enhanced by membership in mutual learning communities, and those same communities, in turn, are strengthened by increased individual capacities; they complement one another toward reciprocal growth. Increasing individual capacities automatically increases the expertise available in the community, which, in turn, multiplies the amount of "teaching"[2] and feedback available to individual students. In fact, these relations and levels of communities, not just the teacher–student relationship, are the vehicles for educational growth: individuals constantly contribute to a community of knowledge and skill building, and, in turn, they constantly absorb and learn from the community. Conceived in this way, individual self-development consists of internal and social processes. As such, individual capacity building is not distinguishable from group community building; both are inseparable and equally important.

The importance of community building alongside capacity building is buttressed by the Japanese notion of self, which prizes the relational aspect of self in interaction with others, as opposed to the independent self apart from others that is foremost in U.S. thinking. The boundaries between self and other are not clearly distinguishable and are constantly negotiated as contexts change. Rather than "self," "personhood" is a better term. Teaching–learning processes in Japan cannot truly be appreciated unless the reader is freed from the hidden assumptions built into the American notions of individual and self.

What notion of self comfortably combines the intrapersonal and interpersonal dimensions?

Kokoro: the notion of personhood

According to Harumi Befu's (1986) concept of "personhood," self-identity contains three vital dimensions: interpersonalism, self-discipline, and role perfectionism. Interpersonalism is characterized by particularism (a notion of self that changes depending on the situation, especially with whom one is interacting), mutuality of trust, and interdependence. Importantly, "it is the interconnectedness of persons and the quality of this interconnectedness that determines who one is. Connectedness is not merely a matter of knowing someone; it also expresses moral commitment to reciprocal support" (Befu, 1986:23). Interpersonalism stresses the relational aspect of self, dependent on others. "Commitment to reciprocal support" is essential for building the mutuality of trust on which self-identity and community identity are based.

Self-discipline, the quality of one's character, is also inextricably woven into the concept of self. Several complex terms capture the essence of this character: *ki, kokoro, tamashii,* and *seishin*. No simple translation is possible (Rohlen, 1974c), but in combination they refer to a positive mental attitude, "vitality to live," a "sympathetic and empathetic soul," and the "determination to overcome all odds" (Befu, 1986:24). Self-discipline must be molded through experience that involves "hardship (*kuro*), endurance (*gaman, nintai, shimbo, gambaru*), effort (*doryoku*), and the utmost self-exertion (*isshokemmei*)" (Befu, 1986:34). Thus, role perfection, or the commitment to do one's best, regardless of the status of one's role and despite all odds, is an important component of personal identity. The stronger one's self-discipline and role perfection are, the greater mutuality of trust can exist. Caring and trust, in this context, can evolve either in the midst of hardship and harsh treatment or in warm, nurturing environments, provided that the underlying and guiding forces of shared goals and mutual concerns for each other are secure. Interestingly enough, these values are precisely those upon which success in school life and education often depend.

Developing the self in Japan is a social process as much as it is an internal process. *Kokoro* (heart) unifies these processes. *Kokoro* is an individually distinct notion (in that one must reflect upon and develop one's own heart or *kokoro*), yet at the same time, it is the centerpiece for self-development that places empathy and consideration of others as integral to self-identity, thereby making community building the basis for capacity building. In fact, knowledge transmission is secondary to a more comprehensive emphasis on developing *ningen* (human beings), the primary teaching goal expressed by principals, teachers, and parents. And at the core of *ningen* is *kokoro* (the center of the physical, cognitive, spiritual, aesthetic, and emotional self). Significantly, "human being" and "person" automatically contain dependent dimensions. The two *kanji* (Chinese characters) used to write *ningen* mean "amid people."

If *kokoro* places a concept of cognition that includes emotion at the foundation of the educational enterprise, and if *kokoro* places empathy with others at the foundation of concerns about oneself, then how is this reflected in schools? These thought-provoking educational conceptions place relations in the forefront, profoundly influencing the ways schools and classrooms are organized and even the ways teacher and student roles are defined.

As one example, organizational design reflects relational priorities, and structural features often decide relations regardless of individual intent. For instance, trying to find "collaboration" time (a common preparation period) is often a struggle for U.S. teachers. Isolation is a presumed and accepted work mode. In stark contrast, in Japan, all teachers' work desks are crowded into one room, clustered by grade-level groupings, and every day begins with a whole-staff meeting. Constant interaction characterizes Japanese teachers' lives, requiring ongoing attention to the quality of adults' professional relations.

With a relational focus, teacher and student roles and responsibilities do not have the same easily identifiable time and space boundaries evident in the United States, where a clear separation between on- and off-campus life and school versus vacation time predominates for both teachers and students. Instead, Japanese teachers and students enter into a web of relations: ideally, bonds that last a lifetime.[3] Spinning this web entails all-encompassing, ongoing attention to mutual obligations, rights, and responsibilities. Hence, Japanese elementary teacher and student roles and knowledge extend beyond subject matter and school walls, including use of vacation time, student appearance, personal habits, motivation, interpersonal relations, and behavior (Inagaki and Ito, 1990; Sato and McLaughlin, 1992; Sato, 1993; and the essays by Fukuzawa, LeTendre, and Lewis in this volume).

Practically speaking, the above translates into teacher practices such as required home visits to all students; all teachers sharing responsibility for teaching swimming during three weeks of their six-week summer vacation; assigning homework and monitoring students' lives during vacations; and apologizing to store owners in person if students are caught stealing.[4]

Blurred boundaries between self and other characterize teaching–learning processes and educational visions set in motion in classrooms on a daily basis. Besides teacher–student interdependent work groups, perhaps the most striking difference is that the blurred boundaries extend to the concepts of teachers and learners themselves. With properly developed, trustful relations between adults and students in classrooms, everyone is constantly teaching and learning from everyone else, both verbally and nonverbally. Teaching and learning become inseparable acts, and each individual is at once a teacher and a learner.

The efficacy of this nexus of teaching–learning processes depends upon the nature of individual inclusion in the community of relations. Any individual or group basis for exclusion weakens the quality of the teaching–learning community, and Japanese are no different in their ability to discriminate amid a notable inclination toward inclusion.[5] A more difficult teacher role is that of fostering a mutual learning community. A strong mutual learning community sustains ongoing, reciprocal teaching–learning processes, requiring an environment (a teaching–learning context) in which individuals can freely seek help from anyone and individuals who give help can do so generously, maintaining equitable, individually validating relations. And ideally, individuals do not need to ask for help; others automatically sense the need and offer without being asked: the nonverbal, empathetic, relational self (*kokoro*) in action.

Relational framework

As the centerpiece of self-development that promotes participation in mutual learning communities, *kokoro* also serves as a central organizing principle for educational programs and for understanding the relational framework postulated in this essay. The central idea of a relational framework is connectedness. *Kokoro* places a premium on the quality of relations.

For each individual, a variety of relations exist, and the interplay between them changes over time: connectedness between various aspects of self and self with the environment (integrated self, capacity building); connectedness between self and others (interpersonal relations, community building); connectedness between oneself and the content to be taught–learned; and connectedness of the content itself (both between subjects of study and within subjects over time).[6] Even on an analytical level, the relations between opposing forces (interplay and complementarity) and appreciating the continuum of relations is important. Although none of these values of connectedness is new to U.S.

educators,[7] one major difference is the ways they interconnect in a systematic fashion in the Japanese setting.

An important transformation of underlying assumptions for school life is evident: the educational enterprise, by definition, is not just individual and is not fundamentally cognitive. Instead, it is fundamentally a series of carefully nurtured relationships, beginning with the family, extending to the school, including identification with successively larger communities, lasting throughout one's life. The starting point, means, and ends of education become caring relationships established between all members of a learning community.

Tracing an elementary school student's life is a journey through carefully nested communities: desk partner, small groups, grade level identification, older–younger student mentor relationships, whole school identification, family and community organizations. They are not members merely by virtue of their presence. Each student and teacher must actively contribute to the creation of mutually responsive, lively communities for all, thoughtfully crafting the reciprocal roles, obligations, and rights of the individuals within them. Students and teachers put their individual and collective mark on the processes as well as the products of schooling.

Through carefully orchestrated delegation of interdependent responsibilities, the teacher can unobtrusively facilitate relationships whereby students negotiate decision making and students develop allegiance to many other students, thus providing multiple means for each student to nurture her/his sense of trust and belonging. Varied groupings create multiple forms of individual and community consciousness. Ready availability of numerous role models automatically multiplies the number of teachers, greatly increasing the potential access to learning opportunities for individuals. As a result, individual concentration on academic work may increase.

This complex, mutually reinforcing network provides a motivation for active engagement and success, as well as a cushion for failed opportunities. Where one relationship or set of relations is failing, others may buffer the pain and become more salient; where concepts and skills are not learned in one teaching–learning context, another set may prevail and succeed. Instances where the network fails to function indicate weaknesses in the educational system, individually or as a group.

The issues shift dramatically. The question is no longer one of individual versus group orientation; rather, it is one of how individual learning generates collective learning and of how adeptly crafted individual participation constitutes the essential building blocks of group information. Educational issues center less on individual rights versus group responsibility and more on how individual rights and group responsibility go hand in hand, necessitating the delicate, tricky process of negotiated trade-offs and involving degrees of sacrifice at every turn. Constant attention to others is both restrictive of individual freedom and yet expansive in terms of the gains made possible through group connectedness and support.

Cognition and cognitive development are inseparable from emotion and human development. Moreover, they are just two of many areas of expertise in the fluid ownership patterns of knowing, teaching, and learning. Maintaining relationships and good working groups is a never-ending process: one that must be validated as much as the knowledge, outcomes, and products it inspires or fails to inspire. The emotional, aesthetic, and physical capacities and sensibilities essential to well-rounded growth and to relationship formation are no longer trivial and incidental. Therefore, ongoing reflection on (*hansei*) and meticulous attention to the quality of experiences and the nature of individual participation in shared activities are imperative.

Besides academic outcomes, other measures attain significant status, especially those honoring connectedness. The characteristics of elementary school programs that become prominent are trust, egalitarian togetherness, harmony, continuity over time, and patience. Characteristics of students that are publicly rewarded are less academic and more relational: ability to get along with others, empathy, humility, commitment, and self-discipline – and taking initiative and assuming responsibility. Nonverbal pedagogical tools and skills become powerful modes not easily dismissed. Silent forms of knowing and displaying knowledge are as validated as verbal, active forms. Occasions for celebrating diverse accomplishments, and for cultivating caring relations that validate individuals and their nested levels of communities, are as valued as test scores.

Instances where teachers and students invoked explicit attention to *kokoro* were quite poignant, often illuminating the soulful, intuitive aspects of education viewed as a relational endeavor. Responding to my query about why mischievous students were not punished, one teacher explained that "punishing a child pushes him further away. If you want to get him to work with you, you must open your heart (*kokoro*) and bring him in." Indeed, punishment as a way to define and exert authority distances people rather than "opening hearts" to promote relations. Punishment as denied participation and isolation takes away the very experiences students need to promote better relations and academic achievement. As one teacher explained, students with behavior or academic problems are the very ones who need more opportunities to socialize, to increase self-discipline, and to assume responsibilities in order to improve.

Essentially, *kokoro* directs our attention to four particular areas noted in this study: (1) diversity in forms of knowing; (2) shared ownership (distributed locus of control); (3) nonverbal pedagogical tools; and (4) process orientation. Why these? By definition, *kokoro* necessitates diversity in forms of knowing (integrated self) set in a social nexus of obligations and a web of relations (shared ownership), whereas the complicated task of nurturing the well-rounded individual and community growth requires attention to nonverbal pedagogical tools and the journeys or processes generated as they collectively strive for such comprehensive goals.

Diversity in forms of knowing refers to curricular diversity (learning environments, materials, activities, and events) and to diversity in the forms of relations. Intricate patterns of nested identity building, group work, role assignments, and interdependence permeate teaching–learning in Japanese elementary classrooms.

Shared ownership is a guiding principle for the ways in which the diversity of forms of relations are constructed and enacted on a daily basis. It denotes the sense of control to which all individuals are entitled as they assume "ownership" of the material forms of learning; of their classroom in assuming mutual responsibility for each other; of the school as an institutional process that they help form; and of the knowledge base that they learn from and contribute to. Shared ownership is a compelling catalyst for peer teaching–learning, as well as an effective class management strategy that frees teachers from the mundane areas of disciplining and housekeeping.

With respectful relations, the desire for inclusion is a persuasive force for soliciting individual initiative, responsibility, and cooperation. Ideally, students accommodate to others' wishes because they want to cooperate (internalized control, or practically, because of peer pressure), not because of adult commands. Heartfelt group membership is strengthened by one philosophy, foremost in daily Japanese elementary classroom decisions: universal participation – the hallmark of Japanese egalitarian sentiments. Participation is a right, not a privilege that may be manipulated for control. Thus, participation in all activities is equal, mutual, and universal, regardless of the inconvenience, cost, and time considerations. Universal participation as community building works best when accompanied by three guiding principles: (1) equality of access to materials, activities, assignments, and duties; (2) validation of everyone's efforts, contributions, and expertise; and (3) attention to individual and group initiative and responsibility.

Potential outcasts retain their dignity and enjoy the security of belonging. Differential inclusion (denied participation, favoritism, special treatment) works against group solidarity because "community" then belongs to some more than others, resulting in differential incentives to contribute. Exclusion and perceptions of lower status erode commitment and motivation, two cornerstones of the will to learn. Where effort, persistence, and integrity are sincerely rewarded along with outcomes, all students can be valued and experience success.

Process orientation

Assessment in a relational framework must account for these significant yet elusive areas of process orientation. In addition to report cards, five additional measures assume significance in Japanese public elementary schools: (1) direct participation in an array of learning experiences; (2) periodic opportunities to display diverse accomplishments, especially authentic activities in context; (3) the quality of one's participation and self-discipline (Japanese use terms such as *gambaru, gaman, chanto, isshokemmei, chikara o awasete,* and *naka yoku suru*),[8] especially the degree of effort and integrity displayed; (4) the quality of one's character (e.g., honesty, sensitivity, and consideration for others); and (5) peer relations and group membership. The last three are directly connected to the important aspects of "personhood." The resulting practices reveal a fascinating U.S.–Japanese difference in the perceived relationship between learning and time.

In Japan, age is the grade level marker; in the United States, academic achievement (specifically, math and reading) is the grade level marker. Underlying the U.S. assumption is that academic achievement is the point of commonality that will enable students to teach and learn together better, whereas the Japanese assumption is that age is the point of commonality. Americans presume that more difficult work cannot be done without having mastered prior skills, whereas Japanese assume that prior skills will be mastered with the increased challenge and repetition necessitated by more difficult work, with additional exposure to other contexts and experiences and with continued support of age-level peers. Practices in Japan therefore prioritize togetherness and relations, while those in the United States prioritize achievement. The Japanese elementary goals are aimed more at building the foundation for learning (exposure to a wealth of direct experiences, cultivating mutual teaching–learning relations, instilling the proper attitude, discipline, character, and the will to learn) rather than demonstrating specified academic achievement levels by a certain age.

The premium placed on the social relations and bonds developed with one's age cohort over time is best evidenced in the facts that teachers and students stay together as a group for at least two years (a typical pattern is first-second, third-fourth, and then fifth-sixth grades),[9] and that students advance to each grade with age-level peers, regardless of achievement. One rationale for this practice is that developing the right relations takes time. As one teacher put it, "the first year you learn how to work together as a group and understand each other, and the second year the real learning can begin." Placing an annual benchmark for achievement is an artificial barrier when learning is conceived as social relations and as an irregular process that is evidenced in varying contexts, not necessarily demonstrable at an annual test-taking time.

Therefore, practices like standardized testing, ability grouping, tracking, retention, and skipping grades are virtually nonexistent within Japanese elementary schools, partly because they represent such a narrow range of standards for achievement but also because *kokoro* demands broader attention to an interactive array of relational standards that render unthinkable such divisive practices. The discontinuity of grouping practices that differentiate learning opportunities creates a relational disturbance affecting self-image and peer relations.

Regardless of academic proficiency, students may not be able to swim backstroke, play and sing melodies in F major and D minor, do handsprings, and carve a wood block, all required in the fifth-sixth grade curriculum. Skipping a grade is inconceivable for four reasons: (1) no one is perfect in all these required skills; (2) improvement is always possible; (3) each grade level has ceremonies and special events not replicated in other grades; and (4) students play indispensable roles in each event. Students benefit from experiences not available in any other grade, and each individual is needed to maintain relations whereby they teach and learn from same-age peers.

Ability grouping does not make sense with instructional activities that require multiple abilities. Changing contexts and maturity thus formulate learning opportunities in more powerful ways than fixed notions of ability and achievement in Japanese schools. Differing contexts stimulate engagement and various connections so that students can more meaningfully embrace the concepts. Some learning can only be construed and displayed in real-life contexts. Sometimes learning simply does not reveal itself until much later or with a change in setting. Maturation is a highly irregular process. Age-level progression allows for this variance: for example, sometimes a key event like starring in the third-grade play will spark motivation to turn a negligent student around, and some slow students suddenly catch up by the sixth grade.

Time is a valued commodity, and time use reflects the priorities that drive educational decisions in any country. Less time spent in school on standardized testing releases time for practices that honor *kokoro* and relations. One practice that predominates in Japanese elementary schools is *hansei* (see also the essays by Fukuzawa and LeTendre, this volume). *Hansei* (reflection) is the primary means for focusing on the journey: encouraging individual and group assessment of processes and of one's participation, thereby highlighting relational standards such as sensitivity to feelings, empathy, diligence, and effort. An essential complement of *hansei* is goal setting. By providing reflective moments to assess participation vis-à-vis goals, *hansei* is a superb way to cultivate self and group discipline and the capacity to evaluate, especially in a constructively critical fashion toward continual self and group improvement.[10]

Afterward or during work in progress, orally and in writing, as an individual, in small groups, and as a whole group, *hansei* was a common discussion method and feedback mechanism in the schools I surveyed. Students reviewed learning activities and, in the process, more firmly assimilated their learning. They developed the abilities to summarize their learning, to postulate the next problem for study, and to set future learning goals. Administrators, teachers, and parents did the same goal setting and reflection after events in their respective groupings. *Hansei* was critical for soliciting meaningful ideas and suggestions from all participants and was used throughout Japanese society.

Reflection also served as a mutual assessment mechanism between students and the teacher. For teachers, reflection was a means to gauge student participation and learning, to engage students as active learners who take responsibility for their own learning, and to provide individual and group feedback. *Hansei* was therefore a powerful mechanism of control as well; teachers had the power to observe and respond to the students' reflections and to make the students rewrite or rethink their responses. Undoubtedly, students felt pressure not only to be honest in their reflections but also to conform to adult expectations. Students had ample practice in the art of *hansei,* so that by the sixth grade, some students were thoughtfully articulate about their performance and could evaluate themselves in relation to others. As such, *hansei* was an effective strategy for developing empathy and moral judgment, along with critical thinking skills.

Reflection worked because it was accompanied by norms that fostered considerate discussion and participation patterns, primarily ones that attended to feelings and produced surface harmony. Rather than self-praise or other-criticism, recommendations for self-improvement were acceptable. When speaking about others, pressure rested on verbalizing the constructive sides and leaving the negative sides unsaid, but implicitly understood. Students were encouraged to relate their ideas to the previous speaker – for instance, "I agree with this part, but . . . ," or "My idea is a little different. . . ." Being aware of silence, students included others without their having to ask: listening, understanding with *kokoro*. Complaining was a sign of weakness; instead, *gaman* was prized: silent endurance.

Hansei is critical for developing shared ownership patterns, and shared ownership enables *hansei* to work as an effective mechanism for accountability. In fact, *hansei* was the major accountability mechanism invoked on a daily basis for building trustful relations, with report cards punctuating the process at the end of each trimester, each measuring different aspects of educational growth. Learning evolves on a continuum of successes and failures, both as individual and as group responsibilities, not dependent on a one-time assessment of success versus failure, solely on an individual basis. As such, *hansei* is the perfect accountability counterpart for *kokoro:* a versatile assessment mechanism authentically adaptable to a wide variety of contexts, capable of validating diverse forms of knowing, sustaining individual and mutual growth.

Diversity in forms of knowing: broader conception of the basics

With *kokoro* at its core, genuine learning depends on direct experience, as reflected in the fascinating variety of Japanese words for "experience." One is *kemmon* or *kembun* (a combination of the *kanji* "to see" and "to hear"): experience through the eyes and ears, meaning visual, aural experience, observation, and information gathering. Another word is *keiken,* experience gained through the passage of time – a word also used for empirical science. The third word, used in contrast to the others, signifies experience gained through one's total body: *taiken.* The two *kanji* for *taiken* are the words for "body" and "testing," so investigation through actual experience involving the whole body and all its senses is a more inclusive way to experience. Several times principals and teachers remarked that the best learning relied on *taiken.*

Use of the total body for learning was significant in two ways: cultivating all sensory capacities and valuing repetitious learning so that certain skills become automatic (see the essays by Peak and Hori in this volume). The wonderful phrase *karada de oboeru* (to remember through one's body) represents this holistic learning and physical automaticity. Other Japanese phrases refer to learning things so well that they become "attached" to one's body. Total knowing was gained through the body, not just through one's mind: a more comprehensive, meaningful, and permanent form of learning.

Sensitivity to total body learning promoted curricular diversity along many dimensions. The core curriculum of the fifth and sixth grades consists of nine subjects. In addition to the four standard subjects considered academic in the United States (language arts, mathematics, science, and social studies), art, home economics, moral education,[11] music, and physical education receive diligent attention in Japanese elementary schools. In my observations, academic subject times were often sacrificed to prepare for music, art, drama, or physical education special events. A review of the list of required content and skills for each subject matter (Ministry of Education, *Elementary School Course of Study,* 1983) attests to the diversity of intellectual and experiential activities to which all students are entitled in their schooling alone.

Besides subject matter studies, the school day includes student responsibilities for whole school cleaning time, service and clean-up of their hot lunch, and classroom management duties. There are also weekly extracurricular activities and responsibilities for all fourth through sixth graders: club activities, student council activities, school work times (for events preparation), and free activity periods. Students stay at school as late as 5:00 P.M., and time spent in these activities remains unchanged regardless of budget constraints and other academic concerns.

One week is busy enough, but throughout the year, events and ceremonies invigorate an already full schedule. Because the school year is sixty days longer in Japan (240 days) than in the United States (180 days), people assume that students spend that much more school time in academic studies, which therefore accounts for the higher achievement levels. However, a U.S. Department of Education report (1987:10) adjusted for the special events and half days and reported a full-time equivalent of about 195 days for Japanese schools. The noteworthy difference is forty-five more days of special events, ceremonies, and extracurricular activities. Contrary to conventional reasoning, the longer year may contribute to greater achievement not because of more time spent on academic studies, but because of an emphasis on nonacademic activities, easily eliminated as "frills" in the United States.[12]

Instead, Japanese teachers welcome these activities as means to develop leadership and organizational skills; to broaden direct experiences; to reinforce academic, artistic, physical, social, and personal skills acquired in other studies; and to secure fresh perspectives on students. Teachers often emphasize the value of this diversity in capturing well-rounded views of students in order to engage them individually in more compelling ways. Many discipline and control problems are averted by increasing opportunities to tap students' interests. Moreover, curricular diversity is less likely to favor the same students; hence, a clear hierarchy of "smart" and "stupid" students is less likely to emerge. As more students experience success, they feel more included in school, and the sense of community may be strengthened.

Capitalizing on the interplay of opposing forces also promotes diversity in forms of knowing. Varied experiences and responsibilities kept each day lively: different academic subjects were interspersed with nonacademic subjects and activities. Lectures and drills were punctuated by plentiful opportunities to demonstrate skills in diverse areas. The same subject taught in a similar fashion each day provided gratifying consistency in an otherwise ever-changing schedule. Sitting to concentrate on reading or drills was a welcome relief from the physical activity. And individual seat work was a nice respite from the interdependence required in other activities. The breadth of experiences was imperative for refining academic skills because students remained eagerly engaged, their bodies and minds vitalized.

In order to promote the academic basics effectively, Japanese seem to prioritize the relational basics, what I refer to as the "four C's": community, connectedness, commitment, and caring.[13] In Japan, the four C's are basic to the development of *ningen* and *kokoro*. These four areas derive their significance and meaning from the process of forming relations: necessitating reciprocity, mutual respect, and simultaneous consideration of self and others.

Finally, the required diversity of materials was irresistable: I wanted to become an elementary student again. Most were the students' own property to use, protect, and otherwise have readily accessible wherever they went. For each subject, students had their own textbooks, notebooks for note taking and other homework, and hands-on activity materials. Students also had their own music instruments (usually recorders), gym uniforms, and kits for art, home economics, and calligraphy.[14] Rich and poor students alike are assured of having more than the basic educational materials available to them. Since they are responsible for their own possessions, students' view of school and their place in it are profoundly affected.

First-grade teachers spent the first few months showing students how to pack their backpacks, how to organize their desks, and how to arrange materials in preparation for each lesson. Importantly, success and failure were shared as individual and group responsibilities (peer and home). Various communication systems helped students and teachers remind each other: monitor duties, daily meetings, memo books, diaries, and phone calls. Although some Japanese complained about the uniformity and conformity promoted by the above standardization, a vital asset was the common set of expectations and consistent requirements that enabled students and parents to cope with the diversity made possible by such standardization.

Shared ownership: distributed locus of control

The above example points to two extremely important areas of shared ownership. In the first case, the material possessions and control of the materials of teaching–learning are not inconsequential. In the second, attention is drawn to the means by which everyone is enabled to take control of the means and ends of their own education: consistency over time, standardization, and well-constructed, interdependent relations are just a few ways.

Another form of ownership cultivated in Japanese schools was that of student leadership and responsibility for the organization, as well as maintenance of school and classroom procedures, rules, events, and property. In delegating authority and control to students, they were placed in charge of constructing and protecting their educational journey, which in turn may have powerfully influenced their view of their roles in fostering their own educational growth: the ultimate capacity building. Attendance was high because of both motivation and obligation.

Regarding knowledge transmission in education, I shifted my focus from the word "knowledge" (a typically American focus) to the "transmission" side. Again, knowledge as a concrete product becomes inseparable from and complementary to the more relational process of transmission, with a commensurate focus on the versatility and significance of varied forms of relations.

How was the locus of control delicately but purposefully shifted under the guidance of an adept teacher? The main method was the variety of interdependent responsibilities and grouping patterns that formed the mainstay of elementary classroom participation. *Han* formed the core unit of classroom organization for doling out responsibilities (such as lunch, daily cleaning, and class management), for forming study groups, and often for bestowing rewards (praise) and punishments (criticism). The basic *han* was determined by the seating configuration, clusters of about six people each. *Han* changed whenever the teacher changed seating assignments.[15]

Other groups were determined by role assignment, such as student councils and classroom monitors, which changed only once or twice per year, and *toban,* which were classroom leader duties that rotated daily so that each class member regularly had opportunities to run classroom affairs. Each day two students were *toban,* responsible for transitions between class periods, running class meetings, and generally maintaining classroom discipline. Even the most irresponsible students had their chance. Usually their demeanor changed with the added responsibility, but if not, peers were expected to quietly assist.

Through student councils, students monitored many aspects of their school, such as athletics, health, lunch, library, and "school beautification" (cleaning). In other groupings, students managed classroom affairs and academic work. These monitor duties and grouping patterns contributed to academic learning by providing opportunities to employ textbook concepts and skills in actual practice, to assess individuals beyond grades and test scores, and to develop their abilities to plan, organize, make decisions, and problem-solve, both individually and as a group.

Success depended upon innumerable duties, roles, and grouping patterns that varied in size, duration, and means of selection: by chance, by student preference, by seating patterns, and, rarely, by teacher designation.[16] Teacher preference and student performance did not factor into role assignments, so students could work together as equals. Assigning duties in groups necessitated collaboration and interdependence, increasing rather than inhibiting individual efficacy. Individual distinctions were minimized; individual contributions to others were emphasized.

In addition to universal participation, three particular features contributed to peer cooperation: the duties and basic organization remained the same from year to year; students rotated frequently; and classroom norms allowed for mutual consultation and assistance. As a result, by the fifth grade, enough students had performed each duty that peer cooperation and mutual supervision were not only possible, they were unavoidable. One received help whether or not one wanted or needed it. In order to experience the benefits of mutual assistance, one also had to bear the burden of peers constantly looking over one's shoulder. Regardless of personal preference or priorities, one was also obligated to sense when timely assistance needed to be offered. Going to school meant togetherness, for better and for worse.

In fact, a major breakthrough in my understanding of Japanese elementary classrooms occurred as I shifted my American point of view of "supervision" to a more relational one. During recesses, before school, and after school, students often exercised, played, or studied on their own, without adult monitors. No substitutes were hired when teachers were absent.[17] Students were often given work, told what to do, and left on their own. Although mischief increased, students managed themselves and eventually completed tasks. I was perplexed but fascinated by the lack of adult supervision. Two questions arise: Why are Japanese students left unsupervised so often? Alternatively, why do American students require supervision?

What I first interpreted as "unsupervised" behavior revealed an American bias that students need adult supervision. After further observation, I realized that students are always supervised, whether or not adults are around, because *peer supervision and self-supervision form an integral part of authority and control mechanisms at work in Japanese schools.* Capitalizing on invisible authority, the most effective form of control, teachers monitor the noise and behavior in quiet, subtle ways.

Invisible authority refers to the respect and control teachers secure by virtue of practices or values that obviate the need to exercise their authority directly or explicitly. All seem to be necessary and work together. One is the shifted locus of control of many class processes and administrative duties to students, as outlined above. Other practices include mechanisms for encouraging students to resolve conflicts and solve problems on their own; developing internal mechanisms of control; cultivating nonverbal pedagogical tools; and establishing familiar rituals and consistent forms of organization. Standardized practices are a form of invisible authority because they set forth consistent expectations that allow peers to supervise themselves equitably.

Significantly, peer supervision is only as effective as the teacher's patient ability to minimize explicit control to allow peer and self-supervision mechanisms to take hold. The most striking feature of Japanese elementary schools was the loud noise levels, not monitored as closely as they would be in America. The range of tolerated behaviors and noise levels was surprising, yet the uncontrolled noise and behaviors were obviously not a sign of lack of control.

Class time was preserved for instruction not necessarily because of more obedient students, but because of greater tolerance. Teachers merely continued their presentation, and eventually (through the guidance of peers) most students followed along. If disruptive individuals did not bring themselves into line, peers assumed the responsibility of dealing with the disruptive behavior of their friends. Once they have prepared students and set expectations in a thorough and thoughtful manner, teacher supervision is unnecessary as peer and self-supervision take control. Thus, teachers seemed to secure more control during crucial times by not exerting control, even relinquishing control at other times.

The primary vehicle for this authority is the trusting relations created as a classroom unit: truly heartfelt group membership. Ray McDermott (1977) makes an important distinction: trust is not the property of an individual; rather, it is a "product of the work people do to achieve trusting relations, given particular institutional contexts" (199). Classroom management is a shared concern, teacher and students together acting as one classroom entity circumscribed by trusting relations, not opposing forces. At the beginning of the school year, teachers spent much time developing relations prior to textbook instruction; some played with their students during recess to model group building behavior and to develop closer relations with their students.

Placing a value on social relations and on mutual assistance inescapably invited greater noise and movement levels. In the "noise continuum," boisterous rowdiness was not a virtue, but it was appreciated as a reflection of friendship, togetherness, school enjoyment, and enthusiasm. One teacher likened the process to a dialectic, yin–yang principle: in order to induce more diligence during class, one must allow the noise to escape during transition times.

For instance, as soon as class ended, students popped out of their seats, laughing, chasing each other, or wrestling on the floor. Angry disputes rarely involved more than a quick glare or a punch in return. They were just having fun. The few tattle-tale cases were met with teacher indifference or with an effective glance or grumble. When teachers ignored rather than controlled these outbursts, peer supervision mechanisms were strengthened: students settled matters themselves. Ongoing dispute negotiation was an integral part of teaching–learning and of "making sense of each other."

Teacher absence therefore becomes as important as teacher presence. Teachers' risk taking included leaving students alone to manage themselves. One first-grade teacher purposely left his class for brief moments. Upon his return, he could hear students yelling, "teacher's coming!," but he deliberately stood outside the door and waited, silently and patiently, until all students had returned to their seats. He then asked, "May I come in?" Then he either praised the students because they sat quickly or he expressed disappointment for having to stand in the hall so long. When students told on others, he ignored the transgressions or simply asked, "Well, what could you have done about it?" When successful, these moments represented opportunities to exercise individual and group initiative and responsibility; when less than successful, they presented opportunities to learn those qualities through reflecting upon and analyzing the problems and incidents that arose.

Teachers garnered control more through repeated patience than repeated punishment.[18] The primary goal is developing the proper attitude toward school life: intrinsic motivation, initiative, and concern for others. Motivation stems from the compelling attractiveness of learning tasks themselves and from each student's relations with others. Once motivated, students can think and act together. Students' voluntary compliance is the goal.

How did teachers develop the internal mechanisms of control that promoted self and peer discipline? Well-placed praise and its complement, silence, were the teachers' most powerful tools. Praise set expectations and drew attention to students who exhibited the desired behavior. Alternatively, teachers just mentioned the problem: "Some people are still not listening" or "Everyone has not turned in their notebooks," calmly pointing out the inconvenience caused to others. Responsibility is left with students to take the initiative. Disappointment or approval often needs no words; people read each other's eyes, face, or body language. Empathy and awareness of one's effect on others should bring students into line. Rather than verbal duels, silent pauses call *kokoro* into action, hence nurturing its development.

In an interesting way, noise and silence are complementary partners in the class management process: student noise, teacher silence. Students admonish their neighbors, help them find an answer, and warn them when the teacher is getting angry. During class, the amount of permissible murmuring and moving bodies without teacher intervention is surprising to an American observer, and it is regulated by silence. The most common way teachers secured attention was standing silently in front, waiting and watching, until students noticed and quieted each other – no matter how long it took. Usually this process took only a minute, though it seemed much longer.

In an important way, equitably delegating authority and control to students helps to reduce the power struggle between teachers and students. Catherine Lewis (1989) observed the same delegation of authority to children in nursery schools. She reveals nice insights about "children's internalization of rules and their attitudes toward authority" with peer rather than adult enforcement of rules (41). Peer supervision lessens the need for teachers to make demands on students, which then allows "the teacher to remain a benevolent figure to whom children have a strong, unconflicted positive attachment" (41). In addition, peer criticism "poses less of a threat to the child's identity as a good child," which may then "be a critical determinant of the child's subsequent willingness to obey rules" (41). This study lends support to her views. Teachers definitely separated the act from the person; even with the most irrepressible students, teachers maintained that the students had "good hearts" and had just done "bad things" due to a lack of understanding or maturity. Their persistent patience and calm demeanor were commendable.

On the other hand, with such a high value placed on inclusion, the pain of exclusion may be exacerbated. In fact, exclusion (informally and in the form of ostracism) is a powerful tool for social control and conformity to group expectations. Despite explicit practices that mitigate status differences, students still create their own status distinctions: strong versus weak, cool versus weird, smart versus stupid. The observed teachers exhibited a clever range of techniques to reduce clique formation. Yet differences in degrees of cooperation and social cohesion must be continually negotiated in a status-conscious world. Better and worse classroom environments reflected Japanese teachers' ability to deal constructively with these divisions.

Nonverbal pedagogical tools

Many smooth teaching–learning processes rely on nonverbal conveyance of information; *the ideal is to understand without being told*. Harumi Befu (1971) identifies four pertinent features of Japanese cultural style: subtlety, simplicity, indirection, and suppression of verbalism. He explains, "Suppression of verbalism, indirection, and emphasis on that which is hidden and can only be intuited are well exemplified in Zen Buddhism, which virtually denies to language the role of communication of information and logical reasoning" (1976).

Learning in the traditional arts and crafts epitomizes these ideals: expertise accrues "as much through informal observation, intuitive understanding, and 'absorption' of the master's techniques as through formal, verbalized instruction . . . this intuitive learning comes about only through a long and intimate relationship with the master" (Befu, 1971:176). Absorption combines the acts of close scrutiny, diligent concentration, observant reflection, and attentive deliberation. The significance of *taiken* (whole-body experience) is clear.

These innumerable nonverbal and implicit forms of communication constitute the heart of many educational processes, cultural transmission, and social control in Japan. The teaching–learning described in this volume reveal their utility and versatility in a variety of settings: in the Rinzai Zen monastery (Hori), in Noh drama (Hare), in the Suzuki Method (Peak), and in businesses (Rohlen). Although Japanese society is rapidly changing, and although verbal expression and public speaking are important in schooling, many classroom practices still rely on features stemming from this tradition. In fact, role modeling and absorption as means of knowledge transmission assume powerful roles in a cultural context that emphasizes subtlety, indirection, and intuition.

Absorption is the ability to acquire understanding and to construe meaning by sentient awareness. One absorbs a holistic combination of information through all the senses. As a process, absorption encompasses a range of "knowing": those moments when we automatically understand and act, yet remain unable to clearly articulate what led us to know. It is an entirely sentient act, yet learning has occurred. Precisely because absorption operates on such indirect communications and sensations, it is a compelling way to accumulate knowledge, interpersonal skills, attitudes, values, motivation, and the will to conform.

The power of absorption lies in its constant underlying presence, complementing verbal instruction and permeating the readily recognizable ways to teach and learn, such as lecture, seat work, consultation, and discussion. Moreover, the mutual teaching and learning continue outside school, as adults and peers are constant role models in the process of daily life. One teacher, who produced magnificent choral singing in his classroom, explained that all students can learn to sing in tune simply with regular practice beside their peers: absorbing, listening.

Consistency in form and order aids the absorption process. One feature of Japanese culture is the important role of form and order: in comportment; in the organization of time, thoughts, and materials; and in the physical environment. Neatness, symmetry, and cleanliness are prized aesthetic values that support this form and order, which includes an emphasis on proper etiquette, personal habits, and rituals. Repeated practice in ways of thinking, organizing, and planning (such as goal setting and *hansei*) also sustained mutual teaching–learning processes. On a practical level, numerous cultural forms of comportment (ways to sit, to stand, to bow, and to eat) make group activities and transitions more efficient.

Ritualistic behaviors and imitation of forms also may be viewed as the outward manifestation of the foundation for deeper understanding. In other words, repetitive patterns of form and order comprise a vital, comforting framework enabling individuals to incorporate new ideas and practices as their own. The framework becomes the channels through which creative conceptual and artistic juices may flow, and in turn is altered as it is adapted on an individual basis. Thus, physical form and order (attention to outward appearance) cultivates understanding and an appreciation that induce mental and spiritual form and order. Hori's concepts of teaching by teaching and teaching without teaching (this volume) offer an excellent illustration of these issues.

For example, to improve memory and refine fundamental skills, repetition and drill have a valued place as direct experience. Engaged repetition and drill entail hard work and suffering, experiences through which one demonstrates patience, dedication, and endurance, all essential to learning and character building. Remembering through the body (*karada de oboeru*) is more permanent. Through repetition, an invaluable absorption leading to whole-body automaticity occurs: the point is to know something so well that it becomes second nature, thereby freeing one's capacity to create. Paradoxically, out of the tension created by repetitive drill and hardship springs creativity. And from mastery of the basics comes the ability to create.

In Japanese classrooms, uniform procedures reflected outward appearance, not necessarily uniformity within the students' hearts and minds. Individuality was evident: I was impressed by students' curiosity, initiative, and creative experiments during and after class. Students may have practiced identical skills until they internalized a common form, but once learned, these basic skills enabled them to become more independent and adventurous. Avenues for individual expression were more prescribed and structured at times, but more open at other times. Trusting, equitable relations encouraged open expression in important ways. In class, teachers encouraged students to voice their own opinions; they asked for dissenting views, and students freely voted on possible answers. (See the essays by Shin-ying Lee et al., Stigler et al., and Tsuchida and Lewis in this volume.)

Conclusion

Kokoro embodies a holistic regard for individual students and for the school as one of many institutions sharing the responsibility of educating students. It calls for a more generous conception of basic skills, valuing relational as well as academic ones. In fact, the curriculum for establishing the relational basics may constitute the basis for acquiring the cognitive basics: the three Rs may be learned more quickly, completely, permanently, and eagerly when complemented by the four Cs. And, in an interesting twist, the three Rs may be acquired by spending more time and energy on the relational basics. Perhaps one determinant of good teaching anywhere is the extent to which the four Cs are cultivated to achieve the three Rs.

The value of *kokoro* and the relational framework for producing further insights into Japanese society and culture, and for education in general, is compelling. This essay offers merely a peek into the potential generative power of a focus on *kokoro;* continued research, dialogue, and analysis are welcome and warranted. In particular, examination of U.S. schooling and teaching–learning processes may benefit from a relational focus. What would educational reforms look and feel like if the emphasis shifted from cognitive development apart from others to cognitive development through one's relations with others? What changes would occur in teachers' professional lives with a conception of teaching and learning as inseparable acts, shared by all members of the classroom? What impacts on students, schools, and communities would occur with shared ownership?

Education must center on the complex enterprise of building nested layers of relations while simultaneously tending to various aspects of self in order to accomplish the spiraling conceptual development of an array of knowledge and skills. In Japanese elementary schools, a few ways they accomplish this dizzying agenda have been discussed in this essay: (1) diversity in forms of knowing; (2) shared ownership; (3) nonverbal pedagogical tools; and (4) process orientation. However, essential as these are to Japanese elementary schools, they are not commonly emphasized in educational discourse in the United States or in our discussions of Japanese education.

Based on my observations, words commonly associated with "group oriented" and stereotypically ascribed to "the Japanese" lose meaning with a more fine-grained analysis. In an ironic twist, in such a homogeneous society with so many uniform practices, the success of its educational system rests on the degree to which diversity is encouraged and exploited. Because individual diversity is so great, the best way to nurture capacity building along with community building is to ensure a breadth and diversity of experiences. Actual achievement becomes more fluid than the rigid nature of categories can reflect. Who is rigid? U.S. educators spend much time categorizing and grouping students in inflexible ways that compromise their individuality. In part, Japanese educators purposely avoid these types of groupings in favor of protecting the individual sense of self. Who is group oriented?

As I saw the interconnectedness prompted by the relational framework, many of the terms used to describe "the Japanese" or "Japanese education" needed clarification in their own cultural context to amplify the underlying multidimensional complexity. Also, terms such as "individual," "authority," "cognition," and "ability" take on new meaning when cast in another cultural framework. In Japan, a relations orientation seeks complementarity where divisions surface and seeks commonality where differences appear, thus concealing the critical role of individual endeavors and diversity within the group. By contrast, an orientation to individual independence conceals the prevalence of group conformity in the United States.

This essay is not meant to be an uncritical testament to the "perfection" of the Japanese system. On the contrary, this essay presents an educational vision inspired by the observed classrooms and schools and extracted from explanations of the admirable practices witnessed on a daily basis over the course of three years. The same practices that resulted in well-constructed, systematic capacity and community building have equally damaging potential, depending on the ability of the Japanese to adhere to their own standards and ideals. Problems evident in their own system result from inadequacies and failure to create equitable, mutual teaching–learning communities. Further explication and investigation into these failures and inadequacies in light of the relational framework would shed further light on this line of analysis.

Any strikingly positive or negative feature mentioned here is not unique to Japan. I have observed comparable excellence in exemplary classrooms in the United States. Likewise, the contradictions and questionable elements reside as tensions within our own society as well. Perhaps the teachers we admire share more commonalities, regardless of their nationality, than they share with teachers we do not admire in either country. My hypothesis is that "expert" teachers probably build mutual learning communities and refine *kokoro,* whether they are American or Japanese. More robust educational questions may point to U.S.–Japanese commonalities rather than distinctions: for example, what are the characteristics of effective and less effective teaching in both countries?

Future research should look more carefully at relational variables and processes in both countries. Most telling may be an emphasis on words and practices that unify rather than divide. Most divisive is the American tendency to set up false dichotomies. Concepts set apart in an oppositional framework are misleading in the oversimplification they invite. Applied to research in general, perhaps the ultimate false dichotomy potentially producing the most damaging implications is that of "the United States versus Japan."[19]

The Japanese case points to potential educational gold mines by appreciating the interplay and integrating concepts that Americans tend to separate in school settings, such as cognition and emotion, mind and body, success and failure, repetition and creativity, uniformity and diversity, individual and group. Looking at these dichotomies in their classroom reality, important nuances emerge. Practitioners effect the delicate balance between individual and group needs, between structure and freedom, and between seeking uniformity for equality's sake and diversity for equity's sake. Admittedly, an uneasy tension exists between the attractive pull of individual diversity and the equally desirable push toward conformity and sacrifice for the collective good.

In closing, the one insight most provocative in its potential impact is considering *kokoro* at the heart of education. Important shifts in conception occur with *kokoro.* School is not just a building but also a process, a shared phenomenon, whose qualities are defined by and for those who congregate together each day. The classroom is not just a place bounded by four walls in which knowledge is transmitted. It is also a community of learners defined by their network of relations and extending beyond school walls.

Kokoro embraces a vision of education that is soulful as well as technical; that attends to feelings as well as knowledge; that thrives on nonverbal, intuitive pedagogical tools as well as on verbal, concrete tools; that honors group as well as individual endeavors; that seeks process as well as outcome measures; and that prizes continuity, long-term consistency, and togetherness alongside change, flexibility, and individuality.

Teachers are not merely government servants mindlessly following curricular prescriptions. They react and interact with fellow teachers, students, and communities to effect lively teaching–learning processes. Teacher expertise is not just a matter of subject matter knowledge. Teachers need consummate interpersonal skills and heightened sensibilities to tune in to students, to touch their souls, to move their hearts, and to inspire their bodies and minds.

Students do not need constant supervision. They can assume responsibilities and supervise themselves if given the carefully crafted chance. And finally, students are not born with a given set of abilities that determine their eventual achievement. They have unknown capabilities, and in working with those around them, their abilities and achievements are born.

The notion of "ability" as an immutable trait of an individual ceases to wield much power in an educational world that stresses combining individual efforts to achieve a greater learning whole and in a culture where the definition of self is highly relational and context dependent. Its lack of utility as an organizing principle in classrooms (so strong a feature in the U.S. educational mindset) actually frees individual potential for capacity building. The locus of power shifts to transforming innate qualities through individual and group efforts, through peer reliance and assistance, and through intelligently learning how to use one's physical and human environments to teach and learn.

Perhaps most memorable from an American standpoint was the exposure to empirically observable evidence that subjects like physical education, art, and music were not primarily ones of talent, so that poor performance could easily be dismissed.

In all grades, I observed outstanding art work, social studies and science projects, and notebooks filled with outlines and reflections that exhibited attention to organization, color, and detail. Coupled with the fact that every student participated, not just select ones, and the fact that the IQ and achievement test scores of these students ranged from very low to very high, these accomplishments were the result of something more than innate ability. With time, patience, assistance from others, and motivated efforts, everyone can sing, compute, read, and draw.

From my observations, learning resulted from an inseparable combination of natural tendencies,[20] of nurturing the appropriate learning relations and conditions, and of effort. In each project, the end products ranged in quality, but the overall, average level of achievement was appreciably high. I wondered if Americans are not doing a disservice to our children and to our teachers by expecting so much less, especially in art, physical education, music, and sharing responsibility. Children are much more capable than U.S. conventional wisdom grants them.[21]

The educational challenge is a two-way street, striving to maintain a meaningful balance between all these goals and forces in order to optimize the potentials within all students: perhaps an art more than a science. Enlisting *kokoro* also as a guide to the research, policy formation, and implementation processes may be informative and may serve us well. In an interesting convergence of school reform trends, the United States is promoting cooperative learning and group work, while Japan is seeking individualized instruction and independence. In their quests, given the fundamental difference in conceptions of the individual self, where will each find its balance? And how similar or different will they look? Needless to say, both sides have much to learn from each other's successes and failures as they embark on similar journeys, interestingly initiated from and set in contrasting contexts.

Notes

1. Research was also conducted in two public schools in Nagano prefecture (one rural town and one isolated mountain school) and two minority public schools in Osaka. Data collection consisted of narratives from observations, interviews, questionnaires, video-

tape recordings, student products, teacher records, document analysis, and student artifacts to provide a comprehensive view of school life. Without long-term, daily research into classrooms, the most important aspect of education in Japanese schools cannot be adequately analyzed: namely, the teaching–learning process. Ongoing contact and a long-term view of the same setting proved necessary to appreciate the complexities and gain the trust necessary to secure as natural and as honest a picture of daily life as possible.

2. This notion is also important in Ann Brown and Joe Campione's work with their Fostering a Community of Learners program, particularly their notion of distributed expertise (Brown & Campione, 1990; Brown, 1992; Brown et al., 1993).

3. One 60-year-old friend, who now lives in America, still attends his elementary school reunion in Japan whenever possible. During my research stay, my 103-year-old uncle, who had been an elementary school teacher, fondly reported that a former elementary school pupil had just traveled a long distance to visit him.

4. In turn, students are obliged to follow school dress codes and rules even during non-school hours and to fulfill their school obligations at home and during vacations. I observed class time used to plan "walking-to-school" groups, led by sixth graders, for safety purposes, and teachers meeting with parents to plan neighborhood watch patrols during vacation, again out of concern for students' safety and time use. In more extreme cases, one teacher reported bringing a girl to school each morning because her parents were unable to get her ready for school; and a principal had been meeting with three errant boys every morning for several months before school to review reflective journals the boys were required to write. The principal felt that a simple apology to the injured parties was insufficient because the pattern of the boys' behavior indicated more serious problems of character he sought to rectify.

5. One need only read newspapers for daily dramatic accounts of some of these abuses and excesses, but each anecdote or scandal must be balanced with further research. Refer to my dissertation (1991:52) for other examples of kinds of exclusion or discrimination and further citations.

6. The importance of relations regarding content should not be overlooked just because the subject cannot be treated fairly and in more depth in this essay. For example, ideally teachers situated the lessons in students' daily lives, and they related the content of the lesson to previous lessons and to those that will follow. Wherever possible, connections were made between subject matters and between academic and extracurricular activities. Almost ev-

ery math lesson I observed began with a question or problem posed to students about something in their lives, followed by the teacher linking the ensuing student-oriented dialogue back to an explanation about how today's math lesson will help solve or understand the problem. (See the essays by Shin-ying Lee et al., Tsuchida and Lewis, and Stigler et al., this volume.)

7. In fact, when asked when some of these practices were instituted, one teacher replied, "We got these ideas from you [meaning the United States]. They come from John Dewey." Ironically, perhaps the Japanese have been more successful at putting Dewey's philosophy of education into practice on a broad basis.

8. Respectively, these terms roughly mean effort (*gambaru*), endurance (*gaman*), properly or just as it should be (*chanto*), to try as best or as hard as one can (*isshokenmei*), combine our strengths (*chikara o awasete*), and get along well with others (*naka yoku suru*).

9. Nagano students and teachers stayed together for three years. I heard of rare cases in which classes changed every year or stayed together for all six years.

10. Sometimes each person is expected to say something. If no one offers an opinion, a facilitator calls on people until everyone has had a chance to speak. Lewis also discusses *hansei* in her chapter.

11. Moral education has its own textbook and basically covers interpersonal relations, the meaning of friendship, appreciating others' feelings, learning to work together, and assuming responsibility.

12. This prompted one Japanese researcher to complain that the problem with Japanese elementary schools was that they did not teach academics, only moral and social education. Little did he know that I felt this was a strength, and that better academic learning seemed to be predicated on the moral and social base that he found distracting and oppressive.

13. The four Cs represent conceptual areas that I derived from the data. They are not an explicitly formulated set of ideas espoused by Japanese educators, though most would agree that these four terms are given priority in Japanese elementary schools. The term "caring" represents any feelings (*kimochi*), emotional bonds, or expression of emotions and compassion. I must thank Nel Noddings for drawing my attention to the importance of caring in education. Her book (1984) contains an important philosophical discussion. The term here, however, is used in a more general sense; its meaning is derived from the Japanese context and refers to the concern for *kimochi* or feelings.

14. Each kit contained innumerable pieces. Additional materials and supplies also had to be brought from home. In cases where stu-

dents cannot afford extra fees or supplies, families may apply for and receive government aid. No one is denied participation due to economic hardship. One priority evident in Japanese schooling is that budgets provide less money for nice-looking premises and for adult salaries and staffing of extra personnel, and more for textbooks and materials for the students.

15. Students had different *han* for studying art, music, home economics, science in the laboratory, and physical education because those subjects often involved moving to a different room. (See Lewis, this volume.)

16. Students volunteered for their preferred assignment, and if more volunteers than slots were available, students usually decided by *jan-ken-po* or another chance game.

17. Of course, teachers are responsible for students, but they do not worry about directly supervising their students at all times. In my two years of observation, substitutes were hired only for long-term absence. Once I observed a first-grade teacher leave her students to finish lunch, prepare to go home, and dismiss themselves. The neighboring teacher popped his head in two times to see if everything was running smoothly. They finished their day and went home just as the teacher had instructed.

18. Surprisingly few concrete rewards and punishments were doled out. In fact, when I asked students to list rewards and punishments, they had difficulty with this type of thinking, especially what was meant by punishment. The few rewards listed were praise and good grades, and no punishments were listed. One reason is that rewards and punishments set up status barriers that work against community-building ideals. Doing well is its own reward; other distinctions and elite groupings are unnecessary.

19. I would like to thank Ray McDermott for his insights into false dichotomies, especially this one.

20. "Abilities" may be too confusing a term here because I sense that it means very different things in the two cultures. I am not exactly clear about the Japanese conception, but one aspect seems to be that it is not an immutable quality of oneself. One can nurture ability or it can be inadequately developed, but one still does not have "it" as though it comes as baggage to carry throughout life. Their conception of intelligence seems to be a good example: intelligence is not an immutable, innate quality of a person; rather, intelligence is a quality that manifests itself in interaction with one's physical, social, and material environments. Therefore, IQ tests are meaningless to Japanese teachers because they do not measure an essential aspect of intelligence: its application in practice. Similarly, IQ tests do not reflect the effort or ways that a

person displays intelligence, and these areas may be more pertinent for assessing intelligence.

21. Many current U.S. educational reforms support the capacity- and
community-building ideals elaborated in this essay. Because this
essay was meant to be an explanation of teaching–learning within
the Japanese context, I did not dwell on the similarities and differences between them. Further comparative research and analysis
into the range of these reforms would be interesting: to mention a
few, Fostering a Community of Learners (Brown, Campione),
Complex Instruction (Elizabeth Cohen), Accelerated Schools
(Henry Levin), ATLAS project (James Comer, Howard Gardner,
Theodore Sizer), the Child Development Project (Eric Schaps),
and the Coalition of Essential Schools (Sizer).

School and classroom models

Up to now, the essays have largely explored metaphors and ideals of teaching within various Japanese contexts. In this section, we look at specific teaching practices in school. All of the authors in this section are interested in comparing how Japanese and American teachers present knowledge. By contrasting the practices of teachers, we can shed some light on how broader assumptions about teaching and learning affect the way elementary and middle schools are organized. We also present a essay on one of Japan's most successful tutoring schools.

All of the authors are fairly positive about the Japanese system. They have not set out to reveal the problems of Japanese methodologies, but rather to describe the more well-founded practices as objectively as possible. All of the authors have had extensive experience in U.S. and Japanese classrooms. That they should all find Japanese education at the elementary and middle school levels superior (in some respects) to American education is not an indication of their lack of impartiality but rather a strong testament to the efficacy of some of the fundamental strategies employed in Japan.

The reader may wish to consider how the following concepts orient Japanese teachers and students in their work. In presenting knowledge to children, Japanese use a fairly compact set of techniques. However, although the tools are simple, they are used in complex and varied ways.

Routines: Rather than assuming that routines are something to be avoided, Japanese teachers use them to reduce work. The top-down curriculum approach and standardization give teachers more time to work with individuals and attend to the problems they have with the materials. Of course, this emphasis considerably reduces the teacher's autonomy in deciding what will be taught, as well as flexibility in altering lessons. But paradoxically, it allows the teacher much more flexibility in working with individual students. Since everyone is on the same path, it is easy to devote attention to those who are struggling.

Formulas: The authors point out that rather than focusing on memorization, math and other subjects are presented in tightly linked sequences that allow the teacher to anticipate children's problems and to guide a public discussion of the problems. By having a clear idea of what formulas children need to know and in what order, teachers can allow students to test the validity of the material. The teacher "knows the path," but rather than presenting a "map," as many American teachers do, she stays ahead of the class, allowing them to explore alternative routes. Eventually, the students will have to come to the right conclusions – the tasks are designed to flow from one level to the next. In the process of finding the formulas, students are allowed considerable leeway in exploring and questioning.

Goals: The students and teachers face a common set of goals – how to understand these problems. By focusing on errors as useful data for reflection (*hansei*), the teacher distances herself from the role of judge or arbitrator. There is remarkably little worry among Japanese schoolchildren about being scolded by the teacher for the wrong answer (at the elementary level). Teachers and children are united in a search. Similarly, teachers' lives are organized to promote a sense of common struggle. By organizing learning as a set of goals to be achieved by a group, much of the invidious comparison found in American schools (and in later Japanese education) is avoided.

Levels of schooling and models for learning

Japanese elementary education stands in stark contrast to the rigid tracking and massive amounts of memorization that form the stock in trade for news stories on Japan. These scenarios are more likely to be found in the high schools and, to some extent, in the last year of middle school. Rohlen (1983) has shown the deleterious effects on students who are unable to enter elite high schools. Okano (1993) shows how working-class Japanese and nonethnic Japanese are tracked in vocational and commercial high schools. Without doubt, entrance into high school ushers children into a vastly different world – one that is far harsher than the elementary and middle schools they have left.

But in elementary and middle school, Japanese education is effective in offering access to a wide variety of students and in getting them to outperform students in most nations on standardized tests. And, in direct opposition to our stereotypes of Japanese education as killing the individual, the elementary school curriculum and classroom organization allows children more time to talk and to interact with the teacher. Unpalatable as it may be to some researchers, Japanese elementary classrooms maintain a boisterous, engaged atmosphere while simultaneously getting children to do significant amounts of academic work.

Critics of the Japanese educational system will, of course, wish to hear more made of the socioeconomic differences in educational access and attainment. While Japan has a relatively ethnically homogeneous society and a low index of economic disparity, working-class, *burakumin* and *gaiseki* students are found in disproportionately high numbers in the low-status tracks (Okano, 1993; Rohlen, 1983). These factors undoubtedly place strains on the school, but they do not explain why Japanese teachers teach the way they do. Attempts to deconstruct the social or political history of Japan do not tell us why Japanese teachers seem to be able to do a range of things that American teachers say they would like to accomplish. The class and racial tensions that affect American education have different expressions in Japan. The essays in this section provide a great deal of comparative information about what teachers do, allowing us to theorize about the "deep" cultural foundation for learning at the elementary level in Japan.

Teachers and teaching: elementary schools in Japan and the United States

SHIN-YING LEE, THERESA GRAHAM,
AND HAROLD W. STEVENSON

Ask typical Americans about Japanese education and the answers usually conform to a stereotyped image: intense, highly pressured children learning under the tutelage of a stern, demanding teacher who seeks conformity and stresses mechanical learning and rote memory. Lectures, group recitation, and daily drill characterize the teaching, they would say, and passive docility describes the children. Japanese students, because of the rote learning, lack the creativity and problem-solving skills of American students. It is through this robotlike perfection, many Americans argue, that Japanese students attain their high level of academic competence. They acknowledge the fact that American students may not be competitive in international comparative studies, but they propose that American schools foster the originality and creativity that have made America the superpower it is.

This stereotyped image of Japanese elementary schools is out of date. It may have had some validity in earlier centuries, when children of the noble and warrior classes were required to master classical Chinese and Japanese texts, and it may describe some Japanese middle schools and high schools. But it is an inaccurate description of what occurs today in Japanese elementary schools. These impressions are typically based on

The research described in this article was supported by the National Science Foundation. We wish to thank James Stigler and Michelle Perry, who supervised the observations in the United States; our Japanese colleagues, Seiro Kitamura and Susumu Kimura; Fong Su, who translated the narrative observations; and David Crystal, Kelton Boyer, and Heidi Weiss, who assisted in coding the observations. We greatly appreciate the willingness of the teachers to allow us to come into their classrooms, knowing that we would observe their teaching practices.

brief visits by Westerners who do not know the Japanese language and who know little about Japanese culture. Indeed, Americans are shocked when they have the opportunity to understand what actually goes on in the typical Japanese classroom.

We have frequently witnessed their shock as they watch a video program that we filmed in Japanese elementary schools or when we accompany them on visits to Japanese classrooms. Except for the large number of students in each class, Japanese elementary schools have little resemblance to what most Americans expect. Many aspects of the schools are uniform, but the rules are not so strict and rigid that they eliminate the expression of individuality by the children or by the teacher. American visitors tell us that they did not anticipate the liveliness of what they saw, especially the noise and wild activity that occur on the playground and in the school before class begins. Nor do they anticipate the readiness with which the children are able to assume a calm, attentive attitude once the lesson begins. They are surprised by the students, their ease in moving from one activity to another, their active participation, their willingness to volunteer their own ideas and answers, and their thoughtful responses when they are called on to give their own answers and to evaluate those of other students. Those who understand what is being spoken in Japanese are impressed by the skill and adroitness with which Japanese teachers guide the students through lessons. They describe the teachers as skilled professionals who approach their classes with calm confidence and who present interesting lessons with vigor and enthusiasm. They are surprised by the teachers' mastery of both subject matter and teaching techniques.

In writing this essay, we have sought to describe the characteristics of the teaching that occurs in Japanese elementary school classrooms in greater detail. We base our discussion on data collected through scores of visits to Japanese schools and dozens of interviews with Japanese teachers. Systematic observations conducted by skilled observers in many classrooms have transformed casual impressions into objective, quantifiable bases for description. In order to provide a better perspective for interpreting these data, we contrast them with comparable data collected in the United States.

Background of the study

Before describing what we found, it is necessary to discuss how we conducted our study. Two questions about methodology inevitably arise: How did we select the classrooms for observation? How did we conduct the observations and interviews?

The sample

Observations were made in 10 elementary schools in Sendai, Japan, and in twenty elementary schools in the Chicago metropolitan area. We selected the particular schools after discussions with colleagues in each city and with members of the administrative staffs of each school system.

We visited a representative sample of urban schools, including some of the best schools, some average schools, and some of the least effective schools in each city. In each school we randomly selected two first- and two fifth-grade classrooms for study.

The ten Sendai public schools represented the broad range of schools found in a large, traditional Japanese city. The Chicago sample included nine public schools and five private schools in the city of Chicago and six suburban schools. The larger number of schools in Chicago was necessary in order to represent the diverse ethnic, racial, and socioeconomic groups residing in the metropolitan area. The Chicago sample ranged from North Shore schools, often considered to be among the best in the United States, to troubled inner-city schools.

The method

We limited our visits in the present study to mathematics classes because their content is similar in different countries and because it is taught in all schools. We also wanted to gain a better understanding of why Japanese children demonstrate such high levels of competence in mathematics. What happens in mathematics classrooms that might help explain why, from kindergarten through high school, Japanese students consistently outscore American students in comparative studies of mathematics achievement (Stevenson, Chen, and Lee, 1993)?

On the basis of our experience in an earlier observational study of schools in Japan and in the United States (Stevenson, Stigler, Lucker, Lee, Hsu, and Kitamura, 1987), we decided that we needed detailed information about classroom teaching procedures. Thus, we had two observers visit each classroom at the same time. One observer wrote a narrative description of everything that transpired in the classroom. This included what the teachers and students said and did, as well as other aspects of the lesson, including the topic of the lesson, the information written on the blackboard, and the materials used. The second observer used a time-sampling method and recorded the presence or absence of predetermined categories of behavior at each minute throughout the lesson. Observers visited each classroom four times over a two-week period.

All observations were conducted by local college students or graduate students. To ensure reliability, observers were trained by a member of our research group until they achieved at least 80 percent agreement with an experienced observer. The narrative observations were later translated into English, and a detailed flow chart of the sequence of activities was constructed for each lesson.

Our interview for teachers was constructed simultaneously in English and Japanese. Before deciding to include a question, bilingual members of our research group had to agree that the Japanese and English versions were as close as possible in terms of meaning and nuance. We were able to interview all of the teachers in the classrooms that we visited, both in Sendai and in Chicago.

The setting

We begin by providing general background information about the schools and the teachers. Without such information, it is difficult to understand the rationale for some of the teaching practices and the context in which they occur.

Schools

One of the first things the visitor to the Japanese elementary school notices is the large size of the school and the large number of children in each class. The average enrollment in the Sendai schools we visited was approximately 1,000 students – 300 more than the average of the Chicago schools. In Sendai, as in all Japanese cities, elementary schools enroll students from grades 1 through 6. The average class in Sendai included 38 pupils at first grade and 41 at fifth grade. Japanese teachers are expected to handle classes of this size by themselves; assistants are never found in Japanese elementary schools, and parents are never called upon to help in class. The corresponding sizes of the Chicago first- and fifth-grade classes were 26 and 28 pupils.

Compared to American elementary schools, the typical Japanese classroom is sparsely furnished: a small desk and a chair for the teacher, desks for the children, and a television set. There may be a magazine rack, a plant or two, and little else other than the cubbyholes at the back of the room for storing some of the children's materials. The classroom is clearly for teaching lessons. The teachers' other work, such as preparing lessons, consulting with other teachers, and correcting papers, takes place in the teachers' room, where each teacher in the school has a desk, books, and other teaching materials. Classrooms rarely have such amenities as carpeting, a drinking fountain, computers, a library corner, or extra tables and chairs.

School buildings are typically made of cast concrete painted a neutral color. The somberness of the building and the sparseness of the classrooms are brightened by children's drawings, self-portraits, wood carvings, and other art products that are hung in the halls or at the back of each classroom. Classes often compete with each other to see who can do the best job of decorating their classroom or a hallway. As a result, classrooms are not the austere, bleak rooms one might expect from the outside of the building. In addition to the large teachers' room, the school usually contains a conference room, a gymnasium, and administrative offices, and there is a large yard for all-school assemblies, exercises, and play. It becomes obvious that a large part of the schools' funds is devoted to the salary of their personnel, rather than to the construction and maintenance of an expensive physical plant.

Schedule

Attendance at elementary school is compulsory in both Japan and the United States, and the average age of students entering first grade is very similar. School lasts 5½ days each week, vacations are shorter than in American schools, and the class typically stays together with the same homeroom teacher for at least two or three years. Even though classes are large, daily interaction over a period of years fosters high levels of social interaction among the children. First graders attend school an average of 5.6 hours a day in both Sendai and Chicago. Fifth graders in Chicago also spend an average of 5.6 hours a day in school, but the average length of the school day for fifth graders in Japan is nearly 7 hours.

All children in Japan, regardless of their academic progress, remain with their classmates throughout elementary school. Retention in a grade is not an option. In contrast, students in the Chicago schools are sometimes held back and required to repeat the year; in fact, in one school we visited, this included 28 percent of the children in a single grade. Japanese teachers, knowing that they probably will be with the children for several years, are highly motivated to understand each child's abilities and problems, and to develop strategies for responding to each child.

The school day in Japan is organized around forty-minute class periods. Every period is followed by a recess of ten or fifteen minutes. On an average day in our study, children in Sendai spent nearly 15 percent of their school day in recesses; Chicago children spent less than 5 percent. In addition to the recesses, Japanese children spend an hour to an hour and a half for lunch, after-lunch cleaning, and recreation. These frequent opportunities to relax and engage in vigorous physical activity undoubtedly play an important role in the sustained ability of Japanese children to respond so attentively to their teachers during the lessons.

Fifth and sixth graders attend supplementary clubs and classes that are held at school each day. These classes, called *kurabu,* include such diverse activities as calligraphy, sports, literature, and art. *Kurabu* meet during the school day, and participation in one of the activities is required. Thus, even though the regular school day is longer in Japan than in the United States, the difference is due primarily to these additional opportunities for social interaction, recreation, and participation in a rich program of extracurricular activities. Partly because of this, Japanese children see school not only as a place to learn, but also as a place where they can play and be with their friends. This view is in marked contrast to the stereotype of tense Japanese schoolchildren who are so busy with their studies that they have little time for fun.

Curriculum

The Ministry of Education defines the curriculum for all Japanese schools. Thus, the schools lack the high degree of local autonomy found in the United States. This does not mean that the curriculum is described in such detail that every first grader throughout Japan will be studying the same lesson at the same time on the same day. Actually, the curriculum is more similar to a set of guidelines, which each school must interpret to fit its own needs. In fact, chapter 1 of the Ministry's *Course of Study for Elementary Schools in Japan* begins with the statement that "Each school should formulate a proper curriculum . . . in order to accomplish the educational aim of well-balanced development of individual pupils as human beings, with full consideration for the actual conditions of the school and its locality, and for the pupils' level of mental and physical development and their individual characteristics" (Ministry of Education, 1983).

In the subsequent 123 pages of the English version of the *Course of Study*, general statements describe the goals of each subject area for each grade. For example, a goal of fifth-grade language classes is to "write passages, differentiating the facts from impressions and opinions" (17); a goal of fifth-grade mathematics classes is "to know that the relation expressed by a formula is applicable to various numbers such as integers and decimal fractions" (51). Only in the specification of the particular Chinese characters (*kanji*) that are to be learned each year does the *Course of Study* provide precise guidelines for the content of lessons.

The detailed development of curricula is left to the schools and private publishers, who use the *Course of Study* as a guide for constructing grade-appropriate materials. The particular textbook series to be used in a city or prefecture is selected by local educational authorities. Teachers do not have the opportunity to choose an alternative textbook, but they are free to develop their own approaches to teaching the content of the required text.

Teachers seriously try to follow the *Course of Study*. For example, only 20 percent of the teachers in Sendai reported leaving out any of the material included in the mathematics text. In Chicago, over half of the first-grade teachers and three-fourths of the fifth-grade teachers said that they left out material. These differences are partly due to different conceptions of the curriculum, especially in mathematics. Writers of Japanese textbooks and teachers assume that lessons should move linearly; that is, each lesson should build upon prior lessons because there will be no opportunity to return to concepts once they have been discussed. Teachers in Sendai believe that they must cover a topic completely the first time and that they should not move on to the next level unless the children have mastered the earlier ones. American textbooks, on the other hand, follow a spiral model: they return to most topics year after year, each time seeking to treat them in greater detail. Teachers know that children will have later chances to cover the material if they do not learn it the first time and may not be concerned if some children fail to grasp the concept. This makes it difficult for teachers to know what their students have covered in earlier lessons and how to gauge their own teaching.

Computers and calculators are not used in Japanese mathematics classes. None of the Japanese teachers said they instructed children in the use of computers in mathematics classes and only 15 percent said they provided experiences with hand calculators.

Teachers

Teachers hold a respected place in Japanese society, and their salaries reflect this high status. Persons enter the teaching profession knowing that their salaries will be competitive with those of their colleagues teaching at universities or working in business or in other professions. As a consequence, teaching is attractive to both men and women. Nearly half of the Japanese teachers in the schools we visited were men; in contrast, only 12 percent of the Chicago teachers were men.

Teachers in both cities were experienced professionals. The teachers we observed in both Sendai and Chicago had taught in elementary school for an average of 16 years. However, their educational histories differed greatly. The average teacher in

Sendai had attended college for 3.5 years; only 70 percent of the first-grade teachers and 85 percent of those in fifth grade had received a bachelor's degree. The remainder had received a teacher's certificate from a two-year college. In contrast, all of the Chicago teachers had received their bachelor's degree and 40 percent had also received a master's degree.

Given this difference in formal education, how do we account for the proficiency in teaching that we observed? The answer lies in the way teachers are trained. In preparing Japanese teachers, colleges mainly provide training in substantive areas, such as language arts, mathematics, and science. Aspiring teachers are expected to enroll in classes dealing with the methods for teaching these subjects, but this requirement is not always enforced. A few weeks are spent in practice teaching, but teacher training does not stop then. Japanese teachers do not acquire their skills primarily through college classes. Real instruction occurs on the job. For example, each new teacher interacts closely with a mentor, a skilled teacher on leave for the year, who is assigned to help several new teachers. Close interaction with other teachers throughout the teacher's professional life results in continuous refinements of teaching skill.

Japanese teachers arrive at school around 8 in the morning and remain at school for 8 or 9 hours a day. Chicago teachers usually arrive by 8:30 and leave 6½ hours later. Despite the fact that Japanese teachers spend more time at school, they actually teach between 25 and 29 hours a week, or somewhat more than 4 hours a day during the 5½-day week. Chicago teachers, in contrast, are in front of the classroom nearly all of the time they are at school. The energy and skill that Japanese teachers bring to their teaching are due in large part to the opportunities they have at school for interacting with other teachers, preparing lessons, working with individual students, and correcting papers. Because their tenure at a particular school is limited to seven years, teachers do not have the opportunity to fall into habitual patterns of interaction. At the end of their tenure at one school they are required to transfer to a different school, where they encounter different teachers, different parents, and new groups of children.

Just as school offers ample opportunities for social interaction among students, the teaching schedule allows Japanese teachers frequent opportunities to interact with each other. Teachers spend some of the time they are at school working together on lesson plans and sharing ideas about teaching techniques. Part of the explanation of why Japanese teachers are so skilled is that their schedule allows them to learn from each other and from more experienced head teachers. In contrast to American teachers, who spend most of their time at school working alone in their own classrooms, Japanese teachers are able to learn and receive help from each other. Their experience with other teachers is also increased through city- and prefecture-wide workshops dealing with teaching techniques and the content of academic subjects.

The Japanese theory of teaching is perpetuated through frequent contacts among teachers and continuous sharing of information. Rather than learning a formal theory or an abstract set of principles, Japanese teachers learn their skills through observation and practice. They do not follow a set pattern but instead adapt what they learn in ways that make them feel most comfortable. As a result, lessons taught by different teachers may be similar in general outline, but may differ in specific content and in the manner and order of presentation.

Teaching mathematics

When we asked both Japanese and American teachers about mathematics, the focus of our study, they told us that they liked to teach mathematics, liked mathematics in general, and thought it was very important for children to learn mathematics. Generally, the Japanese teachers were a little less positive in their answers than the American teachers. For example, when they were asked to rate how important they thought it was to learn mathematics, the average rating made by the Japanese teachers on a 5-point scale was 4.2; for Chicago teachers, it was 4.9.

The biggest differences between the two groups of teachers appeared in their ratings of how well they thought they taught mathematics. American teachers were very confident of their abilities; Japanese teachers were less sure. On a scale where 1 indicated "very unskilled" and 5 "very skilled," the average self-rating made by the Japanese teachers was 3.1 at first grade and 3.5 at fifth grade. American teachers at both grades gave themselves an average rating of 4.4. The difference may reflect the tendency of Japanese teachers to believe that they still have much to learn about teaching. Over half of the Japanese teachers thought their training in mathematics was not appropriate; less than one-quarter of the American teachers shared this belief. In response to the question of what could be done to improve children's performance in mathematics, 94 percent of Japanese teachers mentioned improved teaching methods and 14 percent mentioned factors related to parents. Among the American teachers, the corresponding values were 49 percent and 34 percent.

Classroom organization

Whole-class instruction

The large number of students and the lack of space in Japanese classrooms make it necessary to rely strongly on whole-group instruction. In our observations of the mathematics lessons, Japanese teachers taught the whole class over 95 percent of the time. Even though there is a movement in the United States toward individualizing instruction, American teachers also relied predominantly on whole-class instruction in mathematics classes: first- and fifth-grade teachers worked with the whole class 78 percent and 85 percent of the time, respectively.

The explanation usually offered for favoring the whole-class approach is that it gives the largest number of children the greatest amount of instruction by the teacher. It also provides frequent opportunities for interaction between students and teacher. Paradoxically, the small-group interaction favored by many Western educators actually limits the amount of time that each child can benefit from the teacher, who must move from group to group throughout the class period.

Whole-class instruction is in line with an important precept in the contemporary Japanese philosophy of education: instruction in elementary schools must comply with an egalitarian system of education. This view, developed primarily since World War II, is a reaction to the elitist system that characterized Japanese education earlier in this century. All children are believed to have an equal right to an education, and Japanese schools seek to provide all children with equal opportunities to realize this right. With the whole-class method, all children receive the same type and amount of instruction. The belief in egalitarianism also explains several other aspects of Japanese educational practices. It underlies the practice of not teaching formal subjects during kindergarten – a practice that might give some children an early advantage over others. It is also the basis for the Ministry of Education's providing a curriculum to be followed in all parts of the country. The Japanese believe it is unfair if students in Kyushu, for example, do not have the same access to comparable school facilities and opportunities to learn as children in Tokyo.

Whole-class instruction is also in accord with the strong Japanese belief in the importance of hard work. Japanese teachers generally assume that all children can acquire the basic academic skills if they study diligently. Teachers plan their lessons with this in mind. Teachers present each topic slowly and thoroughly so that all students are given adequate opportunity to master the material. Tracking and ability grouping within a class are never practiced, and little attention is given to children who may have special needs, such as gifted children or slow learners. These children's needs must be met outside the regular classes through after-school clubs and classes, private tutoring, or attendance at special schools, such as the well-known Japanese *juku*.

Teaching practices are oriented, therefore, at raising the general level of achievement of all Japanese students, and Japanese schools have been remarkably successful in achieving this goal. For example, in the mathematics test we devised on the basis of the Japanese and American children's textbooks, 87 percent of the Japanese first graders but only 42 percent of the American first graders were able to answer three-fourths of the first-grade items correctly. At fifth grade, 75 percent of the Japanese students but only 23 percent of the American students were able to answer three-fourths of the items through their grade level.

Attention

The alert responsiveness of Japanese students that catches the eye of the casual observer was evident in our observational records. Our observers judged that Japanese students were attending to the teacher or to the task they were assigned approximately 80 percent of the time. In Chicago, children were attentive only 60 percent of the time. There are several reasons for this. In Japan, basic subjects such as mathematics are always taught in the morning, when children are fresh. In American classrooms, it is not unusual to observe mathematics lessons being taught in the afternoon. Moreover, as we have pointed out, children are more relaxed and are able to be more attentive after vigorous play than if they are required to participate in one class after another in rapid succession. Teachers, too, can bring greater vitality to their teaching if they do not have to be in front of the classroom all day long. Perhaps most important, the structure of the Japanese lesson and the instructional approaches used by Japanese teachers are more likely to engage children's attention and to direct their activities than are the less well-organized approaches of many American teachers.

It is impossible to maintain children's attention if the lesson is repetitious and uninteresting. Japanese teachers know this and use various strategies to maintain the children's attention. Even though each topic is taught slowly, this does not lead to boring, repetitious instruction. What impresses the observer is how lively, dynamic, and engaging the lessons turn out to be. Japanese teachers spend little time lecturing. They present interesting problems; they pose numerous questions; they probe and guide. Not only are children asked to discuss their own solutions to problems, they are also called upon to evaluate the relevance and effectiveness of other children's solutions. Each child, knowing that he or she will be called upon during the course of the lesson, is attentive to the teacher and to the responses made by other children.

Japanese teachers do not linger on any particular approach to the lesson. Knowing that children benefit from different teaching techniques, they change their approach several times during every class period. To illustrate this, we calculated the average number of times the teacher changed the topic, the material, or the activity during each lesson. We defined each change as initiating a new segment. At fifth grade, for example, we found that Japanese teachers broke the lesson into an average of eight segments, each of which lasted an average of 5 minutes. American teachers broke the lesson into an average of six 6-minute segments.

Structure of the lesson

Each 40-minute period into which the Japanese school day is divided is devoted to a particular subject. Close adherence to this system was evident in our observations: the average length of the mathematics classes we observed was 39 minutes, and most classes began and ended within a few minutes of this average. The average for the American classes was similar: 38 minutes. But there was great variation, depending upon the teacher. Some of the American lessons lasted no longer than 6 minutes, and others continued for over 1½ hours.

The coherence of the lessons and the variety of teaching techniques used by Japanese teachers contribute to the success of the whole-class approach. These help to create the integrity of the lesson, a central concept in the Japanese curriculum. Each class period is not devoted simply to discussion of particular subject matter but is constructed around the concept of a meaningful lesson. The goal of each lesson is to present coherent, integrated information about a specific concept or topic. Like any good story, lessons are devoted to the development of a series of logically interrelated themes. What occurs over weeks and months resembles a book with an introduction followed by the development and resolution of the plot. Each lesson is like a well-written chapter that has its own unique content but also adds to the story being told in the whole book.

Japanese teachers in our study often achieved this ideal. For example, they oriented the children to the purpose or themes of the lesson in 65 percent of the first-grade classes and 48 percent of the fifth-grade classes. In contrast, American first- and fifth-grade teachers began by orienting students in only 34 percent and 38 percent of the lessons, respectively. The Japanese lessons were frequently judged to be coherent and clear. In the 450 lessons that were observed, raters judged the degree of coherence, which was defined as the degree of relevance and logical interrelatedness of the activities within the lesson. Raters gave the highest ratings on a 3-point rating scale more frequently to the Japanese than to the American teachers at both first and fifth grades (Figure 1). Similarly, the Japanese teachers were judged to be clear in their presentations much more frequently than the American teachers.

It is easier to present coherent lessons if the teacher does not try to cover too many topics and does not have to deal with frequent interruptions. A single topic was covered in 82 percent of the first-grade and 96 percent of the fifth-grade Japanese mathematics lessons. American teachers were likely to cover several unrelated topics in a single lesson, such as addition, use of the calendar, and telling time; they did this in 40 percent of the first-grade lessons and in 20 percent of the lessons at fifth grade.

Lessons were less frequently disrupted in the Japanese than in the American classrooms. Irrelevant activities, such as announcements on the public address system, fire drill, or collection of lunch money by cafeteria personnel, took place in less than 10 percent of the fifth-grade Japanese lessons but in nearly half of the fifth-grade American mathematics lessons.

Student participation

Two popular Japanese songs for children are *"Suzume no gakko"* and *"Medaka no gakko"* (School of Sparrows and School of Fish). In the case of sparrows, a hierarchy depending upon age exists, and teaching is harsh and demanding ("Teachers of the sparrows' school," says the song, "are swinging their rods, drawing the pupils together to make them recite in unison"). In the school of fish, all are of equal status, and they proceed through their activities peacefully and happily ("Let's take a look at the fish, playing vivaciously as they swim and play games").

Japanese teachers attempt to create *medaka* classrooms, that is, classrooms where the teacher does not attempt to dominate as the sole dispenser of knowledge and arbiter of what is correct. Instead, he or she views the ideas and reactions of students as valid and useful contributions to classroom learning. In this way, Japanese teaching is closely related to contemporary Western constructivist approaches to education. Rather than being passive recipients of information, students are expected to be active participants in the construction of their own knowledge.

Japanese students provided answers or explanations to the whole class in 99 percent of the lessons. In addition, they were

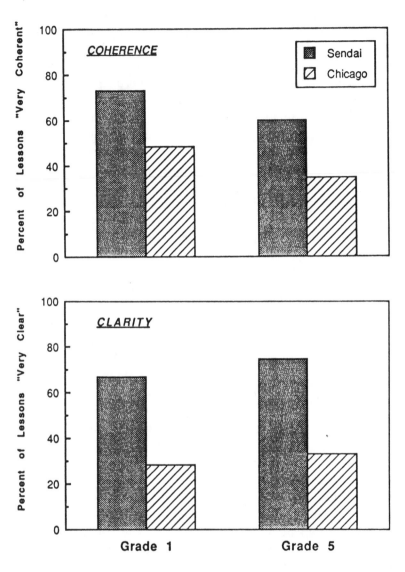

Figure 1. Coherence and clarity of the lessons.

asked to discuss the solution of some problem among themselves in 17 percent of the lessons. American students were called upon to discuss and explain problems in 88 percent of the lessons; in only 1 percent were they asked to discuss or solve problems among themselves.

Multiple activities

Even though a single topic is covered in a typical Japanese lesson, teachers use many different activities in the course of a single class period. They may ask children to use concrete objects to represent the problem or concept being posed or to write their solutions on the blackboard; they may call upon the group to respond in unison; or they may present "thought" problems whose solutions must be done mentally.

The frequent change of activities during the lesson serves two purposes. It offers different avenues for learning, and it maintains children's attention. Some children may learn better through discussion; others may be helped by the use of concrete objects. Slow learners are aided by the thorough and varied approaches. Fast learners may experience a large amount of review, but even they are believed to benefit from being exposed to the many facets of the elementary mathematics curriculum. With these varied activities, Japanese teachers seldom need to lecture to children; instead, they attempt to guide the children toward mastery of the topic. Throughout the lesson, teachers formulate the problems, students respond, and teachers react constructively to the children's efforts. When children begin to engage in irrelevant, off-task activities, the teacher first attempts to direct their attention back to the lesson by starting a different type of activity rather than by changing the topic or scolding them.

Teaching methods

The most common activities used in teaching fall under three general headings: demonstrations with concrete materials, visual representation through diagrams and written rules, and direct verbal instruction and explanation.

Concrete objects

Japanese teachers are sensitive to the fact that young children benefit from the use of concrete objects to illustrate abstract concepts. Whether they are guided by child development theorists or rely on their own everyday experience with children, teachers know that young children learn more readily through manipulation of concrete objects than solely through abstract verbal definitions. Japanese teachers put this knowledge into practice in 68 percent of the first-grade lessons and in 19 percent of the fifth-grade lessons. Although American teachers were probably aware of the importance of using concrete objects, they were less likely to use them. First-grade teachers used concrete objects in fewer than half of the lessons, and fifth-grade teachers used them in only 13 percent of the lessons.

The use of concrete objects is aided by the fact that Japanese elementary schoolchildren are provided with a *Sansu Setto* (mathematics set). This game-like box is full of colorful, well-designed materials to be used in mathematics lessons: cardboard forms of different colors, a clock, a ruler, blocks, rods, dice, and many other attractive items.

Materials in the mathematics set are used frequently, often in unexpected ways. For example, the teacher tells the children to get out their red triangles and to make a design, any design they want. She walks around the classroom, inspecting the children's creations. Then she selects three children and asks them to draw their designs on the board. The first explains that he has constructed a yacht; the second, a butterfly; the third child tells the class that he has made a rectangle out of two triangles. The teacher looked at the rectangle thoughtfully: "Hiroshi has made a rectangle from two identical triangles. I wonder, is there any way we could figure out the area of one of these triangles?" Hands shoot up. "We learned that the area of a rectangle is the length times the width," says one of the children. "Since there are two triangles in the rectangle, the area of one of them is half the area of the rectangle." After assessing whether the other students agree, the teacher explains how to write the formula for determining the area of a triangle. It is very likely that if no one had constructed a rectangle on the first trial, the teacher would have repeated the exercise until she found an example that would illustrate the principle she sought to teach. By using concrete material, the children were able to figure out how to determine the area of the triangle conceptually rather than by trying to learn an abstract rule.

Japanese teachers may use more complex apparatus to illustrate concepts. For example, to introduce the concept of "average," a fifth-grade teacher first presented a word problem. "Four children, A, B, C, and D, had 4, 3, 2, and 1 glasses of juice, respectively. On the average, how many glasses of juice does each child have?" The teacher then displayed a large container separated by partitions into four equal parts. She poured each child's glasses of juice into one of the separate sections. "What will happen if I remove these?" she asked as she pointed to the partitions dividing the container. "The juice will flatten out," responded the students. She removed the partitions to let the liquid reach an even level. She then reinserted the partitions to illustrate how all four children now had equal amounts of juice. She followed this demonstration with an explanation of the concept of "average."

Visual presentations

Reliance is placed not only on the manipulation of objects by the children or the teacher, but also on the frequent use of drawings, diagrams, and demonstrations. As children became older, Japanese teachers use these types of visual presentation as partial substitutes for the manipulation of concrete objects. By fifth grade they used some type of visual presentation in approximately 60 percent of the lessons; American teachers used them in only 38 percent.

Verbal explanations

Verbal explanations of mathematical concepts and rules would seem to be at the core of what most people mean by teaching. Nevertheless, in some lessons the American teachers made no effort to give an explanation or to elicit explanations from students. The mathematical operations could have been explained earlier, but in these classes there was no further reference to or elaboration of the concepts behind the operations; the children spent all of the class time practicing routine operations. This occurred very seldom in the Japanese lessons but was found in an astounding 18 percent of the lessons taught by the first-grade American teachers (Figure 2).

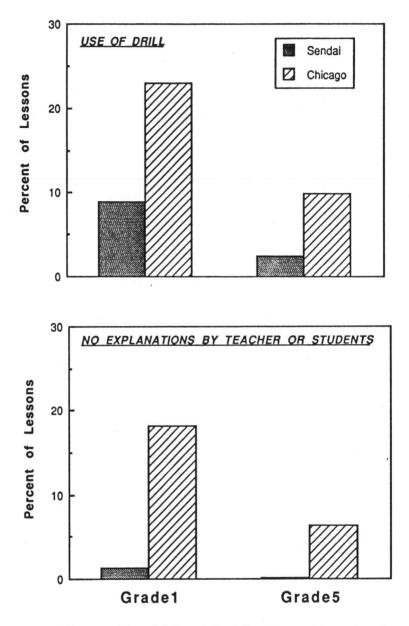

Figure 2. Use of drill and the failure to provide explanations.

Drill

Because Japanese teachers use many different types of activities in each lesson, they do not have to rely on drill as a common teaching method. Drill was used as a teaching device in only 9 percent of the Japanese first-grade lessons and only 2 percent of the fifth-grade lessons – strong evidence against the stereotyped view of mechanical forms of teaching in Japan. Drill was more frequent in the Chicago classrooms (Figure 2).

Conceptual modes of instruction

Japanese teachers frequently tell their pupils something like this: "There are many ways to solve a problem. Think of as many ways as you can. Don't worry about getting the correct answer; just come up with as many different solutions as possible." They place emphasis on thinking about the problem rather than on trying to come up quickly with an answer or solution. This emphasis is challenging to children and seems likely to lead them to a deeper understanding of the concept. Our observations in Japanese classrooms reflect the pervasiveness of this conceptual approach.

Types of information

Two types of information are typically provided in a lesson: information about the steps necessary to solve the problem (procedural information) and information that leads to an understanding of the conceptual basis of a problem (conceptual information). Instruction can include either procedural or conceptual information, or both. With only conceptual information, the child may have a good understanding of a problem but may never learn how to find an answer. On the other hand, if teachers present only the routine, mechanical steps necessary for solving a problem, students may know how to solve a particular type of problem but may be unable to extend their knowledge to other problems involving the same concepts. When both types of information are provided, children are not only able to solve particular problems but are also able to apply their knowledge more broadly.

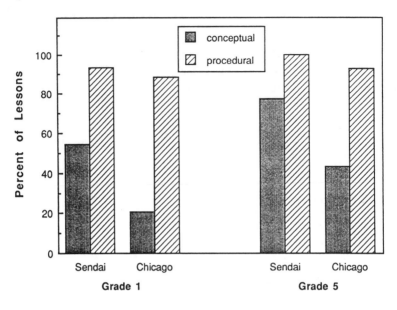

Figure 3. Percentage of lessons in which conceptual and procedural information was presented.

To characterize each lesson, we identified lessons that contained only procedural information and those that included both conceptual and procedural information. Although lessons in both cities were conducted at the procedural level, conceptual information appeared in over twice as many lessons in Sendai as in Chicago (Figure 3).

These are not the results that most American teachers would have predicted. In the minds of American educators, it is American schools, not Japanese or other Asian schools, that emphasize problem solving and conceptual approaches to learning. Even though American teachers claim that teaching and learning should be conceptually oriented, it is the Japanese teachers who are more likely to put these beliefs into practice.

Japanese teachers used several other ways to induce and encourage a conceptual, problem-solving approach. Everyone would probably agree that problems and concepts are more challenging to children and are more readily understood if the problems are presented in a meaningful context, if teachers illustrate concepts with different types of problems, if they utilize children's answers as a basis for further explanations, and if they relate abstract concepts to the child's everyday world of concrete experiences.

Meaningful context

Beginning a lesson with only numbers and mathematical symbols may lower children's motivation to learn mathematics and may force them to rely on rote forms of learning. Knowing this, Japanese teachers typically begin each lesson with some type of problem that is meaningful either in terms of the students' everyday experiences or as an application of the concepts they are learning.

For example, the teacher shows the class two identical beakers; one is half full and the other is a third full of juice. She asks the children how much juice she would have if she poured the juice from the two beakers into a single beaker. Or she may ask them to describe how they would determine the density of two swimming pools with different numbers of people swimming in them. In both examples, the emphasis is on understanding the relevance of certain mathematical operations, not on finding a quick answer or solution.

Japanese teachers were assiduous in embedding the lesson in a meaningful context. By fifth grade, after the children had mastered the rudiments of mathematics, Japanese teachers introduced some type of meaningful problem or task in over 97 percent of their lessons. American teachers used this approach in only a quarter of the lessons we observed (Figure 4).

One of the most common ways of ensuring that mathematical concepts will be meaningful to children is to embed the concepts in word problems. By solving such problems, children gain an understanding of how mathematics is relevant to real-life situations. Because of this, word problems are considered to be a useful component of Japanese mathematics lessons. Japanese teachers presented word problems in 32 percent of the first-grade lessons and in 86 percent of the fifth-grade lessons. Word problems were much less popular with American teachers, who often treated them as a separate topic in the mathematics curriculum. They used them in only 9 percent of the first-grade and 14 percent of the fifth-grade lessons.

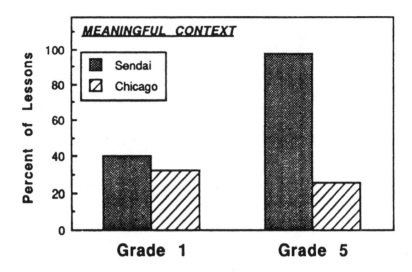

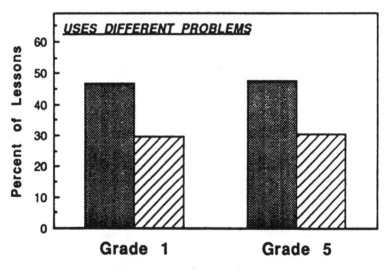

Figure 4. Percentage of lessons in which conceptual and procedural information was presented.

Different types of problems

A second technique for inducing conceptual understanding is to illustrate how the same principles can be applied to different types of problems. The likelihood that the Pythagorean theorem will be applied in a rote manner is greatly reduced if it is used in

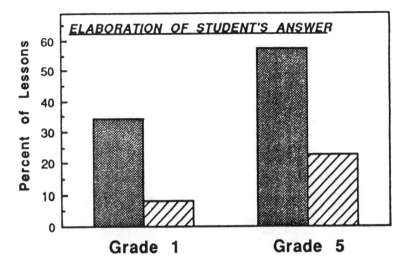

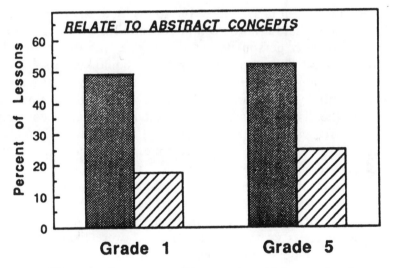

Figure 5. Percentage of lessons in which a student's answer was elaborated and examples were related to abstract concepts.

problems as different as calculating the length of a leaning tree or the distances between each of three cities. Japanese teachers also present the same mathematical concept in many different formats; within the same lesson they may use word problems, diagrams, concrete objects, group activities, and work sheets that each child must handle alone. Japanese teachers used different types of problems to illustrate a concept in nearly half of the lessons. American teachers used them in fewer than a third of the lessons (Figure 4).

Alternative approaches

Japanese teachers invite alternative approaches to the solution of a problem. Here is an example. The teacher told the students about five persons who went fishing. Each caught a different number of fish. The teacher displayed a graph depicting each person and the number of fish the person caught. The teacher then asked the students how they could figure out the average number of fish caught. One student suggested that she would add all the numbers of fish together and divide by the number of persons. The teacher asked if there were other ways to solve the problem. A second student said, "I would take some of B's fish and given them to E, and so on, to even out the numbers." A third student said, "I would first collect all the fish and then give one to each person until the last one was distributed." Another student proposed that everybody should keep the same number of fish owned by the person who has the fewest fish and then redistribute the rest of the fish equally to the others. Rather than stop the discussion after hearing the first student's correct and standard response, the teacher kept the children thinking about the problem. When they were done, the teacher explained and discussed each of the solutions.

Japanese teachers engaged their students in this type of constructive discussion three times as frequently as the American teachers (31 percent versus 9 percent of the lessons). Thus, Japanese teachers created conditions that were likely to lead to a deeper understanding by emphasizing how alternative procedures could be used to solve the same problem and how the same procedures could be used to solve different problems.

Using students' answers

A fourth technique employed by Japanese teachers to help children understand concepts is to elaborate on children's answers (Figure 5). Relying on the suggestions given by a child, regardless of the correctness of the answer, the teacher further explains the child's answer and offers a related but more detailed explanation of why a particular procedure does or does not work. For example, a child suggests that the first step in adding fractions with unequal denominators is to add the two numerators and then to add the two denominators. The teacher uses the approach suggested by the child and demonstrates how, in adding one-half and one-half, the procedure incongruously leads to a sum that is equal to one of the two parts. This type of elaboration is likely to be more effective in increasing children's understanding of the concept than simply restating the rules for solving such a problem.

Relating concrete problems to abstract principles

A final example of the conceptual nature of the Japanese teachers' approach is found in the frequency with which they made an effort to relate the concrete problem to abstract concepts.

In a lesson dealing with rates and ratios, one teacher asked the students about the distances several trains travel and the time it takes each to travel the distance. The teacher asked which train is the fastest. She first guided the students to consider the distance and the time separately in discussing the relation of each to the speed of the trains. They quickly discovered the necessity of examining distance and time together before discussing speed. By the end of the lesson, the teacher and students had translated the word problem into a formula relating the three concepts of speed, distance, and time (Figure 5).

Seatwork

In classrooms all over the world, children are left alone during part of the class time to work on their lessons by themselves. Seatwork was assigned in over 90 percent of the Japanese mathematics lessons and in 85 percent of the American lessons. It occupied somewhat over 30 percent of the time of the first and fifth graders in Japan, as well as of the first graders in the United States. More time (43 percent) was devoted to seatwork by American fifth graders.

Seatwork is handled in very different ways by Japanese and American teachers. Japanese teachers use seatwork as a time for students to practice each segment of the lesson and for the teacher to evaluate the children's level of understanding. It is an integral component of the lesson. Our impression is that American teachers, overburdened and fatigued, use seatwork as a time when they can be by themselves, correcting papers, resting, or working on their next lesson.

Rather than delaying practice until all aspects of the lesson have been covered, Japanese teachers alternate between teaching and practice. After discussing a particular concept with the class, Japanese teachers assign children a few practice problems. The teacher walks around the classroom while the children are doing seatwork, looking carefully at the children's work, making comments to individual students about their efforts, and seeking to determine whether the children understood what has just been discussed. This cycle of following each period of teaching with a short period of practice occurred about three times within an average Japanese lesson, and each seatwork assignment seldom lasted for more than 5 or 6 minutes.

Seatwork is further integrated into the lesson by following it with discussion of the problems being solved. Such discussions occurred in over 85 percent of the Japanese lessons but in only half of the American lessons. The lack of immediate feedback about the seatwork assignment was due to the fact that seatwork was the last activity in 50 percent of the Chicago lessons – a situation that occurred in less than one-fourth of the Japanese lessons. The lack of time made it difficult for the American teachers to have the children correct each other's papers or for the teacher and students to discuss the problems. American children often left their class not knowing whether they had solved their practice problems correctly. It appeared to be the most unproductive use of children's time in American classrooms; typically, it was poorly integrated with the rest of the lesson and failed to provide children with more than repetitive practice.

Evaluation

In addition to discussing the practice problems, it is helpful for students to have an evaluation of the correctness or relevance of their responses. Nowhere is the difference between the Japanese and American approach to evaluation more evident than in their use of errors. Rather than consider errors as an indication of failure, Japanese teachers use errors as an index of what children do not know and what the teacher needs to clarify. Their response to errors is nonjudgmental in terms of children's abilities, for errors are attributed to a lack of study rather than to children's lack of ability. Because of this, children feel little embarrassment about reporting errors and teachers do not worry that pointing out errors will lower a child's self-esteem. Errors are viewed as providing a good opportunity for discussing and correcting misinterpretations. Nor do teachers worry about calling upon students to point out other children's errors. In line with this goal, evaluations by both teacher and students occurred more frequently in the Japanese than in the American classrooms (Figure 6).

When taken together, the sequence of instruction, practice, and evaluation provides an ideal pattern for effective learning and was characteristic of the Japanese lessons. This seemingly simple pattern of activities was frequently not followed in the American lessons (Figure 7).

Individual differences

We have described an approach to teaching that seems to take little account of the fact that every class contains slow learners and fast learners, highly motivated and less motivated children, and children who differ in their responsiveness to the teachers' efforts. Discussions of American education make much of this diversity and of the difficulties American teachers face in teaching groups that are so heterogeneous in terms of ethnic, racial, and socioeconomic characteristics.

It is a mistake to assume that Japanese teachers encounter little variability among their students. They, like American teachers, must accommodate individual differences among children in their teaching. Variability in children's performance on mathematics tests was as great in Japanese as in American first-grade classrooms; by fifth grade, the variability was even greater in the Japanese than in the American classrooms.

How do Japanese teachers respond to individual differences? We have described how they use a variety of materials in order to engage and maintain all children's attention and involvement. Another approach is to organize small groups (*han*) whose membership is purposely made as diverse as possible. By having

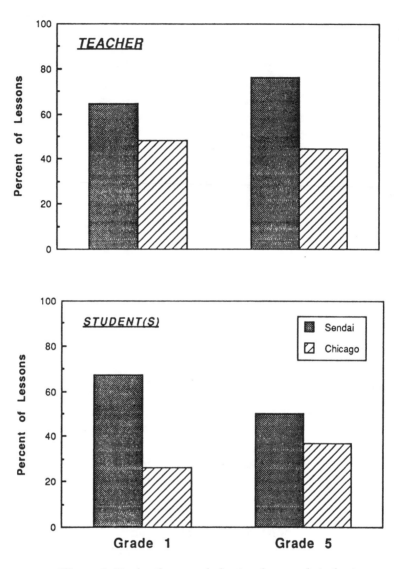

Figure 6. Evaluations made by teachers and students.

slow learners paired with fast learners, both types of student benefit. Slow learners benefit from watching the techniques of fast learners. Fast learners benefit by being forced to clarify their ideas as they try to explain mathematical concepts to slow learners. Similarly, the intense interest and high motivation of some members of a small group may have a contagious effect,

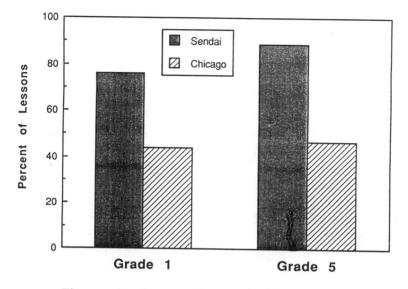

Figure 7. Percentage of lessons in which the pattern, instruction, practice, and evaluation occurred.

spreading to other, less involved members. It is in this sense that they often practice the cooperative learning techniques espoused by many American educators.

Japanese teachers also spend time outside of class helping children who may need extra assistance. The Japanese teachers we interviewed said they worked with individual children outside of class over three times as often as the American teachers said they did (an average of 30 minutes compared to 10 minutes a day). Suggestions may be made to fast learners about some additional references or activities they might find interesting. The needs of slow learners may be met through extra help. These techniques do not necessarily reduce differences among children in terms of their academic achievement, but they have the beneficial effect of raising the level of achievement of all children in the class.

Another useful approach taken in many Japanese schools is for teachers to conduct demonstration classes for parents. These classes have two functions. Through these demonstrations, parents gain a better idea of the actual activities in which their children are engaged. The demonstrations also serve as a means of initiating discussions about individual differences, for after the classes the teachers invite parents to discuss individual differences in children's responses to various approaches to instruction.

Out-of-class learning

In addition to the regular curriculum and extracurricular activities, Japanese teachers make use of other opportunities for informal learning. Even the lunch period, when students and teacher eat together in their homeroom, can serve as an occasion for informal instruction. Students in one fifth-grade classroom, for example, were eating large sweet potatoes, an item that was not on the lunch menu in other classrooms. When the lunch was over, the teacher turned on the television set and showed a videotape about sweet potatoes. The sweet potatoes that had just been eaten were grown by the children in the class. The videotape showed the children planting the sweet potatoes, caring for them, and eventually harvesting them – a much more vivid and meaningful lesson in natural science than could be provided by reading about the cultivation of plants.

Many other opportunities for informal learning take place during the special activities that punctuate the Japanese school year. For example, there is a Sports Day and an Arts Day in most Japanese schools; many schools also have Physical Fitness Day, Marathon Day, a Movie Festival, a Musical Festival, an Arts and Science Festival, and a Cultural Festival. There are walking excursions, overnight field trips, times for gardening and animal breeding, choral contests, school beautification activities, school trips to historical sites, and other activities throughout the school year. All of these experiences contribute to the time children spend in school but are seldom mentioned when the long school year in Japan is discussed in the Western media.

Conclusion

Our observations yielded a very positive picture of the teaching by Japanese elementary school teachers. We found no support for the stereotypes of Japanese teaching practices with which we began this essay. Rather, we have described how Japanese teachers present interesting lessons in remarkably well-organized ways. Far from emphasizing rote learning and drill, the lessons encourage a conceptual, problem-solving approach to learning. We concentrated on mathematics classes, but we feel confident that the approaches we have described also characterize the teaching that occurs in language arts, social studies, and other elementary school subjects.

The teaching techniques we have observed are not esoteric or derived from an exotic Japanese philosophy; they are principles and approaches that would generally be accepted as sensible, productive teaching practices in any classroom. Indeed, when we describe them to American teachers, they insist that they already use such principles to guide their teaching. The question we must ask is why they fail to use them more frequently.

We should point out that a different picture is likely to emerge if we observe high school classes. Because entrance into good universities is very competitive and is almost solely dependent upon obtaining a good grade in the college entrance examination, instruction in high schools is often defined by the content of the college entrance examinations. This tends to result in the abandonment of the teaching practices in elementary classes we have described in favor of more rapid-fire instruction that emphasizes facts and procedures.

Of course, all Japanese elementary school teachers are not equally effective, but generally the quality of persons entering the teaching profession is high and teachers strive to perfect their skills throughout their years of teaching. Given the characteristics of the teachers and the structure and support of the schools, we can begin to understand why Japanese students demonstrate such remarkable levels of academic achievement. Excellent teachers, backed by involved parents and a society that supports education, are a key element in their success.

What emerges is a very optimistic view of education. Japanese assume that all teachers can learn how to teach well if they have proper guidance and good models – that good teachers are made, not born. Similarly, they expect that all children will be able to master the curriculum if they are given proper instruction and study hard. These views and their translation into practice lie behind the success of Japanese elementary school education.

Responsibility and learning: some preliminary hypotheses about Japanese elementary classrooms

INEKO TSUCHIDA AND
CATHERINE C. LEWIS

Academic achievement differences between U.S. and Japanese students have commanded great attention in recent years. Yet, we know relatively little about actual classroom instruction in the two countries. Recently, we coded 100 videotapes of lessons from U.S. and Japanese fourth-grade classrooms, using systems that focus on teachers' motivational and instructional strategies. In the course of coding the videotapes, we were struck by several apparent differences between the Japanese and U.S. classes that are not well captured by our coding system[1] and that seem to merit further investigation.

This essay discusses two issues that struck us as we coded the videotapes of Japanese and U.S. classes: student responsibility for learning and for classroom management. By "student responsibility for learning," we mean the extent to which students actively shape their learning environment by engaging in hands-on learning and active discussion; helping to shape the content and direction of lessons; and actively monitoring and directing their own learning. By "student responsibility for classroom management," we mean student involvement in helping to shape and enforce the norms, rules, and practices needed to keep the classroom running smoothly.

Description of the sample

Our study was conducted in ten Japanese and ten U.S. fourth-grade classrooms. Japanese classrooms were all located within

We wish to acknowledge the support of the Nippon Life Insurance Foundation, the Abe Fellowship Program of the Center for Global Partnership, and the small grant program of the Spencer Foundation.

Table 1. *Total number of students in three Japanese schools*

	School		
Number of students	1	2	3
Male	524	425	278
Female	435	403	236
Total	959	828	514

Source: Gakko kan'rian (1990) from each participating school.

the Kasugai School District, near the city of Nagoya (population: 2 million). Kasugai is a middle-class suburb on the outskirts of Nagoya, with a population of about 260,000. Many residents of Kasugai commute to Nagoya, and others work locally in small- to medium-sized businesses.

U.S. teachers were from schools serving middle-class communities in the eastern San Francisco Bay Area. Despite our efforts to find comparable Japanese and American schools, the American sample included students from a wider range of social, economic, and ethnic backgrounds than did the Japanese sample.

In both countries, information about the schools was obtained from school personnel and records. The nature of available demographic data differed between the Japanese and U.S. schools as well as within each country. All Japanese school reports provided information on the number of students enrolled (from first grade to sixth grade; Table 1) and on parental occupations. However, the parental occupational categories varied among the three Japanese schools (Table 2). Japanese school reports do not disclose parents' socioeconomic status or student achievement level as measured by standardized tests. In contrast, the U.S. school reports did not provide specific information on parental occupations. Table 3 provides data on the ethnic makeup of the U.S. sample, and Table 4 on student achievement in reading, written language, and mathematics.

In both Japan and the United States, teachers needed to conduct classes in both science and social studies to be eligible for our study. In both countries, principals were first recruited

Table 2. *Parental occupations in three Japanese schools*

Occupation	School		
	1	2	3
Public employee	68	81	31
Company employee	—	440	320
Self-employed	—	55	22
Agriculture	2	1	—
Service	132	40	—
Manufacturing industry	206	—	—
Construction industry	75	—	—
Transportation/communication	57	—	—
Retail business	99	—	—
Financial/insurance	25	—	—
Real estate	2	—	—
Teaching/teachers	15	—	—
Utility related	12	—	—
Others	13	—	5
Total	710	617	378

Source: Gakko kan'rian (1990) from each participating school.

for the study, and permission was asked to recruit individual teachers within the school. In the United States, principals permitted the teachers to make the final decision regarding whether or not to participate in the study, with the result that some individual teachers declined to participate despite the enthusiasm of their principals. In contrast, all teachers in the Japanese schools agreed to participate; in effect, the decision to participate in the study was treated as the responsibility of the principals or vice-principals. For that reason, and because not all U.S. classroom teachers taught both science and social studies, it was necessary to recruit teachers in more U.S. schools than Japanese schools to obtain a sample of 10 teachers in each country. The ten U.S. teachers were drawn from six schools in five different school districts. The refusal rate of U.S. teachers was 23 percent. In contrast, no Japanese teachers refused to participate. The ten Japanese teachers were from three schools within the same school district.

Except for a difference in the number of data collection

Table 3. *Ethnic makeup of U.S. schools*

%	School					
	1[a]	2[b]	3[c]	4[d]	5[e]	6[f]
Caucasian	24	61	69	65	83	74
Black	18	11	5	21	—	1
Hispanic	7	63	8	—	3	14
Filipino	35	15	2	—	—	2
Pacific Islander	18	1	2	—	—	3
Asian	1	3	16	—	11	9
Other	—	1[1]	2	14	3	3
Other ethnic traits	—	—	20 different languages spoken	—	4 students with limited English	16% of the students in ESL

[a] The report was not dated.

[b] The data were obtained from the State Report dated October 1991 at the school district office. [1] Five students (approximately 1%) were descendants of Native Americans.

[c] The data were obtained from the State Report dated October 1991 at the school district office. [2] Four students were Filipino, three students were Pacific Islanders, and one student was a descendant of Native Americans.

[d] The data were obtained from the 1991 school year report at school.

[e] The data were obtained from the January 1992 annual report.

[f] The data were obtained from the 1990–91 annual report and State Report. [3] One student was a Pacific Islander and three students were descendants of Native Americans or Alaskan natives.

points, the study was replicated in both countries with the same technical procedures. Data were collected at the beginning and near the end of the school year in both Japan and the United States; one additional midyear data collection occurred in the United States. (Financial constraints limited data collection in Japan to only twice.) In total, forty lessons were videotaped in the Japanese schools (two lessons each in science and social studies by each of ten different teachers). In the United States, sixty lessons were videotaped (i.e., ten teachers conducting science and social studies lessons on three different occasions).

Due to the differences in sample recruitment in the two coun-

Table 4. *Student enrollment and achievement in reading, written language, and mathematics*

	School					
	1[a]	2[b]	3[c]	4[d]	5[e]	6[f]
Total number of students	Approx. 1,000	555	483	Approx. 370	435	500
Grade level	K–6	K–6	K–5	K–6	K–5	K–5
Reading (percentiles)	62	84	97	80	Approx. 88	95
Written language (percentiles)	52	64	85	81	Approx. 92	88
Math (percentiles)	65	74	77	88	Approx. 94	95

[a]The report was not dated. The percentiles for reading, written language, and math were obtained for grade 5 in the report dated April 1992 by the California Assessment Program (CAP).
[b]The percentiles for reading, written language, and math were measured for grade 3 in 1989–90 by CAP.
[c]The report was dated spring 1991. The percentiles for reading, written language, and math were measured for grade 3 in 1989–90 by CAP.
[d]The percentiles for reading, language, and math were measured for grade 6 in 1989 by the Comprehensive Test of Basic Skills (CTBS).
[e]The report was dated January 1992. The percentiles for reading, written language, and math were measured for grade 3 in 1989–90 by CAP.
[f]The data were obtained from the 1990–91 annual report. The percentiles for reading, written language, and math were measured in 1989 to 1990 by CAP.

tries and the small sample size in each country, the findings should not be assumed to generalize to the larger universe of Japanese and American teachers. Rather, we present some preliminary hypotheses that need to be investigated in a larger, representative sample of teachers.

Student responsibility for shared routines

Lois Peak and others have noted that first-grade teachers in Japan explicitly teach routines, such as changing shoes and stowing backpacks, until the whole class can operate almost as a single organism (e.g., Peak, 1987; White, 1987). A striking feature of Japanese classrooms, to Westerners, is that there is often a *single* right way of doing things: of arranging desk contents, taking notes, holding a book to read. Wall posters show, for example, the proper postures for reading, writing, and standing to speak, the proper arrangement of desk contents, and the required belongings to be brought from home each day (pencils, erasers, handkerchiefs, tissues, etc.). At lunchtime, even first graders don white chef hats and aprons and serve hot lunch to classmates, executing a complicated set of maneuvers (fetching the food, moving desks to form dining tables, setting places for the classmates who are serving), with few words from the teacher. Students may conclude the routine by folding their aprons in a particular pattern of folds, following an illustration posted on the classroom wall.

During the Japanese science and social studies lessons we videotaped, students often rapidly rearrange all the classroom furniture on the basis of just a phrase from the teacher ("get into your four-person groups"); sometimes they do this several times during a single class period. Such efficient, practiced transitions give an impression of tight authoritarian control. However, another way of looking at such routines is that they give students a great deal of responsibility because they are utterly predictable and thus can be student managed.

Another striking feature of the Japanese lessons is the ease with which Japanese students seem to perform flexible, interdependent roles within their small groups. As explored by Lewis (this volume), the familylike small groups found in Japanese elementary classrooms stay together for several months and work together on many activities each day, from science experiments to musical performances to lunch preparations. In the Japanese science lessons we videotaped, the teacher often asks the science monitors (one of many classroom jobs for which students may volunteer) to fetch for their groups equipment requiring great care, such as a balance and an alcohol lamp. The remaining students in each group decide among themselves who should get the other equipment and materials needed by their group. Before Japanese students began an experiment, they talked through the procedural steps involved in the experiment and discussed who should take what role: for example, who should get hot water from the teacher; who should pour and measure cold water in containers; who should balance water with weights; and who should hold two containers (one containing cold water and the other containing hot water) and release them in a tankful of water.

In contrast, U.S. teachers were more likely to write on the blackboard specific roles that they wanted students to perform, such as facilitator, recorder, and reporter. They explained to students what each role entailed and asked students to decide who would take each role. Students then decided who would take each role that the teacher had outlined. However, none of the U.S. classes that used this process seemed to have built-in, smooth routines for allocating roles. Consequently, teachers usually spent 10 to 15 minutes of the class period explaining the procedures and the roles of students and having students choose their roles. Often teachers ended up exercising control by making disciplinary statements so that students would quiet down and efficiently make their decisions about roles.

While U.S. classrooms also, of course, have predictable routines (Sarason, 1982), many aspects of American classroom practice – such as the alternation between play and study, the introduction and conclusion of lessons, and so forth – show much more day-to-day variability than their Japanese counterparts. For example, almost all U.S. teachers we observed dismissed individuals or groups of students for recess and lunch. Teachers exercised their authority to select individuals or groups of students to be excused first. That is, leaving for the recess or lunch break was contingent on students' good behavior, as if it were a reward or privilege given to students. In contrast, Japanese student monitors (a position held by all students in daily rotation) called students to order and dismissed them, following schoolwide chimes at the end of each lesson.

Another predictable feature of Japanese classes was lesson length. Japanese lessons lasted for 45 minutes; each 45-minute class period was followed by a 10- or 20-minute break. Teachers sometimes arranged a two-period lesson (a change announced to the students in advance) or went beyond the class period into break time (after obtaining permission from the students). In either case, the students knew when the lesson would end, and were responsible for pacing their work and announcing the lesson's end. In contrast, the length of U.S. lessons varied significantly, from roughly 30 minutes to 1½ hours. The varying length of lessons sometimes seemed to place American students in a passive position, in which they could not pace themselves and were dependent on the teacher for information about when to move on to another part of the experiment or activity.

Flexible lesson duration no doubt has its advantages: it may enable American teachers to plan elaborate, engaging assignments, to adjust lesson length in response to students' attentiveness, and to escape the arbitrary tyranny of the bell. However, this flexibility for teachers may create unpredictability for students, which leaves them more dependent on teachers' management of the lesson. Our overall impression from viewing the videotapes is that American students, in comparison to their Japanese counterparts, play less of a role in classroom management because American teachers initiate and end classes, give specific instructions on how to move desks and accomplish other transitions, and describe, often in great detail, the particular procedures (such as note taking or working with partners) to be used in the day's lessons.

In the unpredictable conditions that prevailed in the U.S. classrooms, teachers often needed to remind their students about the time remaining and about their expectations for progress. We found that in more than half of the American lessons (58 percent), teachers informed students about the time remaining for their tasks. In addition, in 42 percent of lessons, they hurried students to complete their tasks. In contrast, Japanese teachers used fewer time reminders and hurried students less often (18 percent and 25 percent, respectively). In addition, American teachers redirected students' attention more frequently than did Japanese teachers (98 percent versus 52 percent of lessons). In almost all American lessons, teachers redirected students' attention either nonverbally (e.g., by waiting for students to look at them or by pointing at a student) or verbally (e.g., by stating what students are expected to do or by counting while waiting for students' attention). In Japanese classes, however, almost half of the lessons proceeded without any redirectional statements from teachers. (The use of redirectional statements is explored further in the section "Responsibility for Motivation and Attention.") Figure 1 shows the percentages of three types of management statements by teachers in Japanese and American classes: hurries students, provides time information, and directs students' attention.

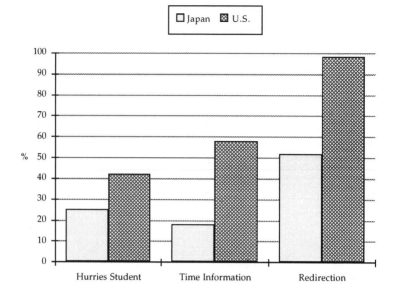

Figure 1. Management statements in Japanese and American classes.

U.S. teachers' more frequent use of management statements may be connected to the less responsible role students play in classroom management and shared routines. A question arises: is there a connection between students' intrinsic motivation to learn and teachers' degree of regulation of students' behavior? The answer to this question may provide insights into the creation of more desirable learning environment for students.

Responsibility for participation

Coherent lessons

Just as Japanese classrooms have well-defined procedural routines, Japanese academic lessons tend to follow a well-defined, coherent script that includes discussion of the lesson's goal and the relationship of the activities to the lesson goal (Stigler and Perry, 1988). Japanese teachers' manuals for science reveal that an individual lesson is part of a larger unit with coherent themes and topics, with lessons built upon previous lessons, many of which occurred in prior grades. These themes and topics are arranged seasonally, so that students can, for example, study tadpole development, rainfall, and plant growth outdoors as they actually occur (Okamoto, Calfee, Varghese, and Chambliss, 1991). In addition, Japanese science manuals lay out students' anticipated responses to each lesson. Using this information, Japanese teachers can prepare their lessons in a way that draws out students' mistakes and misconceptions, and helps students reflect on these as part of their movement toward the concepts teachers want to convey.

Probably due to their experience with such coherent lessons, Japanese students tend to focus their attention on the teacher's lesson-relevant statements, whereas American students attend equally to both lesson-relevant and irrelevant statements made by the teacher (Yoshida, 1991). Like the shared classroom routines, the coherent script of a Japanese lesson (at least in mathematics) may enable students to assume greater responsibility for learning, because students can more easily distinguish important information from unimportant information and thereby allocate their attention.

Teachers' feedback style

A common teaching style in the Japanese lessons was for the teacher to ask a question (e.g., "What are the effects of moving water in a stream?"), to solicit many different ideas and opinions from class members, and to acknowledge each response by saying "I see" (*naruhodo*), without ever indicating whether it was correct or incorrect. Often, Japanese teachers went an entire class period without telling students whether or not answers were correct. Instead, they continued to solicit many different ideas from students, asked students to elaborate on already stated ideas, and encouraged students to debate among themselves. This approach kept students wondering about the issue under discussion and encouraged them to seek better explanations and answers.

Participation as a responsibility, not a choice

We sometimes had the impression that, in Japanese lessons, even individual comfort was sacrificed to the strong norm that *all* students participate. Participation was a responsibility, not a personal choice. For example, in a science lesson on the functions of flowing water (*nagareru mizu no hataraki*), a Japanese teacher asked her students to imagine a word associated with "river." During the first few minutes, the students easily generated associations and quickly raised their hands, to be called upon by the teacher. As their responses became sparse, the teacher challenged them, in a more demanding tone of voice, to think hard. Then, she began going up and down the rows, calling on every student in turn. When a student could not add to the list of the words, the teacher asked the student to remain standing until he or she came up with another word. Several students standing at the teacher's request looked uncomfortable and ashamed.

Japanese teachers frequently conveyed their expectation that all students would participate, and that boys and girls would participate equally. Looking around the classroom after they asked questions, teachers made statements such as "Why do only boys have their hands up?", "Let's hear from the people who don't have their hands up," and "I'm going to wait a little longer until everybody has an idea." In addition, several of the Japanese teachers encouraged widespread participation by having students use special hand signals. The hand signals allowed students to show whether they agreed or disagreed with what was just said or whether they wanted to raise a different point.

Often, discussions were led by the students themselves. The discussion might be led by the daily monitors, or each student who spoke might call on another student in turn. Students often used classmates' hand signals to decide who to call on, and these student-led discussions were remarkably lively and coherent. Compared to U.S. discussions, in which teachers tended to ask most of the questions, these discussions seemed to afford students far more opportunity to participate in the exchange of ideas and opinions. Teachers watched the overall flow of discussion and sometimes intervened with a question or comment; at the same time, they keenly observed the students' progress in thinking, sometimes noting down students' comments.

As noted elsewhere (see Lewis, this volume), reflection is a central feature of Japanese elementary school life. Teachers asked students to reflect, at the end of a lesson, school day, or week, on questions such as "Did I volunteer my ideas sometime today?", "Did I listen carefully to the ideas of others?", "Did all classmates speak up or just the ones who usually talk?", "Are we becoming a class where it's okay to make mistakes?", and "Did we make progress toward our class goal 'Let's think of others' feelings before we speak'?". These reflection questions strongly underlined the expectation that *all* students would participate in class discussions and the conditions (such as kindness and respect) that would support participation.

Cooperative groups

One method of involving all students in lessons is by having them conduct activities in small, cooperative groups. In 45 percent of the Japanese science lessons and 13 percent of the U.S. science lessons, students worked for part or all of the lesson in cooperative groups. In Japanese lessons, the cooperative group activities often gave students considerable opportunity to contribute to the lesson and to shape its content. Students in groups in Japanese classrooms worked *as groups* on tasks that required or benefited from group participation (e.g., brainstorming, debating, conducting and discussing experiments).

In one science lesson on the growth of potatoes (*imo no seicho*), the teacher reviewed the three different conditions under which the students had planted seed potatoes in early spring: (1) with the old potato attached, (2) with the old potato removed, and (3) transplanted to a less crowded garden, with the old potato removed. The teacher spent a substantial amount of time reviewing the three planting conditions with her students (the teacher had prepared three drawings to illustrate the plants in the three different conditions). After helping her students associate their own observations of the plants and her illustrations, the teacher reminded students that new potatoes were produced regardless of the condition and that the new potatoes contained starch. (The students had already done an experiment with iodine and found that starch was present in the new potatoes.) Then the teacher asked the students where the starch in the new potatoes was made. She directed them to discuss this question in their small groups without looking at their textbooks. In one small group, one of the boys started describing his idea about the origin of the starch in the new potatoes:

"things like stems draw nutrients, the starch from . . ." (he could not complete the sentence). Another boy then joined the discussion with a similar statement. Now a girl took a turn and said, "The sprout came out of the old potato and grew bigger. Then the sprout opened its leaves and gathered the sun and sent nutrients down to the stems to produce new potatoes." All group members listened to her opinion carefully, and at last the group said, "Then, shall we agree on it?" to come to a group consensus. Finally, a second girl indicated her support of the group consensus with a nod.

In such small-group discussions in Japanese science lessons, it was common for the members of the groups to take turns expressing their original ideas and opinions. They generally listened to others' points of view in a polite and respectful manner. They were often very active in agreeing or disagreeing with others' opinions. In some instances, teachers encouraged students not to agree easily with group members but to proudly report their different opinions to the whole class. In fact, the teacher in this example commented to this small group that it was strange that they easily agreed on one idea about the origin of starch. Since more opinions were not generated and debated, this teacher intervened and redirected the students to think more deeply and to express more individual opinions. Details of the strategies this teacher used will be elaborated below.

Discussions in which teachers encouraged students to express their agreement or disagreement with one another's opinions were common in the Japanese science lessons (in 20 percent of science lessons, Japanese teachers urged children to express agreement with one another, and in 40 percent of lessons they urged them to express disagreement) but rare in the U.S. science lessons (each occurred in only 3 percent of U.S. classes). Similarly, the Japanese teachers more often encouraged students to elaborate on or respond to one another's responses (40 percent of lessons) than did the U.S. teachers (7 percent of lessons). Figure 2 illustrates the percentages of teacher encouragement statements in Japanese and American classes.

Another interesting feature of the small groups in Japanese classrooms is that they typically are not casual groups, constituted for science alone. Rather, they are family-like small groups that are maintained for several months, working together on a wide variety of academic and nonacademic activities each

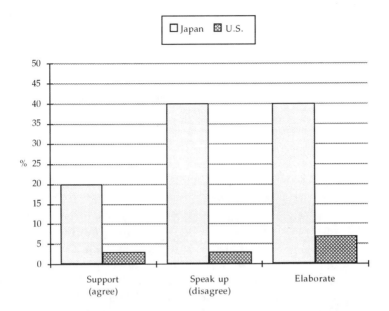

Figure 2. Encouragement statements in Japanese and American classes.

day. Each small group (*han*) brings together children with different abilities and personal qualities. A fourth-grade teacher interviewed by Ineko Tsuchida described her strategies for selecting group members as follows:

> Teacher: These are the third groups this year. At the beginning of the year, I needed to learn the students' names, so I had them sitting in order of the attendance list and formed the groups that way. Then, next, I asked students who had not had a chance to be group leaders in earlier grades to be group leaders. The students formed groups around those leaders in a mutual process in which the leaders and members chose each other. I told them five children per group, three boys and two girls, but let them work out group membership unless they asked my advice on problems. . . . Then, for the current set of groups, I chose the leaders.
>
> Tsuchida: So this time you chose the leaders yourself, and asked students to go into the groups they wished, but to keep groups balanced by gender. How did you choose the leaders?
>
> Teacher: Well, I've had a chance to observe the students for two months now. This month, I'd like to make mathematics

central. I haven't said anything to the students, but I've been thinking that this month I'd like to help the students who are having difficulty in mathematics. So, for each *han* I tried to select a leader who's kind, takes care of others, and who is fairly good at mathematics.

Tsuchida: Why did you choose mathematics?

Teacher: I think mathematics may be the area of greatest ability differences. For a mathematics problem, some children may be able to do it in thirty seconds; others try and try and can't solve it even after thinking for thirty minutes. The gaps are big. I think it's because mathematics builds on previous learning. Social studies and science don't build so much on themselves – students' life experiences or personal interests still contribute quite a bit. Sometimes fourth graders change dramatically in their achievement in science or social studies, depending on the curriculum materials or whatever. But mathematics depends so much on what's been learned previously, so the gap widens with age. So, to shrink the gap, I thought it would be fun for them not to learn just from me, but from their friends as well.

Tsuchida: You've thought quite a lot about this, haven't you?

Teacher: (Laughing) No, no, it's just that I'm just getting the children to help me out.

Standard lessons

In addition to the routines that involve Japanese students in responsible roles in the classroom, the books and materials that are used also suggest a different view of student responsibility. Many U.S. science lessons we saw (including some very interesting, thoughtful ones) had no standard supporting materials, such as a textbook, available to children. Many American teachers relied on hand-out materials. Japanese lessons, in contrast, could be previewed and reviewed in textbooks, and all students owned the textbooks – half-inch paperbacks that were easily toted home. In Japan, dozens of self-tests and reviews aligned with the nationally approved textbooks in each subject area could be bought at any local bookstore.

Japanese students in the classrooms we studied all kept ongoing notebooks for each subject that included, in the case of science, their initial thinking about a problem, their activities, and a summary of the class discussion; teachers gave students time to write in their notebooks as a regular part of lessons. The notebooks accompanying science often provided matching diagrams and illustrations supplementing the textbooks. The notebooks also provided spaces for students to write reviews and summaries of their lessons. In this way, Japanese students routinely had a great deal of responsibility for monitoring and managing the progress of their learning. In contrast, note taking in U.S. lessons seemed to be a much more individual affair. The separate pieces of paper used for activities such as brainstorming, making predictions, or noting experimental results did not seem to become a permanent record students could review and often ended up crumpled in a desk or wastebasket.

Responsibility for motivation and attention

The Japanese and U.S. lessons we videotaped also seem to be shaped by different ideas about responsibility for motivation. U.S. teachers assumed more responsibility for helping students stay on task: they reminded them of time, accountability, rewards, and so forth. For example, in 98 percent of U.S. lessons, teachers used directional statements such as "Look up here," "Shhh," and "Listen!" to maintain students' focus on the lesson; such statements were employed in 52 percent of Japanese lessons (see Figure 2). In conjunction with these directives, some U.S. teachers used stars or points to reward compliance or attentive behavior by groups (23 percent of lessons) (Figure 3). These external rewards were often collected for a week and exchanged for special rewards and privileges such as class raffle tickets or bumper stickers for family cars. In fact, some of the school annual reports gathered in this study proudly announced that their schools had "student recognition programs" to reward students who displayed proper behavior and good academic work. In addition, U.S. teachers more frequently used statements to remind students that their work would soon be carefully checked or tested; such "accountability" statements occurred in 15 percent of U.S. lessons but in no Japanese lessons. The U.S. teachers also reminded students how much time they had to complete their tasks or made "time reminders" (47 percent of U.S. lessons, 18 percent of Japanese lessons) (Figure 4).

In contrast, no external reward system was observed in either

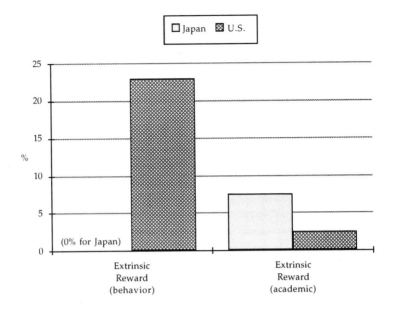

Figure 3. External reward statements in Japanese and American classes.

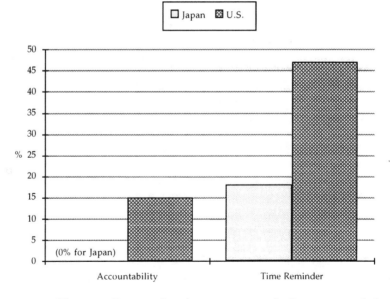

Figure 4. Lesson-framing statements in Japanese and American classes.

Japanese science or social studies classes. The motivational techniques employed by Japanese teachers appealed to students' natural curiosity and inquisitiveness rather than to external rewards. To begin lessons, they often used naive questions, intoned as if students were thinking out loud. For example, a Japanese teacher began a science lesson on the growth of potatoes as follows: "Isn't it strange that iodine on all new potatoes grown in three different conditions changed color? That means . . . ?" (using a rising intonation with a brief pause to solicit students' response). After students responded that it means that the potatoes had starch, the teacher replied, "That's right! They all had starch. What were the three different conditions?" (pause to wait for students' responses). "Yes, yes" (responding to students' reply), "that's right. In the first condition" . . . (posting the illustrations of potato plants growing in three different conditions on the blackboard) "an old potato was kept attached until it became soft and mushy. In the second condition, an old potato was removed shortly after sprouting. And in the third condition, a young plant was transplanted to a less crowded garden. But where was the starch made in these new potatoes? How was starch made in all new potatoes?"

These questioning techniques seemed effective not only to catch students' initial attention to and heighten their curiosity about the critical question, but also to motivate students to think more deeply and more analytically. Hess and Azuma (1991) call this kind of questioning the "sticky probe approach": relaxed, patient, in-depth pursuit of a single issue in which teachers helped students stay on task by asking questions that challenged students' assumptions, by highlighting conflicting ideas, or by adopting a puzzled tone of voice that said "Explain to me why you think that." The following is an example of a Japanese teacher's persistent approach to motivate students to think more deeply. It is an excerpt from the narrative of the same Japanese science lesson on the growth of potatoes.

During a small-group discussion period, the teacher walked up to the group and asked the students how many ideas they had discussed. She said, "Have you finished it? How many opinions did you have? One? That's strange! You should have many different opinions." Walking away from this group, she made a comment to the whole class that group 1 (not the same group as the one she just talked to) was having the most active discussion (*Ippan wa ichiban kappatsu dana*). Then she said,"Science monitors, ask every one of your group members a question like 'Mr. so-and-so (*nani nani-kun*), where do you think the starch was made?' " A minute later, the teacher interrupted the group discussion again and said, "Just a minute; look toward the teacher, please. The issue was *where* it was made. Someone in a group said 'here' and others said 'there.' But don't answer it so simply. Wasn't there an old potato? Wasn't there starch in the old potato? Then, say something like, 'The starch in the old potato went where . . .' instead of saying, 'the leaves (*happa*)' or 'the stems (*kuki*).' Think about it a little bit more deeply."

The assumption behind this approach seemed to be that students are capable of great concentration and perseverance, and that in-depth exploration of ideas requires no external rewards or incentives – that learning is rewarding in itself.

Data from a survey of Aichi Prefecture elementary teachers suggests that alternation between group and whole-class activities is a dominant pattern in Japanese elementary instruction (Kajita, Shioda, Ishida, and Sugie, 1980). Nearly all elementary teachers surveyed by Kajita and colleagues used small groups routinely in science, and most alternated two or more times between small groups and another instructional format within a single lesson. In our small sample of 50 science lessons, 45 percent of the Japanese science lessons and 13 percent of the U.S. science lessons included cooperative group work; frequently in Japan but rarely in the United States, the cooperative group work alternated with a whole-class focus within the same lesson. For example, the Japanese teachers might pose the question of where starch is made in sweet potatoes, have small groups debate this, have the whole class review the groups' hypotheses and figure out how to investigate them, and then have the groups conduct the investigations.

Alternation between whole-class focus and cooperative group activities breaks up the length of time that students need to be passive listeners. During whole-class activities, students are often required to listen to the teachers' instructions, or to listen as the teacher calls upon one student at a time or reviews the important points of lessons. This one-on-one questioning places on nonparticipant students the responsibility to remain attentive. Probably knowing that effect on students, teachers tend to call on individual students as quickly as possible and question as many students as they can. This leads teachers to use the types of questions that students can answer easily and quickly. When the nonparticipant students cannot maintain attention to the didactic exchange between the teacher and other students, however, teachers must use disciplinary statements to redirect their attention.

In contrast to teachers' whole-group presentation, small-group activities often involve all students as active participants. When teachers allow students to work in groups for a lengthy period without teachers' feedback or intervention, however, students often lose their concentration. Consequently, they may socialize among themselves and get distracted from learning. Conversely, when students wait for group activities for a lengthy period while listening to teachers' whole-group presentations, they often wear out their patience and attention by the time the activity begins. Then they may not remember what they are supposed to do and, again, they may socialize with each other in small groups. In order to manage students' inappropriate behaviors in groups, teachers may repeat procedural instructions or choose to delay students' small-group activities until they quiet down. In fact, U.S. teachers often criticized cooperative learning precisely for these reasons: students' increased noise level and loss of attention as a result of social interaction in groups.

In contrast to the exclusive use of whole-group presentations or of cooperative group activities, frequent alternation between these two types of presentations provides students with opportunities both to gain information presented or elicited by the teacher and to participate actively in small-group activities. By interjecting questions and comments between students' small-group activities, teachers also provide appropriate "bridges" between students' hands-on activities and the concepts under study. Japanese teachers often use whole-class time to raise questions and to highlight incongruities in students' thinking. This may enhance students' capacity to learn from the hands-on activities.

In sum, Japanese science lessons often alternate between small-group activities designed to elicit active participation and whole-class segments that provide student groups with feedback on their ideas and questions to stimulate further thinking within their groups. This alternation seems to be an effective way to balance the benefits of participation and "ownership" provided by small-group activities with the benefits provided by the teacher's expertise.

Although U.S. science lessons also had some coherent themes and topics running through individual lessons, it appeared that lesson content was highly influenced by individual teachers' interests, expertise, and experience. Thus, both the content of lessons and the length of instructional units varied greatly in U.S. science classes. For example, one teacher spent several weeks covering the evolution and life cycles of water animals because she herself spent a summer vacation studying them in Hawaii. In contrast, another teacher spent only one short class period on the topic of electric circuits. The amount of supporting or supplementary materials teachers used in classes also varied according to the amount of initiative taken by each teacher.

Conclusions

What assumptions about student learning and motivation might underlie the practices of the Japanese and American teachers we observed? One impression from our small-scale, qualitative study is that the teaching practices of U.S. teachers may be more rooted in behaviorist theories emphasizing reward and punishment than are the practices of Japanese teachers. U.S. teachers' choices of motivational and disciplinary statements may reflect the belief that students need to be prodded, enticed, and/or even threatened to study. Compared to the Japanese teachers, the U.S. teachers seemed to assume more responsibility for helping students stay on task; they reminded them of time remaining, accountability, rewards, and so forth. They also hurried students to complete their tasks within the limited time and frequently offered individual assistance when students needed help. In the U.S. lessons, learning seemed to be seen as an individual matter between a teacher and a student, rather than as something that students could manage among themselves. U.S. teachers also seemed to believe that learning occurs only when students are quiet and under control. In fact, during transitions between activities, they repeatedly used management statements until all students were attentive to them.

The classroom practices of Japanese teachers, however, seem

to reflect a more constructivist view of learning and teaching. Japanese teachers seemed to assume that learning would occur naturally as long as students were exposed to subject matter in a way that piqued their curiosity, built upon what they already knew, and could be explored as part of their social interactions. They seemed to rely on intrinsic motivation to drive learning rather than extrinsic rewards and punishments. Japanese teachers seemed to assume less responsibility for keeping children on task. Compared to the U.S. teachers, the Japanese teachers used fewer time reminders and remarks to hurry students. They also tended to help individual students less frequently than the U.S. teachers did. No external reward system was observed in Japanese science classes. Americans who have viewed our videotapes of the Japanese science lessons – including a group of American fourth graders – uniformly comment on how noisy the Japanese students are as they pursue science. An American third grader who attended a Japanese elementary school for one semester said: "In my class in America, if students are making noise, the teacher quiets them down. In my Japanese class, if kids are making noise so I can't hear the teacher give the assignment, it's my problem. I have to tell them to be quiet." Instead of managing classroom behavior directly, Japanese teachers may rely on the long-term, cumulative impact of the small groups (*han*) of three to five students who work together daily over a period of several months, frequently reflecting on the quality of their cooperation, responsibility, and learning. Their approach can be viewed as an attempt to create a small community of learners within their classrooms.

In sum, we have suggested several hypotheses related to learning and responsibility in Japanese classrooms: that routines and established procedures allow students to manage many aspects of classroom life; that use of small groups, student-led discussion, and class-wide participation further build student responsibility for lessons; that the design and use of books and materials give students independent access to subject matter; and that motivation comes primarily from the interaction of students with subject matter, not primarily from rewards or incentives offered by teachers.

Although these are only hypotheses derived from a small, exploratory study, we think they may provide an important context for future research on Japanese education, as well as for understanding the accounts of Japanese instruction that other researchers have provided.

Note

1. The observation scales used in our study were adapted from H. H. Marshall, "Coding Manual for Lesson-Framing and Management/ Motivation Statements," revised edition, 1987. See also H. H. Marshall, "Motivational Strategies of Three Fifth-Grade Teachers," *The Elementary School Journal,* Vol. 88, No. 2, pp. 135–50, 1987, and H. H. Marshall, "In Pursuit of Learning-Oriented Classrooms," *Teaching & Teacher Education,* Vol. 4, No. 2, pp. 85–98, 1988, for her analyses of teacher motivational and management statements.

Cultures of mathematics instruction in Japanese and American elementary classrooms

JAMES W. STIGLER, CLEA FERNANDEZ, AND MAKOTO YOSHIDA

Historians of education have documented a profound change in the expectations Americans have for their schools (Graham, 1992). Recent dissatisfaction with American education may be due as much to these changing expectations as to any decline in the quality of schools. Now, for the first time in our history, we are concerned with achievement, not just attainment. Whereas previously we judged the quality of our nation's schools according to what percentage of students attended them, we are now concerned that our students learn something in school. Also for the first time in our history, we expect schools to play a major role in the achievement of social justice. Whereas previously we were satisfied if our elite received an education of the highest quality, we are now concerned with fairness: that children from all social, ethnic, and economic backgrounds have the opportunity to achieve academically. America's goals for education in the 1990s can be summed up as high achievement for all students.

Although these goals may be relatively recent in the United States, they correspond closely with the goals of Japan's educational system. Indeed, our new admiration for Japan's educational successes may be partly due to the new hopes we have for our system of education. In previous work done in collaboration with Harold Stevenson and his research group at the University of Michigan, we documented the extent to which Japan

The research reported in this essay is part of a collaborative research project with our Japanese colleagues Giyoo Hatano, Shizuko Amaiwa, and Hajime Yoshida. The project is funded, in part, by the Spencer Foundation. We are grateful to Giyoo Hatano, Paul Cobb, and Tom Rohlen for comments on an earlier draft.

achieves these newfound American goals. Focusing on achievement in mathematics, we found that Japanese elementary schools, by the time they reach the fifth grade, are so far ahead of their American counterparts that the lowest-scoring school in our Japanese sample scored higher than the highest-scoring school in our American sample. Further, we found that variability in achievement across schools, which is one indicator of the distribution of educational opportunity, is far smaller in Japan than in the United States (Stevenson and Stigler, 1992). The quality of education and the quality of students vary far more across schools in the United States than they do in Japan. So, in terms of both achievement and fairness, Japan is a model worthy of our close attention.

In this essay we focus on classroom instruction in mathematics in Japanese and American elementary schools. Because much of the mathematics children learn is learned at school, mathematics is a useful domain in which to ask what it is that Japanese teachers do that results in such high levels of achievement for such a large percentage of Japanese children. We have conducted several comparative studies of classroom instruction (Stevenson and Stigler, 1992). In this essay we focus on preliminary results from a current study in which we are collecting videotapes of math lessons in both Japanese and American classrooms and attempting to characterize the differences. Because so much of teaching and learning is domain specific, we have tried to compare lessons in which Japanese and American teachers are teaching similar topics. For example, we are collecting tapes of 20 Japanese and 20 American fifth-grade teachers teaching a lesson on how to find the area of a triangle. In this essay we report some preliminary analyses of four fifth-grade lessons, two Japanese and two American, dealing with two topics: the area of a triangle and the concept of equivalent fractions. But before we discuss these analyses, we will discuss more generally the context in which these lessons take place.

Cultures of mathematics instruction

Just as we speak of Japanese and American culture, we can also speak of cultures of instruction that differ among classrooms. Although we find Japanese and American lessons differing on a number of dimensions, we also find that these dimensions cohere to form two distinct systems or cultures of classroom instruction resembling what Cobb, Wood, Yackel, and McNeal (in press) have called "traditions of classroom mathematics." What, in general, it means to teach and learn mathematics differs across these societies in a way that resembles the distinction drawn in the American mathematics education community between school mathematics and inquiry mathematics (Richards, in press) or between teaching for understanding and not (cf. Cobb et al., in press). Our challenge is to understand how it is that Japanese teachers and students achieve the kind of instruction that leads to such high levels of achievement.

The culture of instruction, like any culture, comprises numerous elements that are passed down through traditions. Some of these elements are artifacts such as textbooks and other instructional materials. Other elements include instructional routines (i.e., the temporal structures that organize instruction) and the beliefs and expectations held by participants (i.e., teachers and students) about their roles and about the goals of the activity. Together these three elements – materials, routines, and expectations – determine to a great extent what will happen in classroom instruction.

Artifacts of instruction

What transpires in classrooms is partially a function of cultural artifacts that teachers and students use in the course of instruction. Textbooks and the curriculum in general are important determinants of the different instructional cultures found in Japanese and American elementary schools. Other instructional materials, such as concrete representations of mathematical concepts, play a role as well.

One of the most important aspects of Japanese education is the fact that the curriculum is both highly specified and common across all schools and classrooms in the country. What this means is that even though several companies produce textbooks in Japan, the books they produce are almost identical throughout the country. As we will discuss below, this has a great effect on the nature of the teacher's job in Japan compared to the United States. For now, suffice it to say that this commonality in textbooks leads to great commonality in instruction throughout Japan.

In the United States the content of the curriculum is often determined by the individual teacher, school, or school board, so that two first-grade teachers even in the same school often teach using different textbooks and materials, and even cover different topics over the course of the school year. For this reason there is considerably more variability in instruction across classrooms in the United States than there is in Japan, mirroring the variability in achievement.

A shared curriculum does not in itself promote high levels of achievement. But it does ensure greater commonality – and thus equality – of educational experiences.

The teacher's role

Many American teachers would react negatively to the "top-down" imposition of a common curriculum, but Japanese teachers rarely complain. The reason, we believe, is that the role of the teacher and the conception of the ideal teacher are quite different in these societies. In the United States, teaching is considered a highly idiosyncratic profession, and the common lore is that one cannot be taught how to teach because a good teacher is born more than made (cf. Stevenson and Stigler, 1992); a teacher must find her own way. Japanese society views teaching more as a craft, as a skill that can be perfected through practice and that can benefit from shared lore or tricks of the trade. If music were used as an analogy, the Japanese conception of the ideal teacher would be like that of the concert pianist: the great pianist is not expected to write the concerto but only to perform it well. The American teacher, by analogy, is expected not only to teach but also to write the score. An innovative teacher in the United States is one who organizes her own curriculum, makes her own materials, and implements her lessons with independent initiative. In Japan, the innovative teacher is one who skillfully teaches the lesson that is prescribed by the text.

These two distinct conceptions of teaching lead to quite different paths of teacher development in the two countries. Once American teachers finish their student teaching and receive their university degree, they are given their own classrooms over which they have complete control. American teachers complain most of isolation, the price they pay for such total control over their classrooms. American teachers spend most of their hours at school in their classrooms teaching and have virtually no time for interaction with other teachers.

The training of Japanese teachers is not thought to begin until they start their first teaching job, at which point they begin a long period of apprenticeship-like training in which they are supervised closely by master teachers. On the job, teachers in Japan spend more hours per day in school, but they spend only about half of that time teaching. The rest of the time is spent interacting with other teachers about matters of professional interest, chief among these being techniques for teaching the curriculum.

The common curriculum has an important influence on the interactions that Japanese teachers have with each other. Even if American teachers had time for interaction during the day, without a common curriculum there would be little they could share that was not of a general nature. But when all of the fifth-grade teachers have just taught the lesson on how to derive the formula for finding the area of a triangle – which occurs at about the same time each year in Japan – they have much to discuss: Why did my students not arrive at that solution? Did you pose the problem in a different way? Do you think I hurried them through the first part of the lesson? These concrete, specific discussions about teaching can occur only when there is a common experience in the classroom.

Thus, although Japanese teachers relinquish some of the authority that American teachers have, they get back in return more opportunities for sharing knowledge and precise skills and for professional development. The authority in Japan lies in the curriculum and in the forms that constitute the routines of teaching. These common forms relieve Japanese teachers of some of the anxieties about authority faced by American teachers. On their own to a greater degree, American teachers work hard but are often reinventing the wheel, and experiencing more uncertainty, whereas Japanese teachers can focus on perfecting the craft of teaching in a more structured and delimited process.

Goals and expectations

Both teachers and students bring beliefs and expectations to the classroom that have a powerful impact on what goes on there.

Even if Japanese and American teachers used the same textbooks and activities, the resulting instruction would differ because of differing beliefs about what it means to teach and learn mathematics, and even about what mathematics is.

American mathematics educators have pointed out the different conceptions of mathematics held by American teachers and students, on the one hand, and by professional mathematicians, on the other (e.g., Schoenfeld, 1985). American schoolchildren, for example, appear to believe that a math problem always has a single correct answer, that the answer can be determined within 10 minutes if the problem is solvable at all, and that the teacher is the final arbiter of whether or not an answer is correct. The culture of professional mathematicians includes a quite different conception of mathematics. In that culture there may not always be a single correct answer, the solution to a problem may come gradually over a period of months or even years, and the correctness of the solution is determined by mathematical proof, that is, argument and analysis of the process by which the solution was obtained.

Leaving aside the issue of whether the culture of school mathematics *ought* to resemble that of professional mathematics, it is still interesting to note that the culture of mathematics in the Japanese classroom more closely resembles that of professional mathematics. Japanese teachers go to great lengths to get their students to focus on the process of problem solving instead of on the answer. They often work on problems that take longer to solve, sometimes more than a single class period. And they resist taking on the role of arbiter of what is correct and what is not, preferring to let students discuss among themselves the validity of different solutions.

These differing beliefs about the nature of mathematics lead Japanese and American students to construe the purpose of classroom instruction differently from each other. American students tend to focus on getting the answer and attend less to explanations that may be provided, whether by the teacher or by other students. As documented by American mathematics educators (e.g., Cobb et al., in press), American students often construe the goal of instruction to be to learn the procedure for getting the answer, not to understand *why* the procedure is mathematically valid.

Instructional routines

Finally, the culture of instruction is highly influenced by the routines that teachers put together to make lessons and in which students participate. Perhaps the most written-about routine used in American classrooms is the "recitation," a rapid-paced series of short questions and answers by which the teacher leads students through the material at hand (Schneider, Gallimore, and Hyland, 1991). As we will show, this kind of recitation does not appear to characterize Japanese instruction, at least not to the degree it does American instruction.

Japanese mathematics lessons at the elementary level appear almost formulaic, so great is the similarity in routines across classrooms. They almost always begin with a problem, which the teacher poses for the students to think about. She then gives the students 10 or 15 minutes to work at solving the problem, either alone or with peers. After most students have found at least one way of solving the problem, the teacher reconvenes the class and asks students, one by one, to come to the board and explain their solutions. After the class discusses the merits of each solution, the teacher calls on the next student, invariably with the question "Did someone find a different way to solve the problem?" At the end of the lesson, students may be given a few minutes to apply what they have learned to some practice problems in their textbook. The single problem posed at the beginning of the class provides continuity or coherence across the lesson, and rarely does the focus go far astray from the initial problem.

American mathematics lessons are considerably more varied in form but do share some characteristics that differentiate them from the Japanese lessons. American lessons usually do not begin with students trying to solve a problem. Seatwork of this sort is usually relegated to the end of the lesson and is used for practice of the procedure taught by the teacher in the main part of the lesson. The beginning of the American lesson usually involves recitation, with the teacher leading students through direct instruction in how to perform some arithmetic procedure, or sometimes an explanation about a mathematical concept. The topic of the lesson will sometimes shift during the lesson (Stevenson and Stigler, 1992), making the lesson appear less coherent than the Japanese lesson.

Having provided some background on the different cultures of instruction that are manifest in Japanese and American elementary mathematics classrooms, we can proceed to a more detailed analysis of the processes that transpire in the course of instruction. We begin our analysis by presenting overviews of two lessons – one Japanese and one American – on how to find the area of a triangle. Using these lessons as examples, we discuss the qualitative differences we see between Japanese and American lessons. We also present results of objective codings of the lessons that help us to quantify some of the differences we see. The objective codes, which are preliminary in nature, were developed in the context of the triangle lessons; to explore their validity, we also apply them to two additional lessons on a different topic: equivalent fractions.

We organize our analysis around the role that students' thinking plays in instruction. It is our current view that a major difference between the Japanese and American classroom traditions is in the emphasis placed on students' thinking and problem solving during instruction. We present evidence for this view in both qualitative examples and quantitative analyses. Our emphasis is on describing the techniques that Japanese teachers use to promote students' thinking during instruction. Although in the United States teaching that emphasizes understanding also often emphasizes small-group and individualized instruction, Japanese teaching, surprisingly, combines the almost total use of whole-class instruction with a strong emphasis on students' thinking. Similarly, although American teachers are increasingly introducing manipulatives (i.e., concrete materials) into their classrooms because they wish to promote student thinking and enhance understanding, we find that the use of manipulatives in itself does not lead to these outcomes. The ways Japanese and American teachers use manipulatives in instruction differ markedly – again, we will argue, on the issue of student thinking.

The area of a triangle: two lessons

One topic that appears in both Japan and the United States at the fifth-grade level is the method of finding the area of a triangle. Students in both cultures have been introduced to the con-

Table I. *Overview of the Japanese and American lessons on finding the area of a triangle*

Segment	Length (min)	Description
		Japanese Lesson
I	3.5	Presentation of the problem
2	14.5	Students attempting to solve the problem on their own
3	29.0	Class discussion about the solutions that students came up with, leading up to the general formula
4	5.0	Doing further practice problems from the textbook (students working on their own)
Total	52.0	
		American Lesson
I	1.0	Review concept of perimeter
2	8.0	Area of a rectangle: explanation, formula, and practice problems
3	25.0	Area of a triangle: explanation, formula, and practice problems
4	11.0	Students began homework assignment; teacher walked around and helped
Total	45.0	

cept of area, and they know how to compute the area of a rectangle. In the lessons we taped, both Japanese and American teachers used children's understanding of how to find the area of a rectangle in order to develop a method for finding the area of a triangle.

Overview of a Japanese lesson

The Japanese lesson can be divided into four segments (see Table 1): presentation of the problem; students attempting to solve the problem on their own; class discussion about the solutions that students came up with; and students working alone on further practice problems from the textbook. This sequence of activities is prototypical of the Japanese lessons we have observed. The teacher almost always begins the class by posing a problem, and the rest of the lesson is oriented to understanding and solving that problem.

In this lesson, the teacher begins by asking students to name the kinds of triangles they have studied. As they name them – right, equilateral, isosceles, and so on – the teacher puts the corresponding shapes cut out of paper on the blackboard. She then says: "We have various kinds of triangles on the board, and today I would like you to think about how to find out the area of a triangle." She hands out to each student sheets of paper printed with outline drawings of the various kinds of triangles. She instructs the students not to find the area of the shapes, but just to think about what would be the best way to find the area. She tells the students that they can cut, fold, and draw.

Students then spend 14.5 minutes working on the problem on their own, during which time the teacher circulates, mostly observing what the students are doing. Students are actively engaged at this point, and though they are not formally divided into groups, there is a great deal of discussion and interaction among students seated in proximity to each other. At the end of this time, the teacher reconvenes the whole-class discussion by asking a student to go to the board and explain her method for finding the area of a right triangle.

For the next 29 minutes, a succession of students go to the board to explain their methods for finding the areas of the various kinds of triangles. All of the students use cutout shapes and chalk drawings to explain their approaches, and the solutions they have devised are often quite ingenious. After each student explains his solution, the teacher and the rest of the class discuss its viability. The teacher then, in collaboration with the students, writes a formula on the board that summarizes the student's solution, for example, "base × height/2." A total of nine different students present solutions. At the end, the teacher directs attention to the formulas on the board and asks the students if they notice any kind of pattern. A spirited discussion ensues in which students observe and then confirm that the different informal formulas that resulted from the different solutions are really the same across the solutions, regardless of the kind of triangle involved. In the final 5 minutes of the lesson, students use the formula to solve some problems in their textbook.

Overview of an American lesson

The American teacher begins his lesson by reviewing the concept of perimeter: What does it mean? How do you find it? He then makes the transition to area:

So we dealt with perimeter. Today, we are going to deal with area and we are going to deal with the area of two things. We are going to deal with the area of a rectangle and the area of a triangle. Area is how much space is inside a flat shape.

The rest of the lesson is divided into three segments (see Table I): one on the area of a rectangle, one on the area of a triangle, and finally, a period of seatwork.

The segment on the area of a rectangle starts with the teacher holding up a series of rectangles that have been divided into square units. As he holds each one up, he asks the students to tell him the area, which they figure by counting the squares. After several of these examples, the teacher asks the students for a formula: "Now find me a mathematical way of doing it so that I don't have to count all the time. Brian?" Brian responds: "Times the width times the length." The teacher writes the formula on the board: $A = l \times w$. He then gives the students two practice problems that require them to multiply the length by the width to get the area.

The teacher then moves on to the area of a triangle:

Now, let's take off some of this (erases board) and see if we can go on to our next thing, which is, we want to find the area of a triangle. We are going to start out with the same thing. We are going to start out and talk about when we find the area of a triangle, we are still finding units, square units like this (holds up a small square). Well, here is a triangle (holds up a triangle with a grid drawn in), and we have units. Now when you get to triangles, what's the problem? Sue?

The problem the teacher is referring to is that square units are difficult to count with a triangle because they don't fit exactly over the area. Having pointed out this problem, the teacher then introduces a solution, giving a demonstration that involves fitting two pre-cut right triangles together to make a rectangle and showing that the area of each triangle is half the area of the resulting rectangle. The demonstration itself is accomplished quickly, within seconds, and there is virtually no response – either questions or discussion – on the part of the students. The teacher then gives a second demonstration in which he cuts one of the triangles in two and places the pieces adjacent to the other triangle to make a rectangle. Again, he receives no feedback from the students. He then tells the students the formula for the area of a triangle: $A = 1/2 \times b \times h$.

After giving them the formula, the teacher poses three problems and has the students apply the formula. He then starts them on the assignment.

Three differences between Japanese and American lessons

Using these two lessons as points of reference, we can discuss the differences we have observed between Japanese and American lessons. As we indicated above, we have focused increasingly on the role that students' thinking plays in instruction. We will argue that (1) Japanese teachers, in contrast to American teachers, place students' thinking at the core of their lesson-planning process; (2) Japanese lessons provide students with more opportunities to think during instruction than do American lessons; and (3) Japanese lessons create an atmosphere in which students' thinking is valued and legitimized to a far greater extent than do American lessons.

The role of students' thinking in teachers' planning

Lesson plans can provide insight into how teachers conceive of and plan their lessons. In our current project, we ask all of the teachers we videotape to provide us with written lesson plans. The lesson plans provided by the Japanese and American teachers for the lessons described above are very different from each other. However, they are typical of ones we received from teachers in the two countries. The American lesson plans almost always look like outlines or lists of activities that will constitute the lesson; the Japanese lesson plans are far more detailed (Figure 1).

Japanese lesson plans stress coherence of lesson activities. The Japanese lesson plan places the current lesson in the context of

Math Lesson Plan (3/19/91)

1. Correct assignment

2. Review - perimeter

3. Area of a rectangle / square
   A. Introduction
   B. Region marked - find area - counting -3
   C. Mathematical way - multiply   Length × width
   D. Examples
   E. Formula   A = L × W - recipe
   F. Examples   Note: Answer square centimeter / inch

4. Area of a triangle
   A. Introduction
   B. Region marked - count - difficult
   C. Double triangle - put together - rectangle
       find area - find 1/2
   D. Other examples (2) - find 1/2 (×1/2 or ÷2)
   E. Formula A = 1/2bh
   F. Examples

5. Assignment

Figure 1A. The American lesson plan.

lessons that precede and follow it and in the context of the mathematics curriculum. The plan begins by stating that this lesson is the third of six lessons in a unit on the area of quadrangles and triangles. The previous lesson was on the application of the formula for finding the area of parallelograms. The objective of the current lesson is to learn that triangles can be transformed so that the formula used to find the area of quadrangles can be applied to the problem of finding the area of triangles. The next lesson, we are told in the lesson plan, will be on application of the formula for finding the area of triangles.

Planning lessons to be coherent with those that precede and follow facilitates students' thinking by providing them with op-

算数科指導案

5年1組　男16名　女20名　計36名
担任　Teacher#45

1. 単元名　　「四角形と三角形の面積」（6時間扱い中第3時）

2. 主眼　　　三角形の面積を求める場で、切って移動したり、折ったり、2倍したりすると、既習の求積公式の使える形に変形できることに気づき、三角形の面積を求めることができる。

3. 本時の位置

| 前時: 平行四辺形の面積公式の適用 | → | 本時 | → | 次時: 三角形の面積の公式の適用 |

4. 指導上の留意点

- 自分のできそうな問題から取りかからせる。
- 底辺と高さのとらえ方がまちがっていないか確認していく。

5. 展開

段階	学習活動	予想される児童の反応	時間	指導・助言
問題把握	1. 色々な三角形の面積を求めよう。 ・直角三角形 ・正三角形 ・二等辺三角形 ・高さが内にとれる三角形 ・高さが外に出る三角形	・直角三角形ならできそうだ。 ・切ってみよう。 ・折ってみよう。 ・マス目を書いてみよう。 ・高さの線を入れてみよう。	10分	・取りかかれないでいる子には、直角三角形を考えさせる。 ・全部できない子には、できるところまで、考えさせる。
追究	2. 自分の考えを発表したり、友達の考えを聞こう。 A. 直角三角形	 ・二倍したら長方形になる。 ・底辺×高さ÷2	30分	・求め方の式もださせる。

Figure 1B. The Japanese lesson plan.

追究	B. 正三角形 二等辺三角形	・切って移動して長方形にする。 ・底辺÷2×高さ ・折って長方形にする ・底辺÷2×高さ÷2×2 ・マス目を書いて数える。	
	C. 高さが内にとれる三角形	・高さの線を引いて2倍して長方形にする。 ・底辺がわかれてしまうので、言葉で式ができない。 ・2倍して平行四辺形にする。 ・底辺×高さ÷2 ・マス目で数える。	・もう少しまとめられないか考えさせる。 ・長方形の半分であることから、式を導き出させる。
	D. 高さが外にでる三角形	・直角三角形にしておいていらない部分をひいてしまう。 ・式は言葉で書けない。 ・2倍して平行四辺形にする。 ・底辺×高さ÷2	・式は記号を使っても複雑になるので特に出させない。
	3. 三角形の面積の公式をみつけよう。	・どの三角形も底辺×高さ÷2で出ている。	
一般化	4. 色々な三角形の面積を求めよう。	・底辺×高さ÷2にあてはめ	5分	・底辺と高さのとらえ方がまちがっていないかみる。

Figure 1B (continued). The Japanese lesson plan.

portunities to infer connections between different topics in the mathematics curriculum and between different pieces of knowledge that are relevant to the topic being taught. A student who is striving to make sense of the world must work in a sensible world. Otherwise, the task is impossible. In their planning, Japanese teachers work to ensure that the most important links can be made by students.

American teachers place little emphasis on coherence across lessons. In the American plan for the triangle lesson, the teacher writes down nothing about how this lesson relates to those that precede and follow it. He may be thinking about such relationships, but they are not written down in the lesson plan. In fact, the American teacher does begin his lesson by reviewing the concept of perimeter, which the class apparently covered last time. But because there is no direct link between perimeter and the area of a triangle, this order of events renders the American lesson less coherent than the Japanese one, which begins with a review of the different types of triangles that exist. Events within the American lesson are less connected to each other, and the lesson itself is not seen as connected to the surrounding lessons. (The relative coherence of Japanese lessons is a characteristic we have described elsewhere: e.g., Stigler and Perry, 1988; Stevenson and Stigler, 1992.) This lack of coherence in the way the American lesson is planned probably renders it harder to interpret than the Japanese lesson.

Japanese teachers anticipate students' thinking. Children's thinking also plays a central role in Japanese teachers' planning of the activities that comprise the lesson but not in American teachers' planning. As is evident in Figure 1, the American lesson plan lists the points the teacher plans to make or things he plans to do: correct assignment, review perimeter, area of a rectangle. He has laid out a sequence of activities and also a sequence of discoveries or insights that he wants to impart to the students. He has them count square units to find the area of a rectangle and then introduces the formula (what he calls the "mathematical way"). He makes a note to himself that he wants to explain to the students that a formula is like a recipe. He wants to demonstrate that the method of counting square units is difficult to apply to the case of triangles.

The Japanese lesson plan emphasizes what students will think, not what the teacher will say or do. Using a format that is commonly used for lesson plans in Japan, the teacher divides the lesson into three steps: understanding the problem, investigation, and generalization. For each step she enters, in a chart, four kinds of information: the learning activities that she will lead the students through, the expected student reactions to the activities, the approximate time that will be spent on the step, and the guidance or advice that she might offer in response to the students' reactions. In the column labeled "Expected Student Reaction," the teacher carefully lists the solutions – both good ones and less good ones – she expects students to propose. This fascinating exercise in planning primes the teacher to listen to what students have to say and allows her to think ahead of time about how to facilitate students' understanding. The American teacher has planned what he will do but has not started to think about what effect his actions might have on students' understanding. Nor has he anticipated the students' reactions. It is a plan that focuses the process on the teacher's marching orders for himself rather than the less predetermined responses of the students to an unsolved problem.

Opportunities for student thinking during instruction

The concern with student thinking that guides the Japanese teacher's planning of her lesson also manifests itself in the way she teaches the lesson. We have identified a number of ways in which the Japanese lesson provides more opportunities for student thinking than does the American lesson. We will discuss these differences next.

The role of problem solving. One striking difference between the two triangle lessons is in the role played by problem solving. As we saw above, the Japanese teacher – and this applies to almost every Japanese lesson we have observed – begins by posing a problem and then having students work to solve it on their own. Only after students have worked on their own does the teacher begin the more directed part of the lesson, that is, the public discussion of students' solutions. Often – and this is the case in this lesson – the problem posed at the beginning of a

Japanese lesson is the one on which most of the lesson is focused, the problem thus serving as a theme around which the subsequent activities are organized.

The American lesson starts with a series of short-answer questions, first about the concept of perimeter, then about the area of a rectangle. The lesson consists primarily of a series of these teacher–student exchanges designed to lead students to an understanding of the formula for determining area. Only after the teacher has presented a formula does he ask students to solve problems on their own in a period of seatwork at the end of the class.

In general, American teachers put seatwork at the end of the lesson, Japanese teachers at the beginning. This placement corresponds to the different roles seatwork is assumed to play in instruction. American teachers view seatwork as an opportunity to practice what has been learned in the lesson; Japanese teachers view it as an opportunity for students to try solving problems on their own before being exposed to other students' solutions. Our Japanese colleagues point out that the Japanese teachers have the luxury of forgoing the use of seatwork for practice because homework and *juku* (cram schools) provide ample opportunities for practice outside of class, opportunities that American teachers cannot depend on (see Stevenson and Stigler, 1992, and Russell, this volume).

Partly because problems are not posed until the end of the lesson, they take a very different form in the American lesson than they do in the Japanese lesson. In the Japanese lesson, students are given shapes without markings or dimensions and asked to find the area. In the American lesson, students are presented with shapes like the one shown in Figure 2. Because the base and the height are clearly labeled, students never really grapple with the problem of how height should be defined in order to use the formula. Thus, what is actually a challenging conceptual problem is simplified to become a simple calculation problem.

Time to think. We have noted before that Japanese lessons appear to move at an extremely slow pace (Stigler and Perry, 1988). Part of this perception is due to the organization of the lesson. As noted above, Japanese lessons almost always begin with a single problem, the solution to which becomes the focus of the entire lesson. This concentration on a single problem

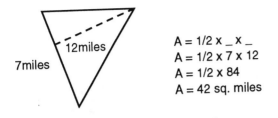

Figure 2. A problem from the American lesson.

lends coherence to the lesson and allows a thorough exploration of the problem. American students work many more problems than do their Japanese counterparts and come to emphasize quantity rather than quality of solutions. Again, Japanese students at *juku* may be drilled to do many problems in order to perfect mental dexterity, but only after first learning the logic of problem solving as described here.

Thinking in classrooms takes time. A lesson planned in reference to what the teacher will say instead of what the students will think inevitably leaves some students behind. In the American lesson described above, little time was set aside for students to ponder the derivation of the formula for finding the area of a triangle. When the teacher did the demonstration with the two cut-out triangles, it happened quickly. The students were expected to follow the demonstration but were not given enough time to discover the relation for themselves. In the Japanese lesson, students spent the entire time thinking about and discussing how to derive the formula for finding the area of a triangle. The expectation was that the derivation would take time for students to construct; it would not be understood by students in a momentary flash of insight.

We have tried to develop ways of objectively coding the pace at which instruction proceeds. One way, of course, is to count the number of problems students solve during a lesson. When we do this, we find the pattern we have already described: Japanese students solve far fewer problems than do American students during the course of a lesson. Another variable we have tried to measure is the rate at which talk proceeds during the lesson. In Figure 3 we present a count of the average number of words per minute spoken, by teachers and students combined, during public discourse in the four lessons we have ana-

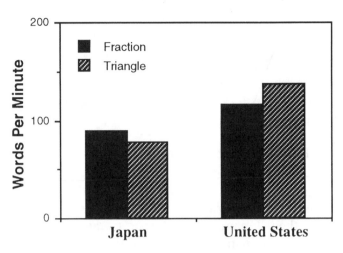

Figure 3. The pace of instruction in Japanese and American classrooms: average number of words (English translation) spoken by teachers and students during a minute of instruction.

lyzed. This is a very rough measure comparing the number of words spoken in the U.S. classrooms with the number of words spoken in the English translations of the Japanese transcripts. Still, we believe that it corroborates one of our recurring observations: Japanese students are less hurried during the lesson; they are allowed more time to construct meaning for the mathematics that goes on around them.

Opportunities to discuss mathematics. Aside from providing time for students to think, the Japanese teacher provides many opportunities for children to describe their own thinking and to hear other students describe theirs. Just as most Japanese lessons begin with a period in which students work to solve a problem on their own, most also follow the problem solving with a period in which students describe and then debate their various solutions to the problem. Students are heard from more, and at greater length, during the Japanese lessons.

It is also important to note that the emphasis in Japan is on *public discourse* (as opposed to private, one-on-one interaction). American teachers do not emphasize public discourse to the same degree, as is evident in the ways teachers and students interact during seatwork. The American teacher views this as a time to work with individual children and to evaluate their work. He walks from student to student, saying such things as "Well you are almost right, but you've got to find half of 90 correctly," "You got it," and "Okay, now you're substituting okay now. . . . You have to go out and put in one-half and put in your base and your height." His talk is private, intended only for the student whose desk he is passing, and not for the other students in the class. He functions as a tutor, going from child to child.

The Japanese teacher talks much less than the American teacher as she walks around the room. When she does talk to individual students, her remarks are brief and vague. She might offer a suggestion; for example, a student having difficulty working with the acute triangle might be encouraged to "try working with the right triangle first." But she never directly instructs a child and never tells children that their solutions are correct or incorrect. Her role is not that of tutor but of researcher, studying the children's thinking about the problem. Discussion of answers – both correct and incorrect – is public, after the class has been reconvened. Everyone is thought to benefit from these discussions; to have them privately would be to deprive most students of valuable opportunities for thinking and learning.

We have developed three ways to objectively code the quantity of student talk within a lesson. The results of these three measures for the four lessons we have analyzed are shown in Figure 4. In panel (a) we have coded the percentage of total words spoken during public discourse that come from students (as opposed to the teacher). Approximately twice as much student talk is observed in the Japanese class discussions as in the American discussions across both the triangle and fraction lessons. We can also see, in panel (b), that the average length of the public conversations engaged in by students and teachers is greater in the Japanese than in the American lessons. Our unit of comparison here is *teacher–student exchange,* a subunit that we have defined within periods of public discourse. When a teacher asks a question and then calls on an individual student to answer, everything from the initiating question through the last utterance of the student is considered part of a single teacher–student exchange. Panel (b) shows the average number

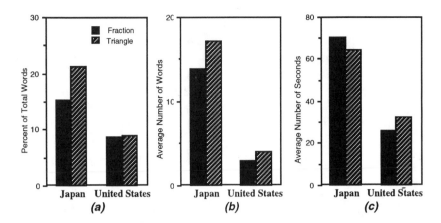

Figure 4. Quantity of student talk. (a) Percentage of total words (student) spoken during public discourse; (b) average number of words spoken by individual students during a teacher–student exchange; (c) average number of seconds in public discourse before teacher calls on a new student.

of words spoken by individual students during one of these teacher–student exchanges. Finally, we see in panel (c) that having lengthier conversations with students leads to another result: American teachers call on new students during public discourse more frequently than do Japanese teachers (once every 20 to 30 seconds in the American lesson versus every 60 to 70 seconds in the Japanese lesson).

The goal of asking questions. Japanese and American teachers appear to have different goals for asking questions: the American teacher asks a question to get an answer, the Japanese teacher to get students to think (Stevenson and Stigler, 1992). Analysis of the two triangle lessons provides rich confirmation of this general point. The Japanese teacher poses a problem, then asks students to explain their thinking about the problem. The explanations she elicits are lengthy and involved. The teacher interrupts as needed to help the student continue or to draw the student out, but never cuts the student off. Incorrect or less efficient solutions are given as much time and focus as correct ones.

The American teacher, in contrast, has a clear idea of where he wants the discussion to go. The kinds of questions he asks

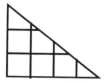

Figure 5. Figure presented by the American teacher to illustrate the difficulty of counting squares method for finding the area of a triangle.

are almost all of the "answer known" variety: there is a single correct answer, the teacher knows what it is, and the student's job is simply to produce that answer. An excellent example of what we mean by this is contained in the transcript of the lesson. Recall that the American teacher, in his plan, had written "Region marked – count – difficult" to guide the beginning of his segment on the area of a triangle. We see from the transcript that his strategy is to show students that counting square units is difficult in the case of triangles: as can be seen in Figure 5, problems arise in counting the fractions of square units that inevitably line the hypotenuse of the triangle.

Now what happens when the teacher tries to implement his strategy? He shows the triangle in Figure 5 and asks a student to tell him the area. His plan is that the student will be stumped, which will then motivate the need for an alternative solution, at which point he can launch into the demonstration he has prepared, in which two right triangles put together become a rectangle. But the students were not so quick to give up on the method of counting square units. Instead, they kept trying to do it, despite the teacher's desire to move on. Here is an excerpt from the transcript:

> Melissa: I have a question.
>
> Teacher: Go ahead, ask.
>
> Melissa: Like 'cause under there is like, uhmm, two like parts of a square, and one is like missing a little corner, and one is missing like a bigger corner, and there is like a bigger corner, and then there is a little corner over there.
>
> Teacher: Okay, so it has to be more than three, doesn't it?
>
> Melissa: Yeah (looks confused).
>
> Teacher: That's a problem we are going to find.

John: There is six.

Teacher: There is six.

Eric: I think that, hmmm, 'cause we have to add a half together to get a whole.

Teacher: That's right, but the question: are they halves? This one is not a half, is it? This one is not a half; this one is way more than a half (pointing at different pieces of squares drawn along the hypotenuse of the triangle).

Mary: There are six, right, if you take the little corner like the triangle off the third one from the bottom.

Teacher: Okay, there.

Mary: No. Yeahh, and you add it to the second one.

Teacher: Here.

Mary: Yeah, that one. Where does the littler one go?

Teacher: Yeah okay, where . . . (laughing) hold on a minute. Let's go, here is the same triangle (he produces a paper cutout of an identical triangle without the squares). Okay, now it is very interesting. In fact, I have two of them. It is interesting when you take two triangles that are identical, like these are – they are exactly the same – and you take and you put them together. What do you end up with (demonstrates), David?

David: A square.

What is evident in this portion of the lesson is that the teacher had no interest in the students' answers to the question he posed: he was looking only for the response that would lead him into his demonstration. Students were actively trying to solve the problem by mentally combining the partial square units, but the teacher was thwarting them at every turn, *even though the students in fact had correctly solved the problem* (getting the answer, six). His goal was for them to memorize the formula, and getting an answer – even the correct one – by another means was to be discouraged.

Coding types of questions asked. What kinds of questions do Japanese teachers ask in order to provoke the long, drawn-out discussions that we observe? We began our coding by listing every teacher question that was asked during public discourse. A teacher question is defined as an attempt by the teacher to elicit a student response. Since it is often difficult to distinguish between rhetorical questions and genuine questions that students are unable to answer, only questions that actually elicited students' responses are included in this coding. Questions need not be in the form of an interrogation. They can be, for example, an instruction such as "please go to the board and show us how you solved the problem."

Once we listed all of the questions asked by teachers we coded them into one of four categories (plus "other").

1. *Name/identify* questions are those in which the teacher asks a student to name an answer without asking for any explanation of how the answer was found. Questions like "What kinds of triangles have we studied so far?" or "What is the length on this shape?" fall into this category.

2. *Calculate* questions are those in which the teacher asks for the solution to an explicitly stated calculation. Questions like "So, to find the area, we do 9 times 12, which is?" or "What is 90 divided by 2?" fall into this category.

3. *Explain how or why* are questions in which the teacher asks for an explanation for answers given or procedures carried out. Questions like "How did you find the area of this triangle?" or "Why is the area here 17?" fall into this category.

4. *Check status* are questions in which the teacher is trying to monitor what everyone else is thinking or doing. Questions like "Who agrees?", "How many people found this?" or "Is anyone confused?" fall into this category.

We then determined what percentage of the questions asked by each teacher fell into each of the above categories.

In Figure 6 we have graphed the percentage of questions in each lesson falling into each of the four categories. The two Japanese lessons are represented in the upper panel, the American lessons in the lower one. First, it is interesting to note the similarity of patterns in the graphs across the two lessons within each culture but the striking difference in patterns across the two cultures. In both American lessons, the most frequently asked type of question was name/identify, followed by calculate and then explain. In the Japanese lessons, the most frequent type of question was explain, followed by check status. Neither of these two Japanese teachers asked a calculate question, and neither of the American teachers asked a check status question.

These patterns of teacher questioning help us to understand why students might talk more and at greater length in the Japa-

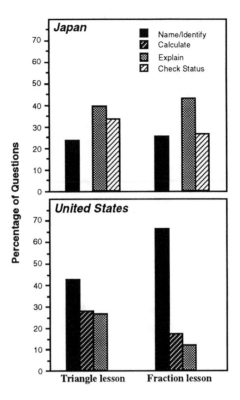

Figure 6. Types of questions asked by Japanese and American teachers.

nese classrooms than they do in the American classrooms. If students are asked simply to name, identify, or calculate, then their answers would be expected to be brief. Asking students to explain how or why they solved a problem in a certain way, on the other hand, should lead to lengthier answers. We investigated this possibility by graphing the number of words students said in response to two types of questions: name/identify and explain. The results are shown in Figure 7.

As we would predict, there is no appreciable difference in length between Japanese and American students' answers to name/identify questions: the average answer, in both cultures, is less than five words. Explain questions, in both cultures, lead to lengthier answers, but the effect is much greater in the Japanese lessons, where students' answers average approxi-

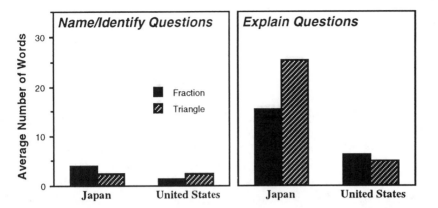

Figure 7. Length of Japanese and American students' responses to questions asking students to name/identify versus explain.

mately 20 words in length. We can think of two reasons for these lengthy answers. First, Japanese students are more accustomed to hearing teachers request explanations than are American students, and they've had more practice answering such questions. Another reason has to do with the nature of the explain questions that teachers ask. In Japan, most explain questions ask students to explain new material or novel solutions to problems. In the United States, the majority of such questions ask students to explain material that has already been explained, either by the teacher or by another student.

The use of errors. Another indication that American and Japanese teachers have different goals in asking questions comes from the way they deal with incorrect answers. As we have noted elsewhere, Japanese teachers treat errors or incorrect answers quite differently than do American teachers (Stevenson and Stigler, 1992). American teachers go to great lengths to keep errors out of the mathematics classroom, and especially out of the public discourse. This may be because of behaviorist learning theories that emphasize the importance of success for learning, or because teachers fear damaging children's self-esteem by exposing their inadequacies. But for whatever reason, American teachers tend to correct mistakes quickly when they do occur, and almost never ask children with incorrect solutions to problems to display their solutions to the class.

Japanese teachers take a very different approach to errors. Instead of seeing errors as indicating lack of ability or potential on the part of the student, Japanese teachers see errors as a natural part of the learning process and as important sources of information about children's mathematical thinking. They believe that discussion of incorrect solutions can play an important role in children's developing conceptual understanding of mathematics. Japanese teachers also think errors should be discussed publicly – not privately, one-on-one – so that all students can benefit by analyzing them.

In our tapes, we have observed two strategies that American teachers employ to deal with incorrect responses to questions. One of these is simply to ignore the response and to let another student answer. This is consistent with the idea, discussed above, that the American teacher's goal in asking questions is to get the answer she needs to move the lesson along. The same purpose is accomplished as well by the second strategy, that of reinterpreting incorrect or inappropriate answers so that they fit the teacher's expectations. Our Japanese colleagues hasten to point out, however, that these strategies may make sense within a cultural system such as the American one, in which mistakes may be interpreted as revealing underlying physical or immutable deficits. If errors arouse anxiety or threaten self-esteem, it may be impossible to use them the way that Japanese teachers do.

The use of manipulatives. Finally, it is fascinating to note the different ways that manipulatives are used by these two teachers. The Japanese teacher gives students paper triangles to work with from the beginning, then has them continue to use them throughout the lesson as they explain their solutions. The manipulatives in the Japanese classroom are used as tools for thinking and as objects for reflection. The American teacher uses the manipulatives for a demonstration: when he gets to the point in the lesson where he wants to explain the derivation of the formula, he pulls out two right triangles, fits them together, and shows the resulting rectangle. In this particular lesson, students get no chance to work with, or even touch, the concrete representation.

The value placed on students' thinking

It is not surprising that in the Japanese classroom an atmosphere is created in which student thinking is valued and legitimized; in the typical American classroom, we find a very different atmosphere. This difference is seen clearly in the way students' solutions are used in the American and Japanese lessons, the way authority is referred to, and the way mathematical formulas are introduced in the two classrooms.

The role of students' solutions. The Japanese lesson on area of a triangle proceeds the same way as virtually every Japanese lesson we have observed in one crucial respect: after students are given a problem to work on at the beginning of the lesson, the rest of the lesson generally involves whole-class discussion of the various solutions – correct and incorrect – that students came up with. In this particular lesson, nine students come to the board, one by one, to explain their solutions to the problem. Inherent in all of these interactions is the value attached to students' solutions. The teacher almost never evaluates the solutions; she simply asks the class to comment on them. She constantly refers to the importance of discovering alternative solutions to the same problem, and relies on students' discussions of the procedures to determine whether each will, in fact, lead to the correct answer. Students themselves learn that much of the content of the class is carried in these student-centered discussions, so they show great patience in listening to lengthy descriptions of sometimes highly idiosyncratic solutions.

Reference to authority. Implicit in the way American teachers ask questions is that the teacher knows the answer and is the authority on what is right or wrong. The view that mathematics is a field in which there are definite answers, and that someone always knows what the answers are, is communicated to children in these patterns of discourse. Thus, it is not important what the child thinks, but whether or not the child's answer is correct. Japanese teachers, in contrast, rarely tell students they are right or wrong, leaving any such evaluation to the children's classmates. (Not that students don't care how their teachers feel about their work: our Japanese colleagues tell us that Japanese students are very sensitive to their teachers' implicit evaluations.) Japanese teachers place great emphasis on asking students to explain how they solved a problem and promote the view that there are multiple ways of solving a problem. Correct solutions, in the Japanese classroom, are those that make sense and are convincing to the students.

One striking characteristic of the American tapes we have viewed is the frequency with which American teachers refer to authority to justify their mathematical assertions. One example of this is in the quote above, when the teacher, in response to a student's suggestion that the width be multiplied by the length to get the area of a rectangle, states that "in mathematical" the order is reversed, that is, length is multiplied by width. In another example from the triangle lesson, the teacher refers to "they" in explaining the proper formula for the area of a triangle:

> Teacher: So now we can go back and find out what we are going to do. We know that the area of a rectangle equals length times width. Okay, that's a rectangle. What are we going to do for a triangle? What would be your guess?
>
> Jack: Take the length and the width of the rectangle and divide that into half.
>
> Teacher: You got it. You got it. You're going to take the length and the width and divide into half.
> Now we have to do a couple of things here 'cause it changes just a little bit. Area equals ½, that's what you said, times, now instead of using length they use base times the height. Okay, so *b* stands for base (writes height under the *h*). Okay, when a triangle is like this and it has a square corner on it (holds up right triangle), then we have what we use to . . . what on a rectangle we call the length and the width. *But on the triangle they are going to call this the base and they are going to call this the height.*

We have never observed Japanese teachers refer to outside authority, or to their own authority, as justification of a mathematical conclusion or procedure. Common to the Japanese lessons is the technique of giving students the authority to decide the validity of mathematical conclusions or procedures. As in the world of real mathematics, the ultimate test of validity for a mathematical argument is how convincing it is to your peers. In the triangle lesson we see the common practice of students: after answering a question or proposing a solution, they ask their classmates if the solution is correct or not. This ritualistic aspect of the lesson is probably just that, yet the implicit message is clear: the teacher is not the judge; the community is. We also see the habit, on the part of both teachers and students, of maintaining the link between an idea and the person who generated it. Teachers and students alike refer to "Kei-kun's solution," "Nozomi-san's approach," and so on. This practice highlights the fact that any particular solution proposed is just one of many alternative solutions and that its validity must be tested. Having more of the crucial information in a lesson come from students, as opposed to the teacher, means that students attend more seriously to what their peers have to say. American students know that whatever is important will come from the teacher, not from other students.

The use of formulas. It is interesting to note the different ways formulas are used in these two lessons. Both teachers want the students to know that the formula for the area of a triangle is $A = 1/2b \times h$. But the point at which they introduce the formula, and the manner of introduction, are quite different. In the Japanese lesson, informal formulas are written to describe each student's solution as he or she proposes it at the board. The goal is to record, in convenient notation, the method that the student used; the form is allowed to vary. Thus, for one student the teacher wrote the formula "base/2 × height"; for another, "base × height/2." The focus is on the problem and the solution; the formula is introduced merely as a summary of what was done. At the end of the lesson, the teacher has students look at the nine formulas that remain on the blackboard and lets them notice the similarity among them: for all the triangles, no matter what kind, the formula for finding their area is essentially the same.

The American teacher introduces the formula early and immediately tries to get it in the canonical form. After the students count the square units in a rectangle, the teacher asks for another way to get the answer, and a student answers with the formula.

> Brian: Times the width times the length.
>
> Teacher: Okay, if I multiply, and in mathematical we are going to turn it around, we are going to say we are going to multiply

the length times the width, so the area of a rectangle equals the length times the width (writes "$A = l \times w$" on the board).

Now from just looking at our three samples here, you know it works every time: you multiply the length times the width and you end up with finding the area of a rectangle, and we could also say a square; the same thing would work on a square, wouldn't it?

Note how the teacher takes a perfectly reasonable answer – "times the width times the length" – and insists on turning it around into the more conventional order of length times width. This amounts to subtle invalidation of the student's thinking and, at the same time, invokes outside authority to justify the move: "in mathematical we are going to turn it around." Note also the the speed with which the teacher states the generalization, "from just looking at our three samples here, you know it works every time." This is in marked contrast to the Japanese teacher, who lets the children ponder, at the end of the lesson, the generality of their solutions.

We also see in the American lesson plan the note "Formula $A = l \times w$ – recipe." In fact, the teacher refers more than once to this analogy, giving students a very different conception of formulas than is conveyed by the Japanese teacher.

> Teacher: 15 sq cm (writes this on the board), now here's how we do that. We say area equals length times width; now that's a formula or an equation, right? What did I tell you? I said a formula was like a recipe. When you are doing a recipe, what do you do with it? You are at home and you are baking cookies and you have a recipe; what do you do?
>
> Miriam: Mix them all together.
>
> Teacher: Yeah, and if it says, if it says "one half cup of flour," what do you do?
>
> Miriam: Add in one half cup of flour.
>
> Teacher: You put a half cup of flour, you don't put in two cups of sugar. So, when it talks about area equals length times the width you put in what it calls for, so you say area equals length, 5 cm, times the width, 3 cm. Now you have a times sign, so you go 5 times 3 equals 15, and notice that they said square cm. (Teacher wrote formula down while speaking.) They remembered 'cause if they just said 15 cm, that's a line measurement; square cm says that is an area measurement.

The teacher goes on to bring in the recipe analogy four more times in the lesson. Near the end of the lesson he says:

Now that is finding the area of a triangle. One thing you want to get use to is, as we go along, we are going to end up with more and more formulas. Tomorrow we are going to work with volume, and we are going to have a formula for a recipe for finding the volume of something, and once you learn to just to substitute – find the base, plug it in; find the height, plug it in – you won't have any trouble with formulas.

If the Japanese children are learning that formulas are tools to guide thinking, and to represent the results of their thinking, the American children are learning that formulas are things given them by the teacher so that they will know what to do in certain situations. The epistemological outlooks that are being socialized in the two lessons differ greatly.

Conclusion

In this essay, we have presented preliminary analyses of part of a new set of data consisting of videotaped mathematics lessons in Japanese and American elementary schools. The most salient differences between the Japanese and American traditions of classroom mathematics are in the degree to which student thinking is stressed. We found three major ways in which Japanese lessons emphasize student thinking. First, Japanese teachers take student thinking into account in their planning of instruction. Not only are their lesson plans structured to facilitate students' coherent representation of the lesson, but Japanese teachers actually anticipate – in writing – students' responses to instruction. Second, Japanese teachers use a number of techniques to give students opportunities to think during instruction. These techniques include providing time for students to solve problems during the lesson, not hurrying students to find solutions, providing opportunities for public discourse about mathematics, asking students the kinds of questions that will elicit lengthy and thoughtful responses, using students' errors as opportunities for reflection and discussion, and using manipulatives as tools for representing mathematics ideas. Finally, Japanese teachers go to great lengths to convey a view of mathematics in which authority lies not in the teacher but in the methods themselves; there are multiple ways to solve a single problem; and the methods of solving problems must be evaluated by mathematical discourse and argumentation.

Why do Japanese teachers teach this way and American teachers, by and large, not? Surely there are a number of reasons. One might be the mathematical preparation of American elementary school teachers. There is no question that American teachers, like the rest of the American population, are less mathematically competent themselves than are the Japanese teachers. Letting students influence the direction of the lesson, as inevitably happens in the Japanese-style lesson, may provoke anxiety in American teachers who may not be sure themselves if children's novel solutions to mathematics problems are justified.

Similarly, the mathematical preparation of the students may affect the quality of classroom discourse. The open-ended requests for explanations that appear so common in the Japanese classrooms may be possible only because Japanese students have the knowledge required to answer the questions. A study of social studies instruction by Schneider, Gallimore, and Hyland (1991) lends validity to this possibility. In that study, short-answer, recitation-type instruction was more prevalent in a class for remedial students than in a class for gifted students, even when the teacher was the same. Thus, the kinds of discussions found in Japanese classrooms might not occur without sufficient knowledge and understanding on the part of both teachers and students.

Another reason American teachers teach the way they do may be the relative lack of resources available to them. Specifically, a good deal of research is required to be able to predict what students' problem solutions will be, as was seen in the Japanese teacher's lesson plan in Figure 1. It is important to note that the Japanese teacher did not have to come up with the anticipated student responses by herself. Reference books and publications available to Japanese teachers describe students' thinking about all of the topics in the mathematics curriculum. A teacher who is unsure about a particular topic, or a beginning teacher, has many sources to go to for help.

This point may be far more important than anyone has realized. In fact, one American teacher development program that is apparently achieving results similar to those we have seen in

Japanese classrooms seems to work in just this way. The program, called Cognitively Guided Instruction, is based at the University of Wisconsin (Carpenter, Fennema, and Franke, 1992; Frank, Fennema, Carpenter, and Ansell, 1992; Peterson, 1992; Stigler, 1992). Although there are other components to the program, the major one provides teachers with information about the different methods students themselves come up with to solve various kinds of problems.

Finally, what we see when we observe in Japanese elementary classrooms looks quite different from what apparently goes on in Japanese secondary schools, where students talk little and where the focus is on rote memorization (Rohlen, 1983). This is an important qualification. It also raises the interesting question of why teaching techniques should change so radically over this age range. One factor, no doubt, is the intense competition associated with entrance exams into college that shape, in a major way, the high school experiences of Japanese students. Another factor is that the values we see embodied in elementary mathematics lessons – values such as the importance of each individual expressing his point of view in public class discussion – are generally not valued in adult Japanese society. Having good ideas is important, but expressing those ideas in public is often frowned upon. Elementary teaching in Japan may thus make more sense when viewed in a life-span perspective. Perhaps elementary lessons are the way they are in order to explicitly teach young Japanese students how to think, analyze problems, and invent solutions. Once they have learned these skills, however, it is no longer necessary to display them publicly, hence the shift in high school. Americans tend to see talking and acting as evidence of thinking. Japanese see thinking as something that goes beyond talk and action. Thinking involves reflection, and reflection is what characterizes instruction in Japanese elementary mathematics classrooms.

The Kumon approach to teaching and learning

NANCY UKAI RUSSELL

Memorization is the beginning of intelligence.

Kumon Tōru[1]

In the early summer of 1954, eight-year-old Kumon Takeshi, a second grader in Moriguchi City, Osaka, came home from school with a poor grade on his arithmetic test. His mother was concerned, but his father, Kumon Tōru, a high school math teacher, was not. "In my opinion, his health . . . was the most important thing during the elementary school years; I planned to put him on a structured course of study after he entered middle school" (Kumon 1981:186). But prodded by his wife, Mr. Kumon began thinking about how to help his son. He reviewed Takeshi's mathematics textbook and was surprised by the way concepts were introduced and then dropped. He turned to commercial drill books, but they only offered repetition of unimportant material. Dissatisfied with what he had found available, Mr. Kumon began crafting a home study program. He wrote out individual worksheets of minutely sequenced computation problems, adjusted to Takeshi's ability level, and assigned one each day. Happily, Takeshi's grades improved, but when they quit the regimen, his scores slipped again. The family returned to using the worksheets but found that if Takeshi skipped a few days of work, he was loath to restart the schedule. Through trial and error, a useful system eventually emerged: Takeshi did one worksheet each day under Mrs. Kumon's supervision. Mr. Kumon corrected it that night and prepared the next day's

This essay is condensed from a version that originally appeared in the *Journal of Japanese Studies* (Winter 1994).

problems, gradually increasing their difficulty. Four years later, Takeshi had completed 1,000 worksheets and was solving problems in differential and integral calculus. When Mr. Kumon gave his son a few university entrance exam problems, Takeshi, by now a sixth-grader, was able to solve most of them.

Today, *Kumon-shiki,* or the Kumon method, is the most widely used supplemental system for studying mathematics in Japan. The self-paced curriculum has been expanded to over 5,000 timed worksheets, taking the learner sequentially and incrementally from prewriting skills and dot-counting exercises to college-level physics problems. The method was developed to teach mathematics and is best understood through this curriculum, the focus of this essay, but also should be seen as a method with broader applications. Approximately 70 percent of Japanese children who study Kumon math also enroll in Kumon's course for Japanese language, and a smaller proportion study English using Kumon. The method is mostly used by young children: approximately 7 percent of Japanese elementary schoolchildren study by Kumon twice a week at after-school tutorial centers. Their numbers, and the longevity of the method, have made the Kumon Institute of Education into Japan's largest private educational enterprise in terms of enrollment and revenue.

The Kumon method is controversial and occupies a special niche in the rich, variegated world of Japanese education. Japanese critics dislike the rote-style progression through skill levels. Its most prominent critic is the Japanese Ministry of Education (*Monbushō*), which emphasizes the development of critical thinking skills in mathematics – while Kumon stresses computation – and which establishes curricular standards for each grade that Kumon then aims to have its students surpass. The individualized nature of the method runs counter to group-oriented methods, and Kumon is famous for nurturing "genius" children who solve calculus problems at age five in a society renowned for its uniformity. Japanese mothers seem either to love the method or to hate it. Nevertheless, several features of Japan's educational culture have worked in favor of its development. The first factor is the cultural acceptance of repetition, memorization, and mastery as valuable and essential aspects of learning. Also, the importance of mathematics in education – central to success in mathematics – is vital to performing well on entrance examinations and in school, and thus a high value is placed on ways to study the subject. Finally, the structure of women's employment in Japan has provided the Kumon company with thousands of active teachers who, denied access to the mainstream economy and not licensed to teach in the public education system, play a crucial role in the method's development and successful execution. Many women have found a personal calling and even spiritual meaning in their jobs, lending an air of near-religious zeal to corporate gatherings and publications. They are supported, on the home front, by Japanese "education mothers" who supervise their children's completion of Kumon homework.

Were the Kumon method used only in Japan, it might be viewed merely as an interesting educational oddity that has lessons but not direct applications for people outside Japan. In fact, Kumon math is used by 350,000 children in 27 countries,[2] with 70,000 in the United States. As might be expected, usage of the method has developed along different lines in the United States. The most profound innovation is the use of Kumon in American public and private schools as a supplement to the regular curriculum. This adaptation has shifted the focus of the program from home to school; from ambitious Kumon franchisee to overburdened public or private school teacher; from a narrowly exam-focused society to one that is not. Kumon also is used in the United States as an after-school program, and here as well, adoption of the method has produced unexpected outcomes.

This essay will describe the Kumon philosophy and how the method is used in Japan, and will examine the interplay of factors that made Kumon effective in Japan and such an intriguing experiment in the United States. Although the technical aspects of the curriculum are the same, different contexts lead to different outcomes, revealing much about the state of the two societies and the assumptions that each holds on how learning should take place.

The Kumon method

The Kumon method represents a clear example of what Western educational psychologists term "guided learning" theory. In contrast to "active learning" theories that stress cognition through the manipulation of materials, the exploration of ideas, and unstructured discovery, "guided," "reception" or "expository" learning draws on a behaviorist approach. This approach emphasizes the mastery of prerequisite skills before continuing to higher levels of difficulty. The goal of Kumon is precisely that: for elementary schoolchildren to master the extensive corpus of manipulative skills that lead ultimately to solving problems in differential calculus. Mr. Kumon's original goal for his son was to help him master this level of mathematics since eventually he would study it in school.

When Mr. Kumon thought about his son's education, he knew that eventually Takeshi would have to learn differential equations in high school, since that would lead him into university-level math. Then he figured that before differential equations comes trigonometry, and before that comes geometry. Before geometry comes algebra, and preceding that is division, multiplication, subtraction, and addition.[3]

After witnessing Takeshi's achievement, which at the time he considered amazing, Mr. Kumon came to believe that all children were capable of solving calculus problems if they were introduced to the material in small steps at their own pace. Mr. Kumon set that objective at the apex of his curriculum pyramid and worked down. This highly sequential presentation is key to the Kumon method and is a key factor in the theory of guided learning, especially as it is applied to mathematics (see Ausbel and Robinson, 1969:143).

To its sequential presentation, the Kumon method adds the principle of automaticity, or "overlearning," which is the measure of whether material has been mastered. Children must practice computation until finding solutions becomes automatic. They progress to a higher level of work only after they show the ability to complete sheets accurately within prescribed time and mistake limits. If either of the limits is exceeded, additional drilling is assigned.

The method is put into practice as follows:

1. The newly enrolled child takes a 20-minute diagnostic test. After the score is evaluated, the child is placed at an extremely low skill level in order to enhance his or her early performance and thereby build confidence and motivation.
2. The child is presented with a new plastic Kumon box that contains several stapled packets of 3 to 10 worksheets. One

packet is to be completed each day, requiring 15–30 minutes' study.

3. Twice a week, the child attends a Kumon classroom (*kyō-shitsu*). The completed homework is turned in, and that day's packet is done at the classroom.

4. The child receives back previous homework and corrects the mistakes until a perfect score is returned. The process of correcting one's own mistakes is seen as an important opportunity for self-teaching.

5. The instructor graphs the child's progress in a detailed record book and, according to the most recent results, assigns more difficult work or repetition of previous pages.

6. Kumon is practiced every day of the year.

The vehicle for learning the mathematics curriculum is approximately 5,000 five-by-seven-inch worksheets whose most striking feature are their long, regular rows of computation problems printed in dark grey ink. The 5,000 sheets are divided into 28 levels, with most containing 200 pages. Each level corresponds to the material and concepts covered in a Japanese grade, as shown in Table 1.

The upper section of every worksheet has a similar appearance, as shown in Figure 1. At the top left corner is a letter and number, designating the curriculum level and page number within that level. Children who do Kumon glance at this corner when they receive new homework to see what level they're at. At the top right is a box with spaces for entering the starting and ending times, date and child's name. There is a noticeable absence (in worksheets above preschool level) of words, pictures and tables. The purpose is to focus the learner's attention on numbers.

Kumon problems are sequenced to an astonishingly minute degree, giving the worksheets the appearance of eye-pleasing order and regularity, if one is sympathetic to the Kumon method, or mind-numbing repetition if one is not. The reasons are two-fold: (1) so that the child is not pressured, since the degree of difficulty increases so gradually, and (2) to help the child discern number patterns.

For example, a child working at Level 3A on preaddition skills will be given many pages containing problems such as $1+1$, $3+1$, $2+1$, $5+1$, $4+1$ and so on. Having firmly mastered

Table I. *Kumon mathematics curriculum by level*

	Curriculum level	Japanese grade level	Material and concepts covered
Preschool level	7a		Number games; recognize, recite numbers 1–10
	6a		Zero; ability to recognize, recite numbers 1–30
	5a		Line drawing, mazes
	4a		Number tracing, dot counting
	3a		Number charts, beginning addition
	2a		Simple addition by mental calculation
Elementary	A	1	Addition, subtraction (mental)
	B	2	Vertical addition (carrying), subtraction
	C	3	Multiplication tables, multiplication, division
	D	4	Multiplication, division, fractions
	E	5	Fractions (reduction, four operations)
	F	6	Four operations, decimal, word problems
Middle	G	7	Positive and negative numbers, algebraic expressions
	H	8	Linear equations, linear functions
	I	9	Polynomials, factorization, square roots, quadratic equations
High	J	10	Higher factorization, quadratic equations
	K	11	Various functions (quadratic, fractional, irrational, exponential, logarithmic, trigonometric)
	L		Plane geometry
	M		Progression, differential/integral calculus
	N		Vectors/linear transformations
	O	12	Applications of differential calculus

Table 1. *Kumon mathematics curriculum by level (cont.)*

Curriculum level	Japanese grade level	Material and concepts covered
College P		Indefinite integral calculus, application
		Integral calculus, differential equations
Q–V		College-level physics, mathematics

that, she will continue practicing "adding 1" until 99 + 1. Then "adding 2," "adding 3," etc. is practiced.

Concepts are not explicitly taught. Rather, through repetition, learners experience insight. For example, the means of solving such problems as 48 ÷ 6 or 132 ÷ 12 will be patently clear, without verbal or written explanation, to a child who has completed several hundred multiplication problems and to whom 6 × 8 and 11 × 12 are operations that have been "overlearned." (My interest in Kumon was frequently stimulated by my son, who occasionally exclaimed "I get it!" as he worked problems.) As children become better calculators and as their body of knowledge grows, some discover shortcuts or different strategies for operations, injecting "creativity" and intuition into what seems to be merely a mechanical operation.[4]

The volume of repetition that is necessary before progressing to more difficult work depends on the individual. Children who quickly and accurately complete the two-digit division worksheets, for example, will advance with little redundancy to three-digit division, while others may repeat the two-digit section dozens of times before moving forward. Even the fastest-progressing students, however, work each 200-page level the equivalent of at least three times (Sherman, 1991:101), according to the company. Completion of worksheets should require less than 30 minutes a day, but if this schedule is adhered to, the pages add up rapidly. I was surprised to learn that my daughter, who started doing animal mazes when she was three-and-a-half years old, completed 2,885 pages in two years, to

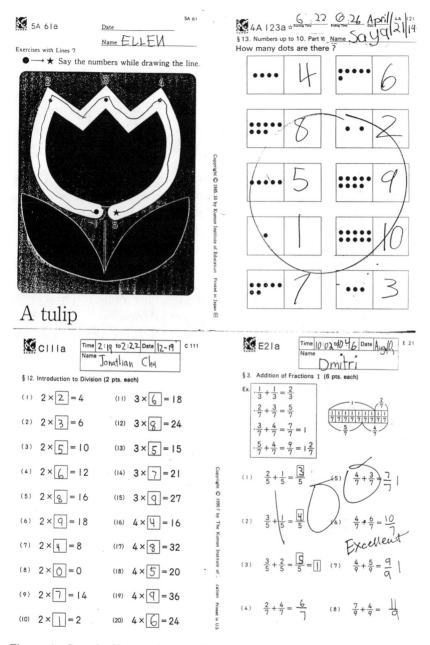

Figure 1. Sample Kumon lesson. These worksheets are from four different levels and provide practice in (1) small motor skills; (2) counting up to 10 and writing numbers; (3) predivision skills, and (4) adding fractions.

finish three levels. A researcher has noted the case of Katō Yukinori, who was enrolled in Kumon when he was four years, nine months old. Five years later, he was solving problems involving vectors at Level O, having completed 800 sheets per level, with backsteps and redundancies in certain areas, for a total of 13,570 worksheets! And he was only "12th best" in Japan for third graders (as judged by how far he had progressed in the materials) (Sherman, 1991:61).

Not surprisingly, Kumon asserts that repetition is fun. Young children enjoy doing the same thing repeatedly; singing a TV jingle or drawing the same picture over and over is satisfying and a crucial part of the learning process (see Montessori, 1964:357). If the child is solving problems at "just the right" (*chodo ii*) level, the act of calculating is effortless and rhythmic. Concentration is intense and, in some cases, the pencil appears to literally fly down the page as the child mumbles meditatively or even laughs with glee.

Repeatedly doing calculations can become a much-hated task, however, when the concept is *not* understood or the skill level is too high. Children who previously zipped through worksheets may rip them up, scribble in frustration, refuse to work, cry, etc. when assigned difficult work.

At this point, sensitive guidance becomes crucial to success. Expert teachers may assign extremely easy work, with a few harder sheets mixed in, to remind children what they are capable of; assign fewer pages per day; ask for closer parental guidance; or, in rarer cases, suggest to the company that possible flaws in the sequencing of problems be repaired. Holding the child's interest during these "hump" periods is the ultimate test not only of the quality of the worksheets but also of the teacher's understanding of the method and skill in applying it. The job of instructors, which will be discussed below in more detail, is not to "interfere" with the child's learning, which will come through internalizing calculation skills, but to offer praise, hints, and individualized feedback on work. Teachers are called *shidōsha* (instructor), literally someone who gives guidance, rather than the traditional *sensei* (teacher), which carries greater instructional authority.

The company also employs psychological strategies, many embedded in the worksheet structure, to keep children motivated. For example, each 200-page level is designed so that difficult "uphill" sections, which introduce new concepts, are followed by "downhill" slopes of repetition. Tedious problems that require several intermediary steps will be followed by a simple one that can be computed mentally, providing a psychological lift analogous to raising a one-pound weight after a strenuous workout pulling 20-pound weights.

New students are started at a level as much as two years, or 400 pages, below their actual ability as determined by the diagnostic test. Starting so low helps develop motivation, speed and concentration since the learner can rapidly complete work that is so easy. Moreover, company studies show that children who begin using easy material advance over the long run more quickly than those who do not. A Japanese manager explains:

> In training for the high jump, a person who can clear 200 centimeters will have trained for a long time at jumping over 150 centimeters. If he starts training at 200 centimeters, he may strain a muscle or hurt himself. Kumon is the same.[5]

In a minuscule but highly celebrated percentage of cases, children aged five and under gradually progress to solving algebra, geometry, and calculus worksheets. According to the company's regularly published Advanced Students List (*Shindo Ichiranhyō*), 600 children aged three years old and under were completing algebra-level worksheets out of a total enrollment of 811,909 in spring 1991. Many adults find it difficult to believe that toddlers can achieve such proficiency, but professional mathematicians say it is not unthinkable, merely unusual since most societies believe that children's time is better spent doing other things. (Nor, perhaps, has there existed a popularized method that consistently produced this outcome.) As a Japanese mathematics professor observes, "For a baby, learning all the rules to speak a language is much more difficult than learning algebra, but language is more important for the child's survival."[6]

Kumon's in-house magazines are filled with disproportionate examples of three- and four-year-olds who are doing algebra, which are meant to instruct and inspire. One such case is that of Shiono Hitomi, whose mother received Kumon song cards, Chinese character (*kanji*) flashcards and puzzles when Hitomi was born. Hitomi recognized the *kanji* for *ninjin* (carrot) when she was nine months old, spurring her mother to enroll her in

Kumon math and Japanese language courses two months later and in the English course when she turned two. Hitomi, at three years old, was doing algebra and solving sixth grade level worksheets in English and seventh grade level in Japanese language. She was doing Kumon worksheets for two hours every day with her mother, completing the Kumon 1–100 magnetic number board in 10 minutes and reading 200 books per month (*Yamabiko*, 1990:32–35).

Is repetition and drill productive use of a child's time? Successful use of an algorithm does not mean that one comprehends the underlying principles. Kumon officials reply that children memorize the alphabet and learn to recognize many letter combinations and words before they begin to read, and that practicing arithmetic skills is the equivalent prerequisite for doing higher levels of mathematics.

Controversy over the Kumon method tends to center, understandably, on the central role of computation[7] and the volume of repetition. In the tendency to focus on educational theory, however, other, less obvious factors that can profoundly diminish or enhance the power of the curriculum may be overlooked, such as the learner's environment and the role played by the instructor and the family. Indeed, Kumon's commercial and educational achievements can be attributed in large measure to the company's canny exploitation of many complex elements that characterize the culture of modern Japanese education. Of particular relevance are the nation's competitive exam-driven system, the social aspirations of Japanese parents, and the availability of a large pool of educated women who supervise and carry out the Kumon method.

The Kumon method in Japan

Kumon has been able to flourish in Japan for several reasons: (1) The Japanese mothers who use it have a positive image of the method; (2) many children seem to enjoy doing it; (3) it is convenient for families; (4) society places a high value on education, and (5) Kumon is seen as a viable after-school program which propels children beyond grade-level work and prepares them successfully for competitive examinations.

According to a 1985 poll taken by the *Mainichi Shimbun*, one of Japan's three largest daily newspapers, 66 percent of 4,200 housewives in Tokyo and Osaka were aware of the Kumon method. Of those whose children were enrolled in the method, 45 percent said they valued the good study habits that the method instills, and 28 percent thought it would help their children learn how to think and concentrate. Nearly 40 percent of enrolled families said they chose the program because it is liked by children, and 35 percent because it has a good reputation among neighbors and friends (Shiba, 1986:311).

The company's user-friendly reputation belies its size and power. It operates 81 regional offices and 18,500 franchises, and in the fiscal year ending March 1992 reported sales of ¥47.5 billion ($475 million). Enrollment figures for September 1992 show that approximately 800,000 children study with Kumon, mostly in three subjects: math, Japanese language, and English. According to the firm, 790,000 children are enrolled in math, 605,000 study Japanese language, and 240,000 study English. (The figures add up to more than 800,000 since many children enroll in more than one subject. Indeed, the company widely advertises a national enrollment of 1.6 million children when, in fact, this figure actually represents the total number of *subjects* that are being studied by the core enrollment of 800,000 children.) Seventy percent of children who study math also study Japanese language, and 63,000 students study all three subjects.

Kumon asserts that its method is appropriate for all ages, but enrollment statistics show that Japanese parents overwhelmingly choose Kumon math as a class for elementary schoolchildren. In fact, this age bracket accounts for 80 percent of all users. Enrollment for math starts to double each year from the two-year-old level until the first grade. It peaks at elementary third grade, as seen in Table 2.

Kumon may be popular for this age level because the method is seen as useful for cementing fundamental arithmetic skills, which are introduced in the early elementary years and which parents consider important to future success in mathematics. Parents who are considering Kumon are told of the method's record of accelerating children beyond grade-level work. Since the method starts new students at such a low beginning point, about six months is required for them to reach their true ability level. By the end of one year, however, 50 percent of children in the top half of their class have surpassed grade-level work. Children in the top quarter of their class are already studying

Table 2. *Enrollment in Kumon math in Japanese elementary schoolchildren (September 1992)*

Age	Grade	Number of students (percentage of all Japanese elementary school students)
≤2		8,146
3		13,217
4		25,755
5	K	50,447
6	1	87,574 (6.3)
7	2	111,710 (8.0)
8	3	119,031 (7.9)
9	4	108,084 (7.2)
10	5	89,020 (5.9)
11	6	74,028 (4.6)

Source: Kumon Institute of Education and Japanese Ministry of Education.

0.75 year ahead. Within two years, children in the bottom quarter are studying ahead of grade level. Since the average Kumon student is enrolled for 28 months, it can be assumed that most children catch up with and eventually advance beyond their grade level. Kumon is used as an accelerated course as well as for remedial purposes, but according to the company, the majority of users can be described as children of average ability.

Of at least equal importance to parents is Kumon's provision of a structured yet low-key format that, properly used, can nurture disciplined study habits and engage a child's attention on an academic subject for a short period of time each day. As many children's first *juku,* or supplementary after-school class, it is a relatively unthreatening experience. Unlike many other big *juku* companies, which have an impersonal, urban image, Kumon *kyōshitsu* are more akin to a neighborhood shop. Virtually all are run by women, half are run out of private homes, and it is common for children to walk directly from schools to their Kumon classes. After arriving, the child greets the teacher, turns in the homework, obtains his or her folder and starts the day's assignment. In one Japanese classroom in Sugnami Ward, Tokyo, a mother sat on the *tatami* with her 18-month-old son on her lap, quietly chanting "1 + 1" problems to him as the children around them chatted and completed worksheets.

Tuition consists of a one-time ¥10,000 (about $100 at ¥100 = $1) registration fee per family[8] and ¥6,000 monthly for primary schoolchildren. The monthly fee is ¥7,000 for middle and high school students, with a discount for more than one subject. Compared to the price of other *juku,* some of which may charge monthly fees of over ¥20,000, Kumon is considered to be moderately priced.

Women account for more than 95 percent of Kumon instructors. Kumon uses a franchise system to spread its network of classrooms, and women who obtain a franchise also serve as that classroom's instructor. Some successful franchisees/instructors operate more than one tutorial center; thus 16,586 franchisees run 18,487 classrooms. The employment structure in Japan offers such limited opportunity for Japanese women, particularly for those who leave the work force to have children and later wish to return, that Kumon is able to select its franchisees from a deep pool of highly educated and willing applicants who are experienced in working with children. Among the group of franchisees hired in spring 1992, for instance, most were homemakers, and 57 percent had graduated from a four-year college and 36 percent from a two-year college. Very few Kumon instructors are professionally trained teachers. Rather, their aim is to earn part-time income in a job that offers the potential to help others. Economist Shiba Shōji has patronizingly described them as "social bench warmers" whose talents have been unleashed by Kumon (Shiba, 1986:324).

The company takes great care in the hiring, training and maintenance of standards in its instructors. Kumon hires fewer than 1 of every 10 applicants. Prospective candidates take a general knowledge exam and a test in the subject they hope to teach, and have a 30-minute interview with a local Kumon manager who judges the applicant's personality and "love of children."

Successful applicants then enter a training period of over one year. Beginning math instructors attend three months of training classes and must complete 2,000 worksheets through Level J (factorization and quadratic equations), starting with 200 pages of mazes and drawing lines between cartoon figures.

For at least several years, instructors also must earn a prescribed number of credits by attending company-sponsored lectures on educational topics and twice a year take an exam in their subject(s). The latter requirement ensures subject mastery, keeps instructors mindful of the students' perspective, and works to enhance their esteem as "professionals." Fujiwara Hideko, a well-known franchisee who now works in Kumon's Houston office, believes that the most diligent Kumon teachers are busier studying, attending seminars, and correcting papers than the average Japanese schoolteacher. In addition, the company has created an elaborate social world to motivate teachers, nurture their sense of professionalism and instill a feeling of participation in a worthy educational cause.

Excellence is encouraged by recognizing exemplary teachers. An elite group of instructors, some of whom earn the equivalent of $100,000 or more from their franchises, become celebrities within the organization. They deliver lectures, earn local fame and may customize their classrooms. For example, Suzuki Mieko of Tanashi City, Tokyo, holds seminars on teaching English to infants. Morita Yukiko of the "Triumph" *kyōshitsu* specializes in working with gifted (*yūshūji*) toddlers who routinely work linear equations and read Japanese essays that use up to 800 *kanji*. Inouye Mayumi of Kyoto Prefecture teaches upper-school students and has published a book of study hints. Her 250 students stay with Kumon for an average of four years, double the average length of enrollment.

Teachers also gain recognition through contributing to or being featured in company monthlies, such as *Yamabiko*, a general newsletter; *Nyūyōji*, about teaching infants; and *Tsukushi*, for teachers of children with learning disorders. All instructors are sent copies, which contain cheery accounts of high-achieving students, complete with baby photos and the obligatory sample of worksheets. One typical article featured the observations of a teacher's poignant experiences with a mentally handicapped boy who enrolled in her classroom as a third grader – crying, unable to hold a pencil, and capable of reading only seven *hiragana*. By the time he turned 15, he was reading *kanji*, solving math problems, and had obtained a job. She emotionally concluded that "there is no other method like Kumon that furthers the intellectual development of handicapped people" (*Tsukushi*, April 1990:26–27).

Expert instructors may be invited by the company to help research a specific topic. "Monitors" (*monitā*) consider a given problem and make suggestions, such as where improvements can be made in sequencing problems or in breaking down concepts into smaller parts.

We found that there is a difficult jump to go from doing $8+3$ to $9+4$ and that more practice is needed on problems that lead up to solving $8+2$. . . . The instructors watch the children and tell us which spots in the worksheets give the children trouble. Sometimes a teacher will say, "one little girl cried when she couldn't do this one." We have the children do the problems and watch their responses. Another teacher told us, "the child was going along very smoothly until this point, when his pencil stopped." (Ozaki Kazuyori, July 18, 1991)

The experience and expertise of past instructors are used in detailed teaching manuals that offer hints and pinpoint trouble spots. For example, instructors are warned that the last 20 pages of Level E (fractions and decimals) are difficult for many children. "They may go forward if they can complete one page within seven minutes. . . . Many children have trouble converting decimals into fractions. . . . Basic problems such as $0.5 = 1/2$, $0.25 = 1/4$, $0.75 = 3/4$ should be memorized through practice."[9]

Some women have complained of feeling exploited by the firm. A company official said that several instructors privately told him that they felt used by the firm since it profits so handsomely from their ideas and observations. Resentment may be directed against company managers who are in supervisory positions yet have little or no actual experience teaching Kumon. In cases such as this, the inspirational example of Mr. Kumon, who, at 80 years old, is the charismatic, hands-on chairman of the firm, can be a powerful salve. He is passionate about spreading his method to help children "learn how to learn" and frequently speaks before Kumon conventions, writes newspaper columns, inquires about worksheet revisions, and holds staff meetings to discuss ways that Kumon can contribute to society, based on his own 70-item list of the method's positive attributes.[10] Admirers compare him to Suzuki Shinichi, the founder of the Suzuki method of violin instruction, which, like Kumon, emphasizes practice and memorization of skills and produces a high level of proficiency in young children. Both men, who are friends, believe that all children have "genius" potential and that it is the responsibility of adults to nurture it to maturity (Peak, this volume).

The Kumon method in the United States

The Kumon method is used by nearly 70,000 children in the United States, about half of whom use it in public and private schools, with the remaining 35,000 students enrolled in after-school tutorial centers. The Kumon method arrived in the United States in the mid-1970s at the behest of Japanese expatriate businessmen who desired a supplement to their children's math education. Gradually the method began to spread among local populations on the West and East Coasts, mostly among children of Asian descent. Two-thirds of Kumon's after-school students in Los Angeles and Orange Counties, for example, are the children of first-generation Japanese and Korean parents. Similarly, children born to Chinese and Korean immigrants are believed to account for two-thirds of the enrollment in New Jersey. In order to expose the method to "real Americans," the firm opened an office in Houston, Texas, in 1988.

The Houston office planned to expand in the U.S. South and Midwest by opening after-school tutorial centers. Ilene Black, an elementary school vice principal in Alabama, irrevocably changed this strategy. Black, of Sumiton Elementary School, viewed a news report on the Kumon method and was impressed by the company's claim of mastery. Despite initial protests of Houston officials that Kumon was not for school use, she persuaded the company to let her try Kumon as an in-school supplemental curriculum, and within one year teachers cited dramatic improvement in standardized test scores. Sumiton first graders, who had routinely scored in the 20th percentile and below in the math portion of standard achievement tests, began to place in the 85th percentile. Before starting the program, Sumiton ranked 19th out of 21 among county schools in a comparison of scores on the Stanford Achievement Test, a norm-referenced test, but after one year of practicing Kumon, Sumiton ranked 9th out of 21 in math.

"None of our teachers changed, and neither did our textbooks. The only thing that was different was Kumon,"[11] Black says. The biggest surprise for her and the teachers, however, was that the children said they liked it, with some even wanting to skip physical education to do Kumon worksheets. Major news media published articles about these outlandish claims of success. The in-school program, which started with 300 students in Sumiton in 1988, was expected to expand to 50,000 children in 36 states for the 1992–93 school year.[12] Sumiton Elementary, in its fifth year of Kumon, is visited by teachers from across the country and even from abroad.

The dramatic displays of success claimed by Sumiton Elementary led to praise and optimism by some observers. The company set a goal of enrolling 2 million American schoolchildren by the year 2000, now viewed as unrealistic. What has become clear over the past few years, however, is that outcomes swing dramatically, depending on the effort and attitude of the classroom teacher. Teachers who like the method and the facts-oriented curriculum tend to produce good results, while those who do not may obtain the reverse outcome.

Enthusiastic teachers and schools report gains in scores on standardized tests.[13] My own random sampling of five schools which had used the method for at least one year also indicated that mathematics scores had increased by varying degrees, but since schools had used the method differently and without using the same control groups, the extent of real change could not be determined.

Successful Kumon schools cite behavioral changes and improved self-confidence, which may then have the effect of lifting the child's performance. An elementary school principal in Atlanta, Texas, whose school uses Kumon for 70 kindergarteners, said, "We felt like it gives the kids a good head start. They get to feeling like they're good at math, and that's about half the ballgame. If you believe you can do it, you can."[14]

The observations of the director of a program for gifted and talented children at the University of Tulsa attracted interest since it is commonly assumed that academically advanced children do not need or like repetition. After using Kumon for 82 students from grades 1–7, for one year, she found in a survey that:

> 68 percent (56 children) said the method helped their concentration,
>
> 54 percent (44) said it helped them stay on task,
>
> 60 percent (49) said it helped them learn how to work hard,
>
> 83 percent (68) said it had increased their speed,
>
> 73 percent (60) said it had helped them improve accuracy,
>
> 91 percent (75) said their math skills had improved.[15]

But Kumon can fail spectacularly where teachers are less convinced of its efficacy. Additional class preparation and the massive amount of grading and record-keeping can be staggering. Grading worksheets for an average class of 21 can take as much as two and a half hours. If immediate grading and record-keeping is not carried out, the wrong level of worksheet may be assigned, destroying the seamless progression of work that successful application of Kumon requires.

Even where teachers devise ways to alleviate the grading problem, such as by having students grade each other's work, rotating grading among work groups, or hiring a part-time grader, students eventually tire of doing worksheets when the novelty wears off or when the problems grow more difficult. Finding ways to handle the dropoff in interest becomes a burden for the teacher, who is not paid to use Kumon and does not have the Japanese support mechanism of active parental interest.

Approximately 35,000 American children study Kumon math in after-school learning centers, which are operated in churches, community centers, schools and malls. Students pay a $30 registration fee and $65 in monthly tuition. Women, often schoolteachers who run centers on Saturdays and professional tutors, account for 70 percent of franchisees. A license and start-up kit costs $300, and the instructor keeps 60 percent of student tuition. The biggest difference is that, until recently, American franchisees have undergone only several hours of training, largely by watching videotapes.[16]

A high dropout rate has plagued many centers. According to U.S. representatives, American students tend to be oriented to short-term results, such as passing an upcoming test or improving a grade, and are not fully accustomed to the idea of extracurricular classes. A Japanese strategist observes that "Japanese mothers want their children to progress beyond their classmates, but when Americans catch up, they feel satisfied and leave the program."[17] An American manager adds, "Most parents feel math is the school's job. . . . When kids leave school, it's hard enough to get them to do their homework let alone extracurricular homework."[18]

The extreme amount of repetition is unacceptable to many parents, and due to the lack of teacher training and absence of a system to educate the user, some parents come to believe that the intent of the extremely low starting level and the voluminous repetition is to collect more tuition. In most U.S. franchises, instructors ask parents to grade the worksheets at home, and if the parents fail to do so, the child's progress cannot be monitored accurately and motivation slackens all around. The task of chauffeurring children to yet another activity, the $65 monthly tuition and the growing trend for children to use computer software to practice math skills are other obstacles for Kumon. First-generation Asian-American parents, however, seem to be less deterred by these factors, and American Kumon centers most resemble their Japanese counterparts where first-generation Korean, Chinese, Japanese and Indian families form the main constituency. Korean parents "are not satisfied with the education system here," says Han Kim, a manager for Kumon in southern California. "In Kumon, they see something very similar to what they learned in Korea. They emphasize this math very strongly for their children."[19] Other foreign-born Asian residents from Taiwan and China have expressed "relief" at finding a program such as Kumon in the United States.

Conclusion

We can increase our understanding of Japanese education by studying why Kumon has been well received for 35 years among a dedicated group of Japanese parents. It may be that Kumon in the Japanese context is a desirable component to school learning, particularly at the elementary level. According to research by Stevenson and Stigler, Japanese elementary schoolteachers use inquiry-based methods to conduct math classes by using small groups to explore concepts, encouraging mistakes and leading open-ended discussions (Stevenson and Stigler, 1992). Class time is rarely spent practicing computational skills. In the evening, however, children practice drill and calculation at *juku*, by doing homework sheets or by filling in practice books sold at corner bookstores. Thus, concepts are considered during the day and practice takes place at night.[20] Recent psychological research indicates that this is a powerful combination for learning (Case, 1985).

Once Japanese children leave elementary school, however, their usage of the Kumon method and the individual and institutional nature of learning change. In contrast to the nurturing female instructors of Kumon, *yobikō* cram school instructors are strict, authoritarian male teachers whose task is to prepare their charges mentally for the narrowly competitive task of excelling on a standardized entrance exam. The option of attending a Kumon *kyōshitsu* is only one component in a complex web of educational choices that Japanese parents make at different points in their children's careers.

Part of Kumon's appeal also can be attributed to the fact that it is a modern expression of deeply held beliefs about how learning should take place. Kumon's emphasis on learning through drill, physical repetition and memorization echoes Japanese instructional traditions that value "doing" as a part of knowing. The phrase *karada de oboeru* (literally, "memorizing through the body") is commonly used in reference to learning processes, whether one is learning to bow, ride a bicycle, master a *nō* dance, or, in the case of Kumon, rapidly perform arithmetic calculations. This phase is the first step for novices and children. A Japanese music instructor who has taught piano to children and young adults for 25 years says, "In methods like Suzuki and Kumon, you are making children learn through their body. They aren't told 'why' yet. When they ask [about concepts] you say, 'just wait a little longer' [*chotto matte kudasai*], and you don't encourage them to think about that yet. Education is a complex process because you must switch to different teaching styles depending on the age of the learner."[21] Repetition also is seen as nurturing positive character traits, such as endurance, patience and discipline. Thus the Japanese teenager who completed 17 levels of Kumon English, and then repeated it for reinforcement, viewed the exercise not only as a way to absorb knowledge, but also as a badge of his diligence and perseverance.

Many traditional Japanese methods of instruction rely on a "guided method" in which a clear goal is set forth with detailed steps that, if closely followed, assure a high level of proficiency. Along the way, learners are rewarded and motivated with an acknowledgment of their incremental advancement, such as special licenses in the tea ceremony, different belt colors in the martial arts, promotion to a higher level of apprenticeship, and, for Kumon students, stickers, certificates of achievement at the end of each "200-step" level, or mention in the Advanced Students List. This incremental approach allows for gradual mastery of a subject while enabling learners to develop a sense of themselves as serious participants in a learning process. For those who endure the two-steps-forward, one-step-backward progression through the curriculum, it guarantees objective measures of success, confirming the view held by most Japanese that personal industry is more important to academic achievement than natural intelligence.

Observing the Kumon method in new contexts provides insight on how the method functions and how users' needs differ. Due to American resistance to intensive repetition, Kumon has considered developing an abbreviated curriculum for U.S. use without the repetition that Kumon deems necessary for "overlearning." "The steps will become rougher."[22]

It has become clear that without Japanese support mechanisms, such as dedicated parental support, and other technical features, such as the uniform training of instructors, the method functions less evenly and effectively. (This became particularly clear to my family when we switched from studying at the Texas office – which was a training center for some of the company's most experienced representatives – to a private New Jersey franchise, where grading was left to parents, guidance was sparse and progression in the curriculum stagnated.) Nor is the method effective for all learners. Ultimately, success in using Kumon may lie in the motivation of individuals. When parents and teachers become closely involved, they achieve high outcomes and open up new areas for application. An Australian instructor suggested the idea for developing an English curriculum for native speakers, Americans were the first to use Kumon in schools and corporations, and Canadians now operate the two largest Kumon franchises of all, in Toronto.[23]

Notes

1. Interview with Kumon Tōru (chairman, Kumon Institute of Education), Osaka, Japan, July 18, 1991.
2. According to October, 1993, figures, the largest enrollments overseas are in South Korea (147,000), the United States, Taiwan (58,000), Brazil (27,000), and Australia (18,000).
3. Interview with Ōzaki Kazuyori (manager, overseas division, Kumon Institute of Education), Osaka, July 18, 1991.
4. In a study by psychologist David Geary et al., Chinese children showed a 3-to-1 performance advantage over American children in their ability to quickly and accurately solve single-digit addition

problems in pencil-and-paper and computer tests. The Chinese children called on a more sophisticated mix of strategies and showed an advantage in speed of processing, abilities that Geary et al. attribute in part to the stronger emphasis on practice of basic arithmetic skills in China (Geary, Liu Fan, and Bow-Thomas, 1992:180–84).

5. Interview with Mori Hiroaki (educational director, Kumon Mathematex), Irving, Texas, May 1991.

6. Interview with Fujita Hiroshi (mathematics professor, Meiji University), Tokyo, July 27, 1991.

7. To some math educators, the reliance on computation alone is a weakness in the method. Miwa Tatsurō, former mathematics education professor at Tsukuba University, explains: "There is only you and a piece of paper. The idea is to look at the examples and find the rule. It's important and necessary for children to find things out on their own, but not all people are capable of doing this" (interview, Kyoto, July 28, 1991).

8. The firm abolished the registration fee in October 1994 in an effort to attract more students amid growing competition in the *juku* industry and a continuing decline in the population of elementary school-age children.

9. Kumon booklet, "Shidō ni Tsuite no Ryujiko," undated.

10. "Kumon-shiki no Tokuchō" (March 1991) is a two-page list of data, opinion and inspirational writing that Mr. Kumon frequently updates. Item 10, for example, "Achieving potential," states that between 1981 and 1991, the number of elementary students solving Level J worksheets (square roots, quadratic equations) grew from 181 to 7,000. Item 25, "I'm glad I became a Kumon instructor," quotes a franchisee as saying that through teaching Kumon, she came to understand the meaning of education and, as a result, developed a stronger love of humanity.

11. Interview with Ilene Black (principal, Sumiton Elementary School), Sumiton, Alabama, May 18, 1992.

12. The North American operations of Kumon were restructured in 1993, and the decision was made to stop marketing in-school programs, which had always operated at a loss. Schools that wished to continue were allowed to do so, and as of October 1994 about 23,000 children were enrolled in U.S. school programs.

13. Such samples are not scientifically measured and cannot be considered representative of other schools. Their common factors are higher test scores in the computation portion of standardized tests, smaller gains in problem solving and an efficient system for grading worksheets. For example, Holy Trinity Episcopal Day School

in Bowie, Maryland, reported that school-wide averages (for 210 students in grades 1–6) increased from an average 72nd percentile in 1990 to the 88th percentile in 1992, and from the 80th percentile in problem solving in 1990 to the 86th percentile in 1992, on the Massachusetts Achievement Test (*Kumon Kronicles*, September 1992, p. 3).

14. Telephone interview with Gus Schulmann (principal, Atlanta Primary School, Atlanta, Texas), Nov. 12, 1992.

15. Patricia L. Hollingsworth, "A Reformer's 'Retrogression': Speaking Out for Kumon Mathematics," *Education Week*, Vol. XI, No 13 (Nov. 27, 1991), pp. 23–25.

16. In 1994, a 300-page training book was introduced into Kumon instructor training procedures in the U.S.

17. Interview with Fujiwara (Houston, Texas), March 28, 1992.

18. Telephone interview with Dave Walker (general manager, Kumon Mathematex, Houston, Texas), May 30, 1991.

19. Anthony Millican, "Presence of Koreans Reshaping the Region," *Los Angeles Times*, Feb. 2, 1992, p. 5.

20. Japanese students indeed score among the highest in many international standardized tests of math. But the Japanese Ministry of Education is concerned that Japanese children also have the highest rate of disliking mathematics. The ministry is recommending in its guidelines that more time be spent in the classroom on *kadai gakushū*, in which children must create their own problems using rules and applications.

21. Interview with Kyūzaki Yukie (piano instructor), Dallas, Texas, Nov. 8, 1992.

22. Interview with Fujiwara, March 28, 1992.

23. As of May 1994, Anne Hui reported enrollment of 1,152 in her franchise and Lynda Montis a total of 946.

Section IV

Path and guidance

As we have seen, the development of strong emotional bonds in early stages of learning is the foundation for the changing tasks of learning in the child's life. The emotional bond is a powerful motivator, and it accustoms the child to being led through the steps of a task without questioning the process as a whole. Teachers move the children from emotional engagement to reliance on the teacher as their guide along the path of learning. Whatever anxiety the child feels is attended to very early in the process. Teachers are free to work on building up a distinct set of traits or characteristics; they are involved in guidance.

Guidance is expressed by the word *shidō* in Japanese culture and covers a wide range of notions. Modern conceptions of guidance appear to have their most recent roots in early Meiji ideas about teaching and learning. Dore argued that in the late Tokugawa there was a widespread belief that *all* human beings were "responsive to moral appeals" (Dore, 1973:401–2). Hall notes that around 1881, teachers were adjured to embody good moral behavior and to exemplify Confucian values (Hall, 1973, 352–3). At the very outset, the nascent Japanese school system was filled with the strong ideal that learning was a moral activity and teachers were moral exemplars.

One of the foremost proponents of strong guidance in education was Mori Arinori, the first Minister of Education (1885–9). Mori was convinced that teachers in his day were undisciplined and weak, unfit to inculcate the virtues needed for leadership. Mori dramatically reformed the nation's incipient normal schools by placing heavy emphasis on military drill (*heishiki taisō*) and by promulgating a series of rules that governed life in these schools with military precision (Hall, 1973, 424). Mori promoted the philosophy that the state and scholars should guide the people in attaining correct knowledge or wisdom. The school, in Mori's view, was a tool for moral instruction. Mori was responsible not only for articulating the state's *right* to educate children but also for demanding that the school be in the business of moral instruction.

Mori's reforms had tremendous repercussions for the school system. Cleaning, practicing drills, and managing the school became an essential part of teacher training and came to be an accepted part of the teacher's work. The increased conformity of teacher training occurred simultaneously with the militarization of the nation and the increasingly rigid school governance. How teachers (particularly left-wing or socialist teachers) responded to the increased rigidity and militarization of the educational system is crucial in understanding the extent to which certain elements of guidance gained powerful legitimacy during the Meiji and Taisho (1912–25) periods. Teachers reacted to the increasing control over their lives and their increased school duties not by refusing extra duties (teachers, by and large, did not advocate the role of teacher as academic specialist) but rather by trying to exert more control over *how* the school would be run and what values would be taught.

Teacher-led reform movements of the Taisho and early Showa (1926–35) periods focused on students developing their own values and attitudes (*taido/kachikan*) while promoting group camaraderie (*nakama zukuri*). These movements, variously designated as "free education" or "free training" (*jiyu kyōiku/kunren*), emphasized that students should learn to govern themselves through their teacher's examples. Already the ideal had coalesced that school and classroom constituted a miniature household or society (*kazokuteki no issho shakai*), an idea very close to *shudan seikatsu,* the group lifestyle that is perpetuated in modern Japanese middle schools. The moral character of the child was to be stimulated and nurtured under the supervision of the teacher.

The teacher as moral guide is still a powerful, if contested, notion in Japanese society (Yang, 1993). The term "guidance" evokes several key concepts: the moral nature of education, teachers as moral guides, and the importance of nonacademic material in schools. LeTendre and Fukuzawa show how notions of guidance are expressed in day-to-day school routines. LeTendre's teachers are concerned with giving children proper *seito shidō* (student guidance). Fukuzawa demonstrates that *seikatsu shidō* (lifestyle guidance) is a central concern of the middle school experience. Both authors pay particular attention to times when there has been a disruption in the normal process.

Russell shows how ideas of guidance have been adopted in one of Japan's largest private cram-school chains. Russell describes methods employed in teaching mathematics – the emphasis being on developing persistence, minute guidance by the teacher, and the ordered presentation of knowledge. The older the child gets, the more emphasis is placed on developing endurance, patience, and determination. The metaphor of learning as a path and of the teacher as a leader or guide is common both in and out of school.

These essays demonstrate that in school or out, *shidō* is a powerful cultural metaphor for learning and teaching as children begin to enter the adult world. In both essays, the overwhelming cultural metaphor driving the role of teacher is that of guide. Whether teachers are to be moral exemplars or to help inculcate certain traits, teaching is far more than the presentation of knowledge.

Shidō: the concept of guidance
GERALD LETENDRE

Introduction

Murata is small even for a 7th grader, and standing before his seniors in the fencing club, Miuchi and Yabushita, he appears a sling-less David facing two Goliaths. But as Mr. Yamagata (Murata's homeroom teacher and coach of the fencing club) and Mrs. Kawaguchi (the chair of the 9th-grade teachers) look on, a tear forms and runs down *Yabushita's* face. With great effort *he* apologizes for taking Murata's money. After Yabushita finishes, Miuchi – the captain of the fencing club – acknowledges that *he* should have returned the $300 that older boys in the club had taken from Murata over the past six months. Miuchi declares:

It was my fault entirely. I did not fulfill my responsibilities as captain of the fencing club. I let the club down.

While the teachers know that Murata offered most of the money to the older boys – and that he stole the cash from his parents' cafe – at this point, they treat the incident as the sole responsibility of the senior boys in the club. In one-on-one interviews with Yabushita and Miuchi, Mrs. Kawaguchi has relentlessly pounded home the point that because they are seniors *(senpai)* it was their duty to set a positive example and ensure that other members of the club did not break club rules. This formal apology, then, has been orchestrated more for their benefit than for Murata's. In Mrs. Kawaguchi's opinion, it is crucial to the educational success of the two older boys that

This essay is condensed from a version that originally appeared in the *Journal of Japanese Studies* (Winter 1994).

they reflect on how they failed in their role as seniors and be prepared to make amends.

The "Murata incident," as I refer to it in my field notes, is a rich example of guidance (*shidō*).[1] In this essay I analyze the basic rationales that constitute the Japanese institution of guidance. Guidance is central to the learning process in Japanese secondary education and appears to function in many other Japanese organizations, such as banks and monasteries (see Rohlen and Hori, this volume). Guidance encodes basic ideas and assumptions about the relationship between teacher, learner, and the task, but it is also a set of procedures and techniques which appear again and again in Japanese learning situations.

The Murata incident is challenging because the learning cycle had clearly broken down inside the fencing club. This situation called for a realignment of ideal and real, and in the teacher's actions we are able to gain a glimpse of the organizational bodies (committees, classes, clubs) and curricular strategies (reflection papers, teacher-as-counselor), as well as the set of rationales teachers and learners asume to inhere in the situation. *Shidō,* as a term, denotes the techniques, organizations and rationales, but I will use the term "guidance" by itself in this essay to refer to the idealized set of rationales.

The expression of guidance in the schools

Student: This morning on my way to school I ran into my senior Maezawa (*Maezawa-senpai*). He said, "Don't give me that look!" I was really upset.

Teacher: What class is he in? Is he a special ed. student? If he continues to bother you, let's talk.

(Excerpt from a student's Lifestyle Diary)

In most middle schools, students fill out daily diaries (*seikatsu dayori/noto*), writing down how many hours they have studied, special things they have done, and problems that are bothering them. Students hand their diaries over to their homeroom teacher on a daily or weekly basis, and the teacher returns the diary with comments. It was through such a diary that Murata's behavior first came to light: members of the fencing club noted that there were odd things going on in the club. Mr. Yamagata, who had just taken over as coach of the club, investigated and discovered just how serious the problem was. These diaries, then, are an essential tool in what teachers call "life guidance" (*seikatsu shidō*).

Life guidance is an informal term used by teachers to denote the basic philosophy that children need to learn a correct style of living – manners, deportment, responsibility, etc. In the official curricular guidelines put forward by the Ministry of Education, this term is rarely used because of its association with left-wing teacher movements before and after World War II. The Ministry of Education prefers to use the term "student guidance" (*seito shidō*) to refer to issues of guidance, though these usually refer to problems that go beyond minor disruptions in the daily routine. When explaining the term "life guidance" to me, teachers emphasized the importance of the daily rhythm and pattern. For teachers, helping students realize a highly routinized regimen of study, extracurriculars and play was key to the educational success of the child.

In their Lifestyle Diaries students are required to detail their activities, often down to the minute. Teachers discourage or encourage certain behaviors. "Aren't you watching a little too much TV?" "You did well in the relay race." The day-to-day life of the pupil becomes a text which teachers comment on and attempt to modify, just as a child's actions and participation were "texts" for the teachers in Kotloff's and Sato's schools (see Kotloff and Sato, this volume). But the diaries also serve as a means of private communication between student and teacher. Several women teachers noted that girls would use the diary as a confidential way to ask about "women's concerns" (menstruation, breast development). Through the use of these diaries, teachers can maintain effective lines of communication with their large classes.

The diaries are part of a series of activities and events that allow teachers to form a strong emotional connection with the homeroom class. In the daily life of the school, the contact between homeroom teacher and class forms the core of the guidance process. In Murata's class, Mr. Yamagata (the homeroom teacher) attends the morning meeting and end-of-the-day meeting. He eats with the class and dons a sweatsuit to take part in the daily cleaning. He accompanies the class on all school outings.[2] When Murata's class sang in the school competition, Mr. Yamagata sang as a member of the class, not as the director. This emotional connection or sense of solidarity is crucial, teachers stated, in motivating and guiding children. Teachers who lacked such connection generally had more disruptive classes.

Students also formed deep attachments with the teachers who supervise the various clubs and extracurricular activities. After the homeroom, clubs are the most common place that teachers attempt to modify student behavior. Mr. Mizuno, a former elementary school teacher and head of the guidance department (*shidō-buchō*), said, "There are some who equate club activity with student guidance." Club participation approaches 90% among first-year middle schoolers in this prefecture – which is partially indicative of the enjoyment children take in these activities. In elementary school, Murata was not successful at sports because of his small size, and upon entering middle school, he joined a club he had not tried. He felt fencing was something he might be good at. Because clubs play such a key role in the overall guidance structure, the fact that Murata's seniors were lax enough to accept money from him was a source of great concern to the teachers.

As Mrs. Kawaguchi remarked, juniors are expected to learn to obey their senior's orders without complaining. The senior member's power can easily be used to pressure or extort junior members, and this kind of problem is not uncommon in middle schools. It was imperative for the teachers to regain the trust of the fencing club members in the senior–junior relationships by calling on Miuchi and Yabushita to take public responsibility for what they had done. Like Mrs. Kawaguchi, most teachers are of the opinion that clubs are crucial to guiding students in learning the adult norms of conduct in socially stratified situations. Club activities are essential in training students to behave in a group (*shūdan seikatsu*). The notion of this kind of group life, however, is distinct from the training described in the early life of the child by Kotloff, Sato, and Lewis (this volume).[3]

From the earliest days of the Meiji on, one function of middle schools or upper-elementary schools was to cultivate and complete the character development of students. Clubs continue to play a vital role in character development within the modern school system. While children in elementary schools are expected to learn to live in groups where mutuality and communality were the overarching concerns, in middle school the concern transfers to functioning as part of a chain of command. One learns to "endure" hardships for the sake of the group and to follow the orders of seniors. While middle schools are no longer the elite training institutions they were 100 years ago, teachers still see that at this age it is appropriate for children to begin to act out distinctions in seniority and differentially assign responsibilities within committees and clubs. Many teachers associate learning this hierarchy with the clubs.

> Mr. Mizuno: A major difference between middle schools and elementary schools is the student's sense of senior–junior relations (*senpai–kōhai*). You really don't find that sense of senior and junior in elementary school.
>
> Myself: What causes this?
>
> Mr. Mizuno: It is the clubs . . . I guess that it is a tradition. There is this idea that seniors should teach juniors. Elementary school children do not have this sense of responsibility for teaching others, but that sense is strong in the clubs.

Clubs are also a primary way of dealing with students who exhibit behavior that disrupts the classroom routine. Clubs offer a way for children with little hope of entering a good high school to meaningfully participate in the life of the school. In direct contrast to American schools, where absenteeism, low grades or breaking school rules are commonly punished by suspension from clubs, students who misbehave were encouraged to take part in club activities in the schools I worked in. If widespread infractions of club rules occur, usually the whole club is punished. Some members of the baseball team at a neighboring high school were caught drinking beer on school grounds. All club activities were suspended for a week, and the members whiled away their time in a classroom writing reflection papers (*hanseisho*) about how they could improve their "character."

Many of the major social events in the school center on club activities or competitions. Although in comparison to American schools, competitions between schools are infrequent. When these events do occur, they are major social events: often a one- or two-day competition in which all schools in the district compete to see who is champion. Teams like Murata's reverberate with the ideal that each member is part of a team, and a team with a long history. This sense of continuity is further emphasized in the prizes awarded.

Individuals and teams receive certificates, but the grand prizes (e.g., trophies and flags) are awarded to the school. Shortly after the Murata incident, the baseball team won the city-wide tournament and brought home the championship flag. The club manager wrote the school name and year on a white banner and attached it to the flag. There were already 30 or 40 banners attached from previous winners, including one from a branch middle school that had ceased to exist. At a school-wide ceremony, the captain of the team officially presented the flag to the principal and the students applauded the team for "winning one for the school."

Because clubs are so vital to the guidance system of the school, Mrs. Kawaguchi and Mr. Yamagata wanted to reestablish the fencing club hierarchy in a correct way to manage and discipline the situation as quickly as possible. As seniors, Miuchi and Yabushita were held responsible and forced to reassert their leadership role. They were ordered to collect money from all the other fencing club students who had taken Murata's money and return it to him, which they did at the time of the formal apology. Mrs. Kawaguchi consciously orchestrated a series of events that illustrated to Miuchi and Yabushita the mistakes they had made and the moral lessons they should learn, including hours of writing reflection papers. She specifically described to Yabushita the shame he should feel and the "resolve" to correct his mistakes that such shame should bring.

As the 9th-grade committee chair, Mrs. Kawaguchi felt it was her responsibility to make sure that 9th graders Yabushita and Miuchi received proper counseling. Both boys were entering a crucial time in their life, preparing for the upcoming high school entrance examination. Coordinating her efforts with other teachers, Mrs. Kawaguchi repeatedly met with the two boys and had them write reflection papers, comparing the papers for minor differences and then sometimes scolding them for up to half an hour. She called an after-school meeting with Yabushita's parents. The next day I asked her how it went.

Oh, it was a great success. His mother cried, and his father got angry and shouted. When we see that [parental reaction] we know the student will change for the better. Yabushita-kun was very moved and he also cried.

Mrs. Kawaguchi and Mr. Yamagata realized that the break-down in the club hierarchy was a far more pressing problem than Murata's troubles. While they did not ignore Murata (Mr. Yamagata spent hours talking with him after school), their immediate concern was re-establishing order in the fencing club. Mrs. Kawaguchi's approach – working on the boys' emotional attitude as well as their overt behavior – was typical. Her scoldings and lectures focused on the attitude and feelings that they should have displayed, as well as on the negative emotional reactions of teachers and club members to their failure. In this way, she attempted not only to remediate the situation but to use the situation as a means to further develop the character of the two boys. Her guidance was as much aimed at developing a proper sense of remorse as recognizing what was wrong with the behavior. Indeed, Mrs. Kawaguchi appeared to place more emphasis on what she deemed to be the correct emotional response.

The intensive attention paid to emotions is central to the operation of guidance, and is readily seen in the duties and actions of other staff members and committees that teachers rely on when things go wrong. The school nurse, for example, often can play a substantial role in student guidance. The image of the nurse is a tender one (*yasashii/shinsetsu*). Ms. Hokubei, the nurse at Murata's school, explained to me: "The chair of student guidance does the strict (*kibishii*) guidance, I do soft (*yasashii*) guidance. Whatever problem children come with, I just listen. I never criticize or scold. I just give the children a chance to talk out their problems."

Mrs. Hokubei plays an important role as an empathetic ear to students. Several times she reported to me that she teamed up with the head of the guidance committee to counsel students. He would do the scolding and admonishing; she would listen to the student's concerns. Mrs. Hokubei also played an important role in that she gave teachers daily reports on who had complained of a headache or stomach ache or who was having her first menstruation. She paid a great deal of attention to physical signs of poor health or stress – the condition of the nails, eyes and hair of students. She also had the duty to weigh and measure all students semi-annually. She coordinated the nutrition campaigns with the health committee, advising parents (mothers) what to put in their child's lunches.

Complaints of stomach aches, dizziness or lack of sleep were taken seriously by Mr. Yamagata and Mrs. Hokubei alike. Teachers believe that lingering illnesses of the body usually indicate problems of an emotional nature. Students who have chronic fatigue, who bite their nails, and whose hair is not shiny and well kept are students that teachers worry about. These outward manifestations indicate that students have some troubles (*nayami*) which they have not expressed. Both homeroom teachers and the nurse may call these children in for private talks in the hopes of getting the children to discuss their troubles. The child's entire range of emotional and physical experiences are studied by teachers and school staff when attempting to guide students. With extremely accurate information from several sources, teachers try to construct experiences that will bring the child's attitudes back in line with the ideal espoused by the school.

The role of the teacher

I'd like to say "Its's not my job" to all this extra work, but if I did, the principal would get very angry with me.
Homeroom teacher in a Nagoya middle school

The overall management of student problems is under the supervision of the student guidance department. A major, time-consuming responsibility of the department is to conduct checks on student uniforms, traffic behavior and inspections of various local "trouble spots." These checks occur on various schedules and with varying degrees of formality. All of them are aimed at preventing problematic behavior or accidents before they occur.

The vast majority of public middle schools have official uniforms, and incorrect attire (e.g., skirts too long or too short, pants too wide or too narrow) is interpreted as an indicator of rebellion and possible affiliation with the wrong crowd. Makeup and earrings are forbidden for girls. All the teachers I interviewed believed that outward appearance was a good indication of whether a student was prone to getting into trouble. Teachers feel that students who are disconnected from school and not intent on their clubs or studies generally do not take care of themselves and are weaker or more vulnerable to the influence of children with problematic behavior (*mondai kōdō*) or juvenile delinquents (*hiko shonen*).

The extent to which school rules and teachers' responsibility extend outside the grounds itself is most clearly seen in the checks that teachers do of local "hot spots" or trouble areas. While it is virtually impossible for urban high school and private middle school teachers to undertake such patrols, public middle schools, even in metropolitan centers, accept children from a limited neighborhood area. Depending on the number of outside school problems, teachers may check trouble spots once a semester or once a month.

During the student guidance meeting in June 1991 the major item on the agenda was the upcoming school vacation. Mr. Mizuno gave each teacher on the committee a circuit of stores and entertainment centers (such as "karaoke boxes" where small rooms can be reserved) to patrol once a week over the summer vacation. The circuits were about 5 miles in length and contained about 20 separate locations. Two female teachers complained about the size of the task and asked that the distance and number of establishments be reduced. However, *none* of the teachers complained about the task itself or remarked that it was an undue imposition or in conflict with their jobs as teachers.

The involvement shown by Mrs. Kawaguchi and Mr. Yamagata is typical. Teachers have many roles and responsibilities that go far beyond our notion of "teaching." That is, they are responsible for counseling students, weeding the school grounds, ordering the kerosene for stoves, and doing much of the accounting. Japanese schools are managed by the teachers with the assistance of one or two secretaries. After their first year, young teachers are expected to teach a full load, assume a homeroom position and sit on several committees. This managing work, which many teachers would like to avoid, constitutes a major way in which guidance is actualized in the school.

Teachers cannot avoid this work because the Japanese school is organized around a set of divisions and committees concerned with managing the school. All tasks necessary to the running of the school are managed by teachers and have a set pattern; most duties are rotated; experienced teachers guide new teachers and students in the correct procedures. Junior teachers, then, expect guidance from their seniors, just as students expect guidance from teachers. All members of the school, from the principal to the cleaning lady, are expected to learn the appropriate tasks and instruct others when their term of rotation ends.

Academic instruction is just one of many components that make up the school. The basis of school organization in middle school is not the academic departments, but the divisions and committees concerned with school management. A teacher's primary affiliation is *not* with his or her department but with the *grade* he or she is a homeroom teacher of. Major curricular goals have both academic and social components. That is, teachers expect children to carry on with their studies of math while increasing their ability to manage and direct their work and the work of peers.

Teachers organize student committees in a pragmatic way that displays the connections they see between various tasks and the education of the students. The Student Guidance Committee, for example, deals with problem behaviors, as well as with student government, garbage disposal and cleaning! The underlying associations between these are not readily apparent to most Americans. When American teachers hear me describe how Japanese students clean the schools, many remark that this is an excellent system to prevent graffiti, as everyone will be "punished" by being forced to clean up the mess if vandalism occurs. Japanese teachers interpret the role of cleaning in a very different way. They believe that there is a strong link between caring for the school, self-governance or self-management and discipline. Cleaning instills in students a sense of pride in the school, and who would want to dirty something one is proud of? The aim is not to "punish" but to instill a sense of "ownership" in the appearance of the school.

The basic academic and counseling unit of the school is the homeroom. Each homeroom has several students "in charge" (*kakari*) who are responsible for day-to-day tasks. There is an "in charge" for taking attendance, for cleaning the boards, and for reporting the assignments in each subject matter. Positions on committees – student council, health committee, cultural festival committee – are elected or rotating positions. While these divisions among teachers and students serve utilitarian needs, they are at the same time activities in guidance. Students learn techniques for self-management (i.e., peer management) by direct experience with and connection to the self-governance of the school. "Teachers-as-managers" direct and model the kind of organizational routine that students should aspire to.

Every aspect of the students' lives – from the milk they drink to the clothes they wear – is supervised and managed by a committee. Crucial to this division of labor is the fact that the entire school is managed *by teachers and students,* with teachers occupying the guiding or managing roles. For each teacher committee, there is usually a corresponding student committee, and students are assigned specific tasks, such as delivering the kerosene to the art room in winter. Moreover, senior students are expected to instruct junior students in the correct way to carry out their tasks, just as a teacher would.

The organization of the school is formed on a parallel hierarchy of students and teachers. Diagram 1 depicts the major roles that students and teachers play in managing the school. By rotating through many positions, teachers learn the entire workings of the school after 5 to 8 years, and can thus instruct new teachers as well as students in how to conduct their duties. Similarly, students will have rotated through all but the top ranks by the end of their 3 years. A major portion of a child's time in middle school is devoted to learning how to work in highly organized, hierarchical patterns of work.

The elaborate organization of committees is not constructed solely for the purpose of getting a task done. Foreign teachers and exchange students alike have voiced their exasperation with the redundancy and inefficiency with which most tasks are carried out. Schools could be cleaned, managed and supplied in a manner much more efficient in terms of cost and time. When I made such "efficiency" suggestions to teachers, they pointed out that the tasks were essential to the students' education and emotional well-being. Teachers regard the various duties as a major part of education – ways to teach students how to work with others and how to care for themselves.

Teachers expect to learn their jobs over time and expect older teachers to guide them. Younger teachers are usually popular with students, but among teachers there is no expectation that a new teacher will be a "star." In our society we have the ideal of the fresh, young teacher pumping "new life" into a school. The Japanese ideal I encountered most often linked an enthusiastic

Diagram 1. *Hierarchy of teacher and student positions*

Principal	Student body president
Vice-principal	Student body vice-presidents
Head of curriculum affairs division	
Head of student guidance division	
Grade committee chairs 9th	Class presidents 9th
8th	8th
7th	7th
Heads of other divisions and various committee chairs	Heads of student committees
Homeroom Teachers	"In-charges"
Teachers without homeroom duties and nonteaching staff	Member of various student committees

Note: Club advisors and/or team captains are also important positions in terms of the school hierarchy but are not directly concerned with *overall* school management. Each club or team is responsible for the care and maintenance of its own equipment and area, as well as its own bookkeeping.

young teacher with a seasoned veteran who guided the youngster's energetic attempts. The idea that one is not a "veteran" *(betoran)* teacher until one has had 15 years or so of classroom experience demonstrates the expectation that teachers, like students, need to learn from their seniors and from years of hardwon experience.

The elements of guidance

The elements of guidance form a package of ideas and rationales that are by definition central to the meaning of middle school. It must be kept in mind that various guidance processes are not isolatable phenomena, and to talk of guidance or *shidō* in an abstract way is to artificially disentangle the word and its meanings from the complex social setting. However, such analysis clarifies the assumptions which underlie the systems of meaning that teachers and students rely on. By clarifying the elements of guidance, we can learn what expectations Japanese have for teaching and learning in schools and perhaps in other organizations as well.

For the sake of brevity, I have outlined the elements of guidance below. These elements have been culled from an analysis of field notes and taped interviews that covered a wide range of actions, activities and year-long processes that occur in classrooms and clubs, in school and outside of school. Through the examples presented in the previous sections, I hope to have given the reader evidence of how these elements come into play in the day-to-day context of schooling. Remember that here teacher does not mean "school teacher" but anyone senior to the learner. Thus, the principal is a teacher to the head of the guidance department, just as the captain of the fencing team (Miuchi) was expected to be a teacher to Murata.

The order and the division of the elements is one that I have imposed:

1. Knowledge is acquired in an experiential process that has mental, emotional, ethical and physical components.
2. Teacher and learner study the same thing: i.e., there is a correct form or order to the acquisition and interpretation of knowledge – one path, one set of discoveries.
3. The teacher is expected to have already successfully completed the path or to be more advanced than the learner.
4. The learner, not knowing the path, is dependent on the teacher.
5. The teacher will model the correct interpretations or correct skills, and the learner will imitate these.
6. Exertion is crucial to knowing – the teacher may set the learner to strenuous and difficult tasks.
7. Basic skills are seen as containing all the elements for complex mastery – the teacher may require a repetition of the basics at any point on the path.
8. Intense effort and a sense of appreciation of effort are necessary to successfully completing the path. But there must be balance or harmony in the learner's emotional relationship with the task at hand.
9. To sustain the learner's emotional balance, the teacher encourages an appreciation of effort and sacrifice in the learner. This is often accomplished by the teacher demonstrating his or her commitment to the learner's progress and affirming that the teacher and learner share one goal: the learner's success.
10. Reflections on past actions – success or failure – are essential for correcting problems and consolidating gains.

The Murata incident alone highlighted many of these assumptions. Mrs. Kawaguchi felt that Miuchi and Yabushita had not been good teachers, and hence Elements 3 and 5 were not holding. This meant that other members of the club could be adversely influenced (E4). Her solution was to instruct the boys in the correct attitude they should have and explain why they should feel this way (E5 and E2). She also put them through grueling interviews and reflection-paper writing sessions (E6 and E10). Finally, she orchestrated a formal apology where Miuchi and Yabushita could demonstrate the "correct" behavior of seniors in such a predicament. Once they had suffered through this process and made amends, Mrs. Kawaguchi was confident that they would be good and successful students. She specifically explained that because the two had demonstrated their resolve and commitment, teachers in the school would not label the boys as trouble-prone or juvenile delinquents (E9).

The second element of guidance sets up the notion that teaching and learning are two sides of one process: guiding and exploring a path. The teacher points out the way for the learner; both are assumed to be on the same path, the teacher having more experience. Teaching and learning are never just intellectual activities – they are part of a process with moral, emotional and physical components: *shidō*. In their concern for the boys' character, Mr. Yamagata and Mrs. Kawaguchi openly displayed their preoccupation with morality. Other scholars have also argued that Japanese schools constitute a moral community (Rohlen, 1983:199–206). Within such a community, the teacher may set the learner to difficult tasks, and the learner is expected to devote all of his or her energies to perfecting the tasks.

As the teacher may at times set the learner to tasks which seem to have no relevance to the path, an effective teacher–student relationship requires trust. Such a relationship is not possible unless learner and teacher have an emotional tie based on a shared set of goals and values. The *ideal* relationship between teacher and learner is that of guide and follower, master and disciple: an emotional relationship where knowledge is slowly built up through correct experience and interpretation.[4] Committees, homerooms and clubs create an atmosphere where teachers can demonstrate the correct usage, skills and manners appropriate to the situation. Hierarchy and complex organization set the stage for teacher–learner interactions.

The elements of guidance encode the notion that individuals share a common path and that coordinated efforts ensure success for *all*. It is too simplistic to assume that many Western educational innovations have failed in Japan because they are based on an "individual" culture and Japan has a "group" culture. Rather, the problem lies in the images or symbols of learning in Japanese culture, which show that people on one path succeed as a group but fail as individuals.

Conclusion

While elementary school socializes children to many of the nuances of Japanese life, middle school is the child's introduction to hierarchical organization and adult patterns of teaching and learning. Many of the incongruencies we have seen in descriptions of Japanese teaching can be better understood if we note the abrupt transition in teaching style and focus that occurs between elementary and middle school. Entry into middle school signifies a child's first steps into adult life, and being a middle schooler means that the child must function in an organization replete with rigid social hierarchies and an intricate system of committees.

The Japanese middle school is a major disjuncture in the educational experience of children. The nurturing and "child-centered" atmosphere of elementary education is replaced by a very formal and rule-laden social setting (Peak, 1989). Up to middle school, children are allowed to just "grow." In middle school, children are trained, guided, and shaped. Within middle school, children experience an academic teaching style that is far less relaxed and comforting than the one they knew in elementary school. Upon entry into high school, the transition is complete. Teachers will no longer try to gain the attention of the learner, as Peak describes in her essay on the Suzuki method. While high school teachers will still guide students in making major decisions or in counseling on their emotional problems, students will be expected to seize whatever academic information the teacher offers. Sacrifice, effort and all-out devotion will be the hallmark of success.

In middle school, Japanese students are exposed to a model of organization and teaching that incorporates the hierarchy and complex social differentiation which we see in many other Japanese organizations. The classroom organization of elementary school does not provide such a model, for it focuses heavily on the close and "wet" emotional relations of peers (Lewis, this volume). Socialization into hierarchical organizations – the Japanese life of senior–junior relations; individual sacrifice; the near-total involvement with the institution – first occurs in middle school.

Many basic Japanese assumptions about social organization and learning in hierarchical situations would appear to be predicated on the model of guidance described in this essay. In diverse areas of Japanese life, expertise is assumed to flow from experienced to non-experienced personnel over a long period of time in a stable social situation. Japanese believe that group interaction is vital to an organization's ability to put knowledge to use. Effort and dedication are emphasized over ability. For most tasks, there is some notion of a pattern or form (*kata*) that should be learned by heart. Senior members are expected to be more versed in these patterns than junior members. And, perhaps most importantly, the social context is not viewed as something separate from learning, but rather as the place where learning occurs.

While students have been well socialized in middle school to expect that specific facts may be acquired by intense study – especially through memorization – they have simultaneously been well socialized in the elements of *shidō*. They will expect to learn from their seniors and to teach their juniors. For, throughout their middle school career, Japanese children have been shown that those who have gone before will guide newcomers along the path.

The *shidō* of the Murata incident was not an isolated incident; rather, it was a complex set of events and procedures which were adjusted to focus on the boys in the fencing club for a period of time. All of the techniques used – the interviews, reflection papers, formal apologies, and after-school counseling sessions – are part of the standard repertoire teachers usually employ in these situations. Underlying these techniques and procedures were the rationales embedded in the ideal of *shidō*. The elements of guidance defined how these processes were organized because the elements encoded or represented assumptions about the nature of the social world that defined the expectations both teachers and students had in their interactions with each other.

In Japanese schools, there is much more to guidance than

dealing with a child's problems. The overall goal of guidance is to promote a student's self-realization that is deeply embedded in networks of family and school (Okano, 1993). This approach is common in a wide variety of settings from schools to company-sponsored training sessions to therapy routines (see Hori and Rohlen, this volume, as well as Reynolds, 1980). Character is built up through various processes – group organization and management, school events, individual counseling and reflection papers. Understanding oneself in a Japanese school takes place in a group – a team readying for a sports festival or a choir practicing for the choral contest. Awareness of oneself and character development are simultaneous. To promote a child's sense of self is to promote a child's sense of duty, responsibility and awareness of his or her capacities.

Personality, a mixture of personal tastes, idiosyncratic traits, preferences, preferred styles of displaying emotions and problem-solving strategies, is understood to be unique to the individual in American schools. It flows from within the person outward – its growth is a process of increasing assertion of control as the individual gains autonomy over his or her life. By presenting a range of choices in the curriculum, the American school can facilitate an environment that encourages self-growth or discovery. But it is assumed in the West that the self will assert its preferences and "naturally" begin to display itself. Most importantly, the child is responsible for his or her own personality. Teachers may affect a child, but they cannot mold him.

"Personality" exists in Japanese classes and school. One boy's taste for *natto* (a pungent dish of fermented soybeans) or a girl's constant fidgeting are all part of the dense display of identity – nicknames, friendship alliances, family connections. School is centered on the development of character and premised on the assumption that children are naturally good, and that by providing them with well-directed and challenging tasks, character can readily be inculcated. The influence of key individuals, especially teachers, precipitates changes in the core of the child, channeling emotions and energy into patience, endurance, thoughtfulness and effort.

There appear to be striking similarities between the theories employed by Japanese teachers and the neo-Confucian philosophy which developed in the later half of the Tokugawa era.

Kaibara Ekken wrote:

Human nature is originally good, but in ordinary people this goodness is lost by the obscuration of the physical disposition and by human desires. The nature of all people is good and, based on this fact, they can be induced to activate their innate goodness. (Tucker, 1989:146)

Teachers regularly tried to activate students' good inner nature. Mrs. Kawaguchi firmly believed that Yabushita and Miuchi were good. The paradigm of guidance, around which the school is largely organized, makes the role of a Japanese teacher a guiding force on the child's character. Maturity implies the development of one's personality or one's character. An immature person is one whose character is "lacking," and a lack of character can be directly remedied by vigorously addressing the deficiency. A deficiency or disruption must be healed in our society by a specialist. Personality disorders are the province of psychologists and psychiatrists; deficits in knowledge are the province of teachers in the American system. In Japanese culture, there is no such distinction – teachers are involved in all aspects of the student's life.

At the heart of the personality–character distinction are fundamentally different ways that Japanese and Americans understand the developing core of the child. Emotional balance is a moral function in Japan because of the notion that a matured human self is integrated with other human beings around him or her. To be excessively independent is to be emotionally unbalanced – to be defective in character. Self-esteem is not the same as *jibun ni jishin ga aru* (believing in one's self). The Japanese emphasis on character-building rather than attention to personality disorders shows up in many areas. There is a struggle in Japanese schools to motivate and push the child to build up a strong inner resolve while strengthening the child's awareness of his or her relations to others.

Epilogue

Months after the incident was uncovered, Mr. Yamagata was still watching Murata. Through the Lifestyle Diary, the homeroom meetings and club time, Mr. Yamagata had ample opportunities to observe the way Murata approached his peers and how they reacted to him. All of the teachers were concerned that Murata be able to make friends and find something in school that he could be proud of. Without such a connection, Mr. Yamagata mused, it might be extremely difficult for him to finish middle school and enter any kind of high school.

Miuchi and Yabushita were successfully ushered into local high schools. To the best of my knowledge, no mention of their role in the incident was passed on to their prospective high schools. Apparently, the teachers were satisfied that they both had displayed the proper remorse and had also shown the resolve to try to be better students and more responsible seniors. Having played a major role in the initial stages of the problem, Mrs. Kawaguchi pulled back after the formal apology and allowed Mr. Yamagata to manage his homeroom and the club. In retrospect, I wonder if her role was meant to be as instructive to him as to the students. In her prompt response to Miuchi and Yabushita's behavior, was she guiding Mr. Yamagata on the path to being a veteran teacher?

Notes

1. *Shidō* is an institution – a reified social process including a core of activities *and* expectations that frame the way certain teaching and learning interactions unfold. Institutions have both symbolic and "logical" power – they are formulated on accepted "truths" and are also indispensable parts of the social reality (Meyer, 1994a; Meyer, 1994b; Scott, 1994). People will resist changing or abandoning an institution both because the rationale it is founded on is accepted uncritically and because to do so would require a dramatic shift in established patterns of meaning (Zucker, 1983; Jepperson, 1991).

2. Middle school and high school students take three major trips a year: short excursions (*ensoku*); overnight stays (*shukuhaku kenshū*); and study trips (*shūgaku ryōkō*). Prior to World War II, the study trips were often excursions to visit military practice areas or to see military equipment. Since World War II, school trips have generally been taken to cultural centers, to see a play, or perhaps even to a nearby park.

3. See also White (1987). As Fukuzawa argues, middle school forms a pivotal experience in the schooling experience of the Japanese adolescent. Historically, the early teens were seen as an appropriate time for youth to begin a stricter form of training than they had experienced at home or in the Temple Schools (*terakoya*). The harshness of middle school life compared with elementary life

reflects the belief that the early teens are a key transition point in the life course.

4. I am not arguing that learning in Japan is some Koan-like experience. The reality of nation-wide chains of prep and cram schools is ample evidence that in many situations learning equals memorizing vast amounts of facts. However, the primary association with learning, the ideal image of learning, is that to learn (*manabu*) is to know (*shiru*), to experience (*minarau*) and to realize (*satoru*).

The path to adulthood according to Japanese middle schools

REBECCA ERWIN FUKUZAWA

Descriptions of learning and teaching in Japanese schools suggest the existence of two different worlds. One labeled "holistic" emphasizes personal development and an experiential approach to learning. The other is a text-centered, lecture format geared to transmitting information necessary for university entrance exams. The first is characteristic of grade schools and preschools, the second of high school. The transition between these two worlds is the middle school (grades 7–9). Middle schools combine a lecture format for academic instruction with a broad range of "nonacademic" activities that emphasize the development of the "whole" person.

Middle schools are accurately labeled. They mark a key transition point in Japanese education. From preschool through the university level knowledge is increasingly specialized, and in this process middle school is the point when for the first time teachers are subject specialists. In Japan middle schools also reinforce a division between the academic and nonacademic sides of the curriculum. Japanese education focuses on the development of the whole person. The curriculum includes a wide variety of nonacademic activities – music, art, sports, field trips, clubs, ceremonies, homeroom time – designed to enhance the full development of the ("whole") person. In fact, the very definition of teaching encompasses not only transmission of knowledge but counseling, guidance and discipline – tasks

I am grateful to Thomas Rohlen, Jennifer Beer, Gerald LeTendre and two anonymous referees for many helpful suggestions on earlier drafts of this essay.

Reproduced by permission of the Society for Japanese Studies from *Journal of Japanese Studies,* 20:1 1994, pp. 61–86.

which in the United States are either viewed as parental or beyond the scope of teachers who are not counseling specialists.[1] Middle school retains the elementary school emphasis on the whole person but also puts increasing emphasis on an efficient teacher-centered approach to instruction geared to future entrance exams.

The nonacademic, enrichment, counseling, and disciplinary activities and the intensifying rigor of instruction establish an apparent set of pedagogical and developmental contradictions. While these are inherent to some degree in any system of education, they are notably polarized in Japan due to the marked emphasis each receives. The middle school sits longitudinally in the middle of this polarity. It also marks a pivotal juncture in the student's educational career (Rohlen, 1983:121). Compulsory education (to ninth grade) is an undifferentiated system – no streaming or special programs for the gifted, learning disabled or any other special group. At the end of middle school, students take entrance exams leading to hierarchically ranked high schools, then to even more extensively ranked universities. The lack of any formal differentiating mechanism before the end of ninth grade has led to the rise of cram schools called *juku* and other developments reflective of the real competition.[2] Thus in middle school the reality of stratification through exams confronts virtually all students and their parents, with future income, prestige and job security riding on the results.

Just as the school system begins to make concerted and high-stakes academic demands on them, middle school students find themselves experiencing the onset of puberty. Friendship, cliques and interest in the opposite sex assume primary importance in their lives, perhaps particularly within public schools which are co-educational. Students begin to develop a varied and independent social life, albeit somewhat tame by U.S. standards. However, unlike the United States, looming high school entrance exams define middle school life as properly an intense, academically focused time. Students are expected to settle down, to face up to the importance of exams and to adapt to the outside adult world in terms of future job and educational realities. The future weighs heavily and they must consider their ambitions, talents, family finances, and above all their own motivation and self-discipline in order to fulfill their ambitions. In the United States, adolescence is seen as a time of awakening individuality and of a gradual introduction to the privileges of independent adulthood. More freedom is the formula and the expectation. The two nations, despite the many similarities in curriculum, thus view teaching and learning in grades seven through nine in very different ways.

This essay asks how the Japanese middle school resolves its pedagogical and other contradictions and sets its stamp on the formation of "adulthood." Academic instruction and the myriad disciplinary and counseling activities labeled life-style management (*seikatsu shido*) are contrasted and their synthesis in a particular systematic approach is analyzed. The descriptions and analysis are drawn from field work done between 1983 and 1986 in three public middle schools in Tokyo referred to as Kita, Higashi and Nishi.[3] All three of the schools were "average" in a number of ways. They were located neither in the affluent central city or suburban districts nor in the poorer "low city" areas to the east. None of them was seriously troubled by major discipline problems of bullying or violence. Each matched the city-wide average of 94 percent for matriculation to high school.

Instruction

The majority of students' time in school is spent in instruction in nine basic subjects: Japanese, Math, Social Studies, Science, an elective (invariably English), Music, Health/P.E., Shop/ Home Economics. Of a total of 32 class hours per week, 27 were classified as instruction. The other five hours a week were allocated to health, moral, educational and occupational guidance, and special activities which are part of student guidance. Despite the importance of these five hours to the middle school goal of personal development, subject instruction dominated the school day.

Japanese public school teachers rarely deviated very far or very long from the text. Unlike teachers in the United States, who often tailor texts to local needs and their own teaching style, Japanese teachers are forced to adhere to the text because (1) the pace required to cover the material does not leave time for extras and (2) the national curriculum is the basis of high school entrance exams. Disregarding the text will handicap students in the competition for places in high school. In short, Ministry guidelines, Ministry approved texts and training for exams wrest control out of the hands of individual teachers and even individual schools.

Classroom organization

Teaching style and classroom organization were almost as homogeneous as the curriculum. All instruction was large group instruction. I found no multi-task organization of classrooms and small group work was rare in academic subjects (Japanese, Math, Social Studies, Science and English). This contrasts with the small group, hands-on approach found in elementary schools and illustrates that teachers are under pressure to provide "equal" education geared to the most efficient transmission of material for entrance exam preparation. Consequently, most classes were text-centered lectures.

Lecture classes in middle schools mean that student participation is limited to teachers stopping to briefly probe students for answers, opinions, or reiterations. There is minimal time for discussion of tangential topics, eliciting student opinions, or for organizing hands-on or experimental projects. This is in strong contrast to student-centered classes typical in early elementary schooling in Japan, where teachers often engage students through lesson-related activities in which students find their way to a teacher-determined awareness or understanding.

Okabe-sensei's English classes at Higashi epitomize the teacher-centered, text-oriented approach. A description of one of his typical classes from my field notes illustrates the style:

When Okabe-sensei walks into the class a few minutes after the bell has rung, the class slowly quiets down for the opening greeting. A student calls out "Stand up!" and the students rise. "Attention!" he calls, and most students stand straight without talking. "Nakamura, be quiet!" Okabe-sensei reprimands one boy. "Bow!" says the voice. Everyone bows and sits down. As the noise subsides, Okabe-sensei says, "Now take out your textbooks and turn to page 14. Today we will begin Lesson 4. This lesson deals with comparatives and superlatives. In Japanese we use *motto* (more) and *ichiban* (the most) plus an adjective to express such differences. Please look at the key sentence at the bottom of the page. 'I am smaller than a whale,' " he reads. He translates the sentence into Japanese and explains the basic rule for forming English comparatives. "In English you add '-er' to some adjectives to form the comparative. Now let's listen to the tape."

He plays the tape recorder, and the students repeat the new words and the six sentences of text after the tape recorder as a group.

At the end of the tape he asks who has looked up the meaning of the words for this lesson. "Have you done your lesson preparation? Nakamura, what does 'ocean' mean?" The boy quickly turns around to face the front. "You don't know? I thought so. You'd better prepare next time. Kubo, what about you?" This student is unable to answer either. "Sasaki," he says, calling on a better student to get the answer. This goes on until the new vocabulary words have been defined. He instructs the students to get out their notebooks and copy what he puts on the board. He puts up the key sentence. Under it he writes "S be (verb) + er than (noun)" and gives a Japanese translation.

"I want you to memorize this sentence." He repeats the sentence and asks five students to stand up and read it from the book and then another two to repeat it without looking. He seems to call on the less able students to read and better students to repeat without looking. Next he reads the first sentence and calls on a student to stand and translate it. "Very good," he says of the performance and repeats the translation. The class is very quiet as students write the translation under the English in their books. He continues to call on better students to translate, correcting and supplementing their translations. All students can answer. He then asks two students to read the whole dialogue. Just as the second student begins to read the last sentence, the bell chimes the end of class. Okabe-sensei has him finish reading. The students stand, bow, and class is dismissed.

Okabe's class was typical in that (1) digressions and discussion did not impede the efficient transmission of material; (2) personal opinions, jokes, [and] practical examples to make classes more relevant were rare; and (3) students were not involved in group problem-solving, trying to figure out the grammatical rule from examples themselves, as they might be in a more student-centered class.

Not all classes were as completely text-oriented and teacher-centered as this. Some teachers paused to bring in practical everyday examples and problems or to relate their personal experiences and opinions. Yet, few classes had even 15 or 20 minutes of really student-centered activities. On occasion, teachers gave students 5 to 10 minutes of independent work time at the end of the period. Invariably this time was spent doing comprehension questions and drills from workbooks designed to reinforce text material. In only 1 out of my 103 class observations used in the analysis did a teacher of Japanese give small groups of students time to discuss the relevance of a reading in the text to a contemporary problem – that of bullying in schools. Only 1 teacher out of 39 teachers regularly had students present text material to the class. This social studies teacher assigned groups of students sections in the seventh grade geography text. He reverted to lecturing the following year when he taught eighth grade history, a subject he deemed too difficult for student presentation. In academic subjects only science labs, scheduled once every two to three weeks, approached the more student-centered or experimental teaching methods.

In sum, compared to both early elementary school in Japan and many American middle schools, instruction in Japanese middle school classes is soberingly intense, fact-filled and routinized. Motivation must come from the student and self-discipline is at a premium. There is little, if any, provision for individual differences either in interests or abilities.

Evaluation

Teacher-centered, text-oriented classes were matched by evaluation methods that stressed individual mastery of material in the text. In academic subjects performance on written, short-answer, multiple-choice or fill-in-the-blank type midterm and final examinations overwhelmingly determined final grades. Neither verbal ability, nor class participation, nor the ability to work in groups, nor the ability to write well significantly affected grades.

Students received term grades on a numerical scale of five to one corresponding to the A to F scale used in the United States. To rule out grade inflation the Tokyo Board of Education set the percentages of each grade teachers could give according to a normal distribution curve. Thus for each subject 7 percent of all students in a grade level received 1's and 7 percent 5's. Another 24 percent received 2's, 38 percent 3's, and 24 percent 4's. Whether everyone does poorly or well, grade distribution stays the same, tying individual scores to the performance of the rest of the class.

Teachers of academic subjects based no less than 60 percent of grades on exam scores. In nonacademic subjects (art, music, health/P.E., home economics/shop), written exams accounted for approximately 40 percent of final grades. Midterms and finals usually accounted for 70–80 percent of grades in academic subjects. One social studies teacher said he calculated 70 percent of grades from midterms and finals, 20 percent from quizzes and homework, and 10 percent from attitude. A science teacher gave two quizzes which counted for 16 percent of the grade. Midterms and finals accounted for the remaining 84 percent. He subtracted points on an ad hoc basis for poor attitude. One English teacher said he derived 90 percent of grades from exams and 10 percent from attitude. In practice, he determined grades solely from exams, then docked students with "attitude problems" as much as a whole numerical score on the report card.

Other nontest forms of evaluation had almost no place in final grades. Teachers did assign book reports in Japanese class and independent science or social studies projects for summer homework, but they contributed little to final grades. One science teacher assigned independent science projects for summer homework but weighted them as only one part of his quiz grade, which comprised only 20 percent of the final grade. Even the teacher who used student presentation of class material counted the presentation as only a nongraded homework assignment. Together with lecture style classes, the weight of examinations in determining final grades stresses individual comprehension of a specific block of codified information, prefiguring, of course, the form of high school entrance examinations.

Juku *and classroom instruction*

The wide variety of types of *juku* which compensate for the public school system's lack of individualized instruction and differentiating mechanisms before the high school level have a substantial yet equivocal effect on classes. On the one hand, *juku* probably dampen the demands for already overburdened teachers to provide extensive after-school or vacation remedial help to students who have fallen behind. At each of my field schools, grade level faculty teams established some kind of informal remedial tutoring for struggling second- and third-year students. Yet as teachers admitted, they could not provide enough help, nor did their help solve the basic problem of what to do with students who were not keeping up with the curriculum. *Juku* fill this gap. They may also heighten students' awareness of the need for serious study, reinforcing the disciplinary and academic messages of school. The more frequent exposure to demands for study and information on the realities of competition may motivate students to pay greater attention to their lessons.

On the other hand, many teachers expressed guardedly negative reactions to *juku*. *Juku* undermine teachers' authority as subject specialists: even though they may be as knowledgeable as *juku* teachers, public school teachers cannot express the extent of their knowledge because they must follow the curriculum. *Juku* teachers can provide more specialized knowledge and training for exams. Teachers also felt that *juku* attendance essentially undermined classroom discipline. A common complaint was that students attending "express" *juku* aiming at entrance to elite schools became bored and disrupted class because they were so far ahead of their regular classes.

Summary

To an American observer this picture of Japanese instruction looks decidedly uninspiring and old-fashioned. At best it seems an efficient approach for conveying masses of information. In the United States the newest pedagogical trends emphasize both student-centered or cooperative learning and incorporation of "enrichment" or nonacademic content – art, music, drama, physical activity – into academic subjects. The goal is the participation of all students in class by teaching to the diverse learning styles of different students.[4] By implication, total reliance on lectures alienates many students who cannot succeed in the traditional classroom setting. If lecture-style classes have been so alienating, why are Japanese schools not plagued by alienation and consequent problems of discipline and deviance?

In fact, by several indices the middle school is the most problematic level of Japanese schooling. Over the past ten years statistics in the Government White Paper on Youth regularly show the highest rates of bullying, violence, and school refusal in Japan among middle school youth. Compared to the problems of drugs and violence in the United States, Japanese school problems of deviance and student motivation seem mild, although they are of great concern to educators and the public in Japan.

Instead of incorporating nonacademic content into academic courses, Japanese middle schools pursue a different approach both to promote student involvement in schools and to create social order conducive to lecture-style classes. The Japanese middle school curriculum includes a large but separate dose of nonacademic activities. Japanese middle school students actually spend proportionately more time on nonacademic subjects and activities than their American counterparts. Some activities, such as the weekly "required club" period or long homeroom periods, are part of the weekly schedule. Others like field trips, ceremonies, special events, and preparation time for special events pepper the school calendar with so many breaks from regular classes that there are few weeks when classes are not cut to accommodate some special activity. Along with extracurricular clubs, these special activities are designed to increase students' participation and sense of belonging to the school. Compared to the United States, Japanese middle schools spend less time on academics but use a more efficient, focused method of information transfer, which in turn allows more time for the nonacademic side of the curriculum. The nonacademic side of middle school also includes the concept of life-style guidance (*seikatsu shido*).

Life-style guidance

Life-style guidance is a set of disciplinary practices meant to mold student life-styles and attitudes both in and out of school. It encompasses the kinds of classroom management or disciplinary activities familiar to American teachers but is more far-reaching in its meticulous regulation of the students' use of time, their appearance, movements and their home life. The goals are healthy social, emotional, and physical development; optimal academic performance; and the early detection and prevention of discipline problems.

Assumptions of life-style management

Several assumptions I have distilled from teachers' comments underlie the methods and philosophy. First, discipline is inseparable from academic instruction. Second, the effectiveness of control rests on warm interpersonal relations between students and teachers. Third, affection alone is not enough; schools can and should engineer a social environment organized to support school goals. Fourth, teachers should guide all students toward one explicit ideal of student behavior. Fifth, the goals of both school and home – the success of the child – are identical, and require home–school cooperation.

While teachers everywhere believe that discipline is crucial to the success of instruction, the lack of any mechanisms to isolate and segregate "problem" students in Japanese schools tightly couples the success of academic instruction for all students to the teacher's ability to maintain control over the most disruptive, unmotivated members of the class. Where mixed ability classrooms are the norm and tracking or programs for students with special needs nonexistent, disruptive students cannot be relegated to lower tracks or classes for the learning or emotionally disabled. Special education classes exist only for the physically and mentally handicapped. Nor can disruptive students be removed from class or suspended from school; teachers maintained that the constitutional guarantee of equal educational opportunity prohibits such action. In lecture classes disruptions can impede the transmission of information to all students more than in a multitask or individualized class, where teachers can deal with individual discipline problems at the same time learning activities are taking place. Thus, the quality and quantity of instruction for the most highly motivated students are directly related to the behavior of the most problematic students, a point most teachers were acutely aware of. . . .

Teachers defined appropriate student behavior as *chūgakuseirashii,* literally "like or the very model of a middle school student." The suffix *rashii,* which can be affixed to most role or status names, implies a single normative ideal and image. Internalization of school rules and norms, realization of the importance of study and a buoyant, cheerful (*akarui*) personality are the marks of a *chūgakuseirashii* student. According to teachers, this is the single image against which all students should be measured.

Teachers everywhere stress the necessity for cooperation and understanding between school and home. In Japan schools set the agenda for cooperation by defining a life-style supportive of education and attempting to socialize parents to agreement with it.

"Understanding" students

These assumptions guide the development of a system of detailed life-style guidance and parent socialization tagged "understanding" (*rikai*) students. Discipline consisted of gathering information on the details of students' lives, feelings and attitudes, then persuading students to adopt the prescribed pattern embodied in the numerous routines of the school. This emphasis on life-style muted discussion of socioeconomic differences in academic performance. Privately teachers acknowledged the effect of socioeconomic status on academic success, particularly in extreme cases. Yet publicly they emphasized how life-style or basic daily habits (*kihontekina seikatsu shūkan*) determine academic success.

Much of the information gathered on students was a combination of daily activity surveys, diaries, and reflection essays (*hanseibun*). Activity surveys monitored the details of student time use and personal habits out of school: how they spent their free time, their money and even what they ate. Diaries monitored student feelings and activities, while essays probed student attitudes toward school.

Students filled out a "Daily Life Notebook" (Seikatsu Noto) every day to remind themselves of their assignments and to allow teachers to quickly evaluate their life-style and attitudes. Spaces for school days were a record of homework assignments, with a place to check review of the day's work and a block to use as a diary of events and feelings. The space for Sunday was a time line which students color coded [to indicate] how they spent their day. In the small section at the bottom entitled "Reflection on this Week," students checked off answers to questions about how virtuous they had been: Had they done good deeds, helped at home, studied enough, done their homework and been healthy? Teachers collected the notebooks at various intervals to check them and gain at a glance what they thought was pertinent diagnostic information to be used to help students improve their academic performance and to predict potential discipline problems.

Some teachers also used unstructured group diaries to tap

into students' after-school activities and private thoughts. Fixed groups of five to seven students in a class (*han*) circulated a bound notebook in which one person each day took turns writing a page or two about anything they wished. Although such unstructured diaries took teachers longer to read, they contained more revealing (and amusing) personal information than the "Daily Life Notebooks" in a way that strengthened the teacher–student relationship by allowing personal comments from both.

For example, one first-year girl wrote about how happy she was joining the band and, in contrast, how bored she was in classes. She added several paragraphs of personal questions and comments to her homeroom teacher: "Why does your hair stand up on end? Why don't you get a perm instead? Have you always been so short?" In response, the homeroom teacher commented in the margins:

> Good for you that you've joined a club. The percussion section is difficult, I hear. I'm sure with lots of work you'll become good. Do persist and don't give up easily. But about your studies. You don't understand why you're studying yet. For whose sake do you study? Certainly not to please me. Everyone has subjects they are weak in. What is important is to begin conquering them, isn't it? At any rate, don't run from your weaknesses. By the way, I'm going to get a haircut next week after the Cultural Festival when I'm not so busy.[5]

The group format also invites peer participation in the process of social control. Opening oneself leads not only to close interpersonal relationships, but to the discipline and scrutiny of society – in this case, one's classmates.[6]

Schools also employed time-use diaries the week before exams to help students learn to budget their time wisely. At the end of each day students color coded their time use: yellow for time in school; blue for personal time, e.g. bath and toilet, etc.; red for meals; green for free time; orange for study time at home; and purple for other lessons or *juku*. Every two or three days the teachers collected the records to check student time use and pencil in comments like:

> Cut your TV time to one hour after dinner! No wonder you stay up too late studying and are so tired the next day at school. You still have time before exams. Change your study habits today!

Good idea to get up early in the morning to study an hour before school. You're fresher in the mornings. I'm sure your efforts will pay off at exam time.

At Nishi, winter vacation reports included a record of New Year's present money (*otoshidama*). This extra page contained columns for the name of the person who gave the money, the giver's relationship to the student, the amount of the gift, and how much money was spent on what. The teachers' rationale for requesting this account was twofold:

Tabiki-sensei: We like to know how much money students have at their disposal and how they spend it. It's not good for middle school students to have too much money. They often buy inappropriate things like expensive clothes, snacks, or computer games which fuel competitive feelings among students who don't have large allowances because of family circumstances. If they save it, it's all right and we encourage them to save most of their money.

By requesting this information we also want to help students remember their obligations to the people that have given them money. We return the sheets to them to keep as a record so that they can refer to them even ten years from now when they will need to begin to repay their obligations.

Teachers used the information gleaned from these types of activity records not only to help students develop better life-style habits but also as an index of the quality of family life. Teachers often stated that "good" homes had a regular life-style where the mother was home to make meals and send children to bed at regular times, following the pattern prescribed by the school. Small details yielded significant information. For example, one teacher said that if a child marked that they were up until 11:30 or 12:00 at night talking, there was almost certainly a problem in the home.

The faculty at different schools also devised special probes to assess home life. For example, at Nishi teachers carried out an extensive survey of eating habits. The real purpose of the study, not conveyed to parents or students, was to assess the quality of family life.

Tabiki-sensei: When I first came to this school I was told that there were a lot of working mothers and single parents. A lot of fast-food (*instanto shokuhin*) or something like tempura on rice (*tendon*) which can be delivered with no salad or soup showed more clearly than anything else that the mother was working. When I asked later if the mother was working, the answer always jibed with the results of the food survey. I don't even need to pay a visit to the home when I survey eating habits.

Mothers who are not cooking well-balanced meals for their families are not sufficiently concerned with their children, the teacher implied.[7]

Each of these forms of information gathering codifies student responses in succinct, concrete terms to allow teachers to easily evaluate thirty to forty students. These small, concrete bits of information about life-style indicate factors teachers believe predict academic performance and discipline problems. Lifestyle is the outward manifestation of socioemotional adjustment.

Frequent essays and questionnaires probed students' socioemotional status more directly by monitoring student feelings toward school events, peers, and home life. At Kita the first-year teachers collected nineteen different kinds of questionnaires and essays over the course of one year. Most of these were "reflection essays" (*hanseibun*) about the various special events or turning points in the year, with titles like "Reflections on First Quarter," "Reflections on Athletic Field Day," "Becoming a Junior High School Student," etc.

The concept of *hansei* and the use of reflection essays are ubiquitous in Japanese society. *Hansei* may be translated as "reflection," but the term has overtones of self-criticism and confession measured against the yardstick of socially defined norms of behavior and emotions. In schools these essays were both a disciplinary tool to encourage errant students to repent their misdeeds and a means of socializing children to appropriate feelings and emotions. Reflection essays assess student attitudes toward school in order to determine understanding of the fundamental lessons of middle school life: the importance of cooperation, group life, doing one's utmost, and the value of all work. Just as there is a "correct" life-style, so there are "correct" emotions for particular events.[8]

Parent–teacher communication

Effective life-style guidance rests heavily on parents' communication with and "understanding" of the school, teachers claimed. Communication included supplying parents with frequent, detailed information on school events, teacher monitoring of home life and concerted attempts at home socialization. Teachers, not parents, set the agenda for communication, and they tell, rather than ask or consult or advise.

Schools sent home a large volume of notices which both informed and socialized.[9] Each grade at every school published a monthly newsletter containing pertinent announcements, teacher advice, and requests for parental support of school discipline. For example, one Nishi first-year newsletter for the month of May began with a list of the upcoming events, a long section on how to effectively study English (a new subject to first-year students) and a warning that forgotten items (*wasuremono*) were becoming a problem. Parents were requested to help their children develop routines to ensure that they would not forget their necessary books and supplies.

Teachers' concerns usually set the agenda in parent–teacher meetings. While face-to-face interaction creates rapport on both sides, most meetings are structured to place teachers in authority and parents in passivity. Formalized home visits were one of the most important of these occasions. During the first term of each year, homeroom teachers visited the home of each of their students. Despite their perfunctory, ten- to fifteen-minute, formal nature, teachers said they learned quite a bit.

Eguchi-sensei: You can tell a lot about the family just by the entrance way. If the entrance way is clean and the shoes neatly lined up, probably the family is proper. But if the shoes are scattered carelessly about or the entrance is quite dirty, then we know that either the mother is working or that the home is undisciplined. On the contrary, when I went to Wake's house it was clean and organized, but totally devoid of any sense of home. When I walked in it was cold and impersonal, as if no one actually lived there. At the time I didn't think anything of it. But when we had problems with Wake, I discovered that her mother is quite aloof and distant from the children. She's too preoccupied with other activities. My first reaction to the home should have forewarned me.

Like the other life-style indices, home visits supplied outward signs or evidence of inner qualities which teachers believed they could read easily and accurately.

Parent–teacher group discussions tended to establish teachers as authorities on the child's behavior rather than focus on parents' concerns. Teachers frequently led parents in confession of their children's inadequacies. Like the use of group diaries among students, parents' public confessions of their children's weaknesses expose behavioral problems to the scrutiny of society – in this case, other parents, where teachers indirectly yet powerfully set standards of evaluation. A class meeting at Higashi began with the teacher's description of the academic and behavioral strengths and weaknesses of the class as a whole. Each of the mothers followed the lead of the homeroom mother chosen by the teacher as the representative of the class to the PTA and talked about her child's life-style problems or personal shortcomings. The teacher either confirmed or disconfirmed the problem behavior, then added her own diagnosis of the student's strengths and weaknesses.[10]

Private conferences between the homeroom teacher and individual parents with their children to talk about academic performance set up teachers as academic authorities. The ability of *juku* and achievement tests by private testing companies to provide more accurate assessments of a student's academic potential and chances on high school entrance exams detract from public school teachers' authority. Yet teachers can diagnose the specific causes for a student's poor performance because of their knowledge of a student's motivation, personality, and life-style. Many teachers said they used this conference to stress the importance of life-style and attitude in determining grades. Moreover, for parents who do not send their children to *juku,* the teacher's advice and analysis are the main source of information for making the third-year decisions about postgraduation schooling or work.

Explanatory meetings before trips were particularly instructional in intent. Teachers repeated to parents the information they had given students about the trip schedule and rules. Infrequently parents questioned the need for a particular rule or practice. During one such meeting the teachers used the question as an opportunity to underscore the connections between school policy and the well-being of their children. They launched into a meticulous explanation of the rationale for the policy, which displayed their expertise and experience as well as (at least publicly) squelching dissent.

The annual "Classroom Observation Day" did allow parents a chance to observe one or two of their child's classes in progress and privately evaluate the teachers. Yet the meeting after class observations was a talk by teachers, not a forum for discussion of parents' criticisms of teachers or reservations about school policies.

Real parental concerns or criticisms rarely come out in any formal or public meetings. Their confessional or highly structured framework, as well as the general unspoken agreement on the need to avoid public controversy, discouraged criticism of teachers and the school. However, parent–teacher communication was not totally one-way. To bridge the communication gap created by the exclusion of parent concerns from official communication channels, one faculty member acted as a liaison to the community, privately and informally ferreting out what parents really thought of school policies. While specific individual concerns perhaps went unmet, general parental concerns might quietly come to the attention of teachers.

Problem management

Despite the efforts of teachers to bind students to them, involve them in school, change their life-style and educate their parents, they did not always succeed. Their disciplinary response depended on the seriousness or type of violation and the number of students involved, with some variation by school. However, we again see several consistent themes.

Teachers believed discipline was most effective by those closest to students. The organization of the school around homerooms and absence of auxiliary counseling or guidance personnel maximize homeroom teachers' roles in disciplinary action. In turn, homeroom teachers often attempted to use peer pressure from classmates or clubmates and build a united front with parents to effect changes in student behavior.

Punishment consisted of lecturing students until they "understood." Physical punishment, suspensions, and expulsions were technically illegal.[11] Discipline consisted of student recognition of the error of their ways, sincere repentance and resolve not to repeat the problem behavior again, hence the centrality of reflection in disciplinary action.

Whether to a whole class or to individuals, teachers used a limited set of appeals for good behavior. They used the term *chūgakuseirashii* as a norm defining appropriate behavior; stressed the tendency of uncorrected, minor problem behaviors to escalate into more serious offenses; invoked the need to avoid inconvenience to others; played up the tendency of society to judge individuals by their group affiliation and groups by the behavior of individuals; and played on the personal bonds they developed with students.

Small, non-chronic breaches of the rules – forgotten items, talking out of turn, tardiness, running in the halls, etc. – elicited no more than a comment to "Bring it tomorrow without fail," "Be quiet you're disturbing the class next door," or "Don't be late again" by whichever teacher was present.

Chronic infractions of minor rules by individuals, class attitude problems, and the interpersonal dynamics of a homeroom were the responsibility of the homeroom teacher. Differences, particularly at this level, existed between teachers' strategies for dealing with classroom management problems. In the union-aligned faction at Nishi or at Kita where the entire faculty leaned toward peer control strategies, teachers established frameworks requiring cooperation and held students accountable for each other's behavior. *Han* were responsible for the behavior of their members and class representatives were responsible for class misbehavior.

These teachers frequently used students to spot and solve problems of classroom discipline by defining a problem and then charging a group of class leaders with the responsibility to solve it. At one such session a union teacher at Kita scheduled a meeting of the class representatives and *hanchō* (group leaders) after school to talk about the perennial problems of poor class attitude, forgotten items, and tardiness. The students began the meeting themselves. When their homeroom teacher came, the students had listed the problems but had not devised any solutions. After much discussion and no solutions, the teacher made two suggestions. The students eventually chose his suggestion to keep track of forgotten items and tardiness by *han* and then punish groups with a large number of violations by having them all stay after school.

A union teacher at Nishi who used student leaders and peer pressure to enforce daily rules raised a similar problem. [From field notes of the discussion]:

Amano-sensei: We have a problem with cleaning.

Yazawa (class representative): Yes, not everyone cleans and that's unfair. Nakayama-kun leaves his work half undone.

Amano-sensei: Is that all right with the rest of you?

Kodaira (*hanchō*): But we can't say anything to our friends.

Amano-sensei: I don't think that [not saying anything] is really friendship. There are a number of boys in this class who mock seriousness. How about a box to report who is not cleaning?

Kodaira: But that would be tattling.

Amano-sensei: Then why don't you just gently chide your friends? Telling someone who is not cleaning is helping them improve themselves. You're responsible for the situation. *Hanchō* are supposed to help the class representative. You're more powerful in teaching your peers what is correct. They may notice their error if a friend points it out.

After much discussion and teacher prodding, the group at last decided to make a suggestion box in which people could put notes without adding their names.

The difficulty both teachers had generating peer pressure to enforce school duties suggests the limits of peer pressure at an age when peer groups are increasingly important. Unlike preschool teachers, middle school teachers cannot count on spontaneous support for minor school rules. Only with lots of teacher prodding did students reluctantly assume the role of their brother's keeper.

Other teachers (usually aligned with the administration) structured work to eliminate the need for cooperation or peer pressure and dealt directly with problem behavior themselves. Teachers with peer control strategies assigned a group of students to clean a particular area during the daily cleaning of the school and then left the division of work and responsibility for completing it to the group. In contrast, teachers with a direct style compartmentalized the work and responsibility in the same situation. They assigned each student a particular area of cleaning responsibility and then reprimanded students who did not complete their work.

Teachers often used peer control for classroom discipline

problems. . . . for more serious incidents involved the teachers of the whole grade. When teachers at Nishi discovered that close to one-fourth of the first-year students had been chewing gum and eating candy in school, they mobilized as a grade. One day at 5:00 there was an announcement over the PA system requesting about eight boys to report immediately to the teachers' room. When several of the students summoned did not appear, their homeroom teachers began calling their homes. In the meantime, the other teachers began to extract informal confessions from the students already gathered. At close to 6:00 they reached the boy who had allegedly given out most of the gum at home. His homeroom teacher got on the phone and ordered him to get to school immediately.

After all the students were assembled, the teachers began questioning the students and discovered that gum and candy had been trading hands for several weeks. The teachers dismissed the students at about 7:00 and stayed until 8:00 planning what they would do the next day.

The next morning in the homeroom period at the beginning of the day, each teacher passed out slips of paper to all the students in the class with instructions to confess whether or not they chewed gum or ate candy at school, and if they did, who they gave it to, who they received it from, and the dates for each transaction. During free periods that day the teachers collated the data from every student on a big chart, cross-checking the information. Some students reported giving or receiving gum or candy from students who did not confess. The teachers marked these students who did not confess for special questioning. Then they divided students into groups of ten to fifteen by sex, homeroom, and receipt or bestowal of the contraband. The next day after school the library was arranged into a temporary courtroom and groups were scheduled for questioning. The four homeroom teachers sat in a line at long desks facing the line of eleven to sixteen standing boys or girls. Along the side at another table sat teachers attached to the grade, the head of the guidance committee who came in and out to hear parts of the proceedings, and myself. Neither the head teacher nor the principal played any obvious role.

The following is an excerpt from my field notes of the interrogation of a group of girls who received something.

Kasuga-sensei: We'll begin the investigation of the facts. Each of you in turn please tell us who you received gum or candy from and when.

The first girl states that she took candy from a friend twice.

Kasuga-sensei: What did you think when you accepted the candy? Did you know that it was against school rules?

"Yes," she replied in a small voice, "so I took it home to eat."

Nezu-sensei: How about the second time?

First girl: I ate it at school.

Nezu-sensei: You knew it was wrong, yet you ate it. And the second time your will power to resist what you knew was wrong lessened. You see how small things anesthetize your conscience into thinking that breaking rules is not a big thing. We're really disappointed in you. Next time, how can you tell us you won't accept sake?

The girl sniffs back a few tears. The second girl brought gum but didn't confess to bringing it yesterday. She says she was asked by a friend to bring it.

Nezu-sensei: Well, if you were asked to bring sake, would you bring it?

She says no.

Nezu-sensei: How can you say you won't? Both candy and alcohol are forbidden in school, but you brought candy, didn't you?

Amano-sensei: Bringing gum is bad but lying about it is worse. Lying is the worst thing in the world. Really shameful and traitorous. It's the worst thing a person can do.

The girl begins to cry. The next two girls had brought cough drops for sore throats. The teachers are less severe with them.

Kasuga-sensei: What should you have done when you had a sore throat?

Two girls: We should have either asked permission or gone to the health teacher.

As they go on, the teachers emphasize how such small things escalate into smoking cigarettes and drinking alcohol.

Kasuga-sensei: Such small things show that your hearts are rotting. What would you think of me if I was a student who ate candy and you were a teacher? You wouldn't trust me, would you? Those of you who are leaders, everyone will do what you do.

Kasuga-sensei: This concludes the investigation of the events. Do you know why you are not supposed to have gum and candy in school?

Girl: Because you can't study if you're eating.

Kasuga-sensei: That's right, but there is also a difference between studying at home in your bedroom and studying at school. In a group at school, small violations of rules can escalate to the point where you can't distinguish between right and wrong.

Nezu-sensei: Rule violations bring shame to both you and the whole school. If people in the neighborhood see you, they will judge you not as an individual but as a Nishi student. If Nishi's reputation grows bad and word spreads, high schools won't want to take Nishi students. How can you jeopardize the chances of the upperclassmen to get into high schools with such selfish behavior? Would you like to go to X Gakuen [a private high school in the neighborhood with a terrible reputation]?

They all answer no.

Amano-sensei: The first time you received gum or candy, wasn't there a small voice inside of you saying no?

All the girls raise their hands. There is lots of sniffing and wiping of eyes.

Amano-sensei: You have both a good heart and a bad heart. This time you listened to the bad one. A murderer is the same; he listens to the bad one. You all haven't gone that far, but you're fueling the growth of the bud of a wicked heart. Show the best of yourselves! You are girls, so you will eventually become mothers. If you can't differentiate between good and bad, how can you possibly raise a child properly? Such moral confusion will be transmitted to the next generation. This is why we teachers want you to reflect on what you've done. Get rid of that budding evil in yourself. In your life now you probably do lots of things half-heartedly – cleaning at school, committee duties. You have not been concentrating on what you have been doing. Mend your sloppy ways now. For your sake we are angry at you today.

Most of the girls are almost sobbing.

Kasuga-sensei wraps up the session: So, from today, try to rethink how you live your daily life. Let this be an opportunity for you to enrich your life.

After the group interrogation, students wrote a reflection essay with a note from either parent. In their notes some parents questioned the school's discipline. In response the teachers called an emergency parent–teacher meeting to explain the school's policy and their actions to parents. Teachers were quite pleased at the outcome of the meeting; many parents frankly expressed misgivings about school policy, but when the teachers explained their position, the extent of the problem and their rationale, they felt they won the support of even the most critical parents. . . .

Conclusions

Japanese middle schools have developed a variety of disciplinary activities to instill in students a disciplined, well-organized life-style. Discipline is personal: teachers state that discipline begins with a caring relationship. Therefore, homeroom teachers who have the greatest knowledge of and close relationships with their students are the primary disciplinarians. Discipline is psychological: students reflect on their misdeeds until they "understand," i.e., internalize school norms and routines. Discipline reaches into the home: life-style management is more penetrating than physical punishment and makes it possible to supervise home life. This intensive program of social control, requiring much time and energy from teachers, attests to the need to build social order. The orderliness ascribed to Japanese society is not given but generated at many points throughout society and over an individual's lifetime.

Detailed discipline of student behavior in and out of school also supports text-centered, lecture-style approach in academic classes where the transmission of knowledge depends heavily on order within the classroom. By the middle school level, academic instruction has moved away from the preschool–early elementary pattern of experiential learning through engagement in concrete tasks to a text-centered approach similar to that in high schools. Lecture-style classes at the middle school level do not mean a lack of emphasis on the whole person. An efficient, teacher-centered approach to instruction is separated from a variety of social, emotional and moral training activities which occupy proportionally more time in Japanese than U.S. middle schools. Both middle schools and elementary schools define learning as a process of personal development. Formal school objectives and individual teachers' definitions of education rephrase the Ministry objective of "students fully realized as human beings." Again and again teachers said that their mission was to "aid human development" or to "help students discover themselves." . . .

Personal development in Japan is a progression through a number of predetermined social roles. This sequence establishes strong expectations of age-appropriate behavior along a predetermined developmental path. Teachers who have traveled further down the path guide students along the same road toward maturity. Along this well-worn path distinct stages mark what is appropriate for one age and inappropriate for another. Gradually the child moves from a quite free, unrestrained existence toward one increasingly defined by social demands. Maturity is the ability to fully adapt to outside social realities and responsibilities which lead not to self-negation or conformity, in the Japanese view, but to personal fulfillment.

The definition of the ideal middle school student reflects the transitional position of this stage between the relative freedom of early childhood and the concerted demands for adherence to the heavy social responsibilities of adulthood. In early childhood, behavioral norms for "good children" emphasize a set of traits which facilitate social connectedness but allow personal autonomy. Words commonly used to describe preschool children, like *genki* "spirited" or "active," *akarui* "cheerful" or "vivacious," and *hakihaki* "clear" or "brisk," imply both sociability and autonomy. Even the term *sunao* "obedient" implies a frankness or naturalness in intent coupled with a cooperative spirit. Within preschools teachers de-emphasize outward compliance with rules while they gradually cultivate children's understanding of socially appropriate behavior. Taken together, descriptions of preschools and terms used to describe the ideal child suggest that early childhood is a time to develop a cooperative, socially engaged child who is at the same time spirited or autonomous.

At the middle school level the characteristics of the ideal student shift. This ideal is one of a well-organized, disciplined life-style built on compliance to and internalization of social norms codified in formal and informal school rules. Middle school is *a priori* a time for study. Thus, a mature student realizes the need to buckle down to serious academic work. Academic classes do not need to be made relevant, entertaining or even intellectually stimulating. At this level study is a sober business. Sociability is defined not only in terms of a cheerful or buoyant personality but as having good manners and a sense of responsibility. Students who are not dependent on teachers' explicit reminders and structuring to achieve these characteristics are described as self-aware. Thus, self-awareness in the Japanese context signifies acceptance of one's socially-defined role and its requirements.

These ideals of maturity for middle school students neatly dovetail with the academic demands of the educational and vocational system but are part of a larger definition of human development that is quite different from that in the United States. As Ruth Benedict observed, in Japan a "U-curve" of development gives the greatest autonomy to young children who are not yet full members of society and to the elderly who have retired from active social participation. The greatest pressures and responsibilities rest on those in the middle – adults in the prime of life who are expected to carry them out with autonomous self-discipline but little latitude for independent action. . . .

Japanese middle school, with its numerous specific behavioral prescriptions and concerted demands for serious study, is a significant step toward an adultlike adjustment to outside social realities. In the United States the ideal of student-centered classes at the middle school level and individual choice of electives embody the increasing freedom and responsibility granted to question, criticize, and choose in pursuit of independent adulthood. These differences between U.S. and Japanese middle schools are obviously intertwined with cultural conceptions. Educational models reflect and recreate cultural conceptions of development, of the social organization of adult responsibility, and of maturity itself.

Notes

1. The broad scope of teaching and learning in the middle school curriculum is based on the concept of *shidō*. Areas of school responsibility are defined as different kinds of *shidō*. *Gakushū shido* refers to academic or subject instruction. *Dotoku shidō* signifies moral instruction, *hoken shido* health education, and *shinrō shidō* educational and occupational guidance counseling. *Seitō shidō* or *seikatsu shido* refers to student guidance, which includes discipline, counseling and myriad activities or events designed to involve students in the life of the school. For a thorough discussion of the concept and its centrality to teaching in Japan, see Le Tendre's essay in this volume.
2. For a full treatment of the significance of *juku* to Japanese education, see Rohlen (1980) and Kariya (1988).
3. All names of places, institutions, and individuals are fictional.

4. For a concrete example of new teaching strategies for classroom teachers, see McCarthy (1987).
5. All individual quotations are taken from formal, tape-recorded interviews.
6. I am indebted to Thomas Rohlen for this observation (personal communication, September 1992).
7. When teachers mentioned working mothers, it was to bemoan their general effect on children. Like comments on "today's family," comments on working mothers expressed a sense of general social decline. In practice, there were working mothers of children with exemplary life-styles and academic performance, which everyone knew existed but failed to mention in conversations on working mothers per se. The prejudice against working mothers focused on the stereotype of mothers working in small family businesses or bars with late hours, which made it difficult to supervise home life. Perhaps the issue of working mothers was a veiled indictment of the inadequacies of homes of lower socioeconomic status where women do tend to work.

Tabiki-sensei herself had been a working mother when she was younger. She seemed to deal with the conflict between the ideal of a full-time mother and the reality of working by becoming a superwoman. Even without children at home at the time of my research her schedule was grueling: up at 5:00 A.M. to cook a traditional Japanese breakfast, at school by 7:30 to supervise early morning club practice, arriving home after 7:00 each night to prepare dinner and do housework before retiring at about midnight.
8. I am indebted to Catherine Lewis for the observation on developing "correct" emotions (personal communication, June 1993).
9. My request for all information sent home with students in one class netted two or three notices per week.
10. See Fujita (1989:82–84) for an almost identical illustration of a meeting for mothers of children at a day-care center.
11. Schoolland (1990) argues that physical punishment and violence are very much a part of Japanese schools today. It is difficult to gauge how widespread violent incidents in schools actually are. In my research I never witnessed violence toward students by teachers. However, physical forms of discipline have been very much a part of Japanese tradition. For a discussion of physical discipline for spiritual ends, see Rohlen (1980:219–220). At one of my field schools physical discipline, particularly the use of *seiza* (sitting in a formal kneeling position), was a common practice until the media campaign against physical punishment in schools in the mid-1980's forced teachers to abandon what they knew had been a technically illegal, but they claimed effective, approach.

Artistic pursuits – old and new

Visitors expect Japan to be filled with evidence of the country's aesthetic sensibilities, but today, short of sightseeing at ancient gardens and temples, most are disappointed. One has to look deep into the recesses of private lives to discover the vibrancy of Japan's famed engagement with the arts, but it certainly exists. Children study music at school as a matter of course. A surprisingly large number also learn an instrument from a private teacher from an early age. On virtually every college campus, one finds student clubs centering on such pursuits as the tea ceremony, ballroom dancing, drama, and flower arranging. The same is true of companies, where similar kinds of clubs are popular. The range of courses in public recreation centers is also impressive, as is the wealth of offerings of private "schools" specializing in a particular traditional art. Cooking classes abound, as do classes in painting and various crafts.

What all this adds up to is a society seemingly saturated with the study of artistic expression. Recall that Japan is home to the Yamaha assemblage of innovative musical instruments, to the Suzuki Method, to some of the world's top classical and jazz musicians, and to schools of tea and flower arranging with millions of dues-paying members. By labeling the subject of all this learning as "art" and "expression," we have imposed a Western idea on a Japanese phenomenon that is actually wider, more inclusive, and different in its basic intent.

Bunka, loosely translated as "culture," includes the study of social dance and the intricacies of an orchestra. The martial arts, to take another example, readily belong to this category, as does the serious study of what we would call "games" (chess, *go, karuta*). Whether they are physical sports or artistic endeavors does not matter. The type of activity is not the key; paramount are the nature of the study itself and its capacity to foster personal growth. "Expression" is the American way of relating art to the individual's psychological needs. In Japan, the relationship for adults centers on enhancing concentration, perception, inner peace, and so forth. These goals are close to the German concept of "cultured" (*gebildet*) but are more concerned with character building and the Zen enlightenment we encountered at the beginning of this book.

The study of noh drama by professionals and amateurs alike is typical of this genre of learning in its organization and basic psychology. Thomas Hare takes us into this work, one he has experienced as a student, showing us how learning and teaching operate within an evolving tradition going back to the sixteenth century. And if the amateur study of noh is old and aimed at the aged, the study of the violin by the Suzuki method is new and focused on the young. Our early contrasts between adult-oriented modes of learning (deriving from the Buddhist tradition of spiritual progress) and modes appropriate to childhood (seemingly akin to the Shinto emphases on spontaneity, energy, playfulness, and natural curiosity) are apparent in these studies – but intermingled. The resonance between education for the very old and very young reveals a "deep" structure to Japanese notions about the progression of learning throughout life.

Try, try again: training in noh drama
TOM HARE

Regimes of training and its theorization in the traditions of noh drama have long been the exclusive and esoteric preserve of professional acting families and have remained, until the twentieth century, generally unknown outside this restricted group. Even after the textual materials relating to such regimes were made more generally available, however, much of the insight they contained was hidden behind a curtain of technical knowledge about stage performance, dramatic convention, and the sociological hierarchy of the noh troupes. Although I am wary of the dehistoricization and decontextualization that can so easily result when we try to look at modern Japan on the basis of traditional, especially textual, materials, I nonetheless regard this as a welcome opportunity to make some observations about training in noh and to speculate on its implications and possibilities outside the world of the theater proper. In the following discussion, then, I will examine the role of training in the arts of noh, with occasional reference to my own modest experience as an amateur who once studied the performance of noh a little in the process of writing my dissertation.

Training and learning

In the context of noh, "training" presents many seeming paradoxes. The devotion to training that is everywhere exhorted in the texts with which we will be concerned could not be effected without a personal, individual commitment, and it would necessarily engage the individual intellect with the highest rigor and intensity; yet the individual must be willing to sacrifice personal judgment, not to mention personal impulse, to a teacher who functions as the embodiment of past mastery in the artistic line. The process of training is not the same as learning about the art, and a comprehensive intellectual understanding of training is not necessarily a goal in the art; indeed, in the first stages of training, such an intellectual understanding might be considered an obstruction. The tools used come from the body, and in a concrete sense it is the body rather than the mind that is being trained, but the tools of the body are abstract forms, not concrete deployments of mimetic technique.

If this is paradoxical, then the value of the paradox lies in its irresolvability, in the tension that forces certain logical or intellectual assumptions to come head to head over a reality that must remain, at best, translucent. It is not the business of this essay to resolve this tension, but rather to ask how we might characterize training and its paradoxes given the evidence in texts on noh training. What features of training might we identify as central, and what social and theoretical contexts do they assume? What activities does training entail, when does it take place, who directs it, and what are its aims, both practical and aesthetic or spiritual? How have social, political, and economic change altered training, and what constants can still be discerned between the training of the past and that of the present?

The word "training" could be said many ways in Japanese. *Kunren, renshu, kyōren, shikomi,* and even *torēningu* are acceptable, depending on the context. In noh, however, two words are definitely applicable. One, *shūdō,* is an old word, hard to find without specialized classical dictionaries. It means "learning the way," and it can be used in the context of religious as well as artistic training. Another word one hears often is *keiko,* also an old word but still in common use today. It is often given a polite (or formal) prefix, becoming *okeiko.*

Okeiko often means "lessons," and it is now applied with equal frequency to piano lessons and lessons in the traditional arts, such as the tea ceremony. But full-fledged professionals, even eminent masters, use the term with regard to their own practice as well, and it doesn't necessarily convey the sense of a beginner's or intermediate's attempts to learn the art. It means, rather, engagement in an artistic activity outside the context of an actual full performance. The philology of the word remains important. It is, in its earliest form, a Chinese two-character, verb–object construction with the sense "think [upon] the past" or "study ancient ways" (*J. inishie o kangau*).

The focus on the past that lies behind the characterization of "training" as *keiko* may seem ironic if we consider noh at the end of the fourteenth century, as it underwent its most dynamic and definitive transition. It was then an upstart art that made its fame and fortune by breaking with the past, yet it is in this context that "training" in noh takes on its most salient characteristics, and it is perhaps here that one may find a broader relevance for training in what has today become a highly cultivated taste, at best, to many, a moribund performing art living a museum existence.

Context

The social and political instability of Japan's medieval era (by which I mean the Kamakura, Muromachi, and Momoyama periods) provided a rich ground for the development, refinement, and elaboration of critical thought and intellectual innovation. In the field of poetics, the end of the Heian period (and the economic hardship it imposed on many aristocratic households) brought a sharply heightened sense of professionalization to the vocation of poet. In the sphere of religious discourse, new or newly prominent conceptions of time and the potential for human action gave rise to the Zen and Pure Land sects, as well as the revivification and reform of earlier sects (such as the Kegon, under Myōe). Political entities with a strong provincial base vied for power with the central authorities who manipulated the imperial throne, creating first (in the Kamakura shogunate) a bipolar power structure and then unequivocally subordinating the imperial court and its *eminences grises* to the political domination of shogunal authority in the first part of the Muromachi shogunate (especially under Yoshimitsu, Yoshimochi, and Yoshinori.)

When, in the late fourteenth century, the authority of the Muromachi shogunate was firmly established in the political sphere, new cultural opportunities arose for classes of society that had been on the margins of cultural production earlier. Yoshimitsu, the third Muromachi shogun, is often depicted as a politically successful leader with a deep sense of cultural inferiority, which he sought to overcome through patronage of new arts that could be seen to rival the grand old traditions of the imperial court. Although such a personalization of the new artistic climate invites skepticism, it is abundantly clear that the late fourteenth and early fifteenth centuries brought a new range of aesthetic possibilities and new groups of artists into prominence. The tea cult came into being and developed a varied practice; linked verse poetry (*renga*) was transformed from a diversion to a high art; and noh drama emerged from the energetic diversity of *sarugaku, dengaku, kusemai,* and other provincial entertainments and rituals. Each of these new representative arts of Japan's middle ages offered new opportunities for artistic careers to members of social classes that had previously been excluded from central participation in the arts of classical Japan (such as *waka* poetry, *gagaku* and *bugaku,* and narrative fiction). With this new social possibility came a new awareness of the role of training in the mastery of an art.

The primary documents for an examination of training in early noh are the treatises of Zeami Motokiyo (1363–1443). Zeami is the central figure in the transformation of *sarugaku* into noh, and his writings on performance, playwriting, and the training of actors provide the earliest and most intimate view of the noh in Muromachi Japan. I am particularly interested in parts of Zeami's first treatise, *Fūshi kaden* (sometimes known as the *Kadensho*), and in another treatise from late in his life, *Kyūi.* Most of the former was written between 1400 and 1402 to record what Zeami learned from his father, Kannami, as well as to distill his own experience from youth through his successful midcareer. The latter is a highly allusive and schematic reflection on artistic achievement written by 1428, when Zeami was sixty-five. In addition to providing a perspective on much of Zeami's career, these two texts maintain an explicit and conscious concern with issues of training and artistic development. And the fact that training and artistic development (rather than, say, aesthetic and metaphysical ideals) occupy a dominant role is itself a commentary on the inseparability of noh from training in noh.

No training to noh training

Fūshi kaden devotes part of its first "book" to the issue of the actor's training at seven stages in his life. This is a good place to begin a discussion of training in noh because of its methodical and clearly staged presentation of the regime of training, but also because it reveals a basic and paradoxical fissure running through the aesthetics and pragmatics of the art. Zeami posits the age of six[1] as the beginning of training, the first attempt of the child to learn about the art to which he is to succeed for his livelihood:

In training at this age, there is always something a child does on his own that shows where his talents lie, and he should be allowed to follow such natural inclinations whether they be toward dance, . . . song, or even the direct display of energy. You should not be too quick to say what is good and what is bad, because if you demand too much, the child will lose interest in noh and weary of it, and make no progress.[2]

This statement presents a form of training that is no training. It proposes merely to exhibit the child on stage, to notice the natural and intuitive basis of performance at this inception of his life as an actor, and to take advantage of his beauty (my choice of the male pronoun is conscious, but it leaves open the underlying sexist assumption that only males are fit for the stage, an assumption rarely challenged in the history of noh). The child, by virtue of being a child, creates interest in what he does. That interest is used most effectively when undiluted by any pretension to imitate or present something other than simply a beautiful child dancing and singing. This may reflect a basic faith in the original nature of the child as good and uncorrupted. This is native to the thought of Mencius and to Buddhist notions of "original enlightenment" (J. *hongaku*), that is, the Buddha nature inherent in all sentient beings (Kojima, 1986:41–42).

This attitude toward children on stage persists today, and informs the "acting" of children on the Kabuki stage as well as that of the noh. No attempt at dramatic subtlety or refinement is expected of a child. One might go further, suggesting a link between such a pattern in the training of an actor and the frequent observation by Americans that Japanese children, before school age, are often given great freedom to behave as they will, and that attempts at discipline come systematically only after the children have entered school, at which time the strictures of social control become, contrastingly, much more apparent than in American society.

Zeami proceeds next to the training of an eleven- or twelve-year-old, and little seems to have changed in the general attitude toward training. Still, it is the natural capabilities of the child that are central to his performance, and the teacher's task is to show these natural capabilities to best advantage:

> About this time, the child will begin to be able to carry a tune, and he will start to understand a bit about the noh, so he should be taught various sorts of noh. First of all, since he is a child, anything he does will be pretty (*yūgen*). Furthermore, his childhood voice will be at its peak during this period. With these two advantages, his bad points will disappear and his good ones blossom.
>
> For the most part, you should not have children do too much dramatic imitation. It neither looks good nor increases the child's ability. However, as the child becomes really skillful, he may be permitted to perform almost anything. A pretty little boy with a good voice who is talented besides can hardly go wrong. (Hare, 1986:18)

Zeami expresses his consciousness of the child actor's future in denying that his present level of accomplishment is any guide to future potential, and while training has become more explicit in terms of proper movement and enunciation, Zeami expects little from the young actor in terms of artistic consciousness or self-awareness. The devotion to training for its own sake is important:

> Such skill is not true skill. It is merely temporary. . . . Consequently, it does not provide any means by which to judge the boy's potential. At this stage, those things the child can do easily should be made the high points of his performance, and major emphasis should be given to his technique. His movements should be exact and his singing understandable syllable by syllable. His basic gestures in the dance should be strictly correct, and he should be resolute in his training. (Hare, 1986:18)

It is only with the transformations wrought by puberty on the body and mind of the actor, before the next stage of his training, that the regularized and systematic training regimen begins, and it is at this point that the young actor's mettle is first put to its strictest test (with a characteristic paradox):

> This period [of age sixteen to seventeen] is of such great importance that you must not practice too much. First, since your voice will be changing, you will have lost one of your dramatic charms. Your body will have gotten much taller, and you will have lost the charm of figure

you had before. The time when you could, with your pretty voice, perform with effortless flair will have passed, and with this transformation, the essential strategy of performance will have changed, leaving you at a loss. You will find yourself in positions that the audience thinks comical, and you will be embarrassed. With one thing and another, all this can be quite disheartening.

In training at this time, even if people point and laugh, pay them no heed. Practice, instead, in private at a pitch our voice will allow and train hard, using your voice in a manner appropriate to the time of day. Be resolute and realize that this is the turning point; commit yourself to noh for life with complete devotion – no other means of training exists. If you give up at this point, your noh is finished. (Hare, 1986:21)

The encouragement to embrace hard work, discipline, and devotion to the art we find here is hardly surprising or unusual to readers familiar with Japan. A self-conscious, formalist, artistic continuity would, in any cultural context, require commitment and the subordination of individual impulse to the authority and conventions of the community. What may be more idiosyncratic here is the clear contrast between the artistic value of a child and that of a postpubescent student of the art.

This can, to some extent, be accounted for by reference to the sexual tastes of the medieval (especially samurai class) aristocracy. The definition of sexuality in medieval Japan did not divide along the lines of heterosexual–homosexual (as it is often seen to do in contemporary America) but more tellingly along lines of age and social hierarchy. The child (especially a beautiful child from a low social class) was one target of sexual interest for older boys and young men (and even older men occasionally) of a higher class, and the resulting relationship could be interpreted to have positive social and educational value, like the institutions of pederasty in classical Greece.

There are significant indications that Zeami himself, in his first appearances in the capital, was the object of more than simply aesthetic interest on the part of his patrons, most importantly the Shogun Yoshimitsu and an important poet and statesman from the imperial court, Nigō Yoshimoto. The biographical details of these relationships are of little immediate relevance here. What is important, however, is the aesthetic idealization of the child as an un-self-conscious locus of beauty. That beauty is, moreover, identified specifically as *yūgen,* a term of great weight and lofty pedigree in the context of medieval Japanese aesthetics.

Yūgen is one of the supreme artistic virtues in medieval Japan, and its embodiment in the child is referred to elsewhere in Zeami's writing as well.[3] The presence of an un-self-conscious and originary beauty, *yūgen,* in the prepubescent child enables the possibility of the loss of that beauty with the onset of puberty and makes necessary a strategy for regaining it. This is the *raison d'être* for training in noh, the fissure between a state of nature and a fall away from it, an un-self-conscious and poignantly ephemeral beauty that must be recaptured or replaced by a long, intensely disciplined, and regimented process of the reconstitution of beauty.

This pedagogical structure is echoed in the dramaturgical theory Zeami posits for the creation of a successful play. It is to unfold in a tripartite process of beginning, break, and fast climax – *jo, ha,* and *kyū,* in Japanese. We have just come upon the break. The actor's career has begun, but until the first transformations of his body in puberty have happened, the actor's potential is uncertain and his training is limited in scope. Then, with the break, the training regimen becomes relatively predictable. By the time a talented young actor is twenty-three or twenty-four, the regimen will have begun to bear fruit:

> About this time a man's artistic potential for his entire life begins to be fixed. Consequently, this is an extremely important time for training. Your voice will have changed already, and your body will have reached maturity. This provides two advantages. . . . Performances worthy of a man in the prime of his youth are possible now. People will begin to take notice and say, "Ah, he's gotten quite good." On occasion you may even win in competitions against famous actors because of the novelty of your dramatic achievement at this particular time. (Hare, 1986:21)

But these first successes of the actor's career are undercut immediately by a cautionary note:

> People will be generous with praise, and you may come to think of yourself as a really accomplished actor. This is very dangerous. . . . Your achievement at this time is not true artistic excellence. It is born of youth and the novelty the spectators see in you. Anyone with a discriminating eye will recognize this fact.
> Your achievement at this time is a beginner's achievement, and it is

a great shame if you mistake it for true artistic excellence and give free rein to your personal eccentricities on stage, thinking yourself a great actor. Even though you are highly praised and win in competition with famous actors, you should realize this is merely [a] temporary achievement born of novelty. You should work at mastering the traditional forms of dramatic imitation and train all the more diligently, inquiring very carefully of truly accomplished actors concerning the fine points. . . . Nearly everyone becomes enthralled with this temporary achievement and fails to realize it will disappear. . . . Ponder this long and hard. If you really have a grasp of your level of achievement at this stage, that achievement will not disappear throughout your life. If you overestimate your level of achievement, even the level once attained will fade away. Think this over carefully. (Hare, 1986:21f)

The reservations apparent in this passage prefigure later developments in a more theoretical and abstract paradigm of artistic achievement, but their experiential base is already clear (and has led to scholarly speculation about the course of Zeami's own career). For our present purposes, it should suffice to note the ambivalence about success in its reliance on the judgment of an audience in what is ostensibly a kind of popularity contest. Zeami is concerned with identifying a stable and reliable foundation for dramatic success, but his choice of metaphor for the successes he has himself experienced is anything but stable and reliable. He chooses *hana,* the flower, and its very ephemerality is the source of its aptness in his metaphorical deployments.

Performance in flower

One of the most ingratiating things about reading Zeami is the (illusory?) sense of a person inside, responding with practicality and intelligence to his own circumstances, even though the things he is talking about are often highly technical or parochial or simply incomprehensible. In the next passage from his account of an actor's training, as we have been following it in *Fūshi kaden,* we come upon the apogee of the actor's career at the age of thirty-three or thirty-four. Or, at least, that is what the text would lead you to believe:

[An actor's] noh around this time is at its highest peak. He who fully understands and masters the various articles in this manuscript and attains true expertise in acting will most certainly gain fame and security in his position. He who does not gain sufficient fame and security, no matter how skillful he may be, should realize that he has not yet brought about the full flowering of his art. If you do not achieve this, your noh will decline after age forty. This will become obvious later. . . . Now is the time for you to take full account of what you have learned in the past to be fully aware of your direction in the future. (Hare, 1986:22)

The heyday of an actor's career, again compared with the flowering of a plant or tree, is the natural consequence of practice and the careful observance of a technical regime, and it virtually guarantees the thirty-something actor success and recognition. The latter is the ratification of a method pursued with exactness and devotion and is the indispensable foundation for later achievement. Consciousness of one's position within the regimen of training is a central feature of Consciousness itself.

There is, moreover, a sense of urgency to what is said here because, like a flower in the natural world, the flower of artistic achievement will inescapably wilt, dry up, and wither away. Already, indeed, in Zeami's remarks on the forty-three- or forty-four-year-old actor, we see an awareness of this:

From this point on, your method in noh should change fundamentally. Even if you've achieved universal praise, and come to the most profound understanding of the art, all the same, you'd better find yourself a good *waki* [i.e., assistant, secondary actor]. Your skill may not deteriorate, but you will unavoidably get older, and you'll lose both the flower of physical power and the flower of your appearance. I don't know about the exceptionally handsome, but for the basically attractive person, it becomes quite unacceptable to perform without a mask when you're old. So you'll have to do without this side of things. . . . Whatever flower you haven't lost by this point must be the authentic flower of your talent. Any actor who hasn't lost this flower by the time he is about fifty must surely have made his name before he was forty. No matter how famous an actor may become, he must be the sort of person who thoroughly understands his own capabilities, and consequently, he will take great care to find a good *waki,* and he won't break his back trying to do this or that, performing some play where his faults are sure to be exposed. The kind of mind which understands its own body's capabilities, that's the mind of a master. (Omote and Kato, 1974:18ff)

At fifty, the irrevocability of change is all the more apparent, and yet an important paradox has appeared in the example of Zeami's own father, Kannami (1333–84):

There's probably no better plan at around this age than to do nothing. "Once grown old, a magic steed's no better than a nag, indeed," so they say. All the same, an actor of true attainment, even though his repertory has dwindled away and, for better or for worse, he has nothing to show off, his flower should still be there. My late father passed away on the nineteenth day of the fifth month when he was fifty-two years old, but on the fourth of that month he had performed before the god of Sengen in the province of Suruga. His noh that day was particularly beautiful and was praised by exalted and humble alike. By that time, I gather, he had already relinquished most roles to the beginners, and he would himself just add a little something here or there where it was easy, but his flower seemed to grow more and more. Because he had attained the authentic flower, that flower remained in his noh without scattering, even until the tree was old and the branches few. (Omote and Kato, 1974:19)

The metaphorical inconsistency here – the flower that does not wilt and fade – stems from the exceptional character of the man who provides the example. Kannami, from all evidence, and certainly from the testimony of his son, was not only an extraordinarily talented and successful individual, but also a teacher of remarkable and lasting success. And yet, what seems an anomaly here may not in fact turn out to be so exceptional after all. Here we turn to the second of the treatises I mentioned earlier, the *Kyūi*, where we find a much richer deployment of metaphor in the description of artistic training and achievement, and a far more egregious transgression of natural reality.

The *Kyūi*, or "Nine Ranks," is a brief text, less than four pages in a modern printed version, schematic, highly allusive, syntactically fragmented, and written partly in a puzzlingly idiosyncratic attempt at Chinese. It opens with a series of notes on the characteristics of nine stages of artistic achievement. The nine stages are divided into three sets of three, marked "the top three flowers," "the middle three ranks," and "the bottom three ranks." For each level, Zeami gives a terse metaphorical characterization in Chinese and a slightly longer Sino-Japanese explanation. We will not quote the latter here, but the former provides a sketch of the treatise that will be useful for us to refer to later:

The Top Three Flowers:
The Stratum of the Miraculous Flower. Silla [the fourth- to ninth-century Korean Kingdom], midnight: the sun is bright.

The Stratum of the Profoundly Cherished Flower. Snow blankets a thousand mountains. Why is that single peak not white?

The Stratum of the Tranquil Flower. Piling snow in a silver bowl.

The Middle Three Ranks

The Stratum of the Correct Flower. The mist is bright, the sun sets, ten thousand mountains are crimson.

The Stratum of Broad Vitality. The mind of the mountain clouds and the moon upon the sea, exhausted in the recounting.

The Stratum of Shallow Patterns. What makes a path a path is not the eternal path.

The Bottom Three Ranks

The Stratum of the Strong and Thin. Shadows flash across the metal hammer, light is cold on the precious sword.

The Stratum of the Strong and Coarse. Three days after birth, a tiger cub would eat an ox.

The Stratum of the Coarse and Leaden. A Tree Rat with Five [Accomplishments]. (Omote and Kato, 1974:174ff)

Zeami now turns to a discussion of the way training in noh relates to this schematic system of artistic accomplishment. Here the extravagant metaphors are given a more comprehensible, though not transparent, interpretation. It is of particular significance that the beginner is required to begin not at the bottom of the latter but at the sixth level, the lowest of the middle three ranks:

Middle first, top second, bottom last, which is to say, in embarking upon the introduction to the performing arts, mastering the articles of training [*keiko*] with regard to the two arts of song and dance comprises the Stratum of Shallow Patterns. The level one gradually arrives at on this path, by thoroughly mastering this and adding patterns to the shallow stratum, is the Stratum of Broad Vitality. Exhausting the matters relevant to this level, and following the path for broad and expansive experience, to arrive at its full fruition is the Stratum of the Correct Flower. This is the rank where one attains the Three Modes [of dramatic imitation] from the Two Arts [of song and dance]. This is the place where it becomes apparent to audiences whether one has grasped the true nature of the flower of this vocation, having attained a secure competence in each [of the technical skills] and become proficient at moving an audience. This is the Stratum of the Tranquil Flower, where, in looking down at one's artistic accomplishments up to this point, one transcends them to the secure attainment of the greatest consequence. Above this is the Stratum of the Profoundly Cherished Flower, where one attains the most wondrous visible effects and performs on the differential between being and nothingness. Hereabove, words no longer avail and one has come to express the internal landscape of the miraculous epiphany of non-duality, the Stratum of the Miraculous Flower. (Omote and Kato, 1974:176)

Despite the extravagant mystical rhetoric of the latter half of this explanation, there is a certain basic logic to the progression of artistic accomplishment Zeami has outlined. In particular, in the middle three levels of training and accomplishment, one masters a body of techniques, explores and expands one's capabilities within their sphere, and proceeds on this basis to the next level. In reaching the top three ranks (or "flowers," as Zeami calls them), this logic holds, even if the artistic accomplishments pointed to are of an overtly religious wonder that may seem remote from our experience. The garnering of artistic success through a measured and gradual mastery of technique underlies the full course of attainment from the Stratum of Shallow Patterns through the Stratum of the Miraculous Flower. Now, however, something surprising occurs:

As for the lowest three ranks, they are the swift undercurrents of artistic performance and are graduated accordingly, but are not of great importance in training. However, once one has gone through the middle three ranks and attained the upper three flowers to attain the secure rank of the miraculous flower, then one may double back and play freely in the bottom three ranks, whereupon the activities one pursues at these levels, too, are harmonized aesthetically. In the past, accomplished performers, though they had mastered the top three flowers, declined to resort to the three bottom levels. This is like the saying "the Majestic Pachyderm disdains the paths of rabbits." In this, nowhere else than in the performance of my late father, have I seen one who followed from the middle three ranks to the top three flowers, and thereupon descended to the bottom three ranks, mastering all. Many others have come to the Stratum of Broad Vitality, and before they have attained the Stratum of the Correct Flower, they have made the descent to the bottom three ranks; in the end, they do not succeed as performers. Moreover, these days there are people in the art who take the bottom three ranks as their introduction to the art. This is not the proper order. Consequently, there are many who do not enter upon any of the levels of artistic accomplishment. (Omote and Kato, 1974:176ff)

Starting at the bottom gets you nowhere in Zeami's way of looking at things. The problem here is one of constraints upon human action. It is important to note that Zeami, like certain Zen masters of his day and of more recent times, posits a certain minimum standard for the pursuit of artistic activity if any improvement is to be made. If that minimum standard is not adhered to in training, then progress is impossible. If the standard is observed and the training regimen is followed regularly and consistently, progress to basic competence is virtually guaranteed. Thereafter, the achievement of artistic virtuosity is a more complicated matter. Much of Zeami's critical vocabulary comes from Buddhism, Tendai, Shingon, and Zen, and as his ideal performer comes to the top three flowers, the increase in this vocabulary is evident. The transition between the Middle Three Ranks and the Top Three Flowers is characterized by a word taken from Zen, *zadan,* and it suggests a break from the gradual and incremental improvement of earlier training into a transcendent and stable virtuosity. More interesting still is the ability of the true virtuoso to descend from his lofty attainments to levels of activity that are not in themselves artistic at all and that have previously been out of bounds. These are the Bottom Three Ranks, and they represent mere action without artistic value.[4]

Zeami's understanding of the sequence of training has antecedents in both religious thought and poetics. In the former sphere, it recalls the system of ten stages of religious consciousness adumbrated by Kūkai.[5] A system more explicitly oriented to training can be found in the "Ten Styles of Poetic Composition" of Fujiwara Teika, the great poet and critic of the late twelfth and early thirteenth centuries. In this case, the styles enumerated are not rigidly hierarchical, but the training regimen is informative for understanding Zeami's view. Teika requires the poet first to master four fundamental styles, the "style of mystery and depth" (*yūgen'yō*), the "style of universally acceptable statement" (*koto shikarubeki yō*), the "style of elegant beauty" (*uruwashiki yō*), and the "style of intense feeling" (*ushintei*). Thereafter, the poet is free to compose in four other styles with which he should have little difficulty, and only after all the previous styles have been mastered is he permitted to go on to the "style of demon-quelling force" (*onihishigitei*) (Brower and Miner, 1963:246–247).

These three traditional approaches share several features relevant to training, whether it be religious or artistic (and the distinction, particularly in Japan's middle ages, is not usually a very meaningful one). Training is to be undertaken following a strict regimen. Specific and discrete fields of activity are to be mastered before proceeding to the next stage; the gradual approach consistently applied will produce good results; and once one has mastered the basic course of training, one will achieve liberation. This liberation is made explicit in Zeami's scheme by the consummate master's ability to descend to levels of activity that would not have been acceptable in a less accomplished artist.[6] All three systems are totalizing systems and give the practitioner a transcendent freedom: "training makes you free." But the seeming similarity to common Western notions of education making the individual free may be deceptive. Training must be differentiated from education because it is not primarily a rational, intellective process but rather a mastery of forms with a strongly kinetic, physical, bodily orientation. Moreover, the freedom attained is not, as most often intended by the Western formulation, political freedom, but rather a spiritual or aesthetic freedom, a freedom that is always enmeshed in a web of obligations within the institutions of noh. That freedom maintains, moreover, an ethical significance that hearkens back to the *Analects* of Confucius. Recall specifically Master Kong's first article:

At fifteen, I set my heart upon learning. At thirty, I had planted my feet firm upon the ground. At forty, I no longer suffered from perplexities. At fifty I knew what were the biddings of Heaven. At sixty, I could follow the dictates of my own heart; for what I desired no longer overstepped the boundaries of right.[7]

The boys from the men

Many of the spiritual concerns of noh have been subordinated to the economic structures of patronage and amateur practice over the centuries. It would certainly have been impossible for noh to survive for the six centuries since it developed its identity were it not for the sense of respect, indeed veneration, that has stemmed from the "reflection on ancient ways" so characteristic of noh. It is important to realize that this is not, or at least not exclusively, the intrusion of a crass (Western) modernity on a pristine (Japanese) tradition, but that for centuries the tradition itself has been able to survive only in reliance on this and related structures of patronage.[8] How does this system of patronage interact with and influence notions of training in noh, and what does it suggest about traditional Japanese attitudes toward training in general?

The ready availability of other kinds of performance art has vastly increased competition for an audience, and in the face of this competition, noh has managed to create and maintain a relatively wealthy and generous audience and patronage base, but that base is far removed from what could, in even the loosest sense, be considered "popular." Most patrons of noh are also amateur practitioners who pay professional teachers monthly tuition for lessons and (high) fees for amateur recitals (usually held once a year).

In my own experience in lessons with generous and patient actors and musicians, the sense of the past was never without paradox. In those lessons intended for amateurs, almost all of the students had seen a good deal more of the past with their own eyes than had the teachers. The majority of my fellow students were women of a certain age. Occasionally a businessman (also a fairly older individual) would attend. The ladies were beautifully dressed in kimonos with an immaculate white *tabi* for use in their dance lessons on the expensive cypress stage. They spoke slowly in exceptionally polite Japanese – "*zāmasu-kotoba*," as my home-staying mother used to call it. They were much like my grandmother's friends – rather well-to-do, well preserved, and well intentioned. There was virtually no expectation that any of us would attain professional rank. Indeed, the time and place for professional training are generally altogether separate from those for amateur training.

The bifurcation of professional and amateur has many practical consequences for training in noh. One concrete example relates to such basic components of noh as its musical rhythm and how this is conveyed to students of the art.

The rhythmic structures of noh are rather complex and, in a majority of cases in a given play, require the marriage of a twelve-syllable line of verse with a basic musical unit counted in eight beats.[9] In effect, certain syllables in a given verse are allotted a full beat of the musical unit, whereas others are given only a half-beat. There is a stereotypical pattern that is referred to for general reference, but in any given performance the actual verse will vary from that pattern, depending upon the vocal embellishments of certain syllables, the particular combination of "schools" of acting, drumming, flute playing, and so on, as well as the individual actor's interpretation of the piece.

In amateur training, however, these fine (but crucial) rhythmic details are for the most part ignored, and students are urged simply to try their best to imitate the teacher. In advanced stages of training, when the amateur is allowed (for a price) to perform a full play or a significant portion of a play, such instruction as may be necessary for that particular play is given, but even in these cases, the responsibility for understanding and articulating the underlying rhythmic structure is held back from the amateur student. This is illustrated perhaps most acutely in the double fee structure used in noh for professional versus amateur performances. Professionals pay far less to their instrumentalists for the performance of any particular play than do amateurs because, in the words of one instrumentalist, "we expect the professionals to understand how the music works and sing accordingly, whereas with amateurs, *we* have to do all the work to keep up with the way they chant."

There are historical and sociological reasons for this discrepancy. The instrumentalists of noh were traditionally considered of lower social class than the actors, and the actors were themselves often of lower social class than their amateur patrons. The chanting of noh texts was considered perfectly appropriate even for high-ranking members of the shogunal court, but the instrumental music was considered fit only for the professionals. This attitude has persisted well into the twentieth century and is one reason for the serious shortage of professional instrumentalists in the world of noh today.

In more general terms, the result is a kind of infantilization of the amateur. Expectations for amateur performances are low, and it is exceedingly rare for an amateur to break through into professional ranks. As a consequence, there is a high degree of exclusiveness and nepotism in professional noh circles.

Some would suggest that this is one of the corruptions of modern life, but already in Zeami's separation of the child actor from the adolescent and postadolescent actor, the seed of this dualism exists. A kind of "natural" beauty exists in the world and is exemplified by the beauty of a child, but it is highly perishable, like the flower so prevalent in Zeami's aesthetic theory. The creation of a more controllable and long-lasting beauty depends on a strict, long-term regimen of training, which must, moreover, follow along the lines of one's seniors in the art. The *transmission* from generation to generation not only of techniques and conventions but also a "spirit" of noh is the lifeblood of the art. In this context, one learns by imitation and strict attention to the way one's superiors perform. Training is a recursive, iterative process, experientially based. The body learns the art first, and in mastering its kinetic structures enables the "spirit" or the "heart" to come to an understanding. Getting the outward behavioral form correct may eventually lead to cognitive understanding, but a comprehensive, intellectually based understanding of the art is considered neither necessary nor desirable. An understanding of even the basics of the plot of a given play is not always considered necessary. Consider, for instance, the anecdote about a venerable old actor who was reported to have figured out the story of a play he had performed many times only by listening to an account of it given by another actor during the intermission, while he himself waited inside a prop for his second-act appearance. This is, no doubt, an extreme case, but it is repeated frequently in discussions of noh, only partly for comic effect.

Horse before the cart

There are many possible pitfalls in trying to characterize the pedagogical strengths of Japan from a perspective that grows out of the gnawing awareness that American educational institutions seem to be failing in many areas. Among them one might mention the unquestioned assumption that national identity is a more important factor in such an enterprise than, say, the discipline being taught, the particular individuals involved, the broader historical context in which the instruction or training and the criticism of it occur, the definition of success or failure in the enterprise, and so on. Aware as I am of these pitfalls, I would suggest, all the same, that the traditional arts, specifically noh, offer several possible areas of inquiry that might provide us with a surer and more effective understanding of the differences between American and Japanese pedagogical ideologies and, consequently, possibilities for rethinking what is done in contemporary American education. In conclusion, then, I would offer the following summary of the pedagogical characteristics of training in noh, not because I think they are necessarily ideal or appropriate for all other educational and training contexts, but because they may provide a useful ground for further discussion and elaboration.

1. Training defers and subordinates a comprehensive intellectual grasp of the subject to a mastery of specific, practical details necessary for various tasks associated with performance.
2. Training is centered on the body. The body is the ground from which intellectual, aesthetic, and spiritual understanding grows, and the first order of business is to achieve mastery of the body within the conventions of noh – its sounds, movements, and visual and spatial vocabulary.
3. The pattern for training exists in the example of past masters. The student must try to bury or forget individual impulses and opinions in favor of the insights and instructions of the teacher. The teacher must be trusted and obeyed until one has achieved a comprehensive competence of the physical skills necessary to the art.
4. The tools of the actor are the abstract tools of form, not conscious, intellectually communicable tools of content. The mastery of forms enables the actor to communicate content in the end, but form must be privileged over content in the process of training.
5. Creativity, although manifest in any fine performance, is not a conscious aim of the actor. It is the result of a complete technical mastery and an un-self-conscious response to the specifics of any performance.
6. Serious training is an activity that demands full vocational commitment. Amateur involvement is purely for enjoyment and carries neither the responsibility nor the potential for professional engagement on the art.
7. Training is an unnatural activity that frequently runs counter to individual impulse. With complete mastery, however, it carries the potential of a reunification with nature, which allows unrestrained artistic freedom.
8. Training is different from learning. The latter centers on the intellectual ratification of propositions and the development of a capacity to understand or process more and more complex propositions, many of them unique to one's individual experience. Training is the internalization of technique, allowing one a more and more accurate realization of the conventions and ideals of a traditional body of knowledge.

In conclusion, I would like to consider a certain break with tradition that is central to Zeami's philosophy of training. The tradition in question is that of the practice and poetics of *waka* poetry, the preeminent classical form of thirty-one syllables (5/7/5/7/7). The founding statement of classical poetics in Japan is the preface to *Kokin wakashū*, a collection of *waka* commissioned by the imperial court and eventually completed in 905 C.E. The preface opens with the following sentence: "The poetry of Japan has its roots in the human heart and flourishes in the countless leaves of words."[10]

This statement operates at one level through a sort of pun. The word for "word" is written with graphs meaning "word leaves," and this natural image is made yet more explicit in the notion that intention and affect, rooted in the heart, can "leaf out" in language. The idea can be traced to earlier Chinese poetic theory, but it became in time the central pillar of traditional Japanese aesthetics.

Zeami, however, turns the idea around, substituting "flowers" for "leaves" and transforming the whole to *hana wa kokoro, tane wa waza nari*, "the flower is the mind, the seed is technique" (Omote and Kato, 1974:37). The affectively centered tradition of Japanese poetics is topsy-turvy here. It's not the mind (or heart) that produces the words or art, but the artistic forms and techniques that ultimately cultivate the mind. "Training," then, "is the basis of identity," a statement that might well have been revolutionary in its time but that has now settled into the foundational orthodoxy of Japanese thought.

Notes

1. I have converted Zeami's *kazoedoshi* renderings into Western ages, but it should be remembered that these are all approximate.
2. All translations from Zeami are mine. Some have appeared previously in Hare (1986), as is the case here. This quote is taken from Hare (1986:15ff.). The others were done for this occasion. I base my translations on Omote and Kato (1974).
3. Most importantly in a treatise entitled *Nikyoku santai ningyōzu, Zeami Zenchiku*, 124.
4. At the very bottom, for example, is the Stratum of the Coarse and Leaden, characterized by the somewhat puzzling "tree rat with five [accomplishments]." This makes more sense when glossed via

allusion to Xunzi: "The flying squirrel has five talents, but it is reduced to extremity." This was further annotated by one Guo Pu:

The five talents of the flying squirrel are its abilities to fly, climb, swim, dig, and run. They are deficient in that though it can fly, it cannot fly well enough to get over a roof; though it can climb, it cannot get to the top of a tree; though it can swim, it cannot cross a gorge; though it can dig, it cannot build a safe shelter; and though it can run, it cannot outdistance a man. Thus, none of its talents amounts to real ability. *Xunzi*, I (Stanford, Calif.: Stanford University Press, 1988), pp. 139, 270.

5. In that system, all human thought and activity is parceled out among ten hierarchical levels:

   10. Shingon Sect
    9. Kegon Sect
    8. Tendai Sect
    7. Sanron (Madhyamika) Sect
    6. Hossō Sect
    5. Pratyekabuddha Vehicle of Hīnayāna Buddhism
    4. Śrāvaka Vehicle of Hīnayāna Buddhism
    3. Brāhmanism or popular Taoism
    2. Confucianism
    1. The Person with no moral or philosophical constraints.

   Kūkai, *The Recapitulation of the Ten Stages of Religious Consciousness,* quoted in *Sources of Japanese Tradition,* I (New York: Columbia University Press, 1958), pp. 150–1. Kūkai's concern is not explicitly with training in this scheme, but rather with establishing the hierarchy of wisdom and spiritual attainment. He does not, however, exclude progress up the ladder of understanding within the life of the single individual, and it is noteworthy that the first level of Buddhist undertaking in this scheme is about one-third of the way up from the bottom.

6. In Teika's scheme, the *onihishigitei,* or "style of demon-quelling force," which is taboo for less accomplished poets, becomes acceptable and effective. In Kūkai's version, although the hierarchy is not explicitly a course of training, the attainment of Shingon wisdom gives one Buddhahood in this life, and one can posit, given the fundamentals of Mahāyāna soteriology, that the said Buddha can descend as a Bodhisattva to the aid of beings in the lower levels of the hierarchy.

7. Arthur Waley, *The Analects of Confucius* (New York: Grove Press, 1966), p. 88. The Confucian system is perhaps different, however, in its explicit training of the individual mind to desire only within the "boundaries of right." Zeami's, Kūkai's, and Teika's understanding suggests that the true master of the field knows no boundaries, and indeed, the notion of boundaries itself is highly problematic in a nondualistic system such as Mahāyāna. We can see here a clear rationale for Tantric Buddhism, which, though never fully developed in Japan, comes from the same

religious roots as Kūkai's Shingon to its exfoliation in Tibetan Buddhism.

8. In the Tokugawa period, a structure of shogunal economic patronage and control was far more important than the patronage by students that supports noh today, but the seed for patronage, and its bifurcated system of expectations and training methods, existed then as well, especially in the professional–amateur relations of a noh actor and his daimyo patron.

9. A brief account of the rhythmic structure of noh can be found in Hare (1986:3–6).

10. Translation by Brower and Miner (1963:3).

The Suzuki Method of music instruction

LOIS PEAK

Talent Education, or the Suzuki Method, as it is better known internationally, is an interesting and highly successful method of teaching young children to play musical instruments. Although developed only forty years ago in Japan by Shinichi Suzuki, a Japanese violinist, it now has branches in twenty-three countries and approximately 300,000 students [use it] worldwide. The method's very young students have attracted considerable public notice through their mass performances of difficult works for violin and piano which were previously the province of professional musicians and occasional child prodigies. Although the method itself remains a quintessentially Japanese approach to education which embodies deeply rooted Japanese cultural assumptions, its successful implementation in numerous foreign countries demonstrates its widespread appeal and ability to survive transplantation to other cultures. In the process of being adopted by other countries, certain aspects of the method have been modified to fit the indigenous educational attitudes and practices of the recipient cultures. This is particularly evident in the United States, where the method differs in a number of important respects from the way it is practiced in Japan.

This [essay] will briefly describe the Suzuki Method, and then

Field research for this [essay] was generously supported by a Japan Foundation Fellowship and a Sinclair Kennedy Travelling Fellowship from Harvard University. I am indebted to Merry White, John Singleton, Munir Fasheh, and Senichi Tsuge for their comments on earlier versions of the [essay,] and to Shinichi Suzuke and the members of the Talent Education Institute in Japan for their kindness and cooperation with the research.

From *The Cultural Transition: Human Experience and Social Transformation in the Third World and Japan.* Edited by Merry White and Susan Pollak. Routledge and Kegan Paul, Boston, 1986.

consider various aspects in which the method demonstrates particularly striking continuity with traditional and contemporary Japanese educational attitudes and practices. Finally, some observations on how the American Suzuki Method has been adapted to better fit typical American cultural attitudes and practices will be presented.

A consideration of this particular method of musical training is pertinent to this volume's consideration of the role of education in developing human potential from several perspectives. Because the performance ability of students in the method challenges traditional assumptions about the limits of young children's potential to learn sophisticated skills, it is a striking example of the high level of ability which can be achieved in an optimally structured learning environment. Also, the considerable continuity between this newly developed method's beliefs and practices and traditional Japanese cultural attitudes may suggest new avenues of research concerning the manner in which each culture's own educational institutions reflect deeply rooted indigenous attitudes concerning the appropriate nature of teaching and learning. Finally, the manner in which the Suzuki Method as practiced in America has been modified in the direction of greater consonance with American beliefs and practices may serve as an interesting case study for policy makers who are considering transplanting their own culture's educational institutions to other countries. Previous discussions of the transfer of educational institutions have typically focused on the process of adapting western institutions to fit non-western cultures. The Suzuki method represents a case of educational institutional transfer in reverse – a non-western institution which has been widely adopted in the west and modified to better fit indigenous western educational beliefs and practices. Consideration of this example may illuminate aspects of the process by which imported institutions are modified to better fit different cultures, as well as reveal some of the implicit cultural attitudes about teaching and learning which shape educational institutions in the United States.

Data for this case study were collected during twelve months of participant observation at the Talent Education Institute headquarters in Matsumoto City, Nagano Prefecture, Japan. In addition to class and lesson observation and interviews with Suzuki and other teachers, interviews were conducted with mothers of local children taking lessons and [with] visiting teachers and parents from the United States. The author also lived in Matsumoto from 1973 to 1975, studying as an apprentice violin teacher under Suzuki, and subsequently taught Suzuki Method violin in the United States for a year.

Description of the Suzuki Method

Shortly after the end of the Second World War, Shinichi Suzuki, a German-trained Japanese violinist, began to teach the violin to children in Matsumoto City according to a new educational concept which he had been gradually developing over the previous ten years. Noticing that all normal children learn to speak their native language easily and fluently by the age of five or six, he concluded that if this teaching method were adapted to other subjects, young children could learn equally effectively. This "mother-tongue approach" became the inspiration for the founding of the Talent Education Method in 1946.

Suzuki's mother-tongue approach can be summarized in the following manner (Suzuki, 1974):

1. Structuring the home environment from birth in such a way that the child is in constant contact with the medium to be learned.
2. Beginning instruction with very simple tasks, using imitation and repetition as the basis of the teaching process.
3. Arranging for abundant daily practice.
4. Encouraging the child's interest in the medium to be learned by making it an integral part of positive interaction between the child and the family, especially the mother.
5. Making learning fun by showering praise and affection at each sign of increasing competence, and making lessons and practice sessions challenging and enjoyable.

The Suzuki Method implements this mother-tongue approach in its teaching of violin, piano, cello, and flute to students beginning at the age of two years. Ideally, Suzuki recommends that children be exposed daily from birth to many repetitions of a selected number of recordings of great musical works, as well as the instrumental repertoire which they will later learn. More commonly in practice, when a mother decides that her child is ready to begin lessons, usually at around three years of age, the mother and child initially spend a month or two observing other children's lessons and listening at home to recordings of the repertoire.

When the child's interest in the instrument has been aroused, the *mother* begins lessons a few weeks before the child, and continues her lessons for several months to acquire a basic grounding in the instrument. Once the child's own lessons begin, the mother assumes the role of the child's home teacher, attending all lessons, directing all home practice sessions, and assuming primary responsibility for the child's progress on the instrument.

The first lessons involve only very basic and simple skills and explicit training in building the child's concentration ability. Each tiny step is repeated for several weeks at a time until the child can perform it easily and accurately many times in a row. Typically, it takes a three-year-old child about a year of hard work to accomplish all the steps necessary to play "Twinkle Twinkle Little Star," the first song in the repertoire. After this point, however, the child's fundamental playing position, tone, and rhythmical sense have been solidly established, and progress through the repertoire rapidly snowballs in speed. Children continue to study and practice earlier pieces as they advance and on request can perform from memory any piece they have ever learned.

Weekly lessons occur in a small group, and group playing and instruction are interspersed with short individual lessons, with the other children and mothers looking on. Children progress through a set sequence of musical repertoire, learning the material completely by ear from the recordings until they reach an intermediate level.

Mothers are encouraged to maintain the amount of practice time at the upper level of their children's concentration and stamina, and to disguise the hard work in the form of games that they play together, with inculcation of the teaching points as the objective. Beginning with numerous one- or two-minute sessions per day, parents gradually build their child's ability to concentrate for longer periods. Over an hour of practice per day is not uncommon even for four-year-olds, and enthusiastic mothers may practice even more. Not surprisingly, progress is rapid and children quickly progress to playing difficult professional concert repertoires. Average violin students master Vivaldi concertos at age seven or eight and Mozart concertos at age ten or eleven; faster students perform these works at age five or eight, respectively.

Although the method is better known for its teaching of very young children, many students continue to study within the method through adolescence. As children mature, mothers gradually play a smaller role in home practice sessions and children frequently begin to practice largely on their own after the age of eight or ten. Although some students do go on to enter conservatories and make a career of music, Suzuki avows that the goal of the method is not to produce professional musicians. Rather than emphasizing career training, Suzuki desires to develop sensitivity, fine character, and well-developed general abilities in his students through the study of music.

American interest in the Suzuki Method began during the early 1960s, and by 1965 a few qualified teachers had begun to accept students. Membership in the method rapidly mushroomed, and currently there are approximately 150,000 students in the United States and Canada, outnumbering those in Japan by a factor of four or five. Although most American teachers attempt to model themselves on the method as it is taught in Japan, in a number of respects modifications have been introduced which better fit American cultural beliefs and practices. The following discussion will describe these modifications, as well as the ways in which the Suzuki Method as originally conceived in Japan is a product of Japanese educational beliefs and practices. These topics will be considered in regard to the following aspects of the method: early education and tailoring instruction to the very young child, the role of the mother, teaching techniques, theories of talent and ability development, and the ultimate goal of musical training.

Early education

The Suzuki Method typifies indigenous Japanese folk psychological beliefs in its recommendation that children begin their formal training in the arts well before school age. Although Suzuki's recommendation that children begin formal lessons between the ages of two and three (Suzuki, 1982) anticipates common Japanese custom by a year or two, there is a widespread and very ancient belief that children learn many subjects, particularly music, second languages, and complex physical skills, most easily and naturally during the pre-school years. . . .

In contemporary Japan, the Suzuki Method is only one of several popular musical training methods for pre-school children. In addition to nearly universal enrollment in at least two years of parent-financed pre-school or day care centers (National Institute for Educational Research of Japan, 1983), during the past twenty years, extra enrichment lessons have also become very common for pre-school children. A recently completed pilot survey of the educational histories of all first-grade children in two Tokyo elementary schools (Taniuchi, unpublished, 1983) suggests that a large majority of the 142 children surveyed began attending extracurricular lessons during pre-school. In School A, a laboratory school attached to a well-known educational university which draws students from generally well-educated, upper-middle-class backgrounds, 99 percent of the children had taken extracurricular lessons during pre-school. In School B, a local elementary school in a middle- and working-class neighborhood, 72 percent of the children had taken extracurricular lessons during pre-school. The most popular types of lessons, in order, were swimming, piano, calligraphy, and gymnastics.

When attempting to teach sophisticated skills in a formal lesson situation to pre-school children, considerable care is required in structuring and presenting the lesson material in such a way that the child's interest and motivation are maintained. The Suzuki Method has borrowed from a long Japanese tradition of folk teaching psychology in consciously stimulating the student's motivation to the greatest possible extent before allowing lessons to begin. New Suzuki students and their mothers observe the weekly lessons of the beginner's group that they will later join for a month or two, meanwhile listening daily at home to a recording of the first songs in the repertoire. During weekly lessons, the mother and child watch the other children from the back of the room, and the teacher and other mothers combine in telling the new child how much fun it is to learn to play the violin. Mother explains that if the child is very good, he or she may someday be allowed to join in the fun.

Once the child's interest has been aroused, the *mother* receives from the teacher a tiny violin just the child's size, and the *mother* begins lessons and daily home practice sessions. The child is required to wait a few weeks longer, watching alone from the back of the room during weekly group lessons, and hearing and seeing the mother practice at home the same exercises that he or she will soon learn. At this point it is a rare child who does not daily beg to be allowed to practice the violin too. When the mother and teacher see that the child's motivation is at a fever pitch, the first lessons begin.

With the ingenious twist of adding the mother as primary role model for the pre-school child, the process just described is that of the time-honored *minarai kikan,* or "period of learning through watching." Such varied contemporary institutions as Zen temples, junior-high-school tennis clubs, and salaried employment typically begin with a more or less rigorous and lengthy period during which the prospective applicant is expected to stand on the sidelines and watch the older members' activities. New applicants must demonstrate the seriousness of their intent to join the group by regular attendance, careful observation of group activity, and enthusiastic desire to be included. Once the group has judged a prospective applicant to have demonstrated sufficient staying power and seriousness of intent, he or she is invited to join the group and provided with the necessary equipment.

Once lessons begin, Japanese teachers recognize the importance of maintaining the student's initial enthusiasm for the subject by not dampening the beginner's clumsy but wholehearted attempts through excessively harsh correction. Most teachers believe that teaching is ineffective and the child's ability will not develop unless the child enjoys the learning process and therefore tries hard to learn the material presented. Six hundred years before Rousseau ushered in an era of child-oriented, humanistic educational practices, [Zeami, a famous Japanese philosopher of the arts,] recommended that teachers approach young students beginning the study of Noh drama in the following way:

Allow children to develop their ability naturally by letting them follow their own inclinations freely. Don't excessively point out "this is good" and "that is bad." If children are corrected too excessively, they lose their desire to learn and find Noh tedious and uninteresting. When this happens, their abilities cease to develop.(p. 108)

Suzuki (1981) echoes his twelfth-century predecessor when he urges mothers and teachers of beginning violin students to remember that:

Adults may want to teach numbers or mathematics, but a child wants to be petted and have fun playing. Tasks which are done happily are internalized and in this manner talent is grown carefully. The problem is how to combine interest and training. If a child is always scolded, his ability will not grow. (pp. 21, 23)

In contrast, Americans seem to have a different folk theory of the nature of motivation and interest. Interests are believed to arise primarily from an individual's personality and natural propensities, rather than being largely developed by the surrounding environment. American parents typically wait for their child to spontaneously evidence an interest in and readiness to undertake music lessons through such behavior as special interest in music-oriented play or occasional requests for an instrumental toy to play with. Training in the arts or the choice of a particular type of enrichment lesson is believed to be properly the product of the child's individual choice, rather than the result of a carefully orchestrated parental attempt to arouse the child's interest. Spending several months calculatedly stimulating a small child's desire to play the violin on the basis of a parental decision that the child should take lessons strikes many Americans as overly manipulative. Partly because American parents typically wait for the child to evidence spontaneous interest, children usually begin lessons slightly later, at age four or five.

The Suzuki Method as practiced in America rarely requires a substantial period of observation and daily home listening before the child is allowed to begin lessons. When a preliminary observation period is required, it is frequently considered more a test of the mother's demonstrated interest in the method than an orchestrated attempt to create strong motivation in the child. A child's simple indication of casual interest and willingness is usually sufficient for lessons to begin, without further delay for artificial inflation of the child's motivation.

Japanese Suzuki teachers believe that without an extremely high level of initial motivation, the child is unlikely to be willing to reliably produce the effort necessary to sustain the difficult process of daily coaxing the fingers and body to learn new and difficult combinations which constitutes violin or piano practice. Because a high level of student effort is seen as indispensable for the teaching process to translate into the development of abilities, the child's level of motivation is not left to the vagaries of individual differences and chance, but consciously maximized before beginning the teaching process. While the American reliance on the child's spontaneous interest may serve perfectly well in undertakings such as music lessons, where a child who does not evidence interest may not be forced to take lessons, such an approach may come aground in situations such as public school, where children are required to learn subjects in which they may not be spontaneously interested. In such situations, Japanese folk psychological notions of gradually introducing the child to the subject in a manner carefully calculated to stimulate motivation may be of considerable use. It is worthy of note that a similar process of gradual introduction to the subject matter, designed to elicit the child's interest and motivation, is common in Japanese pre-schools and first grades (Peak, 1991).

The role of the mother

The mother's role in assisting her child's learning is central to the teaching process of the Suzuki Method. Indeed, the method could be summarized by saying that the Suzuki method teaches the mother how to teach her own child to play the violin at home. Mothers attend weekly lessons with a notebook and tape recorder and come forward with their child to sit under the teacher's scrutiny during lessons. During the lesson, the teacher explains directly to the mother what should be practiced at home during the week and demonstrates the process with the student. The lesson ends with the child reciting a promise to practice hard according to the mother's instructions. Mothers are held solely responsible for their child's progress on the instrument, and although children themselves rarely receive less than generous praise and encouragement at weekly lessons, mothers may be quite strictly admonished by the teacher if the child has not been practicing hard enough.

Suzuki holds parents directly responsible not only for the development of their children's abilities, but for children's personality characteristics as well (1981). Stubborn, disobedient children are said to have acquired their parents' own habits of scolding and intransigence, just as cheerful, obedient children reflect their parents' happiness and agreeability. He therefore encourages parents to continually examine their personalities, honestly admit their own faults and openly strive for self-improvement as an example to their children. This idea that parents (particularly mothers) should constantly work to overcome their own personal weaknesses for the sake of their children has deep cultural roots in Confucian moral teachings for women such as Kaibara Ekken's *Onna Daigaku* (*Great Learning for Women*).

However, the idea of mobilizing the mother as a sort of full-time auxiliary private music teacher for the child is probably unique to the Suzuki Method. Traditionally, children who attended abacus, music, or any other types of lessons either did not practice outside of the lesson situation or usually practiced at their teacher's house (Tsuge, 1983). Furthermore, the pattern of intense maternal involvement in children's educational achievement which is characteristic of contemporary Japanese families (E. Vogel, 1963; S. Vogel, 1978; DeVos, 1973) apparently has emerged only during the past few decades (Norbeck, 1978) as academic success has replaced family affiliation as the chief determiner of a child's occupational future.

Contemporary Japanese middle-class mothers are typically heavily involved in their child's educational activities. Although the Suzuki Method expects more maternal participation than do most extracurricular enrichment lessons, the previously described pilot survey of the educational histories of first-grade children (Taniuchi, 1983) showed that 65 percent of first-grade children's extracurricular lessons were either "always" or "frequently" observed by the mother. In addition to after-school lessons, most mothers maintain a busy schedule of school-oriented activities such as frequent PTA meetings, parent visitation days, and the like. At home, the pattern of the Suzuki violin practice session is recapitulated with school assignments through elementary school, as mothers assist with daily homework, monitor assignments, and ensure that the child is prepared for the next schoolday.

This habit of studying together with the child is established during the pre-school years. Japanese mothers informally teach their children many quiet games and activities which develop experience with educational materials such as writing and counting games, drawing, origami paper folding, and listening to story books. Most children also learn to read and write the basic phonetic alphabet (*hiragana*) and do simple arithmetic at home. A 1967 survey (Sakamoto, 1975) of five-year-old children who were to enter elementary school in five months showed that on the average, children could read 36.8 of the 48 *hiragana* letters. This average has risen over the past seventeen years, and currently most children can read almost all 48 letters by the time they enter first grade. This achievement is largely the result of mothers' assistance at home, as pre-schools rarely teach these skills.

Although in the United States mothers also assist their children's homework, they rarely do so to such an extent. Many parents may believe that it weakens a child's self-reliance and lessens the value of the child's achievement if parents are too heavily involved in the daily learning process. In contrast to Japanese theories of achievement, which tend to emphasize an interdependent network of co-operative effort and planning (Glazer, 1976), Americans prefer to emphasize individual effort and ability. Because American parents typically make a clearer distinction between the child's hobbies and learning tasks and those of the parent, the demands of Suzuki music lessons frequently become a heavy burden for American parents. American Suzuki teachers find that only rarely are mothers willing to seriously practice the violin themselves for several months in preparation to teach it to their child. Observing all lessons and leading daily practice sessions often becomes much more than the mothers bargained for when signing their child up for lessons. One of the questions most frequently asked of teachers by American mothers is "How soon will my child be old enough to practice by him (or her) self?"

Teaching techniques

From the point of view of classical western violin and piano pedagogy, perhaps the most unique aspects of the Suzuki Method's teaching techniques are the emphasis on group instruction and the practice of having children initially learn to play by ear. In these respects, the Suzuki Method represents a grafting of traditional Japanese music teaching techniques onto the study of a western instrument. When the Suzuki Method was transplanted to the United States, these Japanized aspects have usually been modified to resemble more closely typical western methods of music pedagogy.

For example, in Japan, Suzuki violin students usually receive their lessons as a member of an informal group of approximately ten or fifteen children whose lessons overlap each other on a given afternoon. Three or four less advanced students and their mothers arrive shortly before the teacher appears, and prepare their instruments and the lesson room for the teacher's arrival. Once the teacher arrives, relatively brief (five- to twenty-five-minute) individual lessons are interspersed with group instruction and remarks addressed informally to the entire group. Students carefully observe each other's lessons to pick up points which may be relevant to their own performance. Gradually, more advanced students arrive and begin observation and participation in the group activities. Earlier students linger once their lessons have finished to observe later students' lessons, usually spending most of the afternoon in the lesson studio. Scheduling is vague and flexible, and the length of an individual lesson may vary greatly depending on the child's attention span and the weekly assignment. The atmosphere is relaxed and friendly, and lessons may be broken off while the teacher chats with the students over tea and cookies. Suzuki teachers believe that this type of group learning is more enjoyable and effective than exclusively private lessons because students have a chance to associate with and learn by modeling for other students, and to pick up hints for their own playing by watching the teacher work with other children.

This type of group lesson scheduling closely resembles that described by Malm (1959) as typical of traditional Japanese music lessons at the turn of the century. Even contemporary extracurricular lessons for children in traditional subjects such as abacus and calligraphy typically follow this scheduling pattern. In America, however, this type of group lesson is notoriously difficult to institute because many parents believe that private instruction in which the teacher's undivided attention is focused on only one child is more effective than either group activities or observation of other children's lessons. The tuition fee is seen as obligating the teacher to spend a fixed amount of time with a student each week, rather than being similar to a membership fee which allows the child to participate in group activities and to receive as much individual attention as the teacher deems his or her attention span and rate of progress require. American teachers therefore experience pressure to schedule an individual half-hour lesson for each child, with the option of observing other children's lessons or participating in separately scheduled group rehearsal sessions. This relieves American parents of the frustration of "waiting around" while other students have their lessons but also deprives the children of the chance for observational learning and fostering of relationships with other students.

To music educators trained in classical western music pedagogy, perhaps the most controversial aspect of the Suzuki Method is that the children initially learn to play by ear from listening to records which they hear daily at home. Typically, Suzuki-trained children do not learn to read music until they are at least seven or eight years old and studying on an intermediate level. Even after an advanced student becomes able to read music easily and well, musical scores are not used during the lesson, and the teacher hears only that part of a piece which the student has learned from memory. The decision to postpone teaching children how to read music until they are seven or eight is understandable in view of the practical difficulties of trying to explain to a pre-school child why there are eight sixteenth notes in a half note. However, Suzuki holds that the main reason for this practice is to avoid focusing students' attention on the process of transcribing written symbols into sound and encourage their attention to musicality and tone production. He insists that because music is an aural medium, the performer should also experience it primarily aurally rather than visually (Suzuki, 1983a).

It is significant, however, that traditional Japanese classical music was also primarily an oral tradition in which students learned to play by ear. Although an incomplete and rudimentary notation existed for traditional instruments, musical scores were typically preserved as privileged objects and only the most advanced students were instructed in their use. Beginners learned pieces by imitating their teacher passage by passage, and through such additional teaching cues as singing and clapping

(Malm, 1959). This is typical of the teaching and learning of traditional instruments in many other cultures, as well as western jazz and folk music (Trimillos, 1983).

For the past several centuries, however, western classical music has been passed on in written form, and taught and learned primarily through decoding musical scores. Such habits die hard, and currently in the United States, the Suzuki Method's postponement of teaching note reading and emphasis on learning by ear is one of the aspects which draws the most serious fire from the method's critics. It also causes considerable uneasiness among American Suzuki teachers themselves, and many teachers try to develop or borrow methods of teaching note reading to shore up what many consider a major weakness of the method. To address this problem, the American *Suzuki Journal* features a regular column on teaching note reading, which is not included in the Japanese monthly journal.

Suzuki has ingeniously adapted this traditional method of teaching by ear to the widespread modern availability of inexpensive record players and cassette tape recorders. Students can listen at home to the pieces they are studying until they learn them by heart. In addition, through constant exposure, they also absorb the musicality and interpretation of the models. For this reason, even advanced students who read music easily are encouraged to listen daily to professional recordings of the works they are studying. Suzuki likens this process of absorption of musical sensitivity to the process of acquisition of the lilt and subtle intonation of one's native dialect (1982).

Many American observers, however, feel uncomfortable about the degree to which Suzuki students are encouraged to listen to and imitate recorded models. In the western artistic tradition, "creativity" or the ability to develop a uniquely individual rendition of even very well-known works is one of the most important goals of the artistic process. Conscious imitation of even artistically superior models is believed to be inimical to the development of such creativity. Perhaps for these reasons, American parents rarely play the recordings as frequently as recommended, and American teachers rarely encourage students past the beginning stages to use the recorded models as daily examples for direct imitation.

Japanese teachers, however, do not consider imitation in such a negative light. They believe that in the effort to approximate an ideal model, students will gain the superior qualities of a great performer, rather than lose that which is distinctive about themselves. Imitation of a superior model has traditionally been the core of the teaching–learning process in almost every Japanese art form or discipline (Malm, 1959; Gutzwiller, 1974). "Creative" or merely different interpretations are not valued solely for their distinctive quality if they lack a concomitant excellence of artistic taste and a high level of technical skill. Students are believed to gain such technical control through tireless attempts to approximate a worthy model, and to develop taste by becoming so imbued with the style of an excellent performer that it becomes their second nature. The Japanese approach does not altogether eschew creativity, but rather considers it more appropriate to the final stage of the learning process when the advanced student has acquired an exquisite control and understanding of the medium and therefore has the skills to produce a significantly important new interpretation rather than merely an idiosyncratic performance.

Theories of talent and ability development

The Suzuki Method holds that all normal children can develop the ability to give a fine violin or piano performance of concert-level repertoire provided they have a conducive home environment and proper training and practice well. Suzuki's belief that musical talent is the result of education rather than heredity is reflected in his choice of the name "Saino Kyōiku," or "Talent Education" Method. He is unshakably optimistic that just as all children learn to speak their native language fluently and confidently, any child can develop comparable musical abilities if proper effort is expended in molding the environment and providing daily practice. For example (Suzuki, 1981):

I am asked, "Is there no superior or inferior ability?" I did not say, "All children are the same." There is no mistake in the genetical rule that there are no two people alike on earth. I am only saying that "Inborn greatness or mediocrity is not known." When looking at a newborn baby, absolutely nobody can say, "This child will be a talented musician" or "This child will be a talented literary person." Every healthy child in Japan has the ability to speak excellent Japanese by the age of six or seven. I ask all mothers, "Does your child speak well?" If the answer is "Yes," then I say, "If so, then that is the evidence that your child can develop excellent abilities with a good education. Have confidence."(pp. 1–2)

As a Japanese, Suzuki is not unique in his belief that abilities are primarily determined by environment and training rather than heredity. A large-scale Japanese government-sponsored survey questioned 4,500 parents from a broad range of social classes in three different prefectures concerning various beliefs and attitudes related to intelligence (Miura, Nagano, and Watanabe, 1976). Overall, 80 percent of respondents indicated that they believed that intelligence is primarily determined by experience and education after birth rather than heredity.

Cummings (1980) reports the prevalence of similar attitudes among teachers in his . . . study of Japanese elementary schools. He notes the total absence of ability grouping of children within the classroom and remarks:

Japanese teachers are, comparatively speaking, well qualified and experienced, and are confident in the learning potential of all students. They are not impressed by the scientific evidence that suggests school achievement is genetically determined. Instead, they believe anyone can learn if he tries and is appropriately guided. (p. 159)

Beginning in junior high school, many Japanese children experience increasing pressure to pass entrance examinations for prestigious high schools and universities (E. Vogel, 1962). In the popular imagination, gaining admission to a top university is the result of almost superhuman diligence and effort rather than inborn ability. Such popular sayings as "pass with four (hours of sleep per night), fail with five" attest more to belief in the crucial role of hard work and perseverance than the actual sleeping schedule of successful applicants. Despite evidence of strong correlations between social class, financial background, early school achievement, and acceptance at elite universities (Cummings, 1980; Rohlen, 1983) the public continues to believe that any given child's chances of success are largely a matter of daily study until late in the evening, with special tutors and attendance at after-school cram schools.

This Japanese belief in the necessity of great persistence and large quantities of hard work for the development of abilities has been noted by numerous writers, particularly Morsbach (1983), who describes the high esteem with which persistence is regarded by the Japanese. Continued effort in the face of a nearly impossible task is an indication of singleness of purpose and great strength of character, and is glorified in many traditional and contemporary stories and sayings. In any type of study or learning situation, it is commonly accepted that the more valuable the skill to be learned, the harder it will be to acquire. Years of intensive self-discipline and training are expected to be necessary to acquire any really important ability.

Suzuki (1969) echoes this attitude when he writes:

> Ability does not just come by nature without training. We have to educate it in ourselves. Stop lamenting lack of talent and develop talent instead. (p. 52)
>
> Practicing according to the correct method and practicing as much as possible is the way to acquire ability. If one is faithful to the principle, superior skill develops without fail. Those who fail to practice sufficiently fail to acquire ability. Only the effort that is actually expended will bear results. There is no shortcut. (p. 109)

Repetition is central to this activity of diligent, persistent practice. Although the word in English connotes doing the same thing again and again in the same way, when a Suzuki teacher tells a student to repeat a particular passage 100 or 1,000 times, they expect that each time the student will strive to play it better than the last. Repetition is continued long past the point at which reasonable competence is reached, until correct performance becomes automatic. This is the process termed "overlearning" in western educational psychology. Suzuki students for this reason continue to review and study every piece in the repertoire on a comprehensive review schedule. Even advanced students are never considered to "outgrow" the most elementary pieces, and Suzuki frequently reteaches how to play open strings and "Twinkle Twinkle" to students playing on a professional level. He asserts that ability is more effectively developed through time spent in repetition and perfection of previously learned material than through learning new material. . . .

In contrast, Americans prefer to de-emphasize the sheer volume of diligent daily practice which is necessary to develop competence in virtually any field. Textbooks for the popular market carry such titles as "Learn German in Sixty Days" or "Ballroom Dancing in Ten Easy Lessons." Folk beliefs and popular stories usually describe superior abilities in already developed forms, or the progress of students who possess natural genius rather than focusing on accounts of average people who achieve prominence through years of determined hard work and perseverance. In learning situations, teachers and parents usually refrain from encouraging children to exert intense, sustained effort in the absence of talent or affinity for a subject, preferring to scale the goal to their estimation of the child's abilities. Morsbach (1983) observes that American culture typically stereotypes those who spend years of intense self-discipline in pursuit of faraway goals as possessing rigid, compulsive personalities, rather than as examples to be admired and emulated.

The American Suzuki Method also tends to de-emphasize repetition and sheer volume of practice. Parents and teachers of pre-school and lower-elementary-school-age students frequently believe that encouraging large amounts of practice (Suzuki recommends one to two hours per day for this age group) is not necessarily good for a child. Rather than building character through training in diligence and persistence, Americans feel that so much practice by such a young child may somehow be vaguely harmful. Perhaps for this reason, young American Suzuki students tend to practice less than they do in Japan.

Furthermore, the American cultural attitude that repetition is usually boring, whereas learning new material is fun, means that Suzuki students and parents become oriented toward rate of progress through the material rather than quality of performance. Students are less willing to continue to practice and study earlier material, and teachers meet resistance from both parents and students in spending lesson time in continued study of "easy" songs. American Suzuki teachers are also less likely to prescribe their Japanese counterparts' favorite prescription for difficult passages: "Practice it 1,000 times this week and then see if it still seems hard." Daily repetition of the records for home listening also suffers, with American parents being less willing to play the same record five or six times every day.

The goal of training

Although most Talent Education students develop surprising proficiency at very young ages, Suzuki asserts that the primary goal of the method is not to train children to become professional musicians, but rather to cultivate the qualities of sensitivity, service to others, and nobility of character in its students. . . .

An emphasis on the spiritual rather than utilitarian goals of artistic training is common in traditional Japanese arts such as archery (Herrigel, 1953), *chadō* (tea ceremony), *kendō* (Japanese fencing), and *shodō* (calligraphy). The suffix *dō* is written with a Chinese character meaning way or path, and when used in this sense connotes a spiritual discipline. Suzuki shares this view of the goal of studying music and in his early writings coined the term *"ongakudō"* or "Path of Music" to describe the properly spiritual nature of musical training. . . .

Rather than mere professionalism or technical expertise, Suzuki's goal is to raise noble human beings who are splendid in mind and heart through the discipline of musical training. He frequently asserts, "to attain high art and musical sense, a pure mind is indispensable" (1969:44). He directly links style and characteristics of violin playing to personality attributes and attempts to change students' personal weak points through prescribing certain techniques of violin practice. In pursuing such training, he concentrates intensively on the more subtle aspects of violin technique, such as tone quality, musical sensitivity, and intonation. For example, a student who lacks the ability to carry out her intentions self-confidently may find herself required to spend months practicing how to produce a clean attack on an open note, repeating a single note 10,000 times each week. A student with an egotistic and self-aggrandizing playing style may find himself the object of Suzuki's frequent teasing and be used as a model in public teaching demonstrations focusing on his weakest points until he learns to be more humble.

Although in his own teaching Suzuki actively attempts to develop students' character through musical training, in practice few other Suzuki teachers even in Japan pursue this goal so purposefully. Most teachers continue to espouse Suzuki's attitude that the primary goal of the method is to develop fine character in their students but pursue this through less radical methods, such as encouraging respect for the teacher and other students, using polite language and greetings, and maintaining a cheerful and positive lesson environment.

Suzuki frequently writes poems and inspirational sayings for distribution to students and presentation at graduation ceremonies which reflect the direct relationship he perceives between a musician's character and the quality of performance, and the almost mystical connection between the quality of a player's tone and the quality of their heart.

"A string has no heart, it sings only with the soul of the player." (*Gen ni ha kokoro nashi, narasu mono no kokoro wo utau nomi.*)

"Tone has a living soul without form." (*Oto ni kokoro ari, sugata naku ikite.*)

Contemporary students of traditional Japanese instruments such as the *shakuhachi* (Japanese bamboo flute) attest to a similar linking of the study of an instrument and spiritual discipline (Gutzwiller, 1974). Learning the instrument is a process of lifelong study of a few basic works of great antiquity which are studied and restudied at gradually deeper levels. The goal is personal and spiritual maturity, and mere musical pleasantry or technical brilliance in the absence of a concomitant spiritual understanding is devalued as empty mechanical wizardry. The quest to produce pure tone or "the true sound of the bamboo," assumes a function similar to that of a Zen *kôan* (a riddle-question whose solution accompanies enlightenment) in itself. The goal is *ichi on jō butsu,* the attainment of enlightenment through perfecting a single note.

The path to achieving this enlightenment through the study of a particular skill requires patient practice of the medium until its component techniques can be performed effortlessly and infallibly, without the benefit of conscious thought. This requires countless repetitions of fundamental techniques concentrating on achieving control of their minutist aspects (Morsbach, 1983). As described above, Suzuki frequently requests such practice from his students, prescribing, for example, 10,000 repetitions of an open tone, concentrating on improving the beauty of the after echo. The goal is for students to transcend the need for their conscious mind to monitor their efforts to achieve a high quality performance, at which time the medium can be practiced as a spiritual exercise in a selfless meditative state of transcendent calm and detachment. The discipline of practicing to attain such a level of performance as well as the insights gained in the transcendent state are believed to positively affect all other aspects of daily life.

Herrigel (1953) beautifully chronicles this learning process in his description of six years spent as a student of a master in the art of Japanese archery. Four years of intensive daily training were necessary before Herrigel could draw the bow and loose the shot with the required unconscious detachment, effortless strength, and infallible timing. The object of this arduous training was the psychological and spiritual attitude of Herrigel himself, and only after considerable spiritual maturity and flawless instinctive control in loosing the arrow had been attained was he allowed to turn his attention to where the shots landed. The goal of the years of patient practice is to become able to abandon the controlling self and to allow perfectly trained ability to function in a state of spiritual transcendence.

Such overtly spiritual goals are quite foreign to American training in the arts. Learning to play an instrument is undertaken either for enjoyment or the utilitarian purpose of pursuing a career. In its transplantation to the United States, the Suzuki Method has so completely lost its original spiritual aspects and character-molding techniques that few American teachers or parents are even aware of their existence. The method focuses on the concrete task of teaching children to play an instrument and rarely espouses higher goals for molding character than helping children learn to enjoy music and providing a warm, supportive lesson environment. This is in consonance with the typically pragmatic American approach to education, and disinterest in spiritual and quasi-mystical quests for self-improvement through long practice and discipline.

The goals of the American Suzuki Method are also not inimical to the pursuit of a musical career. Indeed, in the eyes of many observers, the number of students who go on to pursue careers in music is in some way a measure of the method's success or failure. Many Americans perceive something wasteful in a child who plays concert repertoire at the age of ten, yet does not go on to become a career musician but plays only for the enjoyment of family and friends or personal satisfaction. Also in contrast to Japan, U.S. teachers and students in the Suzuki Method are not isolated from mainstream musical careers, and several conservatories and university music departments sponsor programs in the method.

The Suzuki Method in perspective

Besides those similarities enumerated in this [essay,] there are other aspects in which the Suzuki Method resembles traditional Japanese educational methods. For example, the relationship between Suzuki and his adult students resembles in some aspects the traditional master–disciple relationship, and the method's organizational structure shares many characteristics of the traditional *iemoto* system of fictive kinship. However, every educational institution shares aspects of continuity with its cultural roots, and the evidence of cultural continuities presented in this [essay] is not meant to suggest that there is nothing new about the Suzuki Method.

Particularly in the blending of traditional and contemporary practices, there is much that is innovative. The method's basic approach of teaching western instruments and classical concert repertoire through methods adapted from traditional Japanese instrumental and spiritual training is unique and diverges considerably from Suzuki's own western-style musical training in pre-war Germany. There are many ingenious examples of the blending of traditional and modern elements, as in using the widespread availability of inexpensive cassette tape recorders in the home to supplement the time-honored oral tradition of teaching by ear and greatly increase students' exposure to the music they must learn. Suzuki's idea of recruiting and training the contemporary educationally oriented mother as an auxiliary home music teacher also very effectively ensures that pre-school children will practice in a regular and efficient manner.

Furthermore, this [essay's] description of changes which the method has undergone in its transplantation to the United States is not meant to suggest that the American version of the method is incorrect or inappropriate within the American setting. This judgmental view is particularly common among both Japanese and American participants in the Suzuki Method, who tend to discount the legitimacy of culturally different educational attitudes and practices in favor of a unidimensional value system in which the original Japanese method is "good" and the aspects in which the American version differs are "bad" or "wrong." Perhaps, by understanding how these changes reflect deeply rooted American cultural beliefs and practices we may understand them not as mistakes or perversities, but as arising from different conceptions of the nature of the process of teaching and learning which contributes to the strength and vitality of other American educational institutions and practices. In a different context, for example, the American penchant for utilitarian rather than character-building goals of training and emphasis on non-repetitive short-cut learning procedures may allow for a broader dissemination of practical skills and a greater willingness to attempt to learn things oneself without relying on a teacher's authority.

However, a teaching method as complex as the Suzuki Method functions as a carefully-balanced inter-related whole, and by changing some aspects of the method, one subtly changes the internal dynamics of the system and achieves a different end product. One example of how this has occurred in the adaptation of the Suzuki Method to American cultural values is the effect of different beliefs about the appropriate role of the mother in the child's learning. Because American mothers are in general less willing or able to be extensively involved for several hours a day in their children's music practice, they spend little time practicing the violin themselves, play the practice tapes less often, and find it difficult to supervise lengthy practice sessions. This means that American children either practice less or must accept more responsibility for their own music lessons at earlier ages, and this pays off in less efficient and careful practice, which in turn affects the average level of American students' performance.

Rather than stubbornly attempting to urge the ultimately unsuccessful process of changing American mothers' conception of their own role so that it becomes more Japanese, successful practitioners must modify and readjust the method to compensate for highly resistant cultural beliefs and practices. By attempting to modify culturally discrepant demands and introducing new techniques which serve a similar teaching function, the method can adapt itself to the new culture without seriously decreasing its effectiveness. However, it is important in this process that the method does not only borrow those aspects which are congenial and ignore others, as this can create serious imbalance and inefficiency in the overall system. For example, American reluctance to encourage students to learn primarily through imitation of models and impatience with large amounts of repetition means that many parents do not daily play and replay the practice recordings at home. This makes it difficult for children to learn new material and to memorize thoroughly that which they have learned. In compensation, many American Suzuki teachers have found it necessary to develop methods of teaching music reading to young students so that they can efficiently learn new pieces.

Perhaps this [essay's] description of the Suzuki Method can provide some ideas for those practitioners who contemplate transporting educational institutions across cultures. Ideally, in the process, both cultures can learn from each other and combine their own strengths with new ideas developed in different traditions. In the case of the Suzuki Method, a basically traditional Japanese method of music instruction has been adapted to local beliefs and customs in numerous countries throughout the world. In the process, it has demonstrated not only that very young children can learn a highly complex skill such as playing the violin, but also that they can learn to experience the joy of making music. This in itself is perhaps the most significant contribution of the method.

Conclusion: themes in the Japanese culture of learning

THOMAS P. ROHLEN AND
GERALD K. LETENDRE

There is no single stereotypical experience that defines the Japanese process of learning, but as we have seen, there are many themes that appear in the various contexts we have been considering. Together these make larger patterns of practice that one encounters frequently when looking closely at learning and teaching in Japan. The preceding essays have presented a rich variety and raised many questions about how such variety is to be understood. In this Conclusion, we highlight the underlying patterns that organize the diversity – the unifying themes, contradictions, complementarities, discontinuities, and challenging issues before Japan. These constitute key aspects of the temporal and spatial dimensions of a landscape of learning and teaching.

Put another way, certain expressions or models of learning or teaching in Japan evoke expectations, patterns, and associations that are identifiable across situations. Within these patterns, both teachers and learners express themselves in terms of certain ideal concepts that shape an inherent dialogue and guide attention to shared expectations.

Play

Much of Shinto ritual is about play (*asobi*) as entertainment for the gods, just as play is a natural avenue for growth and vitality in the teaching approach to early education. Along with the notion of just letting the child grow, there is the notion that in the early years, children should just play. *Asobi* has connotations of unstructured, renewing activity – activity with a creative or energizing potential. This focus on allowing natural energies to flow freely and strongly is part of very old ideas about learning as well as health. The three words that encapsulate this orientation – *asobi, akarui,* and *genki* – are three of the most, if not the three most, important themes in the adult construction of what is desirable in the way learning occurs in the early life of the child.

Group lifestyle

Across virtually the entire sequence of organized learning from school to company, one encounters an ideal of group living (*shudan seikatsu*). Children in first grade are not the only ones to be put through a routine of ordering shoes at the entrance to a room. The same instructive experiences can be seen throughout all levels of schooling, in student clubs and athletics, in company training, and in all forms of spiritual training. Indeed, it seems that this initial concern with socialization to the group (whatever organization the new member is joining) signals that a learning process is beginning. This model is one that appears to hold for virtually all forms of Japanese teaching and learning. Contrary to our current stereotypes, the most common mode of teaching and learning in Japan is not the impersonal lecture – rote memorization and test cramming – but rather the collective learning in elementary school experienced as group living. The continuities between grade one and year one of employment are remarkably parallel in this regard. This does more than set in place an orderly compliance, it also sends the critical message that learning will be shared, that it will be a collective experience. This "socialization model" is utilized in the various clubs, activities, and social organizations in which Japanese participate as children, adolescents, and adults.

Mutuality and imitation

In this schema, learning is pervaded by the assumption that it is a mutual process; the advancement of one's teacher or one's seniors also opens up the way for one's own advancement. Learning functions as an egalitarian principle for all members of the learning collective. This principle helps to modify or counteract the tension produced by the fact that seniority hierarchies are common and that there is much competition to succeed. Full participation of all members is encouraged and desired. Differentiation of ability is downplayed, as it is divisive. What is crucial to the group is the continued general advancement that all members can share. It follows, then, that "imitation is the highest form of praise" in the Japanese cultural logic. Whereas Americans relegate imitation to a position inferior to creativity, Japanese culture elevates imitation as a powerful road to mastery.

This concept of mutuality does not extend simply to persons. The term "mastery" has meanings far different from our Western sense of domination and rule. Mastery is a process of adapting oneself to the material rather than of controlling or subordinating the material to oneself. Conversely, it may be argued that the learner must first accept his or her subordination to the material, task, or form. The advanced potter says he has *learned from the clay*.

Energy

The notion of vitality (*genki*) expressed in such things as curiosity and energetic play is central to Japanese understanding of the child's self and learning potential in the schooling years. This vitality should not be interfered with or inhibited if the child is to progress correctly. The main thrust of teaching is to socialize the child to group circumstances (thus weaning the child, to an extent, from its family circumstances) while not interfering with the flow of individual vitality that is understood to basically define the learning capacities of young children.

Brightness

Akarui, the flow of energy, which is a constant focus of teacher and parental concern, is also a key concern of Shinto. Shinto rituals often focus on efforts to facilitate natural vitality in all manner of living things and to undo (often through rituals of purification or consolation) whatever inhibits or clogs the paths to such expression. Second, one frequently hears teachers and parents speaking of "brightness" in both the classroom environment and the children. A lively, positive atmosphere in class, in the faces of the children, and in their interaction is highly desirable, just as in Shinto there is a cosmological preoccupation with generating light and serving the forces of light over darkness for purposes of fertility and health. Renewing energy in adults is also an aspect, as is the kinds of character training in which initiates are subjected to extremes of cold and heat.

Form

Almost every kind of learning begins with a set form (*katachi*). Training in the form is to be repeated over and over. This is viewed as the outward embodiment of teaching (*oshie*) that is being transmitted. "Learning starts with form" (*kata de hajimeru*) is a common phrase in the traditional arts and crafts (Hori and Hare, this volume). It is the form itself, not the teacher, that seems to be the highest authority. Forms have been perfected by generations of teachers and are therefore the essence of accumulated experience transmitted across time, transcending the individual. Almost all teaching and learning rest on various kinds of forms as crucial media of transmission. Form is, after all, the most concrete way of embodying experience, directly enjoining the learner to repeat a pattern that countless others have experienced.

If we examine this notion closely, we find two very interesting differences between our own attitudes and those of the Japanese. Initially we want explanations, and we feel we need to give much explanation to new learners. The form we tend to rely on most heavily is verbal, whereas the Japanese give greater emphasis to physical activities. Witness the seemingly endless repetition of *kata* (form) that would-be martial arts experts must undergo in judo, karate, and aikido. We as Americans do not like the idea of form as authority (note our preference for informality), and this is manifested in our seeking to change or ignore forms in the name of spontaneity, independence, and creativity. We feel that the Japanese treat forms with undue respect. When we think of what is learned, we tend to think that it arises from allowing the learner to exercise choice, whereas in Japan it arises from the experience of following the form repeatedly until the wisdom or truth embodied in the form become apparent and identification occurs.

Experience

Learning is inherently a matter of experience, and this experience involves the whole person. The Anglo-American inclination to separate cognitive and emotional aspects has not taken hold in Japan. Phrases like "memorizing with one's body" (*karada de oboeru*) indicate that there is less reliance on verbal transmission. Many forms of learning begin in less explicit ways than we would expect. This emphasis on experience also leads to prizing experience over theory and adds authority to the ideas of one's seniors, the group's history, and the weight of the past.

Repetition of basics

How does one gain the experience of the form? How do we enter through form (*katachi de hairu*)? In all the learning situations we review, we see a consistent emphasis on mastery of the basics (i.e., the training forms) through repetition. Mastery of basics (*kihon, moto*) is the motto of every middle school math teacher, potter, and line supervisor. There is nothing more important than the basics. From geometry to the violin and Noh, until the learner masters the basic forms there can be no true progress. This is embodied in the Kumon approach as well. The quick accomplishments of a *wunderkind* are suspect – houses quickly built on sand that will not stand. The solid performance of one skilled in the basics – a person to whom the basics are physical responses, ingrained reactions from years of repetition – is valued.

Authority of teachers

A teacher is anyone who has the authority of experience, the mastery of basics and form. More loosely, anyone who is a senior has at least some qualities of the master (*sensei*), the guide (*shidosha*), and the elders (*senpai*). This is not simply a question of age but reflects the length and quality of experience. Age simply implies more time to accumulate facts, but the Japanese conception is based on a notion of the actualization of wisdom. The teacher or *sensei* is steeped in the forms or experience, and it is evident in his body and his actions. All persons are teachers and learners simultaneously – all travelers along a shared path of forms.

Effort

A crucial linchpin that unites the ideology of equality with competition is that of effort (*doryoku*), especially effort as exhibited in self-discipline. First, consider how Japanese notions of form and experience make more natural an acceptance of effort explanations over ability explanations for achievement in every learning sphere. In Anglo-American culture, which highlights the unique, the creative, and the individual, ability has powerful connotations. It is a distinguishing, inborn quality rather similar to a concept like self or personality and therefore is consistent with individualism in general. In Japanese culture, ability is certainly recognized, but as with the tortoise and the hare, ability is not what wins in the end. Only by effort can one master the forms and gain the experience. Ability in itself does not engage the learner in many of the crucial aspects of the process.

Struggle

There is no good way to translate a set of words (*dodrokyu, nintai, gambaru,* and so forth) that one runs across with stunning frequency in learning situations, and that may be roughly approximated by English terms like "hanging in," "giving one's best," "toughing it out," "not giving up," and similar notions. Nor can we as Americans hear the Japanese term for suffering (*kuro*) without wondering how such a notion is so central to learning situations. We ourselves are only a generation or two removed from the educational ideal of "spare the rod and spoil the child," yet we today are thoroughly predisposed to think of learning as necessarily pleasant, if not exciting. Teachers are responsible for making their classes "interesting," "fun," and "engaging." We have embraced the notion that the inherent labor and pain of learning are to be avoided, disguised, and denied.

Gambaru (effort), *kuro* (suffering), and *gaman* (persistence) are words that are widely used in the spiritual or character-building contexts ubiquitous to Japanese learning. These terms are used in a specifically physical sense – we must note just how physical learning actually is – and often when endurance or exhausting repetition are involved. Exertion is necessary for progress, and to progress in the form, to gain the experience it embodies, it is crucial that one persist and not give up; and that one experience the pain of such a struggle. The new monk, the new potter, or the aspiring third-year middle school student persist through painful repetitions because they fully believe that without experiencing these hardships or trials, nothing can be achieved. Advancement in learning is not assumed to be fun or easy. Rather, it is the challenge and difficulty that provide personal growth – confidence, commitment, and character.

Perfectibility

Absolutes are rarely attainable in the human realm; yet in Japan, in many realms, with continual actions directed at perfection (*kaizen*), this is viewed as always possible. The process of learning continuously is normal. There is no final end point. Persons at any stage have the ability to progress if they study and devote their energies to it. Even among Zen adherents, a fully enlightened master is rare. There is a continual search for improvement, a looking outside oneself (*hansei*) or one's company for renewed dedication and insight. The increments of improvement are often minuscule, but they are real all the same. Perfectibility builds on past accomplishments. It is an inherent property of all human activity, a slow and painstaking process of refinement. It is such a sense of perfection that led Akira Kurosawa, at seventy years of age, to remark that he still had "much work" to do in order to make truly great films.

This is substantially different from American ideas of change and renovation. We assume almost automatically that, to improve, we have to "break out of" our old ways of doing things and forge a new way. We see – in our seemingly endless cycles of educational reform in this country, for example – a tremendous emphasis on finding a new and better way that makes old ways obsolete.

The Japanese themes we have just discussed form a core of expectations about learning out of which myriad learning situations are constructed. They are like old, tried-and-true methods that require only a little innovation and stand ready to be applied to any set of new circumstances, be they computer chip production or maintaining the health of a rapidly aging population through social education programs. By knowing these themes, we can increase our understanding of the power their logic holds in Japanese schools, training programs, traditional arts, and so forth. They comprise a web of mutually sustaining sets of meanings that form the particularly Japanese foundation of learning as social action.

References

Adler, P. 1993. "Time and Notion Regained." *Harvard Business Review* 71, 97–108.

Arai, P. 1993. "Innovators for the Sake of Tradition: Zen Monastic Women in Modern Japan." Ph.D. dissertation, Harvard University.

Ausbel, D. and Robinson, F. 1969. *School Learning: An Introduction to Educational Psychology.* New York: Holt, Rinehart & Winston.

Azuma, H. 1979. *Kodomo no Nōryoku to Kyōiku Hyōka (Children's Abilities and Educational Assessment).* Tokyo: University of Tokyo Press.

1986. "Why Study Child Development in Japan?" In H. W. Stevenson, H. Azuma, and K. Hakuta, eds., *Child Development and Education in Japan.* New York: W. H. Freeman, pp. 3–12.

Befu, H. 1971. *Japan, An Anthropological Introduction.* New York: Harper & Row.

1986. "The Social and Cultural Background of Child Development in Japan and the United States." In H. W. Stevenson, H. Azuma, and K. Hakuta, eds., *Child Development and Education in Japan.* New York: W. H. Freeman.

Benedict, R. 1946. *The Chrysanthemum and the Sword: Patterns of Japanese Culture.* New York: New American Library.

Berger, P., Berger, B., and Kellner, H. 1974. *The Homeless Mind.* New York: Vintage Books.

Boocock, S. S. 1986. "The Social and Cultural Background of Child Development in Japan and the United States." In H. W. Stevenson, H. Azuma, and K. Hakuta, eds., *Child Development and Education in Japan.* New York: W. H. Freeman, pp. 13–27.

1987. "The Privileged World of Little Children: Preschool Education in Japan." Paper presented at the annual meeting of the Comparative and International Education Society, Washington, DC, March.

Brower, R. and Minor, E. 1963. *Japanese Court Poetry*. Stanford, CA: Stanford University Press.

Brown, A. L. 1992. "Design Experiments: Theoretical and Methodological Challenges in Creating Complex Interventions in Classroom Settings." *Journal of the Learning Sciences* 2:2, 141–78.

Brown, A. L., Ash, D., Rutherford, M., Nakagawa, K., Gordon, A., and Campione, J. C., 1993. "Distributed Expertise in the Classroom." In G. Salomon, ed., *Distributed Cognitions: Psychological and Educational Considerations*. New York: Cambridge University Press.

Brown, A. L., and Campione, C. 1990. "Communities of Learning and Thinking, or a Context by Any Other Name." In D. Kuhn, ed., *Developmental Perspectives on Teaching and Learning Thinking Skills*, Vol. 21, 108–26.

Carpenter, T. P., Fennema, E., and Franke, M. L. 1992. "Cognitively Guided Instruction: Building the Primary Mathematics Curriculum on Children's Informal Mathematical Knowledge." Paper presented at the annual meeting of the American Educational Research Association, San Francisco, April.

Case, R. *Intellectual Development: Birth to Adulthood*. Orlando, FL: Academic Press, 1985, chap. 15.

Cobb, P., Wood, T., Yackel, E., and McNeal, E. (in press). "Characteristics of Classroom Mathematics Traditions: An Interaction Analysis."

Cummings, W. 1980. *Education and Equality in Japan*. Princeton, NJ: Princeton University Press.

Developmental Studies Center. 1992. *Dissemination Baseline Study*. Oakland, CA: Developmental Studies Center.

DeVos, G. 1973. *Socialization for Achievement*. Berkeley: University of California Press.

Dore, R. 1965. *Education in Tokugawa Japan*. Berkeley: University of California Press.

1973. *British Factory, Japanese Factory*. London: Allen and Unwin.

Douglas, M. 1986. *How Institutions Think*. Syracuse, NY: New York University Press.

Duke, B. 1986. *The Japanese School: Lessons for Industrial America*. New York: Praeger.

Easley, J., and Easley, E. 1983. "Kitamaeno School as an Environment in which Children Study Mathematics Themselves." *Journal of Science Education in Japan* 7, 39–48.

Educational and Cultural Exchange Division. 1983. "Course of Study for Elementary Schools in Japan." Tokyo: International Affairs Department, Science and International Affairs Bureau, Ministry of Education, Science and Culture, Government of Japan, Tokyo.

Eisner, E. 1982. *Cognition and Curriculum*. New York: Longman.

Elam, S. 1989. "Second Gallup/Phi Delta Kappa Poll of Teachers' Attitudes Toward the Public Schools." *Phi Delta Kappan* 71, 787–798.

Erickson, F. 1984. "School Literacy, Reasoning, and Civility: An Anthropologist's Perspective." *Review of Educational Research* 54:4, 525–46.

Everhart, R. 1983. *Reading, Writing and Resistance: Adolescence and Labor in a Junior High School*. Boston: Routledge and Kegan Paul.

Foreman, R., ed. 1990. *The Problem of Pure Consciousness*. New York: Oxford University Press.

Foucault, M. 1979. *Discipline and Punish: The Birth of Prison*. Trans. by Alan Sheridan. London: Penguin Books.

Foulk, T. G. 1988. "The Zen Institution in Modern Japan." In K. Kraft, ed., *Zen: Tradition and Transition*. New York: Grove Press, pp. 157–77.

Frank, M. L., Fennema, E., Carpenter, T. P., and Ansell, E. 1992. "The Process of Teacher Change in Cognitively Guided Instruction." Paper presented at the annual meeting of the American Educational Research Association, San Francisco, April.

Fujita, M. 1989. "It's All Mother's Fault: Childcare and the Socialization of Working Mothers in Japan." *Journal of Japanese Studies* 15, 1.

Gardner, H. 1985. *Frames of Mind*. New York: Basic Books.

Geary, D. F. L., and Bow-Thomas, C. 1992. "Numerical Cognition: Loci of Ability Differences Comparing Children from China and the U.S." *Psychological Science*, 3:3, 180–4.

Glazer, N. "Social and Cultural Factors in Japanese Economic Growth." In H. Patrick and H. Rosovsky, eds., *Asia's New Giant: How the Japanese Economy Works*. Washington, DC: Brookings Institution, 1976, pp. 813–16.

Goodlad, J. 1984. *A Place Called School*. New York: McGraw-Hill.

Graham, P. A. 1992. *S.O.S.: Sustain Our Schools*. New York: Hill and Wang.

Guilford, J. 1968. *Intelligence, Creativity, and Their Educational Implications*. San Diego: Knapp.

Gutzwiller, A. 1974. "Shakuhachi: Aspects of History, Practice and Teaching." Ph.D. dissertation, Wesleyan University.

Hall, I. P. 1973. *Mori Arinori*. Cambridge, MA: Harvard University Press.

380   *References*

Hallinan, M. T. 1987. "Ability Grouping and Student Learning." In M. Hallinan, ed., *The Social Organization of Schools*. New York: Plenum, pp. 41–70.

Hara, H., and Wagatsuma, H. 1974. *Shitsuke [Childrearing]*. Tokyo: Kobundo.

Hare, T. 1986. *Zeami's Style*. Stanford, CA: Stanford University Press.

Hendry, J. 1986. *Becoming Japanese: The World of the Preschool Child*. Honolulu: University of Hawaii Press.

Herrigel, E. 1953. *Zen in the Art of Archery*. London: Routledge.

Hess, R. D., and Azuma, H. 1991. "Cultural Support for Schooling: Contrasts Between Japan and the United States." *Educational Researcher* 20, 1–12.

Hill, D. 1990, April. "Order in the Classroom." *Teacher Magazine*, 70–7.

Horio, T. 1988. *Educational Thought and Ideology in Modern Japan: State Authority and Intellectual Freedom*. Ed. and trans. by S. Platzer. Tokyo: University of Tokyo Press.

Inagaki, T., and Ito, Y. 1990. "Teacher's Roles and Responsibilities." Paper presented at the Third Annual Symposium, University of Tokyo, July 8–12, 1990.

Jackson, P. W. 1990. *Life in Classrooms*. New York: Teachers College Press.

Jackson, P. W., Boostrom, R. E., and Hansen, D. T. 1993. *The Moral Life of Schools*. San Francisco: Jossey-Bass.

Jepperson, R. 1991. "Institutions, Institutional Effects and Institutionalism." In W. Powell and P. Dimaggio, eds., *The New Institutionalism in Organizational Analysis*. Chicago: University of Chicago Press, pp. 143–64.

Kajita, M., Shioda, S., Ishida, H., and Sugie, S. 1980. "Shō-chūgakkō ni okeru shidō no chōsateki kenkyuu I (Survey of Teaching Methods in Elementary and Junior High Schools I)." Nagoya University *Bulletin of the Faculty of Education* 27, 147–82.

Kapleau, P. 1965. *The Three Pillars of Zen*. Tokyo: John Wethermill.

Kariya, T. 1988. "Institutional Networks between Schools and Employers and Delegated Occupational Selection to Schools: A Sociological Study of the Transition from High School to Work." Ph.D. dissertation, Northwestern University.

Katz, S., ed. 1978. *Mysticism and Philosophical Analysis*. New York: Oxford University Press.

1983. *Mysticism and Religious Traditions*. New York: Oxford University Press.

Kim, H.-J. 1985. "Introductory Essay: Language in Dogen's Zen." In

Flowers of Emptiness: Selections of Dogen's Shobogenzo. Lewiston/Queenston, Australia: Edwin Mellen Press.

Kliebard, H. 1987. *The Struggle for the American Curriculum.* New York: Routledge and Kegan Paul.

Kohn, A. 1993. *Punished by Rewards.* New York: Houghton-Mifflin.

Kojima, H. 1986. "Child-rearing Concepts as a Belief-value System of the Society and the Individual." In H. Stevenson, ed., *Child Development and Education in Japan.* New York: Freeman, pp. 39–54.

Kotloff, L. 1988. "Dai-ichi Preschool: Fostering Individuality and Cooperative Group Life in a Progressive Japanese School." Ph.D. dissertation, Cornell University.

Kumon, T. 1991. *Yatte Miyō, Kodomo no Chiteki Kanōsei wo Tsuikyushite (Try and See: Exploring the Possibilities of Children's Understanding).* Tokyo: Seikosha.

Kurita, Y. 1990. "The Culture of the Meeting: The Tradition of *yoriai* or Village Meeting." *Senri Ethnological Studies* 28, 127–40.

Lebra, T. S. 1976. *Japanese Patterns of Behavior.* Honolulu: University of Hawaii Press.

Lepper, M. 1981. "Social Control Processes, Attributions of Motivation, and the Internalization of Social Values." In E. T. Higgins, D. Ruble, and W. Hartup, eds., *Social Cognition and Social Behavior: Developmental Perspectives.* San Francisco: Jossey-Bass.

Lewis, C. C. 1984. "Cooperation and Control in Japanese Nursery Schools." *Comparative Education Review* 32, 69–84.

——— 1988. "Japanese First Grades: Implications for U.S. Theory and Research." *Comparative Education Review* 32, 69–84.

——— 1989. "From Indulgence to Internationalization: Social Control in the Early School Years." *Journal of Japanese Studies* 15, 139–57.

——— 1992. "Creativity in Japanese Education." In R. Leestma and H. J. Walberg, eds., *Japanese Educational Productivity.* Michigan Papers in Japanese Studies, 22, pp. 225–266. Ann Arbor: University of Michigan Center for Japanese Studies.

——— 1995. *Educating Hearts and Minds: Reflections on Japanese Preschool and Elementary Education.* New York: Cambridge University Press.

Lynn, R. 1988. *Educational Achievement in Japan.* Armonk, NY: Sharp.

Malm, W. 1959. *Japanese Music and Musical Instruments.* Rutland, VT: Charles E. Tuttle Co.

McCarthy, B. 1987. *The 4-MAT System: Teaching to Learning Styles with Right/Left Mode Techniques.* Barrington, IL: Excel.

McDermott, R. P. 1977. "Social Relations as Contexts for Learning in School." *Harvard Educational Review* 47:2, 198–213.

Meyer, J. 1994a. "Rationalized Environments." In R. W. Scott and J. Meyer, eds., *Institutional Environments and Organizations.* Thousand Oaks, CA: Sage, pp. 28–53.

1994b. "Social Environments and Organizational Accounting." In R. W. Scott and J. Meyer, eds., *Institutional Environments and Organizations.* Thousand Oaks, CA: Sage, pp. 121–36.

Meyer, J., Boli, J., and Thomas, G. 1994. "Ontology and Rationalization in the Western Cultural Account." In R. W. Scott and J. Meyer, eds., *Institutional Environments and Organizations.* Thousand Oaks, CA: Sage, pp. 9–27.

Ministry of Education, Science and Culture, Japan. 1983. Science and International Affairs Bureau. UNESCO and International Affairs Department. Educational and Cultural Exchange Division. *Course of Study for Elementary Schools in Japan.* Tokyo: Ministry of Education, Science and Culture.

Miura, K., Nagano, S., and Watanabe, K. 1976, February. "Parents' Beliefs and Attitudes about Intelligence." In *Bulletin of the National Institute for Educational Research of Japan,* No. 38. Tokyo: NIER.

Monbusho. 1988. Research and Statistics Division. Minister's Secretariat. *Statistical Abstract of Education, Science and Culture.* Tokyo: Ministry of Education, Science and Culture.

1989a. *Outline of Education in Japan, 1989.* Tokyo: Ministry of Education, Science and Culture.

1989b. *Shōgakkō gakushū shidō yōryō* [*Course of Study for Elementary Schools*]. Tokyo: Ministry of Education, Science and Culture.

Montessori, M. 1964. *The Montessori Method.* New York: Schocken Books.

Morsbach, H. 1983. "Socio-Psychological Aspects of Persistence in Japan." In *Essays on Japanology, 1978–1982.* Kyoto: Bunrikakau.

Nagano, S. 1983. "Docility and Lack of Assertiveness: Possible Causes of Academic Achievement in Japanese Children." Paper presented at the Conference on Japanese Education and Child Development, Center for Advanced Study in the Behavioral Sciences, Stanford, CA, April.

Nakane, C. 1970. *Japanese Society.* Berkeley: University of California Press.

National Institute for Educational Research of Japan, Section for Educational Cooperation in Asia. 1983. *Preschool Education in Japan.* NIER Occasional Paper 04/83. Tokyo: NIER.

Nicholls, J. G. 1989. *The Competitive Ethos and Democratic Education.* Cambridge, MA: Harvard University Press.

Nihon Kyōshoku linkai. 1974. *"Hyōka to Testo: Shinhan Testo Furiyo Undo no Zenshin no Tame ni"* ("Evaluation and tests: For the Advancement of the Non-testing Movement"). Tokyo: Okumura Insatsu Kabushikigaisha.

Nitobe, I. 1905. *Bushido: The Soul of Japan.* Rutland, VT: Charles Tuttle Co.

Noddings, N. 1984. *Caring, a Feminine Approach to Ethics and Moral Education.* Berkeley: University of California Press.

Norbeck, E. 1978. *Country to City: The Urbanization of a Japanese Hamlet.* Salt Lake City, UT: University of Utah Press.

Okamoto, Y., Calfee, R., Varghese, S., and Chambliss, M. 1991. "A Cross-Cultural Comparison of Textbook Designs." Paper presented at the Annual Meeting of the American Educational Research Association, Washington, DC, April.

Okano, K. 1993. *School to Work Transition in Japan.* Cleveland: Multilingual Matters.

Omote, A. and Kato, S. 1974. *Zeami, Zenchiku, Nihon Shiso Taikai,* Vol. 24 Tokyo: Iwanami Shoten.

Peak, L. 1987. "Learning to Go to School in Japan: The Transition from Home to Preschool Life." Ph.D. dissertation, Harvard University Graduate School of Education.

1989, Winter. "Learning to Become Part of the Group: The Japanese Child's Transition to Preschool Life." *Journal of Japanese Studies* 15:1, 93–124.

1991. *Learning to Go to School in Japan.* Berkeley: University of California Press.

1992. "Formal pre-elementary education in Japan." In R. Leestma and H. J. Walberg, eds., *Japanese Educational Productivity.* Michigan Papers in Japanese Studies, No. 22. Ann Arbor: University of Michigan Center for Japanese Studies, pp. 35–68.

Pelzel, J. C. 1970. "Japanese Kinship: A Comparison." In M. Freedman, ed., *Family and Kinship in Chinese Society.* Stanford, CA: Stanford University Press, pp. 227–48.

Peterson, P. L. 1992. "Using Teachers' and Learners' Knowledge to Transform Teaching." Paper presented at the annual meeting of the American Educational Research Association, San Francisco, April.

Plath, D. W. 1975. "From the Zabuton: A View of Personal Episodes." In D. W. Plath, ed., *Adult Episodes in Japan. Journal of Asian and African Studies* (Special Number) 10:1–2, 1–9.

1980. *Long Engagements: Maturity in Modern Japan.* Stanford, CA: Stanford University Press.

Proudfoot, W. 1985. *Religious Experience.* Berkeley: University of California Press.

Reischauer, E. 1977. *The Japanese*. Rutland, VT: Charles Tuttle Co.

Reynolds, D. K. 1980. *The Quiet Therapies*. Honolulu: University of Hawaii Press.

Reynolds, R. 1969. "Directed Behavior Change: Japanese Psychotherapy in a Private Mental Hospital." Ph.D. dissertation, UCLA.

Richards, J. (in press). "Mathematical Discussions." In E. von Glasersfeld, ed., *Constructivism in Mathematics Education*. Dordrecht: Reidel.

Rohlen, T. P. 1970. "Sponsorship of Cultural Continuity in Japan: A Company Training Program." *Journal of Asian and African Studies* 5:3, 184–92.

———. 1974a. *"Seishin Kyōiku* in a Japanese Bank: A Description of Methods and Consideration of Some Underlying Concepts." In G. Spindler, ed., *Education and Cultural Process*. Ft. Worth, TX: Holt, Rinehart and Winston, pp. 219–29.

———. 1974b. *For Harmony and Strength: Japanese White-collar Organization in Anthropological Perspective*. Berkeley: University of California Press.

———. 1974c. Ki and kokoro: Japanese perspectives on the nature of the person. Paper presented at the regional seminar on Japanese Studies, University of California, Berkeley.

———. 1975. "The Company Work Group." In E. F. Vogel, ed., *Modern Japanese Organization and Decision-making*. Berkeley: University of California Press, pp. 184–209.

———. 1977. "Is Japanese Education Becoming Less Egalitarian?" *The Journal of Japanese Studies* 3, 37–70.

———. 1980. "The *Juku* Phenomenon: An Exploratory Essay." *The Journal of Japanese Studies* 6:2, 207–42.

———. 1983. *Japan's High Schools*. Berkeley: University of California Press.

———. 1989. "Order in Japanese Society: Attachment, Authority and Routine." *Journal of Japanese Studies* 15, 1, 5–40.

Sakamoto, T. 1975. "Preschool Reading in Japan." *The Reading Teacher* 29:3, 240–4.

Sarason, S. B. 1982. *The Culture of the School and the Problem of Change*. Boston: Allyn and Bacon.

———. 1983. *Schooling in America*. New York: Press Press.

Sato, G., and Nishimura, E. 1973. *Unsui: A Diary of Zen Monastic Life*. Honolulu: University of Hawaii Press.

Sato, N. 1991a. "Ethnography of Japanese Elementary Schools: Quest for Equality." Ph.D. dissertation, Stanford University School of Education.

Sato, N. 1991b. "Cooperative Learning and Teaching in Japanese

Elementary Schools." Paper given at the meeting of the American Educational Research Association, Chicago, April.

1993, Summer. "Teaching and Learning in Japanese Elementary Schools: A Context for Understanding." *Japanese Teacher Education, Part II.* Issue editors: T. Kobayashi, C. A. Hawley, and Willis D. Hawley. *Peabody Journal of Education* 68, 4.

Sato, N., and McLaughlin, M. W. 1992. "Context Matters: Teaching in Japan and in the United States." *Phi Delta Kappan* 73, 359–66.

Schneider, P., Gallimore, R., and Hyland, J. 1991, Fall. "Assisting Narrative Performance in Two Eighth-Grade Classrooms." *The International Journal of Dynamic Assessment and Instruction.* 2:1.

Schoenfeld, A. H. 1985. *Mathematical Problem Solving.* Orlando, FL: Academic Press.

Schoolland, K. 1990. *Shogun's Ghost: The Dark Side of Japanese Education.* Westport, CT: Gergin and Garvey.

Scott, R. W. 1994. "Institutions and Organizations: Toward a Theoretical Synthesis." In R. W. Scott and J. Meyer, eds., *Institutional Environments and Organizations.* Thousand Oaks, CA: Sage, pp. 55–80.

Sherman, Craig. 1991. "Japan's Latest Export: Can Japan Help Improve U.S. Mathematics Education?" Senior thesis, Princeton University.

Shiba, S. 1986. "The Excellent Education System for One and a Half Million Children." *Programmed Learning and Educational Technology.* 23:4.

Shields, J. J., Jr., ed. 1989. *Japanese Schooling: Patterns of Socialization, Equality, and Control.* University Park: Pennsylvania State University Press.

Shigaki, I. S. 1983. "Child Care Practices in Japan and the United States: How Do They Reflect Cultural Values in Young Children?" *Young Children* 38, 13–24.

Shimahara, N. K., and Sakai, A. 1995. *Learning to Teach in Two Cultures: Japan and the United States.* New York: Garland.

Shulman, L. 1970. "Psychology and Mathematics Education." In E. G. Begle, ed., *Mathematics Education.* Chicago: NSSE.

Singleton, J. 1967. *Nichū: A Japanese School.* New York: Holt, Rinehart & Winston.

1989. "Japanese Folkcraft Pottery Apprenticeship: Cultural Patterns of an Educational Institution." In M. Coy, ed., *Apprenticeship.* Albany: SUNY Press, pp. 13–30.

Smith, R. 1983. *Japanese Society: Tradition, Self and the Social Order.* Cambridge: Cambridge University Press.

Solomon, D., Watson, M., Battistich, V., Schaps, E., and Delucchi, K. 1992. "Creating a Caring Community: Educational Practices that Promote Children's Prosocial Development." In F. K. Oser, A. Dick, and J. L. Patry, eds., *Effective and Responsible Teaching: The New Synthesis.* San Francisco: Jossey-Bass.

Somucho (Seinen Taisaku Honbu). 1991. *Seinen Hakusho (White Paper on Youth).* Tokyo: Okurasho Insatsu-Kyoku.

Spindler, G. D., ed. 1974. *Education and Cultural Process: Toward an Anthropology of Education.* New York: Holt, Rinehart & Winston.

Steinhoff, P. G. 1989. "Hijackers, Bombers and Bank Robbers: Managerial Style in the Japanese Red Army." *Journal of Asian Studies* 48:4, 724–40.

Stevenson, H. W. 1991. "Japanese Elementary School Education." *The Elementary School Journal,* 92, 109–20.

Stevenson, H. W., Chen, C., and Lee, S. Y. 1993. "Mathematics Achievement of Chinese, Japanese, and American Children: Ten Years Later." *Science,* 259, 53–8.

Stevenson, H. W., Stigler, J. W. 1992. *The Learning Gap: Why Our Schools Are Failing and What We Can Learn from Japanese and Chinese Education.* New York: Summit.

Stevenson, H. W., Stigler, J. W., Lucker, G. W., Lee, S. Y., Hsu, C. C., and Kitamura, S. 1987. "Classroom Behavior and Achievement of Japanese, Chinese and American Children." In R. Glaser, ed., *Advances in Instructional Psychology.* Hillsdale, NJ: LEA, pp. 153–204.

Stigler, J. W. 1992. "Transforming Teaching by Focusing on Student Thinking: Similarities between CGI and Japanese Classrooms." Paper presented at the annual meeting of the American Educational Research Association, San Francisco, April.

Stigler, J. W., and Perry, M. 1988. "Mathematics Learning in Japanese, Chinese, and American Classrooms." In G. Saxe and M. Gearhart, eds., *Children's Mathematics.* San Francisco: Jossey-Bass.

Suzuki, D. T. 1959. *Zen and Japanese Culture.* New York: Random House.

    1965. *The Training of the Zen Buddhist Monk.* New York: University Books.

Suzuki, S. 1969. *Nurtured by Love.* New York: Exposition Press.

    1974. "The Law of Ability and the 'Mother Tongue Method' of Education." Pamphlet privately published by Talent Education Institute, Matsumoto, Japan.

    1981. *Ability Development from Age Zero.* Athens, OH: Ability Development Associates, subsidiary of Accura Music.

1982. *Where Love Is Deep.* Saint Louis: Talent Education Journal, Inc.

1983a. *How to Teach Suzuki Piano.* Matsumoto, Japan: Talent Education Institute.

1983b. Opening remarks at the sixth International Suzuki Conference, Matsumoto, Japan, July 17.

Taniuchi, L. 1983, June. Unpublished results of a pilot survey of the educational histories of first-grade children in two Tokyo first grades.

Tobin, J., Wu, D. Y., and Davidson, D. H. 1987. "Class Size and Student/Teacher Ratios in the Japanese Preschool." *Comparative Education Review* 31:4, 533–50.

1989. *Preschools in Three Cultures: Japan, China, and the United States.* New Haven, CT: Yale University Press.

Trimillos, R. 1983, May. "The Formalized Transmission of Culture: Selectivity in Traditional Teaching/Learning Systems in Four High Skill Music Traditions." *East-West Culture Learning Institute Report* 9:1/2, 1–9.

Tsuchida, I. 1993. "Teachers' Motivational and Instructional Strategies: A Study of Fourth Grade U.S. and Japanese Classrooms." Ph.D. dissertation, University of California, Berkeley School of Education.

Tsuge, G. (Professor of Musicology, Kunitachi College of Music). 1983. Interview, June 16.

Tsukushi. 1990, April. "Yōgō Gakkō Ippan Kigyo Shūshoku," 54.

Tucker, M. E. 1989. *Moral and Spiritual Cultivation in Japanese Neo-Confucianism.* Albany: SUNY Press.

Umesao, T. 1990. "Tradition of Culturedness in Modern Japan." *Senri Ethnological Studies* 28, 1–12.

United States, Department of Education. 1987. OERI Japan Study Team. *Japanese Education Today.* Washington, DC: U.S. Government Printing Office.

Vogel, E. 1962. "Entrance Examinations and Emotional Disturbances in Japan's 'New Middle Class'." In R. Smith and R. Beardsley, eds., *Japanese Culture: Its Development and Characteristics.* Chicago: Aldine.

1963. *Japan's New Middle Class.* Berkeley: University of California Press.

Vogel, S. 1978. "Professional Housewife: The Career of Urban Middle-Class Japanese Women." *Japan Interpreter* 12, 16–43.

Waley, A. trans. 1938. *Analects of Confucius.* London: Allen and Unwin.

White, M. I. 1987. *The Japanese Educational Challenge: A Commitment to Children.* New York: Free Press.

White, M. and LeVine, R. "What Is an *Ii Ko* (Good Child)?" In H. Stevenson, H. Azuma, and K. Hakuta, eds., *Child Development and Education in Japan*. New York: Freeman, pp. 55–62.

Wold, E. 1988. "Inventing Society." *American Ethnologist* 15, 4.

Yamabiko. 1990, November. "Kyoshitsu Arabamu: Anna Seito, Konna Seito, Eigo E, Kokugo G, Hoteishiki Nisaiji de Gakushu." No. 125.

Yang, H. 1993. The teacher's job: A comparison of U.S. and Japanese middle school teachers. Ph.D. dissertation, Stanford University, School of Education.

Yearley, L. H. 1990. *Mencius and Aquinas*. Albany: State University of New York Press.

Yoshida, M. 1991. "Japanese and American Students' Representations of a Mathematics Lesson." Manuscript, University of California, Los Angeles, Department of Psychology.

Zucker, L. 1983. "Organizations as Institutions." In S. Bachrach, ed., *Research in the Sociology of Organizations*. Greenwich, CT: JAI Press, pp. 1–47.

Index

ability
  de-emphasis in classroom setting,
    148, 304
  downplay of differences, 371
  Japanese view of, 374
  mixing of, 88, 131
absorption
  See also drill; repetition
absorption, teaching-learning process, 142–5
academic achievement, U.S. grade
  level marker, 130
academic instruction
  linked to discipline in life-style
    guidance, 303–4
  middle school level, 317
accountability
  hansei concept in context of, 133
  reminders to U.S. students, 205
active learning theory, 250–1
Adler, P., 47, 48
adolescence, U.S. perceptions, 296–
  7
age, Japanese grade level marker,
  130, 162
akarui (brightness), 371–2
all together goal, 76
Ansell, 247
Arai, P., 24
artistic training, Japan, 363
asobi (play)
  early childhood learning, 369–70
assessment, relational framework,
  129
Ausbel, D., 251
authority
  American teacher as, 241–3
  American teacher exercise of,
    196
  invisible, 138–9
  Japanese teacher as, 91
  in mathematical methods, 241–3,
    246
  mechanisms of peer and self-
    supervision, 138–40
automaticity principle, Kumon
  method, 251–4
autonomy, teacher, 154–5
Azuma, H., 207

Befu, H., 122, 123, 142
behavior
  appropriate middle school (*chuga-
    kuseirashii*), 304, 311–12
  discipline in and out of school, 317
  public scrutiny of problems in, 310
  ritualistic, 144
  tolerated, 139–40
Benedict, Ruth, 319
Boocock, S. S., 92
Boostrom, R. E., 95
Brower, R., 336

Calfee, R., 199
Carpenter, T. P., 247
Case, R., 267
ceremonies
  adding to length of school year,
    134
  elementary school, 83
Chambliss, M., 199
character
  See also kokoro (heart); *seishin-
    shugi* (spiritualism)
  character-building activities, 12, 18
  development of, 291–2
  quality of one's, 129
  self-discipline, 122–3
  teaching development of, 52
Chen, C., 159
children
  boys on noh or kabuki stage, 327–
    31
  family relations before entering
    school, 6
  learning Suzuki Method, 347–50
  using Kumon method math curric-
    ulum, 259–60
Christian preschools, 101
classroom organization
  See also groups, small fixed; *han*
    (fixed groups); whole-class in-
    struction
  ability downplayed, 88, 131, 148–
    9, 304, 371, 374
  comparison of Japanese and Amer-
    ican, 167–9
  han groups in elementary school,
    87–9